The Death of the
Irreparable Injury Rule

The Death
of the Irreparable
Injury Rule

DOUGLAS LAYCOCK

New York   Oxford
OXFORD UNIVERSITY PRESS
1991

Oxford University Press

Oxford   New York   Toronto
Delhi   Bombay   Calcutta   Madras   Karachi
Petaling Jaya   Singapore   Hong Kong   Tokyo
Nairobi   Dar es Salaam   Cape Town
Melbourne   Auckland

and associated companies in
Berlin   Ibadan

Copyright © 1991 by Oxford University Press, Inc.

Published by Oxford University Press, Inc.,
200 Madison Avenue, New York, New York 10016

Oxford is a registered trademark of Oxford University Press

Library of Congress Cataloging-in-Publication Data
Laycock, Douglas.
The death of the irreparable injury rule / Douglas Laycock.
p.   cm.   ISBN 0-19-506356-2
1. Remedies (Law)- United States.
2. Injunctions—United States.   3. Specific performances—United States.
4. Equitable remedies—United States.
5. Equity—United States.   I. Title
KF9010.L39   1991 ˙ 34c.7303′23—dc20
[347.306323]

90-6944

9 8 7 6 5 4 3 2 1

Printed in the United States of America
on acid-free paper

For John,
who arrived in the middle
of this project and brought irreparable change.
But no injury.

Preface

The irreparable injury rule has been a fixture of Anglo-American law for half a millenium. In its most obvious application, it says that courts will not prevent harm if money damages could adequately compensate for the harm. It says that I am free to destroy your property as long as I can pay for it.

I suspect that this rule sounds absurd to people who are neither lawyers nor economists. When it comes time to actually apply the rule, it seems absurd to courts as well. Courts do prevent harm when they can. Judicial opinions recite the rule constantly, but they do not apply it. After surveying more than 1400 cases, I conclude that the irreparable injury rule is dead—dead in the practical sense that it almost never affects the results of cases.

Plaintiffs usually get the remedies they seek, because courts usually find that other remedies are inadequate. When courts reject plaintiff's choice of remedy, there is always some other reason, and that reason has nothing to do with the irreparable injury rule. We can identify the real reasons for decision, and use those reasons to explain old cases and decide new cases. This book concludes with a tentative restatement of those reasons, and with a proposal for formal legislative repeal of the irreparable injury rule.

This book has a unified negative thesis—the irreparable injury rule is dead. It also has an affirmative thesis—nearly all the operative law of remedies can be stated without reference to the irreparable injury rule. This affirmative thesis is an umbrella for a host of small and middle-sized insights. For me at least, explaining remedies law without the irreparable injury rule has clarified all sorts of things. I hope some of my readers have similar reactions.

Chapter 1 sets out the theoretical framework for the rest of the book. I seek to complete the assimilation of equity, and to eliminate the last remnant of the conception that equity is subordinate, extraordinary, or unusual. The distinction between legal and equitable remedies is irrelevant except where it is codified, most notably in constitutional guarantees of jury trial. Outside that context, I would not ask whether a remedy is legal or equitable. Instead, I would ask functional questions: Is the remedy specific or substitutionary, is it a personal command or an impersonal judgment, is it preliminary or permanent? Most important, does it impose unnecessary costs in a particular case?

Chapters 2 through 9 test the claims of Chapter 1 against the actual behavior of courts. I explore the relationships among remedies, and identify the real policies that motivate choices among alternative remedies. I explore the relationships between these real policies and the rhetoric of irreparable injury. Chapter 10 tries to integrate the real policies into larger patterns, and emphasizes that the phrase "irreparable injury" can describe all these policies only if it has no meaning of its own.

Chapter 11 examines the the legal-economic theory of efficient breach of contract. The death of the irreparable injury rule removes the positive law support for the most important applications of efficient breach theory. This edifice of contemporary legal scholarship is based on a misunderstanding of the law of remedies, a misunderstanding induced by the misleading rhetoric of the irreparable injury rule.

Finally, Chapter 12 offers proposals for reform, including my tentative restatement of the operative rules.

The chapters on the cases are supported by citation to most of the 1400 cases—by multiple citations to many of them. Why so many citations, and what jurisprudential theory underlies them? String cites are out of style among academics; for some legal theorists, reading cases is out of style. Academic lawyers rarely marshal cases in support of normative claims.

I marshal the cases in support of a positive claim. I cite the cases more for what they do than for what they say; indeed, I cite them principally to show that they almost never do what they say. My colleague Sandy Levinson tells me that my use of the cases is "relentlessly realist." This characterization scores a point in our endless friendly argument over indeterminacy and formalism; I am the one who thinks that doctrine sometimes matters.

In fact the book is both realist and doctrinal. One of its goals is to conform doctrine to reality. Bad doctrine matters because it confuses us—scholars, judges, and practitioners alike. The irreparable injury rule distracts analysis from the real relationships among remedial choices. It highlights the obsolete distinction between law and equity, and subordinates more functional schemes for classifying remedies. It treats the rule as the exception and extraordinarily rare exceptions as the rule. An intuitive sense of justice has led judges to produce sensible results, but there has been no similar pressure to produce sensible explanations.

It remains to explain why I cite so *many* cases. I initially envisioned an article of moderate length, citing only a modest number of illustrative cases. It soon became clear that such an approach would suffice for some readers, but not for others. The traditional understanding had too strong a hold; a significant minority was simply unconvinced. I suppose it would have been easy to pick a few examples consistent with my theory. To the skeptical, a few examples were not enough.

And so the project expanded, with more research, more analysis, and especially more notes. One serendipitous byproduct is that the book now offers a thorough survey of the role of injunctions in contemporary litigation. The notes provide a repository of information for further research, and I have tried to facilitate further research with a detailed index and a table of cases arranged by jurisdiction.

I have generally omitted multiple cases on the same point from the same jurisdiction. Even so, the notes are massive. Readers so inclined can safely ignore them. The notes contain citations, parenthetical information about the sources cited, and nothing more. The rare textual footnotes are generally at the bottom of the page. In a few cases where that was awkward, I state in text that the note contains additional explanation.

Even so, I urge readers to at least browse in the notes. The best way to get your own sense of what the courts are really doing is to sample the parenthetical descriptions of the cited cases. To facilitate browsing, the notes are at the end of each chapter, and each note is identified by a caption as well as by a number. In citing all these cases, I have taken advantage of the flexibility and simplicity of The University of Chicago Manual of Legal Citation.

Despite the invaluable help of my research assistants, I personally read every cited case. I read most of them at least twice. Reading so many cases was burdensome, but it was not dull. I found striking examples, and I found whole lines of cases and fact patterns that I had not known about. Not surprisingly, I found that a large sample of cases is richer than any treatise.

I have tried to offer readers the benefits of that richness without the burdens. The text identifies broad patterns in the cases, and offers a few of the best illustrations; I have tried to keep it readable and brief. For those sufficiently interested, there are plenty of further examples in the notes.

A preliminary draft of parts of this project appeared as an article in the Harvard Law Review for January 1990. I am grateful to the Harvard Law Review and Oxford University Press for cooperating in the publication of both the article and the book.

Austin   D. L.
June 1990

Acknowledgments

This book has a long history, and I have accumulated many debts along the way. The book would still be unfinished were it not for a generous series of research leaves in 1989. The Shell Oil Company Foundation supported my treatment of specific performance of contracts, which is integrated throughout the book and culminates in Chapter 11. The University Research Institute at The University of Texas supported a leave to work on religious liberty, but graciously acquiesced when irreparable injury swallowed most of the semester. The Allan Shivers Research Fund at The University of Texas Law School supported the final stages of writing and editing. Dean Mark Yudof was supportive at every step, both financially and intellectually.

The roots of this project go back almost twenty years, when I was first convinced that the Supreme Court had misused the irreparable injury rule to regulate federal interference with state prosecutions. Two of my early articles were on that problem. Shortly thereafter, I reviewed Owen Fiss's book proposing abolition of the irreparable injury rule. My review concluded with a crude and premature formulation of the thesis of this book.

I remember Frank Zimring urging me to expand the point into a major article, but I looked at him blankly. At that stage in my career, I had said all that I knew how to say. Richard Posner said I should have offered more examples of cases that misused the rule. To my embarrassment, I realized that I did not have any more examples, and that I could not readily find any. There is no digest number for "rule misused." I assume that these former colleagues quickly forgot those conversations, but I did not.

I read more widely for the irreparable injury chapter of my casebook, and the pattern in the cases persisted. Legal remedies were never adequate except when there was some other reason to deny equitable remedies. I formulated the thesis more ambitiously, but also more precisely, and I developed more confidence in it.

I presented the thesis to faculty workshops at Duke in 1983, at Boston University in 1985, and at Texas in 1987. I wrote the first draft of an article at the University of Hawaii in the summer of 1986. I am grateful for the helpful reactions of these four faculties, and for office space and library privileges at Hawaii. I also presented the project to the Remedies Section at the meeting of the Association of American Law Schools in 1990. I benefitted from formal commentary by Alan Schwartz and Doug Rendleman, and from spontaneous audience reaction. I did most of the technical manuscript preparation during a visit at Michigan in winter semester 1990.

I am especially grateful to the skeptics who were not persuaded by the summary treatment in those early versions, and to Dan Dobbs, Tom Rowe, and Scot Powe, who had disparate but vigorous reactions. These three scholars were helpful and encouraging in the usual ways, but each of them let slip one uncompromisingly blunt sentence that went to the heart of what I thought I was doing. Perhaps without realizing the full implications of their comments, they made clear that I had utterly failed to communicate my own vision of what I was about. These reactions led to a quantum expansion of the project.

Fortunately, these reactions were balanced by that of Jay Westbrook. Jay was as excited about the project as I was—more so, because he did not have to read all the cases. He reinforced my judgment that I was on to something more important than I had communicated in early drafts. He read two complete drafts and many substantial fragments; he served as strategic consultant, writing coach, and one-man booster club.

Jack Balkin, Owen Fiss, Sandy Levinson, Bill Powers, and Charles Silver also read drafts and offered help. Mary Kay Kane and Jean Love made extraordinarily detailed comments on a hybrid draft halfway between article and book. Hal Bruff and Tom McGarity read Chapter 6 and tried to protect me from error with respect to administrative law; Mark Gergen, Dick Markovits, Dick

Wright, and Mark Yudof performed the same service on Chapter 11. Jim Treece helped me unravel the commercial disparagement and false advertising cases in Chapter 7. Lea Vaughn saved me from a misreading of Michigan labor law in Chapter 8.

Karen Patton Bogle, research assistant extraordinaire and now an associate at Sullivan & Cromwell, undertook to find and classify the 400 most recent irreparable injury cases. Despite her best efforts, my classification scheme eventually broke down in the face of the real world's complexity. But her work created the core of the project's empirical base, and her count of permanent and preliminary injunction cases still appears in Chapter 5. Subsequent cohorts of research assistants helped to solve unsolved mysteries, find missing sources, check citations, and update Karen's sample of cases. These indispensable helpers included Debbie Backus, Denise Brady, Deborah Coldwell, William Cunningham, Dana Elfin, Georgia Harper, Jay Harper, Larry Pascal, Susan Waelbroeck, and Mark Walker at Texas, and Audrey Anderson and Kathleen Bradley at Michigan. Joan Baron, Mari Campos, and Peter Smits at Texas pinch hit when my own research assistants were unavailable. The Alice McKean Young Regents Chair in Law and the Shell Oil Company Foundation funded extra research assistance in the final push to completion.

Cheryl Harris, my industrious and overqualified secretary at Texas, created tables of cases out of raw footnotes and helped in many other ways as well. Darlene Lentz cheerfully leaped into the breach during my semester at Michigan.

To all these people, who helped in so many ways, thank you.

Contents

The Death of the
Irreparable Injury Rule

1

A Functional Approach to Choosing Remedies

[E]ven though a plaintiff may often prefer a judicial order enjoining a harmful act or omission before it occurs, damages after the fact are considered an "adequate remedy" in all but the most extraordinary cases.[1]

[J]udges have been brought to see and to acknowledge . . . that the common law theory of not *interfering* with persons until they shall have actually committed a wrong, is fundamentally erroneous; and that a remedy which *prevents* a threatened wrong is in its essential nature better than a remedy which permits the wrong to be done, and then attempts to pay for it.[2]

One of these statements comes from Pomeroy's *Equity Jurisprudence*, a leading nineteenth-century treatise. The other comes from the United States Reports for June of 1988. Which is which? And which better describes the current state of the law?

The first statement is the recent one, from a dissent by Justice Scalia. Two other justices joined him. But it is not the law. It is not even close to the law. It is merely a spectacular example of the confusion created by one of our archaic "rules" for choosing among remedies. It states an extreme but recognizable version of the traditional understanding, even though it is wildly wrong as a description of what courts do.

The second statement is not quite right either, but it captures an important part of the truth and it comes much closer to describing judicial behavior. Remedies that prevent harm altogether are often better for plaintiffs, and are always closer to the ideal of corrective justice. A plaintiff should have such a remedy if she wants it and if there is no good reason to deny it. A general preference for damages is not a reason, but a statement of the conclusion. Courts should not prefer damages unless there is some reason to prefer damages. Pomeroy thought that courts had recognized this a century ago. But neither his treatise nor the accumulating cases have had much impact on the traditional understanding.

The traditional understanding is a product of the most general and most misleading of the rules for choosing remedies, the irreparable injury rule. This rule says that equitable remedies are unavailable if legal remedies will adequately repair the harm.[3] Frequent repetition of the rule seems to imply that legal remedies are generally adequate; otherwise, the rule would not be so important. Thus an able scholar writes, "Our materialistic society considers money an acceptable substitute for most recognized interests."[4] If damages are generally adequate, then equitable remedies are generally unavailable. Justice Scalia's conclusion seems to follow: that our legal system prefers damages after the fact.

Our legal system does not prefer damages. I will develop and defend this thesis on the basis of a large sample of recent cases. I will first show how courts have escaped the irreparable injury rule without repudiating it. Then I will show the quite different purposes for which courts invoke the rule's misleading rhetoric. In the process, I hope to clarify the choice between damages and injunctions across the whole range of modern law—clarify it in a way that is helpful to scholars, judges, and practitioners alike.

Courts have escaped the irreparable injury rule by defining adequacy in such a way that damages are never an adequate substitute for plaintiff's loss. Thus, our law embodies a preference for specific relief if plaintiff wants it. The principal doctrinal expression of this preference is the rule that damages are inadequate unless they can be used to replace the specific thing that plaintiff lost. Damages can be used in this way for only one category of losses: to replace fungible goods or routine services in an orderly market. In that context, damages and specific relief are substantially equivalent. Either way, plaintiff winds up with the very thing he wanted, and the preference for specific relief becomes irrelevant. In all other contexts, there is ample basis in precedent and principle for holding that damages are inadequate.

Courts ignore this body of precedent, and find damages adequate, only when there is some identifiable reason to deny specific relief in a particular case. The largest group of such cases arise on motions for temporary restraining orders or preliminary injunctions. Denying relief at that stage serves the important purpose of protecting defendant's right to a full hearing, and a stringent variation of the irreparable injury rule lets the court openly balance the risks to each side. The vocabulary of adequate remedy and irreparable injury is common to both stages, but the competing considerations are quite different. Preliminary relief is best considered as a separate issue, only distantly related to the choice of remedy at final judgment.

At final judgment, specific relief is problematic only occasionally. Sometimes it imposes undue hardship on defendant; sometimes it interferes with the authority of another tribunal or bypasses a more particularized remedy; sometimes it is impractical to supervise; sometimes we have special reasons for preserving jury trial; sometimes the court does not really want to grant any relief at all. The irreparable injury rule may be offered in support of these results, but that is misleading. These real reasons for denying equitable remedies are not derived from the adequacy of the legal remedy or from any general preference for damages. The meanings of "irreparable" and "adequate" are constantly manipulated to achieve sensible results.

I conclude that the irreparable injury rule is dead. It does not describe what the cases do, and it cannot account for the results. Equally abandoned are such corollary expressions[5] as "injunctions are an extraordinary remedy."[6] Injunctions are routine, and damages are never adequate unless the court wants them to be. Courts can freely turn to either line of precedents, depending on whether they want to hold the legal remedy adequate or inadequate. Whether they want to hold the legal remedy adequate depends on whether they have some other reason to deny the equitable remedy, and it is these other reasons that drive the decisions. Courts may balance the costs of the equitable remedy against plaintiff's need for it, and in that sense the degree of inadequacy may matter. But this balancing process is triggered by variations in the cost of the equitable remedy, not by variations in the adequacy of the legal remedy.

Instead of one general principle for choosing among remedies—legal remedies are preferred where adequate—we have many more specific rules. There is a rule about fungible goods in orderly markets, a rule about preliminary relief, a rule about undue hardship, and so on. These rules are often stated in the cases. But when courts invoke these rules, they often go on to invoke the irreparable injury rule as well. And sometimes they rely solely or principally on the irreparable injury rule, leaving the application of some more precise rule merely implicit in their statement of the case. Analysis would be both simpler and clearer if we abandoned the irreparable injury rule and spoke directly of the real reasons for choosing remedies. I will conclude with a preliminary restatement of these operative rules.

A defender of the traditional understanding might deny that I have identified a set of operative rules capable of replacing the irreparable injury rule, and claim instead that I have merely identified the policy reasons for the traditional rule. That is, perhaps the irreparable injury rule survives, and its modern justifications are these problems with specific relief that I call the real reasons for decision. Recent defenses of the traditional rule may be read in this way.[7] If these defenders would agree that the policy reasons for the rule should control and limit its application, then the difference between us is largely one of characterization. But their characterization does not fit the cases.

The irreparable injury rule is stated as a rule of general applicability for choosing between legal and equitable remedies, expressing a preference for legal remedies over the whole range of litigation. The operative rules that I have identified each apply to a specific and limited set of cases. None of these rules has any effect in the vast range of cases reviewed in Chapters 2 and 3.

Even within their scope, the operative rules do not express any consistent preference for legal remedies. The real reasons for decisions are to avoid difficulties in particular cases, and these difficulties are not limited to equity. Some operative rules prefer legal remedies, but a few prefer equitable remedies, and others use different categories altogether. These rules cannot be derived from any coherent version of the irreparable injury rule, and the irreparable injury rule cannot account for the results. Irreparable injury rhetoric has survived only as a label, to be affixed to opinions after the court has chosen the remedy on other grounds.

In my analysis of the operative rules, I aspire to be more positive than normative, but more conceptual than descriptive. The analysis is positive in the sense that I describe what courts actually do. I do not argue merely that the irreparable injury rule *should be* abandoned; I argue that it *has been* abandoned in all but rhetoric.

Even this claim has normative components. I assert that my account of the cases is the best account—best in the sense that it explains the cases in the simplest and most direct way, in the sense that it leaves the smallest number of "wrong" or "exceptional" cases unaccounted for, and in the sense that it produces better results than an account that would take the irreparable injury rule at face value and designate a different set of cases as wrong or exceptional.[8] These normative elements are real, but they should not obscure the dominant positive element. I am explaining the results of existing cases. I argue for an important change in explanation, but for few changes in result.

My analysis is conceptual in the sense that it is not bound by existing conceptual categories. Our existing conceptual categories are historical rather than functional. They are left over from a time when law and equity were administered in separate courts, or even from a time when each legal remedy was administered under a separate writ. The conventional rules are stated in terms of these ancient categories. In a radically changed judicial system, these rules have become obstacles to decision instead of guides. The courts have generally manipulated such rules to achieve just and functional results, but the formal rules, the vocabulary, and the conceptual categories have become dysfunctional. By emphasizing different conceptual categories, I hope to reverse the conventional relationship between the exception and the rule, and to clarify and simplify the entire field.

A. The Irreparable Injury Rule

1. The Equivalence of the Two Formulations

The irreparable injury rule has two formulations. Equity will act only to prevent irreparable injury, and equity will act only if there is no adequate legal remedy. The two formulations are equivalent; what makes an injury irreparable is that no other remedy can repair it.[9]

Attempts to distinguish the two formulations have produced a variety of proffered distinctions but no common usage.[10] One of the proffered distinctions deserves emphasis, because it highlights an important point. The irreparable injury formulation is said to be more general than the no-adequate-legal-remedy formulation, because it omits the qualifier "legal."[11] The rule that equity will not act if there is no adequate *legal* remedy does not literally cover cases where a court denies a preliminary injunction because a permanent injunction will be adequate, or denies a receivership because an injunction will be adequate.

The rule that equity will act only to prevent irreparable injury does not describe these cases either. When a court chooses between two equitable remedies, equity will act whatever the choice. A general formulation that does include these cases is that courts will grant an intrusive remedy only to prevent injury that cannot be prevented by any less intrusive remedy, or only when no less intrusive remedy is adequate. When the principle is formulated accurately, it remains the case that irreparable injury is equivalent to no adequate remedy.

The adequacy and irreparability formulations become different only when they are stated at different levels of generality—when one is stated in terms of the dysfunctional distinction between law and equity, and the other is stated in terms of a functional choice between two remedies, such as preliminary and permanent injunction. "*Equity* will act only when there is no adequate legal remedy" is assuredly not the same as "a *preliminary injunction* will issue only to prevent irreparable injury." But the difference is not between irreparability and inadequacy; the difference is between equity and preliminary injunction.

I emphasize the point so that no reader can misunderstand my usage. I believe that no significant distinction can be drawn between the irreparable injury and no adequate remedy formulations. Nothing in my thesis requires readers to accept that judgment. But clear communication does require readers to understand that I will use the two formulations interchangeably.

2. The Possible Meanings of the Rule

The irreparable injury rule has received considerable scholarly attention. In 1978, Owen Fiss examined the possible reasons for the rule and found them wanting.[12] A vigorous debate over the economic wisdom of applying the rule to specific performance of contracts began about the same time,[13] and soon came to center on the transaction costs of administering the two remedies.[14] Both Fiss and Dan Dobbs have noted that the rule does not seem to be taken very seriously,[15] and in a review of Fiss's book, I argued that the definition of adequacy pulls most of the rule's teeth.[16] The Restatement (Second) of Torts dropped the rule from the black-letter and condemned it as misleading, but replaced it only with a long and unstructured list of factors to be considered.[17] Doug Rendleman[18] and Gene Shreve[19] offered separate defenses of the rule, arguing that equitable remedies are generally more troublesome than legal remedies. But Rendleman conceded that the usual formulations of the rule divert analysis from the real policies at issue,[20] and Shreve also seemed to think the rule is generally misunderstood.[21]

In all this policy debate, no one has extensively examined how the rule actually works. In my experience, many sophisticated lawyers believe that the rule continues to reflect a serious preference for legal over equitable remedies. The elaborate debate over the wisdom of the rule would be pointless unless the debaters thought the rule made a real difference in the results of cases. The three justices quoted at the beginning of this chapter are not the only modern lawyers to assume that the rule requires plaintiff to accept remedies that are plainly inferior but in some sense "adequate."[22]

This traditional understanding can be stated with varying degrees of stringency. Indeed, enormous elasticity has been a central part of the rhetoric of irreparable injury and adequate remedy, essential to its survival. This elasticity threatens to make the rule nonfalsifiable; its supporters seem capable of assimilating any combination of results into the rule.

A nonfalsifiable rule is like a nonfalsifiable scientific theory. If all possible results are consistent with the rule, then no case is decided by the rule, and it is not a rule at all. For the rule to be alive, it must be at risk of being proved dead. I cannot specify the rule for its defenders, but I can specify my own understanding of the minimum possible scope of the rule. What would I accept as proof that the rule is still alive, and what do I mean when I claim it is dead? These questions require a brief survey of the range of possible meanings.

Adequacy seems to imply an absolute standard: Does the legal remedy reach the threshold of adequacy? Such a threshold might be low or high or in between. But adequacy may also imply a range of comparative standards: Is the legal remedy as good as the equitable remedy, or nearly as good, or half as good? Adequacy could even mean something like "good enough in light of the costs of doing better," and that formulation could lead to case-by-case balancing of the effectiveness of the remedy awarded against the costs of the remedy plaintiff prefers. The rule has evolved in precisely this direction. It has evolved beyond the point where it can reasonably be called the irreparable injury rule.

Perhaps the clearest statement of this trend appears in Edward Yorio's book on specific performance. For Yorio, "the adequacy doctrine remains the linchpin of the rules governing specific performance."[23] He defends the rule at length, but he defends it as the first step of a cost-benefit analysis.

> The purpose of the adequacy test in a system of contract remedies is to provide input on the marginal benefit that the promisee would derive from equitable relief. A finding that damages are inadequate means that the promisee would derive *some* marginal benefit from specific relief. . . . For specific performance to be proper, however, the marginal benefit to the promisee must be sufficiently great that it outweighs the marginal costs imposed on the promisor and on the legal system.[24]

I can accept that standard, but its substance is not the irreparable injury rule. Yorio's standard is simply to pick the best remedy in each case after balancing the costs and benefits to plaintiff, defendant, and the court.*

The weakest claim recognizable as a version of the irreparable injury rule is that courts balance costs, benefits, *and* a preference for legal remedies. The irreparable injury rule creates a hierarchy of remedies; it says that legal remedies are preferred over equitable remedies.[25] If courts are simply balancing costs and benefits and picking the most appropriate remedy in each case, then they are doing exactly what Owen Fiss urged when he proposed to abolish the rule.[26] Unless some preference for legal remedies operates across a wide range of cases and actually influences results, there is no remedial hierarchy and the irreparable injury rule is dead. If a weak preference for legal remedies is only a minor factor in a general balancing of costs and benefits, the irreparable injury rule is more misleading than helpful.

In fact, except for the loss of fungible goods or services in an orderly market, there is not even a weak preference for legal remedies. Irreparable injury talk conceals a weak preference for the remedy preferred by plaintiff, and it conceals the focus on countervailing costs that can override plaintiff's preference.

B. Refining the Question

1. Functional Choices in Remedies Law

The irreparable injury rule distorts analysis by asking the wrong question. It purports to choose between legal and equitable remedies, but that is no longer a functional choice. History has its claims, and lawyers should understand the history of equity. But

---

* Yorio may retain a procedural version of the irreparable injury rule. His book implies, and he has confirmed in conversation, that he would require plaintiff to make some showing of irreparable injury to initiate the cost-benefit analysis. Thus, a bursting-bubble presumption would favor the legal remedy, and plaintiff would bear the burden of coming forward with some reason why that remedy is inadequate. My own view is that a bursting-bubble presumption favors plaintiff's choice of remedy, and that defendant bears the burden of coming forward with some reason why that remedy should be denied. The merits of this disagreement are considered at the end of Chapter 10.

law and equity have been merged for half a century in federal courts and for well over a century in many states. The legal or equitable origin of a remedy should no longer be the starting point for analysis.

The law-equity distinction functions as a crude proxy for a set of more functional distinctions—for all the characteristics traditionally associated with equity. The choice of an equitable remedy is commonly thought to embody the choice of specific relief, a personal command to defendant, enforcement by the contempt power, the availability of preliminary relief and discretionary defenses, and the impossibility of jury trial. The choice of a legal remedy is thought to embody the opposite choices: substitutionary relief; an impersonal judgment; the unavailability of the contempt power, preliminary relief, and discretionary defenses; and a constitutional right to jury trial.

There are two things wrong with using the law-equity distinction as a proxy for the underlying functional distinctions. First, there are many exceptions to the presumed relationships among law, equity, and the functional distinctions. Most of the characteristics associated with equity are sometimes available at law, and most of the characteristics associated with law are sometimes available in equity. Using law and equity as proxies for these characteristics is so crude that it is more misleading than helpful.

Second, using law and equity as the analytic categories forces us to choose the whole bundle of characteristics as a unit. If in a particular case we want to preserve jury trial, or avoid the contempt power, then it appears that we must also give up specific relief, personal commands, preliminary relief, and discretionary defenses. If a personal injury victim desperately needs preliminary relief to pay for medical care, that is thought to be impossible because her claim is at law. Forcing courts to choose between legal remedies and equitable remedies is like forbidding voters to cast split-ticket ballots. In fact courts and legislatures sometimes unbundle the functional choices embedded in the law-equity distinction, and they should be free to unbundle further when appropriate. It is time to quit thinking in terms of the law-equity proxy, and to begin thinking directly in terms of the functional choices among remedies.

The most fundamental remedial choice is between substitutionary and specific remedies. With substitutionary remedies, plaintiff suffers harm and receives a sum of money. Specific remedies seek to avoid this exchange. They aspire to prevent harm, or undo it, rather than let it happen and compensate for it. They seek to prevent harm to plaintiff, repair the harm in kind, or restore the specific thing that plaintiff lost. Substitutionary remedies include compensatory damages, attorneys' fees, restitution of the money value of defendant's gain, and punitive damages. Specific remedies include injunctions, specific performance of contracts, restitution of specific property, and restitution of a specific sum of money.[27]

The essence of the difference is illustrated by the closest case, restitution of a specific sum of money. Consider the choice of remedies for sale of defective goods. Plaintiff's substitutionary remedy is damages, measured by the difference between the value of the goods as promised and the value of the goods as delivered.[28] His specific remedy is either specific performance or cancellation. Specific performance, if it is available, will give him goods that fully conform to the contract in exchange for his payment of the price. Cancellation will give him a full refund of the price—restitution of the sum of money—in exchange for his returning the goods.[29]

This example illustrates the two hallmarks of substitutionary relief. First, plaintiff gets neither what he started with—his money—nor what he was promised—goods conforming to the contract. Instead, he gets defective goods and money to compensate for the defect. Second, the sum of money he receives is based on a fact finder's valuation of his loss. The relief is substitutionary both in the sense that the sum of money is substituted for plaintiff's original entitlement, and in the less obvious sense that the fact finder's valuation of the loss is substituted for plaintiff's valuation. Specific relief aspires to avoid both these substitutions, giving plaintiff the very thing he lost if that is what he wants.

The choice between specific and substitutionary remedies is not equivalent to the choice between legal and equitable remedies. Equitable remedies are a crude proxy for specific remedies, because most specific remedies are historically equitable: injunctions, specific performance, constructive trusts, subrogation, quiet title, and cancellation. But some are historically legal: ejectment, replevin, mandamus, prohibition, and habeas corpus. At least one, rescission, was historically available in either law or equity. Another, declaratory judgment, is a statutory creation that has been called legal,[30] equitable,[31] neither,[32] or both,[33] depending on the circumstances and the commentator. Orders to pay money were sometimes available in equity, and courts and legislators sometimes use equitable monetary relief to manipulate jurisdiction or avoid jury trial.[34]

The law-equity distinction duplicates the substitutionary-specific distinction in the most common cases, where the choice is between damages and injunctions or damages and specific performance. That is why Justice Scalia could plausibly state the irreparable injury rule in terms of preventing harm and awarding damages after the fact. Where the two distinctions overlap, I may refer to either. But replevin and ejectment are important sources of specific relief not subject to any version of the irreparable injury rule, and it distorts analysis to ignore them. The belief that our law prefers damages to specific relief is less plausible when one considers ejectment and replevin as well as injunctions and specific performance. Whenever it matters, I will emphasize the functional choice between substitutionary and specific relief instead of the historical choice between law and equity.

A second fundamental remedial choice is whether to make the contempt power available for enforcement. It is generally equitable remedies that end in a personal command, and personal commands are generally enforceable by the contempt power. This is sometimes offered as a reason for the irreparable injury rule.[35]

Personal commands also tend to be associated with specific relief, because both are associated with equity. But there are exceptions to both links in this chain of association; neither link is either inherent or functional. Courts can grant specific relief without a personal command, if that is thought to be appropriate; replevin, ejectment, and declaratory judgments are examples. Replevin and ejectment traditionally order the sheriff to restore specific property to plaintiff, but do not order defendant to turn it over.[36]

On the other side of the traditional equation, courts can grant personal commands at law and enforce them with the contempt power; mandamus is an example. Some specific relief requires a personal command to be effective, but whether we call such a command legal or equitable—mandamus or injunction—is a matter of history and doctrine, not a matter of function.[37] When a state supreme court denies a writ of prohibition on the ground that an injunction would be an adequate remedy at law,[38] historical categories of law and equity have simply produced confusion.

The historical link between personal commands and equity has been further blurred by a trend to greater use of personal commands in aid of traditionally legal remedies. Plaintiffs have long been entitled to postjudgment discovery to find defendants' assets, and defendants must answer on pain of contempt.[39] Most states now have procedures for compelling defendants to turn over hidden or intangible assets that are hard to reach by traditional means of collection.[40] Illinois has actually authorized courts in all cases to compel defendants to pay judgments out of income,[41] and it has converted replevin into a personal command to turn over the goods.[42]

The source of this trend is surely legislative exasperation with traditional means of collection. It is not easy to extract money without coercing defendant's person. Defendant may have no assets; assets may be easily hidden; if assets are found, a forced sale will bring an inadequate price. These difficulties tend to be ignored when the difficulty of enforcing specific decrees is offered as a reason for the irreparable injury rule. When one considers the difficulties of both kinds of remedies, it seems impossible to generalize about their relative workability. Defendants tend to obey court orders,[43] and solvent defendants tend to pay judgments. The problems of coercing recalcitrants and collecting from insolvents must be compared case by case.

Whatever the comparative virtues of personal commands and impersonal judgments, it is a mistake to think that that choice is inextricably linked to the choice between substitutionary and specific relief. Much of the association depends on the historical links to equity, links that are changeable in theory and changing in fact. The choice of the contempt power can be unbundled from the choice of specific relief, because both can be unbundled from equity.

I obviously cannot ignore the distinction between law and equity. The irreparable injury rule talks about it, and the cases talk about it. Sometimes it is codified in statutes or constitutions, most notably in the guarantees of jury trial. But I am more interested in functional distinctions, and especially in the choice between specific and substitutionary relief.

2. The Universe of Cases in Which Choice Is Possible

One reason the rhetoric of the irreparable injury rule has survived is that it is consistent with the armchair empirical observation that our courts award damages more frequently than specific relief. The explanation is that in most of the cases that reach our courts, there is no meaningful choice between damages and specific relief. Specific relief is often impossible, unrequested, or functionally equivalent to damages.

First, specific relief is impossible when the harm has been done beyond anyone's power to prevent or repair in kind. This is true of all personal injury cases. It is true of most consequential damages whatever the underlying wrong. Whether defendant has injured plaintiff's person, damaged his tangible property, breached a contract, or interfered with his business, consequential damages begin to accrue immediately. Specific relief—restoring the damaged property, enforcing the contract, or ending the interference—may prevent the accrual of future damages, but the claim for damages already suffered will remain.

Second, plaintiff may not seek specific relief because it is not in his interest to do so. Self-help followed by a suit for damages is his quickest remedy, so that the lawsuit when it comes is limited to past harm that can be remedied only by damages. The avoidable consequences rule strongly reinforces this tendency. Plaintiff cannot recover consequential damages that he could have avoided by reasonable effort.[44] And sensibly enough, courts have also refused specific relief to cure avoidable consequences that plaintiff should have avoided by self-help.[45] If it were otherwise, specific relief could be used to evade the avoidable consequences rule.

The tendency to self-help is especially strong in suits for breach of contract. Plaintiff will usually be able to make other arrangements and go on with his business more quickly than he can litigate a specific performance suit. This is almost certainly true where the goods or services promised under the contract can be readily replaced. This is also the only situation where settled doctrine holds the legal remedy adequate. The result is that plaintiffs rarely seek specific performance where the goods or services are readily replaceable.

Indeed, as Alan Schwartz has argued, if plaintiff prefers coerced performance, after the delay of litigation, from a defendant who has already breached once, to immediate replacement and a subsequent suit for damages, there must indeed be something seriously inadequate about the legal remedy.[46] The other side of this insight is that specific performance is useful only in cases where performance can await the outcome of a lawsuit, and in a few cases where the court can order essential partial performance on a motion for preliminary injunction.

A third set of cases where plaintiffs seek only money are suits to collect debts. In this large category of routine cases, specific relief and damages are functionally equivalent: a fixed sum of money is the specific thing plaintiff lost. But the availability or unavailability of the contempt power is crucial in these cases. Our courts will usually give an impersonal judgment on the debt, collectible by execution, garnishment, and the like,[47] and generally dischargeable in bankruptcy.[48] They will set aside fraudulent conveyances,[49] and even order defendant to turn over specific hidden assets.[50] But except for highly preferred debts, such as the support of children and spouses,[51] our courts have traditionally refused to order defendant to pay on pain of contempt.[52] Legislatures have tinkered with this rule,[53] but it remains largely intact, and it is supported by a compelling policy.

The policy source of this rule is aversion to imprisonment for debt.[54] The adequacy of the legal remedy is irrelevant; the rule is simply that courts do not use the contempt power to coerce the payment of money. This is an important rule for choosing among remedies, but it has nothing to do with irreparable injury.

If the rule were that we use the contempt power only when legal remedies are inadequate, the protection for debtors would be hollow indeed. The legal remedies for collection of debts are notoriously inadequate; most debtors are judgment proof. Moreover, the poorer the debtor and the greater the need for protection from the contempt power, the more hopeless the legal remedies are. But we do not make the contempt power more available as debtors get poorer. Rather we make it less available: when it is impossible for a debtor to pay, he has a defense to any contempt sanctions that would otherwise be available.[55]

The rule against imprisonment for debt nicely illustrates the judicial capacity to unbundle the choices embedded in the law-equity distinction. Courts can grant injunctions ordering defendants to pay money without intending to imprison defendants who fail to pay, and increasing numbers of cases do just that, usually without discussing the issue. Most of these cases order government agencies or corporations to make periodic payments on a continuing obligation.[56] These orders are personal commands to make specific payments, but because the defendant is not a human being, there is no risk of imprisonment for debt.

A fourth category of cases also deserves mention here. These are the cases holding that replevin is an adequate remedy to recover personal property, and refusing equitable remedies that would recover the same property.[57] Like the other cases described in this section, the cases limiting plaintiff to replevin do not present a choice between specific and substitutionary relief. Plaintiff gets specific relief either way.

The replevin cases do present a choice between personal commands and impersonal judgments; the contempt power is reserved for cases where the goods are unique. The relevant policy is similar to the policy against imprisonment for debt. But present practice may be an overbroad prophylactic response. An injunction that orders defendant to turn over a specific item of property, known to be in his possession, does not present the dangers of imprisonment for debt and would usually be easy to enforce.

However, there are a few difficult cases with defendants determined to resist, and especially with defendants who claim that the property has been lost. The danger here is the risk of imprisonment for contempt on uncertain facts. The court says defendant will be released when he turns over the property, and defendant says he no longer has the property and will never be able to turn it over.[58] If defendant is telling the truth, and if the court does not believe him, defendant can stay in jail without hope of release. That is what makes these cases like imprisonment for debt. Context drives the analogy home, for most of the reported cases of this sort involve insolvent fiduciaries ordered to turn over sums of money and debtors ordered to turn over collateral.

Granting replevin instead of an injunction avoids the risk of encountering these problems. But it does so at a cost. The limitation to replevin rewards undetermined resistance to the court's judgment. The cases where an injunction would work and replevin would not are the cases where defendant is willing to hide the goods but would not be willing to defy an order to turn them over. The effectiveness of hiding the goods depends in part on plaintiff's aggressiveness in searching for them, through self-help and post-judgment discovery. But there is some set of cases where hiding the goods works. The award of replevin instead of injunction enables some defendants to successfully defy the court.

The cases considered in this subsection are irrelevant to the choice between substitutionary and specific relief. Three of these categories—cases where specific relief is impossible, not sought, or functionally equivalent to damages—account for the bulk of all litigation. When they are eliminated, there remains a set of cases in which courts and litigants have a genuine choice between preventing harm and compensating for it. This book is about that set of cases, and it is with respect to that set that I believe our law treats substitutionary relief as generally inadequate.

3. The Historical Origins of Current Law

The death of the irreparable injury rule is not the product of recent judicial activism. Declining respect for civil juries may have pushed matters along, the merger of law and equity may have made equity judges more accessible to litigants in ordinary cases, and the explosive growth of substantive protection for intangible rights created more cases in which only specific relief would do. But the erosion of the irreparable injury rule is much older than the merger of law and equity, a point I will illustrate with occasional citations to older cases and treatises. A brief review of the familiar history of equity shows why the irreparable injury rule came under pressure from an early date.

Equity developed in the court of chancery, a court that emerged in the fourteenth century, when the chancellor began to regularize a procedure for dealing with petitions for the king's personal justice.[59] Not surprisingly, there were intermittent complaints about this bypass of the regular courts. One obvious source of complaints was the judges and other officials of the regular courts,[60] concerned about their turf. Another source of complaints must have been defendants in chancery. Petitioners presumably went to chancery because they expected to fare better there than in the regular courts. For that expectation to continue, defendants in chancery had to fare worse than in the regular courts. Objections to chancery could be tied to fear of centralized power and royal prerogative.

But the intermittent attacks on chancery did not preclude co-operation between chancery and the common law courts.[61] Chancery was doing important judicial work that the common law courts were ill equipped to do.[62] Gradually, the two courts reached an accommodation. Chancery would not duplicate the work of the common law courts, but it would do other judicial work that the common law courts had never done. In short, equity would take jurisdiction only if there were no adequate remedy at law.[63]

This is the origin of the irreparable injury rule. The need for a rule dividing jurisdiction between equity and common law arose from the existence of two separate systems. The preference for common law in the resulting rule has two possible sources. One was simple priority: the common law courts were there first, and the equity court had to justify its existence. The second was a preference for decentralized power, and a corresponding fear of royal prerogative.

So far as I can tell, a preference for legal remedies over equitable remedies played no part in the evolution of the rule. It is true that equity offered a broader range of remedies from a very early date,[64] but the most important differences between law and equity in the formative period were substantive. Equity developed the law of trusts,[65] fraud and mistake,[66] lost documents,[67] and mortgage re-demption and foreclosure.[68] In all these cases, the defect in the legal remedy had little to do with the law of remedies. No legal remedy existed because the substantive common law did not rec-ognize the claim. We tend to forget how much of our substantive law is equitable. In Maitland's famous lectures on equity in 1906, nineteen of twenty-one lectures were devoted to substantive eq-uity. He relegated specific performance and injunctions to the last two lectures.[69]

The most important thing to understand about the evolution of the irreparable injury rule is that its enforcement was entrusted to the chancery. King James I confirmed this power relationship in the famous dispute between chancery and King's Bench in 1616.[70] Chancery controlled the relationship between the two sets of courts by enjoining proceedings at common law. A litigant who attempted to prosecute his legal action in defiance of such an injunction could be imprisoned for contempt. The common law courts failed in their efforts to develop a comparable weapon against chancery.

Common law's most promising possibility was to grant writs of habeas corpus to imprisoned litigants. On return of the writ, the common law court could have reviewed the need for the underlying injunction, and thus decide for itself whether its own remedy would have been adequate. Had that practice become established, the common law courts would have gotten the last word on the adequacy of the legal remedy, and enforcement of the irreparable injury rule would have been entrusted to them. Thus, the ultimate issue in 1616 was whether the common law judges or the equity judges would determine the scope of equity.[71] Equity won.[72]

The resulting relationship between law and equity is not easily described as the subordination of equity. The common law system was primary, and equity was merely supplemental, forbidden to act unless the law was inadequate. But equity was the sole judge of the common law's adequacy. In any case of conflict between legal and equitable rules, the equitable rule controlled, because the equity court could enjoin the proceedings at law. The rules of the common law were enforceable only so long as the equity judges did not become dissatisfied with them. The limits on equitable jurisdiction were enforced only by equity's sense of self-restraint and by the risk of political reaction.

This relationship between law and equity was transmitted to the colonies and adopted in the United States. Colonial hostility to equity focused on executive rather than legislative control of the creation and staffing of equity courts; no one sought to eliminate equitable doctrines and remedies from the judicial system.[73] "Equity law was accepted by all concerned—the dispute was over the constitution of the courts that dispense equity."[74] After law and equity were committed to the same judges, or at least to judges selected by the same political process, the political reasons for restraining equity largely faded away. As Lawrence Friedman said of colonial attacks on equity, "procedural abuses, once wrenched from political context, lost their power to stir revolt."[75]

4. The Definition of Adequacy

It should not be surprising that equity interpreted the irreparable injury rule in ways that expanded its jurisdiction. Once equity established a substantive equitable right, it enforced that right without any inquiry into whether some legal right might be just as good in a particular case.[76] Similarly, once equity began to enforce a right or grant a remedy, it continued to do so even if the same right or remedy later became available at law.[77] Equity decided that damages are never an adequate remedy for a disappointed buyer of real estate,[78] and then it decided that mutuality required it also to take jurisdiction over all suits by disappointed sellers of real estate.[79]

The most important and most general rule limiting the impact of the irreparable injury rule is the definition of adequacy. A legal remedy is adequate only if it is as complete, practical, and efficient as the equitable remedy. This definition of adequacy was well established before the merger,[80] and it is the prevailing definition today.[81] As a defender of the traditional understanding acknowledges, the legal remedy almost never meets this standard.[82]

Once this definition of adequacy was in place, the irreparable injury rule did not embody much preference for legal remedies. In 1979, I characterized the rule as a tiebreaker.[83] If two remedies are equally complete, practical, and efficient, then the legal remedy will be used. That is true as far as it goes, and a far better approximation of reality than the usual statement that equitable remedies are unavailable if legal remedies are adequate. But to call the rule a tiebreaker puts the emphasis on the wrong point, because ties are so rare. One remedy is usually better than the other, and specific relief is granted or denied because of the difference. The tiebreaker functions of the irreparable injury rule rarely come into play.

Moreover, the tiebreaker function fails to explain the ubiquity of irreparable injury talk. If the rule is only a tiebreaker, and if the tiebreaker is rarely needed, then there are few occasions to invoke the rule. Yet any reader of opinions knows that courts talk about irreparable injury all the time. More is going on than tie-breaking. Courts talk about the irreparable injury rule when they deny specific relief for other reasons.

Before we can identify those reasons, we must clear away the factor that does not guide the choice. Courts do not deny specific relief merely because they judge the legal remedy adequate. The irreparable injury rule almost never bars specific relief, because substitutionary remedies are almost never adequate. At the stage of permanent relief, any litigant with a plausible need for specific relief can satisfy the irreparable injury rule.

5. Testing the Thesis

Skeptical early reactions to this thesis persuaded me to test it against a large sample of cases selected more or less randomly. Research based only on working backwards and forwards through citation patterns from the cases I knew about might limit me to a subgroup of cases unrepresentatively consistent with views I had already tentatively formed. A technically random sample is impossible, because there is no way to identify all the cases in the population. I settled for a reasonable approximation of a random sample.

In 1985, I asked a student, Karen Patton Bogle, to compile a list of cases with digest entries under the principal West Key Numbers reciting the irreparable injury rule.[84] She was to gather from that universe the most recent one hundred federal and one hundred state cases granting equitable relief, and the most recent one hundred federal and one hundred state cases denying equitable relief. Other students updated that effort in 1988.

To these lists I added the fruits of screening United States Law Week, the Supreme Court, Federal, Texas, and Northeastern advance sheets, and cases in the literature. Then we worked backwards and forwards through citation patterns, taking care to sample all American jurisdictions and to get a reasonable number of cases on each issue that emerged in the sample. Thus, the sample is somewhat analogous to a stratified sample, in which small subgroups are overrepresented so that each subgroup can be adequately studied.

This sample of cases does not statistically represent some larger population. There is no way to estimate how many other cases are represented by each case in the sample. Reliance on reported opinions is also a source of bias; the proportions of various fact patterns may be different in unreported or unfiled cases. But I doubt that there is a significantly different fact pattern that occurs with some frequency in the real world and never makes it into reported opinions. The reported cases cover a very broad range of strong and weak reasons for granting specific relief matched in every combination with strong and weak reasons for denying specific relief. We can have some confidence that all the important fact patterns are included, even though we cannot estimate their relative proportions. I believe that the cases are broadly representative, and that there is no other line of cases—reported, unreported, or even unfiled—that would give a significantly different picture.

I did not limit this search to a predetermined set of issues. Indeed, I found new issues and whole lines of cases I had not anticipated. We never exhausted the supply of cases, but we exhausted ourselves, and eventually I became confident that we were not finding any new issues or patterns.

In the chapters that follow, I use the cases as data to test the claim that the irreparable injury rule is dead. First I examine the cases granting equitable relief, and the sweeping range of defects said to make legal remedies inadequate. Then I examine the cases denying equitable relief, and identify the alternative explanations that make the irreparable injury rule irrelevant to the result.

Notes on Choosing Remedies

1. [damages are usually adequate] Bowen v. Mass., 487 U.S. 879, 925 (1988) (Scalia dissenting).

2. [preventive remedies are better] John Norton Pomeroy, 3 *A Treatise on Equity Jurisprudence as Administered in the United States of America* § 1357 at 389 (Bancroft-Whitney Co. 1883) (emphasis in original).

3. [statement of the rule] Dan B. Dobbs, *Handbook on the Law of Remedies* § 2.1 at 27, § 2.5 at 57 (West 1973).

4. [money adequate for materialists] Doug Rendleman, *The Inadequate Remedy at Law Prerequisite for an Injunction*, 33 U. Fla. L. Rev. 346, 348 (1981).

5. [corollary expressions] Rizzo v. Goode, 423 U.S. 362, 378 (1976) ("injunction is 'to be used sparingly, and only in a clear and plain case,'" quoting Irwin v. Dixion, 50 U.S. (9 How.) 10, 33 (1850)); Ghandi v. Police Dep't, 747 F.2d 338,

343 (6th Cir. 1984) ("permanent injunctive relief is an extraordinary remedy which should be granted only sparingly and only for compelling reasons"); Wong v. Nelson, 549 F. Supp. 895, 896 (D. Colo. 1982) ("severe remedy which should be granted only sparingly and only for clearly compelling reasons"); Bodenschatz v. Parrott, 153 Ill. App. 3d 1008, 1012, 506 N.E.2d 617, 620 (1987) ("should only be granted when a plaintiff's right to relief is clearly established"); Hollenkamp v. Peters, 358 N.W.2d 108, 111 (Minn. App. 1984) ("only in clear cases, reasonably free from doubt, and when necessary to prevent great and irreparable injury"); Gross v. Conn. Mut. Life Ins. Co. 361 N.W.2d 259, 265 (S.D. 1985) ("reasonable certainty").

6. [injunctions extraordinary] In Matter of Special March 1981 Grand Jury, 753 F.2d 575, 581 (7th Cir. 1985); Ghandi v. Police Dep't, 747 F.2d 338, 343 (6th Cir. 1984); Evenson v. Ortega, 605 F. Supp. 1115, 1120 (D. Ariz. 1985); Paloukos v. Intermountain Chevrolet Co., 99 Idaho 740, 745, 588 P.2d 939, 944 (1978) (specific performance is extraordinary); Crawley v. Bauchens, 57 Ill. 2d 360, 364, 312 N.E.2d 236, 239 (1974); Greenberg v. De Salvo, 254 La. 1019, 1026, 229 So.2d 83, 86 (1969); Grein v. Bd. of Educ., 216 Neb. 158, 168, 343 N.W.2d 718, 725 (1984); Murphy v. McQuade Realty, Inc., 122 N.H. 314, 316, 444 A.2d 530, 532 (1982); Garono v. State, 37 Ohio St. 3d 171, 173, 524 N.E.2d 496, 498 (1988); O'Connors v. Helfgott, 481 A.2d 388, 394 (R.I. 1984); System Concepts, Inc. v. Dixon, 669 P.2d 421, 425 (Utah 1983); Carbaugh v. Solem, 225 Va. 310, 315, 302 S.E.2d 33, 35 (1983); Vt. Div. of State Bldgs. v. Town of Castleton Bd. of Adjustment, 138 Vt. 250, 256–57, 415 A.2d 188, 193 (1980); Tyler Pipe Indus., Inc. v. State Dep't of Revenue, 96 Wash. 2d 785, 792, 638 P.2d 1213, 1219 (1982).

7. [defenses of the rule] See Edward Yorio, *Contract Enforcement: Specific Performance and Injunctions* (Little, Brown 1989) (treating rule as requiring courts to identify and weigh plaintiff's need for specific relief, preparatory to balancing that need against costs of specific relief); Rendleman, 33 U. Fla. L. Rev. 346 (cited in note 4) (treating rule as label for balancing competing interests); Gene R. Shreve, *Federal Injunctions and the Public Interest*, 51 Geo. Wash. L. Rev. 382 (1983) (analysis similar to Rendleman's).

8. [normative elements in positive theory] See J.M. Balkin, *Too Good to Be True: The Positive Economic Theory of Law* (Book Review), 87 Colum. L. Rev. 1447, 1449–54 (1987).

9. [two formulations equivalent] U.S. v. Am. Friends Serv. Comm., 419 U.S. 7, 11 (1974) ("inadequacy of available remedies goes only to the existence of irreparable injury"); Youngstown Sheet & Tube Co. v. Sawyer, 343 U.S. 579, 585 (1952) ("these two contentions are here closely related, if not identical"); K-Mart Corp. v. Oriental Plaza, Inc., 875 F.2d 907, 914 (1st Cir. 1989) ("The necessary concomitant of irreparable harm is the inadequacy of traditional legal remedies. The two are flip sides of the same coin"); Enterprise Int'l, Inc. v. Corporacion Estatal Petrolera Ecuatoriana, 762 F.2d 464, 472 (5th Cir. 1985) ("injury is 'irreparable' only if it cannot be undone through monetary remedies"); Vogel v. Am. Soc'y of Appraisers, 744 F.2d 598, 599 (7th Cir. 1984) (irreparable injury required for preliminary injunction, "but all it means is that the plaintiff is unlikely to be made whole by an award of damages or other relief at the end of the trial"); Triebwasser & Katz v. Am. Tel. & Tel. Co., 535 F.2d 1356, 1359 (2d Cir. 1976) ("irreparable harm . . . is a fundamental and traditional requirement of all preliminary injunctive relief, since equity cannot intervene where there is an adequate remedy at law"); Lewis v. S.S. Baune, 534 F.2d 1115, 1124 (5th Cir. 1976) ("often times the concepts of 'irreparable injury' and 'no adequate remedy at law' are indistinguishable"); Bannercraft Clothing Co. v. Renegotiation Bd., 466 F.2d 345, 361 n.9 (D.C. Cir. 1972) ("the very thing which makes an injury 'irreparable' is the fact that no remedy exists to repair it"), rev'd on other grounds, 415 U.S. 1 (1974); Vietnamese Fisherman's Ass'n v. Knights of the Ku Klux Klan, 543 F. Supp. 198, 218 (S.D. Tex. 1982) ("Victims of discrimination suffer irreparable injury, regardless of pecuniary damage. Accordingly, plaintiffs have no adequate remedy at law"); Gulf & W. Corp. v. Craftique Prod., Inc., 523 F. Supp. 603, 607 (S.D.N.Y. 1981) ("if the injury complained of may be compensated by an award of monetary damages, then an adequate remedy at law exists and no irreparable injury may be found"); Int'l Ass'n of Firefighters, Local 2069 v. City of Sylacauga, 436 F. Supp. 482, 492 (N.D. Ala. 1977) ("the requirements of irreparable injury and lack of adequate legal remedy merge"); Miller v. Am. Tel. & Tel. Corp. 344 F. Supp. 344, 349 (E.D. Pa. 1972) ("there can be no irreparable injury if the plaintiff has an adequate remedy at law"); Gorham v. City of New Haven, 82 Conn. 153, 157, 72 A. 1012, 1014 (1909) ("injury is irreparable when there is no legal remedy furnishing full compensation or adequate redress"); Gonzales v. Benoit, 424 So.2d 957, 959 (Fla. App. 1983) ("irreparable injury is an injury of such nature that it cannot be redressed in a court of law; an injury for which monetary compensation will not suffice"); Justices of the Inferior Court v. Griffin & W. Point Plank Road Co., 11 Ga. 246, 250 (1852) ("a trespass is irreparable, when, from its nature, it is impossible for a Court of Law to make full and complete reparation in damages"); Greenberg v. De Salvo, 254 La. 1019, 1025, 229 So.2d 83, 86 (1969) (injury that "can not be adequately compensated in damages, or for which damages cannot be compensable in money"); R.I. Turnpike & Bridge Auth. v. Cohen, 433 A.2d 179, 182 (R.I. 1981) (requirement that legal remedy be inadequate "is often labeled irreparable injury"); Dobbs, *Remedies* § 2.10 at 108 (cited in note 3) ("the term [irreparable] is not applied literally where permanent injunctions are involved and only refers to the normal adequacy test"); Owen M. Fiss & Doug Rendleman, *Injunctions* 59 (Foundation Press, 2d ed. 1984) (" 'irreparable injury' is defined as harm that cannot be (fully?) (adequately?) repaired by the remedies available in the common law courts"); Douglas Laycock, *Modern American Remedies* 335–36 (Little, Brown 1985) (two formulations are equivalent); Douglas Laycock, *Injunctions and the Irreparable Injury Rule* (Book Review), 57 Tex. L. Rev. 1065, 1070–71 (1979) (" 'irreparable injury' should mean simply injury that cannot be repaired (remedied) at law").

10. **[proffered distinctions]** See Amoco Prod. Co. v. Village of Gambell, 480 U.S. 531, 545 (1987) (irreparable injury is injury that cannot be "adequately remedied by money damages" and is "permanent or at least of long duration"); Bannercraft Clothing Co. v. Renegotiation Bd., 466 F.2d 345, 356 n.9 (D.C. Cir. 1972) ("The irreparable injury rubric is intended to describe the quality or severity of the harm necessary to trigger equitable intervention. In contrast, the inadequate remedy test looks to the possibilities of alternative modes of relief, however serious the initial injury."), rev'd on other grounds, 415 U.S. 1 (1974); Albert E. Price, Inc. v. Metzner, 574 F. Supp. 281, 289 (E.D. Pa. 1983) (irreparable injury is "substantial injury to a material degree coupled with the inadequacy of money

damages"); Charles Alan Wright & Arthur R. Miller, 11 *Federal Practice & Procedure* § 2944 at 401 (West 1973) (irreparable injury "is only one basis for showing the inadequacy of the legal remedy;" difference between this and other bases not specified); Shreve, 51 Geo. Wash. L. Rev. at 392–94 (cited in note 7) (irreparable injury formulation covers the case where plaintiff might avoid the harm through a proceeding that is not sensibly called a remedy, such as defense of a criminal prosecution). See also note 11.

11. [irreparable injury more general] Roland Mach. Co. v. Dresser Indus., Inc., 749 F.2d 380, 383 (7th Cir. 1984) (irreparable injury formulation covers the case of preliminary relief, where permanent injunction may provide an adequate remedy in equity).

12. [no reason for rule] Owen M. Fiss, *The Civil Rights Injunction* (Ind. Univ. Press 1978); see also Laycock, *Remedies* at 335–39 (cited in note 9).

13. [debate over specific performance] Richard A. Posner, *Economic Analysis of Law* § 3.11 at 61 (Little, Brown 1973) (arguing that specific performance prevents efficient breach, and that postjudgment transfer to more valuable use imposes transaction costs); Anthony T. Kronman, *Specific Performance*, 45 U. Chi. L. Rev. 351 (1978) (arguing that parties would bargain for specific performance only where goods are unique); Peter Linzer, *On the Amorality of Contract Remedies—Efficiency, Equity, and the Second Restatement*, 81 Colum. L. Rev. 111 (1981) (arguing that specific performance is more efficient because it correctly allocates subjective costs that damage measures ignore); Alan Schwartz, *The Case for Specific Performance*, 89 Yale L.J. 271 (1979) (arguing that damages are often undercompensatory, that plaintiff is in best position to know when this is true, and that specific performance is no more costly than damages); Edward Yorio, *In Defense of Money Damages for Breach of Contract*, 82 Colum. L. Rev. 1365 (1982) (arguing that damages are more flexible than specific performance, and thus more easily fitted to the equities of individual cases); Yorio, *Contract Enforcement* (cited in note 7) (expanding and refining the argument in his 1982 article).

14. [debate on transaction costs] Laycock, *Remedies* at 369–71 (cited in note 9) (arguing that either damages or specific performance requires two negotiations to reallocate resources covered by contract, and that there is no basis to assume that transaction costs of one generally exceed those of the other); William Bishop, *The Choice of Remedy for Breach of Contract*, 14 J. Legal Stud. 299 (1985) (arguing that negotiations over specific performance will generally be more expensive than negotiations over damages); Daniel Friedmann, *The Efficient Breach Fallacy*, 18 J. Legal Stud. 1 (1989) (arguing that efficient breach theorists implicitly assume that contract damages can be assessed and paid without transaction costs); Ian R. Macneil, *Contract Remedies: A Need for Better Efficiency Analysis*, 144 J. Inst'l & Theoretical Econ. 6 (1988) (criticizing all law-and-economics scholars for paying insufficient attention to their assumptions and the resulting limitations on their conclusions); Ian R. Macneil, *Efficient Breach of Contract: Circles in the Sky*, 68 Va. L. Rev. 947 (1982) (arguing that damages and specific performance differ only in transaction costs, that analysis of transaction costs is highly manipulable, and that emphasis on efficient breach increases litigation); Timothy J. Muris, *Comment: The Costs of Freely Granting Specific Performance*, 1982 Duke L.J. 1053 (arguing that under certain conditions, transaction costs of specific performance exceed transaction costs of damages); Steven Shavell, *The Design of Contracts and Rem-*

edies for Breach, 99 Q.J. Econ. 121 (1984) (offering mathematical argument for efficiency of specific performance); Thomas S. Ulen, *The Efficiency of Specific Performance: Toward a Unified Theory of Contract Remedies*, 83 Mich. L. Rev. 341 (1984) (arguing that specific performance is more efficient than damages where transaction costs of further bargaining are low, and that this is generally the case in contract disputes). For an attempt to extend this debate to new issues, considering the impact of remedial rules on earlier decisions about price and the degree of care to be taken in performance, see Richard B. Craswell, *Contract Remedies, Renegotiation, and the Theory of Efficient Breach*, 61 So. Cal. L. Rev. 629 (1988).

15. [rule not taken seriously] Fiss, *Civil Rights Injunction* at 43 (cited in note 12); Dobbs, *Remedies* § 2.5 at 61 (cited in note 3).

16. [definition of adequacy pulls teeth] Laycock, 57 Tex. L. Rev. at 1071–72 (cited in note 9).

17. [dropped from blackletter] Restatement (Second) of Torts §§ 933, 936 (1979). For the statement that the rule is misleading, see § 938 comment c.

18. [defense of rule] Rendleman, 33 U. Fla. L. Rev. 346 (cited in note 4).

19. [defense of rule] Shreve, 51 Geo. Wash. L. Rev. at 388–90, 392–94 (cited in note 7).

20. [rule diverts analysis] Rendleman at 358 ("the legal conclusion that the legal remedy is inadequate masks the intellectual process of identifying and evaluating interests").

21. [rule misunderstood] Shreve at 388 (two traditional justifications for irreparable injury rule "have nothing to do with" contemporary justifications); id. at 394–95 (irreparable injury rule should be part of "a framework of considerations that is sensitive to the way factors in the injunction dispute will register and combine differently in each case").

22. [rule requires inferior remedies] Carroll v. El Dorado Estates Div. No. Two Ass'n, Inc., 680 P.2d 1158, 1160 (Alaska 1984) (irreparable injury not shown, even though "as a practical matter injunctive relief is the only way to adequately enforce" condominium restrictions; injunction issued because authorized by statute); Johnson v. Murzyn, 1 Conn. App. 176, 181, 469 A.2d 1227, 1230 (1984) (requiring proof of irreparable injury "would seriously undermine" power to enforce zoning laws); Sadat v. Am. Motors Corp., 104 Ill. 2d 105, 117–20, 470 N.E.2d 997, 1003–04 (1984) (Simon dissenting) (irreparable injury can never be shown even though serious defects of legal remedy required corrective legislation); Fiss & Rendleman, *Injunctions* at 77 (cited in note 9) ("judges prefer to recognize most substantive rights with money, but they want people to enjoy other rights in fact"); Randy E. Barnett, *Contract Remedies and Inalienable Rights*, 4 Soc. Phil. & Policy 179, 180–81 (1986) (specific performance is "exceptional," and courts are "reluctan[t] to award" it); E. Allan Farnsworth, *Legal Remedies for Breach of Contract*, 70 Colum. L. Rev. 1145, 1156 (1970) (despite trend toward specific performance of contracts, "for the present, the promisee must ordinarily be content with money damages"); Amy H. Kastely, *The Right to Require Performance in International Sales: Towards an International Interpretation of the Vienna Convention*, 63 Wash. L. Rev. 607, 625–29 (1988) (United States and United Kingdom successfully moved to exempt their courts from specific performance provisions of United Nations Convention on Contracts for the International Sale of Goods, on grounds that specific performance was economically inefficient, and exceptional in their domestic law); Shreve,

51 Geo. Wash. L. Rev. at 387 (cited in note 7) ("The irreparability-adequacy requirement permits courts to deny injunctive relief to some plaintiffs who face certain and substantial wrongs. In such cases, the courts will devalue plaintiff's rights").

23. **[rule as linchpin]** Yorio, *Contract Enforcement* § 3.1 at 27 (cited in note 7).

24. **[rule as cost-benefit analysis]** Id. § 2.5 at 41 (emphasis in original).

25. **[hierarchy of remedies]** Fiss, *Civil Rights Injunction* at 1 (cited in note 12).

26. **[pick remedies case by case]** Id. at 90–91.

27. **[specific remedies]** See Larson v. Domestic & Foreign Commerce Corp., 337 U.S. 682, 688 (1949) (contrasting damages with "specific relief: *i.e.*, the recovery of specific property or monies, ejectment from land, or injunction either directing or restraining the defendant officer's actions").

28. **[damages for defective goods]** UCC § 2–714(2).

29. **[cancellation for defective goods]** UCC § 2–711(1). For illustrations of the difference, see Sadat v. Am. Motors Corp., 104 Ill. 2d 105, 470 N.E.2d 997 (1984), discussed in ch. 4 at notes 19–29, and First Nat'l State Bank v. Commonwealth Fed. Sav. & Loan Ass'n, 610 F.2d 164, 173–74 (3d Cir. 1979), discussed in ch. 2 at notes 102–03.

30. **[declaratory judgment legal]** Simler v. Conner, 372 U.S. 221, 223 (1963) (declaratory judgment suit raising legal issues is legal, so that jury trial is available).

31. **[declaratory judgment equitable]** Abbott Labs. v. Gardner, 387 U.S. 136, 155 (1967) (declaratory judgment suit challenging administrative action is equitable, so that equitable defenses are available).

32. **[declaratory judgment neither]** Patten Securities Corp. v. Diamond Greyhound & Genetics, Inc., 819 F.2d 400, 404 (3d Cir. 1987) ("neither equitable nor legal"); Gulf Life Ins. Co. v. Arnold, 809 F.2d 1520, 1523 (11th Cir. 1987) ("statutory creation . . . neither inherently legal nor equitable"); Am. Safety Equip. Corp. v. J.P. Maguire & Co., 391 F.2d 821, 824 (2d Cir. 1968) ("statutory creation . . . neither legal nor equitable"); Moss v. Moss, 20 Cal. 2d 640, 643, 128 P.2d 526, 528 (1942) ("not strictly legal or equitable"); Mut. Drug Co. v. Sewall, 353 Mo. 375, 379, 182 S.W.2d 575, 576 (1944) ("sui generis, and while not either strictly legal or equitable, yet its historic affinity is equitable"); Walter Houston Anderson, *Actions for Declaratory Judgments* § 216 at 471 (Harrison Co., 2d ed. 1951) ("proceedings under the statute are usually denominated as 'sui generis' to indicate they are neither purely legal nor purely equitable").

33. **[declaratory judgment both]** OB-GYN, P.C. v. Blue Cross & Blue Shield, 219 Neb. 199, 202, 361 N.W.2d 550, 553 (1985) ("sui generis and may involve questions of both law and equity"); Anderson, § 56 at 160 (1st ed. 1940) ("the only sound position that can be taken with respect to such classification is that it partakes of the properties of both legal actions and suits in equity, and that the court will apply the rules with respect thereto as the nature of the case seems to demand").

34. **[equitable orders to pay money]** Bowen v. Mass., 487 U.S. 879, 911–12 (1988) (injunction to pay sums due to state under cooperative state-federal health insurance scheme); Mitchell v. Robert De Mario Jewelry, Inc., 361 U.S. 288 (1960) (injunction to pay wages lost due to discharge or other discrimination in violation of Fair Labor Standards Act); Dominic v. Consol. Edison Co., 822 F.2d 1249, 1256–59 (2d Cir. 1987) (holding that compensation for lost future wages is equitable); Business & Prof. People for the Public Interest v. Ill. Commerce Comm'n, 171 Ill. App. 3d 948, 525 N.E.2d 1053 (1988) (injunction ordering utility to refund overcharges is not a damage award, so postjudgment interest does not accrue); Laycock, *Remedies* at 1268–69 (cited in note 9) (describing Civil Rights Act of 1964, 42 U.S.C. § 2000e-5 (1982), in which Congress avoided jury trial by characterizing all relief as equitable). See also cases cited in note 56.

35. [avoid personal commands] Rendleman, 33 U. Fla. L. Rev. at 355–58 (cited in note 4).

36. [replevin and ejectment] Restatement (Second) of Torts § 945 comment a (1979) (ejectment); id. § 946 comment a (replevin); Farnsworth, 70 Colum. L. Rev. at 1152 (cited in note 22) (replevin); M.T. Van Hecke, *Equitable Replevin*, 33 N.C. L. Rev. 57, 57 (1954). For a typical statute, see N.Y. Civ. Prac. L. & R. § 5102 (1978).

37. [mandamus and injunction] See Orange County v. N.C. Dep't of Transp., 46 N.C. App. 350, 384–85, 265 S.E.2d 890, 912–13 (1980); Dobbs, *Remedies* § 2.10 at 112 (cited in note 3).

38. [injunction as legal remedy] State ex rel. Barton v. Butler County Bd. of Elections, 39 Ohio St. 3d 291, 292, 530 N.E.2d 871, 872–73 (1988) ("relators have an adequate remedy at law via an injunction").

39. [postjudgment discovery] For typical provisions, see Ill. Rev. Stat. ch. 110, ¶ 2–1402(a) (Supp. 1988); Tex. Rule Civ. Proc. 621a (1988); Va. Code § 8.01–506 (Supp. 1984). For an illustrative case, see U.S. v. Hatchett, 862 F.2d 1249 (6th Cir. 1988) (delinquent taxpayer imprisoned until he answered postjudgment interrogatories).

40. [turnover orders] For typical provisions, see Fed. R. Civ. Proc. 69(a); Ill. Rev. Stat. ch. 110, ¶ 2–1402(b)(1) (Supp. 1988); N.Y. Civ. Prac. L. & R. § 5225(a) (1978); Tex. Civ. Prac. & Rem. Code Ann. § 31.002 (1986). For illustrative cases, see Clarkson Co. v. Shaheen, 533 F. Supp. 905 (S.D.N.Y. 1982); U.S. v. Ross, 196 F. Supp. 243 (S.D.N.Y. 1961), modified on other grounds and aff'd, 302 F.2d 831 (2d Cir. 1962).

41. [order to pay judgments out of income] Ill. Rev. Stat. ch. 110, ¶ 2–1402(b)(2) (Supp. 1988).

42. [replevin converted to personal command] Ill Rev. Stat. ch. 110, ¶ 12–301 (1984) ("any person who . . . on the officer's request therefore, refuses to deliver property to the officer having an order or judgment for the taking of the property is guilty of contempt of court"). See Cent. Prod. Credit Ass'n v. Kruse, 156 Ill. App. 3d 526, 509 N.E.2d 136 (1987) (defendant imprisoned for contempt for failing to produce replevied tractor; judgment reversed when appellate court believed his story that tractor had been stolen).

43. [defendants tend to obey] Rendleman, 33 U. Fla. L. Rev. at 358 (cited in note 4).

44. [avoidable consequences] UCC § 2–715(2) (consequential damages for breach of contract to sell goods limited to losses "which could not reasonably be prevented by cover or otherwise"); Restatement (Second) of Contracts § 350(1) (1981) ("damages are not recoverable for loss that the injured party could have avoided without undue risk, burden or humiliation"); Restatement (Second) of Torts § 918(1) (1979) ("one injured by the tort of another is not entitled to recover damages for any harm that he could have avoided by the use of reasonable effort or expenditure after the commission of the tort"). For an illustrative case, see S.J. Groves & Sons v. Warner Co., 576 F.2d 524, 528–30 (3d Cir. 1978) (stating that plaintiff cannot recover consequential damages that could have been avoided by reasonable effort, but holding that difficulties of finding alternate supplier and defendant's continued promises of timely delivery made it reasonable to continue relying on defendant in this case). For a reversal of the usual relationship between specific and substitutionary relief, see Westhart v. Mule, 261 Cal. Rptr. 640, 644–45 (Cal. App. 1989) (plaintiff who did not seek court order authorizing removal of feeding tube cannot recover damages for emotional distress from artificial prolonging of her husband's life) (not officially published, by order of state supreme court).

45. [mitigation and specific relief] See Weathersby v. Gore, 556 F.2d 1247, 1250–51, 1257–59 (5th Cir. 1977) (specific performance denied, even though at time of trial goods were irreplaceable due to shortage, where buyer could have replaced goods after seller's repudiation and before beginning of shortage); Sprecher v. Weston's Bar, Inc., 78 Wis. 2d 26, 50, 253 N.W.2d 493, 504 (1977) (refusing to enjoin transfer of liquor license to third party, where plaintiff failed to mitigate loss by purchasing identical liquor license when chance to do so was offered).

46. [suit in equity shows inadequacy] Schwartz, 89 Yale L.J. at 277 (cited in note 13).

47. [execution and garnishment] See generally Elizabeth Warren & Jay Lawrence Westbrook, *The Law of Debtors and Creditors* 35–70 (Little, Brown 1986). For illustrative cases, see In re Karlen, 885 F.2d 479 (8th Cir. 1989) (garnishment); Credit Bureau, Inc. v. Moninger, 204 Neb. 679, 284 N.W.2d 855 (1979) (execution).

48. [discharge in bankruptcy] 11 U.S.C. §§ 727, 1141, 1328(b) (1988).

49. [fraudulent conveyances] See Uniform Fraudulent Conveyance Act, 7A Unif. Laws Ann. 427 (West 1985); Uniform Fraudulent Transfer Act, 7A Unif. Laws Ann. 639 (West 1985). For an illustrative case, see Jackson v. Farmers State Bank, 481 N.E.2d 395, 403–09 (Ind. App. 1985).

50. [turnover orders] See authorities cited in note 40.

51. [family support] See Hicks v. Feiock, 485 U.S. 624 (1988) (in coercive civil contempt, state may impose on defendant burden of showing inability to pay child support); Johansen v. State, 491 P.2d 759 (Alaska 1971) (child support); Harris v. Harris, 58 Ohio St. 2d 303, 390 N.E.2d 789 (1979) (division of marital property); Ex parte Gorena, 595 S.W.2d 841 (Tex. 1979) (division of marital property); Ex parte Kollenborn, 154 Tex. 223, 276 S.W.2d 251 (1955) (child support). For accounts of the evolution of this exception, see Brown v. Brown, 287 Md. 273, 286–88, 412 A.2d 396, 399–401 (1980); McNulty v. Heitman, 600 S.W.2d 168, 172 (Mo. App. 1980). For studies of its effectiveness, see David L. Chambers, *Making Fathers Pay* (Univ. Chicago Press 1979); David L. Chambers, *Men Who Know They Are Watched: Some Benefits and Costs of Jailing for Nonpayment of Support*, 75 Mich. L. Rev. 900 (1977). For the federal directive to rely on wage withholding instead of coercion, see 42 U.S.C. § 666 (Supp. V 1987); People ex rel. Sheppard v. Money, 124 Ill. 2d 265, 529 N.E.2d 542 (1988) (upholding wage-withholding order against constitutional attack); John J. Sampson, *Title 2. Parent and Child*, 17 Tex. Tech L. Rev. 1065, 1210–30 (1986).

52. [no orders to pay] Compute-A-Call, Inc. v. Tolleson, 285 Ark. 355, 687 S.W.2d 129 (1985) (dismissing suit for injunction to pay money, explaining result in terms of irreparable injury rule); Lake Tippecanoe Owners Ass'n, Inc. v. National Lake Dev., Inc., 390 So.2d 185, 187 (Fla. App. 1980) (vacating order to pay money on grounds that suit for damages for failure to pay would be adequate remedy); CDT, Inc. v. Greener & Sumner Architects, Inc., 453 So.2d 1252, 1255–56 (La. App. 1984) (vacating injunction to pay future installments). See also Cantrell v. Henry County, 250 Ga. 822, 826, 301 S.E.2d 870, 872–73 (1983) (reversing a judgment authorizing county to disconnect water supply to subdivision if developer failed to pay fees).

53. [legislative tinkering] See Ill. Rev. Stat. ¶ 2–1402(b)(2) (Supp. 1988) (authorizing courts in all cases to compel defendant to pay judgment out of income); N.Y. Civ. Prac. L. & R. § 5226 (1978) (authorizing coercive order to pay where defendant's apparent standard of living or employment allegedly without compensation indicates existence of hidden income). See also text at notes 39–42.

54. [no imprisonment for debt] Ex parte Thompson, 282 Ala. 248, 252–54, 210 So.2d 808, 811–14 (1968) (marital debts allocated to ex-husband are not part of obligation to support ex-wife, and contempt citation for failure to pay such debts would result in unconstitutional imprisonment for debt); Risk v. Thompson, 237 Ind. 642, 651, 147 N.E.2d 540, 545 (1958) (enforcement of order to pay installment note would result in unconstitutional imprisonment for debt); Brown v. Brown, 287 Md. 273, 412 A.2d 396 (1980) (promise to support stepchild is contractual, and enforcement by imprisonment is unconstitutional imprisonment for debt); Sainz v. Sainz, 36 N.C. App. 744, 748, 245 S.E.2d 372, 374 (1978) (separation agreement is contractual, and not a support decree, so that specific performance would lead to unconstitutional imprisonment for debt); Bauer v. Bauer, 39 Ohio App. 3d 39, 41, 528 N.E.2d 964, 967 (1987) (after child becomes adult, lump sum judgment for past due child support is a debt, and imprisonment to coerce payment is unconstitutional imprisonment for debt). For typical constitutional prohibitions of imprisonment for debt, see Mich. Const. art. 1, § 21 ("No person shall be imprisoned for debt arising out of or founded on contract, express or implied, except in cases of fraud or breach of trust"); Tex. Const. art. 1, § 18 ("No person shall ever be imprisoned for debt"); Vt. Const. ch. 2, § 40 ("No person shall be imprisoned for debt").

55. [inability to pay as defense] See Hicks v. Feiock, 485 U.S. 624 (1988) (child support); Bearden v. Ga., 461 U.S. 660, 664–73 (1983) (criminal restitution); Johansen v. State, 491 P.2d 759, 765–69 (Alaska 1971) (child support); Palumbo v. Manson, 35 Conn. Supp. 130, 400 A.2d 288 (1979) (body execution); Mueller v. Butterworth, 393 So.2d 1158, 1159 (Fla. App. 1981) (failure to turn over misappropriated fund); Brown v. Brown, 237 Ga. 122, 123–24, 227 S.E.2d 14, 16 (1976) (alimony and child support); Landrigan v. McElroy, 457 A.2d 1056 (R.I. 1983) (body execution). See also Kinsey v. Preeson, 746 P.2d 542, 545–50 (Colo. 1987) (body execution is unconstitutional because it discriminates against the poor).

56. [orders to make periodic payments] Briggs v. Sullivan, 886 F.2d 1132, 1142–48 (9th Cir. 1989) (welfare benefits); Sockwell v. Maloney, 554 F.2d 1236, 1237 (2d Cir. 1977) (foster-care benefits); Cent. States, Southeast & Southwest Areas Pension Fund v. Admiral Merchants Motor Freight, Inc., 511 F. Supp. 38, 43–49 (D. Minn. 1980), aff'd as Cent. States, Southeast & Southwest Areas Pension Fund v. Jack Cole-Dixie Highway Co., 642 F.2d 1122 (8th Cir. 1981) (pension contributions); Hurley v. Toia, 432 F. Supp. 1170, 1175–76 (S.D.N.Y. 1977) (welfare benefits); Howell Pipeline Co. v. Terra Resources, Inc., 454 So.2d 1353, 1357–58 (Ala. 1984) (payments for natural gas as pumped); Robbins v. Superior Court, 38 Cal. 3d 199, 204–07, 218, 695 P.2d 695, 698–700, 707, 211 Cal. Rptr. 398, 401–03, 410 (1985) (welfare benefits); Hull Mun. Lighting Plant v. Mass. Mun. Wholesale Elec. Co., 399 Mass. 640, 641, 506 N.E.2d 140, 140 (1987) (payments on agreement to build nuclear power plant). See also Atwood Turnkey Drilling, Inc. v. Petroleo Brasileiro, S.A., 875 F.2d 1174 (5th Cir. 1989) (ordering defendant to reinstate letter of credit for benefit of plaintiff), cert. denied 110 S. Ct. 1124 (1990). See also cases cited in note 34. For further analysis of these cases, see ch. 5 at notes 14–15.

57. [replevin or ejectment adequate] Charles Simkin & Sons, Inc. v. Massiah, 289 F.2d 26, 29 n.1 (3d Cir. 1961) (refusing preliminary injunction ordering defendant to return plaintiff's tools; "equitable jurisdiction in these cases really rests upon the fact that the only relief which the plaintiff can have is possession of the *identical* thing, and this remedy cannot *with certainty* be obtained by any common law action," quoting Pomeroy, 1 *Equity Jurisprudence* § 185 at 265–66 (5th ed. 1941) (cited in note 2) (emphasis in Pomeroy's original)); Haavik v. Farnell, 264 Ala. 326, 87 So.2d 629 (1956) (refusing injunction ordering defendant to return plaintiff's personal property, "which we consider to be nothing more than a substitute for an action in detinue"); Alger v. Davis, 345 Mich. 635, 76 N.W.2d 847 (1956) (denying constructive trust and receiver because replevin would be adequate remedy to recover personal property). For analysis, see Van Hecke, 33 N.C. L. Rev. 57 (cited in note 36).

58. [resistance to personal commands] See Maggio v. Zeitz, 333 U.S. 57 (1948) (bankrupt claimed he no longer possessed inventory from his business, but would not or could not account for its disappearance); Oriel v. Russell, 278 U.S. 358 (1929) (bankrupts claimed that critical set of account books had been lost); Cent. Prod. Credit Ass'n v. Kruse, 156 Ill. App. 3d 526, 509 N.E.2d 136 (1987) (debtor failed to produce tractor for lienholder, claiming that it disappeared from his field one night and must have been stolen); Tegtmeyer v. Tegtmeyer, 292 Ill. App. 434, 11 N.E.2d 657 (1937) (trustee refused to account for trust assets); Drake v. Nat'l Bank of Commerce, 168 Va. 230, 190 S.E. 302 (1937) (defendant claimed to have lost $18,000 in cash while bird hunting). See also People ex rel. Feldman v. Warden, 46 A.D.2d 256, 362 N.Y.S.2d 171 (1974) (foster mother refused to produce child, and later claimed not to know where he was).

59. [emergence of equity] Frederick Maitland, *Equity: A Course of Lectures* 4–5 (Cambridge Univ. Press, 2d ed. 1936); Theodore F.T. Plucknett, *A Concise History of the Common Law* 180–81 (Little, Brown, 5th ed. 1956); Joseph Story, 1 *Commentaries on Equity Jurisprudence as Administered in England and America* §§ 41–49 at 41–53 (Little, Brown 1835).

60. [complaints about equity] Maitland at 6; Plucknett at 187–95; 1 Story § 46 at 49–50.

61. [cooperation between law and equity] See Maitland at 8, 153; Plucknett, at 188–89, 210–11, 686–88, 692.

62. [work that common law could not do] Maitland at 6–7; Plucknett at 194–95.

63. [origin of rule] Maitland at 7; 1 Story § 49 at 53.

64. [early equitable remedies] Pomeroy, 1 *Equity Jurisprudence* § 37 at 30 (1881) (cited in note 2); 2 Story § 716 at 23 (1836).

65. [trusts] Maitland at 6–7, 23–42; 1 Pomeroy § 38 at 31; 2 id. §§ 978–81 at 519–24 (1882); 2 Story §§ 960–82 at 228–45.

66. [fraud and mistake] Maitland at 7; 1 Story §§ 110–440 at 121–422.

67. [lost documents] Maitland at 7; 2 Pomeroy § 824 at 285–86; 1 Story §§ 78–88 at 94–105.

68. [mortgages] 3 Pomeroy § 1180 at 147–48; 2 Story §§ 1004–34 at 270–301.

69. [two lectures on remedies] Maitland at 301–29.

70. [crisis of 1616] For analysis of the controversy, see John P. Dawson, *Coke and Ellesmere Disinterred: The Attack on the Chancery in 1616*, 36 Ill. L. Rev. 127 (1941). The documents are reprinted with explanatory text in James Spedding, 5 *Letters and Life of Francis Bacon* 380–99 (Longman & Co. 1869). For a summary with citations to contemporary pamphlets, see 1 Story § 51 at 56–57.

71. [which judges would decide adequacy] See Dawson at 148–51.

72. [primacy of equity] See Maitland at 9, 321 (this quarrel "finally decided that the Court of Chancery was to have the upper hand over the courts of law").

73. [colonial attitudes toward equity] Stanley Katz, *The Politics of Law in Colonial America: Controversies over Chancery Courts and Equity Law in the Eighteenth Century*, in *Law in American History* 257 (5 *Perspectives in American History Series*, Donald Fleming & Bernard Bailyn eds.) (Harvard Univ. Press 1971). See Lawrence M. Friedman, *A History of American Law* 47–48, 130–31 (Simon & Schuster 1973); Plucknett, *Common Law* at 687 (cited in note 59).

74. [equity accepted by all] Katz at 282.

75. [equity wrenched from political context] Friedman at 48.

76. [substantive equity not subject to rule] See Pomeroy, 1 *Equity Jurisprudence* § 219 at 218–20, § 1402 at 443 n.1 (cited in note 2) (equity will enforce express or implied trust over common chattels, "since the court will always enforce a trust"). For other examples, see Estate of Cantonia v. Sindel, 684 S.W.2d 592, 595 (Mo. App. 1985) (equitable conversion); Laycock, *Remedies* at 336 (cited in note 9) (mortgage foreclosure).

77. [expansion of law did not contract equity] Buzard v. Houston, 119 U.S. 347, 352 (1886) ("the assumption of jurisdiction by the courts of law, by gradually extending their powers, did not displace the earlier jurisdiction of the court of chancery"); Smith v. Whitmire, 273 Ark. 120, 122–23, 617 S.W.2d 845, 846 (1981) (foreclosing equitable lien despite alleged legal remedy under Uniform Commercial Code); Hempstead & Conway v. Watkins, 6 Ark. 317, 355–68 (1845) (extensively reviewing the cases); Everhart v. Miles, 47 Md. App. 131, 137–38, 422 A.2d 28, 31 (1980) (unjust enrichment claim in equity); 1 Pomeroy, § 182 at 169–71, §§ 276–78 at 300–02; Story, 1 *Equity Jurisprudence* § 63 at 80–81 (cited in note 59); Fleming James, Jr., *Right to Jury Trial in Civil Actions*, 72 Yale L.J. 655, 659 (1963) ("borrowing by each jurisdiction from the other was not accompanied by an equivalent sloughing off of functions," leading "to a very large overlap between law and equity"). For modern cases limiting this rule, see Ross v. Bernhard, 396 U.S. 531 (1970) (holding that seventh amendment and merger of law and equity combined to repudiate traditional rule); Dairy Queen, Inc. v. Wood, 369 U.S. 469 (1962) (same); Beacon Theatres, Inc. v. Westover, 359 U.S. 500 (1959) (same); Koperski v. Husker Dodge, Inc., 208 Neb. 29, 37–39, 302 N.W.2d 655, 660 (1981) (equity has jurisdiction, but generally will not exercise it if new statutory remedy is adequate).

78. [buyers of real estate] 3 Pomeroy, § 1401 at 441–42; 2 Story, § 717 at 24, § 746 at 51. See ch. 2 part A.1.

79. [sellers of real estate] Richman v. Seaberg, 353 Mass. 757, 231 N.E.2d 380 (1967) (granting specific performance without discussing irreparable injury); Hopper v. Hopper, 16 N.J. Eq. 147, 148 (1863) (specific performance is "a matter of course"; "doctrine is well established that the remedy is mutual"); Belilove v. Reich, 102 R.I. 250, 257, 229 A.2d 775, 779 (1967) (seller has no duty to seek other buyers before suing for specific performance); Maitland, *Equity* at 302–03 (cited in note 59); 2 Story § 790 at 99. See also Trachtenburg v. Sibarco Stations, Inc., 477 Pa. 517, 521–25, 384 A.2d 1209, 1212–13 (1978) (seller of real estate can sue in assumpsit for full purchase price plus consequential damages; this is legal remedy, equivalent to specific performance but tried to jury); 2 Story § 723 at 29–30 (sellers of chattels are entitled to specific performance in cases where buyer would have been entitled to specific performance). But see Suchan v. Rutherford, 90 Idaho 288, 295–98, 302–03, 410 P.2d 434, 438–40, 444 (1966) (rejecting "majority rule" of specific performance for sellers of real estate, and refusing specific performance on grounds of adequacy of legal remedy and difficulty of supervising payment of purchase price over eighteen-year period); Centex Homes Corp. v. Boag, 128 N.J. Super. 385, 389–94, 320 A.2d 194, 196–99 (1974) (repudiating settled New Jersey rule and refusing real estate developer's request for specific performance against consumer who had been transferred to another state after contracting to buy condominium unit; plaintiff was plainly in better position than defendant to resell unit).

80. [premerger definition of adequacy] Am. Life Ins. Co. v. Stewart, 300 U.S. 203, 214–15 (1937); Terrace v. Thompson, 263 U.S. 197, 214 (1923); Boise Artesian Hot & Cold Water Co. v. Boise City, 213 U.S. 276, 281 (1909); Rich v. Braxton, 158 U.S. 375, 406 (1895); May v. LeClaire, 78 U.S. (11 Wall.) 217, 236 (1870); Boyce's Executors v. Grundy, 28 U.S. (3 Pet.) 210, 215 (1830); Nat'l Marking Mach. Co. v. Triumph Mfg. Co., 13 F.2d 6, 9 (8th Cir. 1926); Michener v. Springfield Engine & Thresher Co., 142 Ind. 130, 132–33, 40 N.E. 679, 681 (1895); Sumner v. Crawford, 91 Tex. 129, 131–32, 41 S.W. 994, 995 (1897); Butterick Pub. Co. v. Rose, 141 Wis. 533, 537, 124 N.W. 647, 649 (1910); 1 Pomeroy § 180 at 166–67; 1 Story § 33 at 32. See also City of Chicago v. Collins, 175 Ill. 445, 453, 51 N.E. 907, 909 (1898) (test is whether "adequate relief can best be had in the forum of a court of equity").

81. [postmerger definition of adequacy] USACO Coal Co. v. Carbomin Energy, Inc., 689 F.2d 94, 99 (6th Cir. 1982); Laclede Gas Co. v. Amoco Oil Co., 522 F.2d 33, 40 (8th Cir. 1975); Weathersbee v. Wallace, 14 Ark. App. 174, 176, 686 S.W.2d 447, 449 (1985); Hicks v. Clayton, 67 Cal. App. 3d 251, 264, 136 Cal. Rptr. 512, 520 (1977); Jefferson Chem. Co. v. Mobay Chem. Co., 253 A.2d 512, 515 (Del. Ch. 1969); Liza Danielle, Inc. v. Jamko, Inc., 408 So.2d 735, 738 (Fla. 1982); Middlebrooks v. Lonas, 246 Ga. 720, 721, 272 S.E.2d 687, 689 (1980); Thomas v. Campbell, 107 Idaho 398, 404–05, 690 P.2d 333, 339–40 (1984); Bio-Medical Labs., Inc. v. Trainor, 68 Ill. 2d 540, 549, 370 N.E.2d 223, 227 (1977); Hatcher v. Graddick, 509 N.E.2d 258, 260 (Ind. App. 1987); Potucek v. Blair, 176 Kan. 263, 270, 270 P.2d 240, 244 (1954); West v. Town of Winnsboro, 252 La. 605, 620–21, 211 So.2d 665, 670–71 (1967); Alger v. Davis, 345 Mich. 635, 641, 76 N.W.2d 847, 850 (1956); Ganser v. County of Lancaster, 215 Neb. 313, 317, 338 N.W.2d 609, 611 (1983);

D.C. Trautman Co. v. Fargo Excavating Co., 380 N.W.2d 644, 645 (N.D. 1986); Hein v. Marts, 295 N.W.2d 167, 171–72 (S.D. 1980); Brazos River Conservation & Reclamation Dist. v. Allen, 141 Tex. 208, 171 S.W.2d 842, 846 (1943); Chevron U.S.A., Inc. v. Stoker, 666 S.W.2d 379, 382 (Tex. App. 1984); In re C.B., 147 Vt. 378, 380–81, 518 A.2d 366, 368–69 (1986); Allegheny Dev. Corp. v. Barati, 166 W. Va. 218, 221–22, 273 S.E.2d 384, 387 (1980); Restatement (Second) of Torts §933 comment a, at 560–61 (1979); Dobbs, *Remedies* §2.5 at 60 (cited in note 3); John F. Dobbyn, *Injunctions in a Nutshell* 38 (West 1974); Henry L. McClintock, *Equity* § 43 at 103 (West, 2d ed. 1948); 42 Am. Jur. 2d *Injunctions* § 40 at 779 (1969); 30 C.J.S. *Equity* § 25 at 824–25 (1965).

82. [definition never satisfied] Shreve, 51 Geo. Wash. L. Rev. at 387 n.33 (cited in note 7).

83. [rule as tiebreaker] Laycock, 57 Tex. L. Rev. at 1071 (cited note 9).

84. [West Key Numbers] These were Injunctions §§ 14–19, Equity §§ 43, 45–46, and Specific Performance § 5.

2

Irreplaceability

Injury is irreparable if plaintiff cannot use damages to replace the specific thing he has lost. This is by far the most important source of irreparable injury. It has many applications and several formulations. Courts may say that plaintiff has lost something unique, that he has lost something unavailable on the market, or that he has lost something he should not be required to do without. They may say defendant rather than plaintiff should bear the burden of replacement. They may say damages are too hard to measure. Some of these formulations are thought of as independent rules. But they all emphasize different facets of the same underlying principle: damages are inadequate if they cannot be used to replace the specific thing plaintiff lost.

A. Losses That Cannot Be Replaced

1. Real Property

The classic example of a loss that cannot be replaced is land. Thus, contracts to sell real estate are specifically enforceable;[1] this rule is so well settled that it is rarely litigated anymore. The rule is traditionally explained on the ground that no other piece of land would be an adequate replacement for the one under contract, because every parcel of real estate is unique.[2]

This explanation is sometimes belittled as fictional,[3] but most fictional applications are hypothetical and of recent origin. The standard example is a New Jersey opinion that describes "hundreds of virtually identical" condominium units, sold to the public "by means of sample, in this case model apartments," at a fixed price schedule. The court concludes that these units "share the same characteristics as personal property."[4] But it did not actually hold that money is an adequate substitute for a condominium unit. The ground of decision was that a seller seeking only money is not entitled to specific performance against a defaulting buyer. And the best explanation of the result is that the seller was in far better position to resell the unit than the buyer would have been. Seller was the developer, in the business of selling other units at the same site; the defaulting buyer was a consumer whose employer had transferred him to another state.

The rule that damages are never an adequate substitute for land originated when land was the dominant form of wealth in the society and the key to social and political status,[5] and when tract houses and condominiums did not exist. In those circumstances, it probably did not seem at all fictional to say that one horse could substitute for another horse but no piece of land could substitute for any other. Even today, there are few cases in which an exact substitute is actually on the market and available to a disappointed buyer. When there is such a case, plaintiff is unlikely to spend his time and money suing for specific performance.

Most land cases involve wrongs less extensive than refusal to convey a fee simple. A wide range of wrongs relating to land are regularly held to inflict irreparable injury. These include encroachments,[6] nuisance,[7] and continuous or repeated trespasses;[8] removing timber,[9] minerals,[10] or lateral support;[11] violating restrictive covenants,[12] zoning laws,[13] condominium restrictions,[14] or lease agreements;[15] interfering with easements;[16] and wrongfully foreclosing liens.[17] Courts offer a variety of explanations for why the injury is irreparable in these cases:[18] that all land is unique,[19] that any injury that changes the "substance" of the estate is irreparable,[20] that damages are hard to measure,[21] or that a legal remedy would require a multiplicity of suits.[22] Whatever the rationale, injunctive relief is almost never withheld in these cases on the ground that damages are an adequate remedy, although it is sometimes withheld on other grounds, especially the disproportionate expense of removing an encroachment or abating a nuisance.[23]

There may be some remaining force to the rule that a genuine dispute over title will not be determined in a suit to enjoin trespass.[24] But this rule does not reflect any preference for damages. The legal remedy is ejectment or some modern equivalent, which culminates in an order putting the winner in possession.[25] The only plausible policy explanation is that plaintiff is entitled to specific relief, but that defendant is entitled to jury trial if title is at risk.[26] Even this policy is limited; if plaintiff is in possession, ejectment would not lie at common law, and a bill to quiet title will still be heard in equity without a jury.[27] Moreover, courts regularly issue preliminary injunctions to prevent irreparable injury pending trial of the title action.[28]

The view that equity is reluctant to enjoin a trespass is perpetuated by Chancellor Kent's well-known opinion in *Jerome v. Ross*.[29] Kent refused to enjoin the builders of the Erie Canal from taking rock from nearby wastelands. Presumably, the real reason for the decision was that he wanted not to hinder the canal. But his opinion seemed to say that damages are usually an adequate remedy for trespass.

The opinion still appears in a well-known casebook,[30] but its rationale has long been repudiated. Pomeroy's nineteenth-century treatise,[31] and several turn-of-the-century opinions,[32] rejected *Jerome* as wrong in principle, inconsistent with the great majority of the cases, and at least in tension with an earlier opinion of Chancellor Kent.[33] I found no modern case refusing to enjoin a continuing trespass because of the irreparable injury rule.

2. Personal Property

Damages are often an adequate remedy for the loss of goods, but only because plaintiff can use the money to buy identical goods.[34] When plaintiff gets identical goods either way, the choice between legal and equitable remedies hardly matters.

If the goods cannot be replaced with money, then money is not an adequate remedy for their loss. The classic illustration of irreplaceable goods is goods that are obviously unique, such as heirlooms or works of art.[35] Equitable relief to recover such goods is sometimes explained on the ground that they have a *"pretium affectionis,"*[36] or sentimental value.

The same reasoning has been applied to more contemporary subjects of litigation, including unique commercial products,[37] customized cars[38] and boats,[39] a custom stereo set,[40] breeding stock,[41] franchises,[42] businesses,[43] closely held corporate stock,[44] and controlling blocks of publicly traded stock.[45]

Perhaps most revealing, specific performance is available for goods that cannot be replaced because of monopoly[46] or shortage.[47] Thus, courts have decreed specific performance of contracts for the sale of cotton,[48] aviation fuel,[49] and industrial chemicals.[50] A famous case holds that no other variety of carrot can substitute for Chantenay red-cored carrots, so that specific performance is appropriate when Chantenays are in short supply.[51] During the shortages caused by World War II, some courts specifically enforced contracts for the sale of automobiles.[52] Courts that refused specific performance generally viewed the shortage as less severe,[53] considered it adequate to buy a different kind of car,[54] or expected plaintiffs to buy in the gray market.[55] No court suggested that it would be adequate for plaintiff to do without a car and recover damages instead.

Replaceability of goods is principally at issue in actions for specific performance of contracts. If plaintiff has been deprived of property rights, he can invoke legal remedies that give specific relief. He can recover personal property in replevin, and real property in ejectment.[56] Defendant cannot defeat recovery of the property by paying damages.[57] Defendant can sometimes defeat recovery of the property by defiance or evasion; the means of enforcing replevin and ejectment are less effective than the means of enforcing injunctions. Where the property is unique, this difference in enforcement is sometimes invoked to justify an injunction.[58] Despite this difference between personal commands and impersonal judgments, both the legal and equitable remedies aim to provide specific relief.

Modern ejectment and replevin are descended from ancient writs that predate the development of anything like a general law of contract.[59] Perhaps that is why they protect only property rights and not contract rights. I doubt that there is any good contemporary reason for requiring disputed goods to be irreplaceable as a condition for specific performance of a contract to sell them but not as a condition for recovering them from a converter. But if there is such a reason, it will be found in the substantive policies of contract law and in the view that tangible property deserves more protection than promises.[60] It will not be found in any general preference for damages over specific relief.

If defendant threatens to damage, destroy, or convert property still in plaintiff's possession, there is no anticipatory version of replevin or ejectment to prevent the harm. This is so even though we are dealing with property rights and not contract rights. The anticipatory remedy is an injunction, and the injunction is formally subject to the irreparable injury rule. But I doubt that a modern court would let defendant destroy plaintiff's goods for no better reason than the likelihood that they could be replaced later. I found only a few cases, most of which enjoined the tort.[61] A minority of mostly older cases denied the injunction;[62] at least one of those may be better explained by skepticism about plaintiff's claim on the merits.[63]

3. Intangible Rights

The principle that damages are an inadequate remedy for the loss of something irreplaceable is not limited to unique tangible property. The principle even more obviously applies to intangible rights that are never bought or sold in any market. This is why injunctions are the standard remedy in civil rights or environmental litigation.[64] Plaintiff cannot use a damage award to replace the right to vote,[65] equal representation,[66] an adequate hearing,[67] integrated public facilities,[68] minimally adequate treatment in a state prison,[69] free speech,[70] religious liberty,[71] education,[72] freedom from employment discrimination,[73] freedom from unreasonable searches and seizures,[74] or any similar civil or political right.[75] Neither can a damage award replace clean air[76] or water,[77] a lost forest[78] or species,[79] or the cautionary effects of an environmental impact statement.[80] In all these kinds of cases, damages are obviously inadequate, awarded only as a second-best in cases where it is too late for an injunction to do any good. No one seriously argues that damages are adequate in such cases, and the opinions often fail to discuss the issue.

Injuries to the person fall under the same rationale. Plaintiffs cannot replace defective body parts, and awards for pain and suffering do not make the pain go away. Damages are the standard remedy for personal injury only because personal injuries can rarely be anticipated in time to prevent them by injunction. But where an injunction is possible, the irreparable injury rule is obviously satisfied: if it happens, the physical injury to the plaintiff will be irreparable. The most common examples are injunctions against family violence.[81] Forty-eight states now authorize such orders by statute.[82] Another clear example is a Georgia case enjoining a white landlord from driving a black sharecropper off the land. The opinion's explicit rationale is to avoid violence.[83]

The issue also arises when courts are asked to enjoin conduct that creates a risk of serious injury. When the risk is great enough, those injunctions are routinely granted.[84] Courts also enjoin unlawful conduct that will cause emotional distress, and occasionally note the obvious point that emotional distress is irreparable injury.[85]

B. Losses That Can Be Replaced Only with Difficulty

There is no bright line between what is replaceable and what is not. Specific relief is not limited to goods like the Mona Lisa, which is certainly and absolutely irreplaceable. Replaceability is often a matter of degree. Even in severe shortages, some goods are produced and some customers will be supplied. Plaintiff may argue only that her ability to replace the goods is uncertain, unreliable, or difficult. Defendant may argue that similar but not identical goods would be adequate, or that plaintiff could get identical goods if she would go to enough trouble and pay a high enough price.

At this point, courts begin to divide. A significant minority hold that damages are adequate if replacement is difficult, so long as it is possible.[86] But most courts have not required a showing that replacement is absolutely impossible at any price. Courts granting specific performance frequently say that replacement would be difficult, without concluding that it would be impossible.[87]

Many courts have recognized the difficulty and unreliability of procuring scarce goods, and they have recognized plaintiff's need for a steady supply. In an early case involving a farmer's contract to sell his crop to a tomato cannery, the court noted that the purpose of buying the entire crop was to keep the cannery running at full capacity through the short harvest season, and it commented that the very existence of such contracts showed the need for their specific performance.[88] Similarly, in a case involving aviation fuel during the embargo occasioned by the Yom Kippur War, the court saw only "chaos" if the plaintiff airline were left to scramble for fuel in the spot market.[89] Each of these courts granted specific performance.

An especially revealing case is *Kaiser Trading Co. v. Associated Metals & Minerals Co.*,[90] granting specific performance of a contract for the sale of two thousand tons of cryolite. The seller showed that several hundred tons were available on the world market, so at least partial cover was possible. Far more was committed to other buyers under long-term contracts. Efficient breach theorists might assume that plaintiff could buy from those buyers or their sellers by simply bidding a high enough price.[91] But the court sensibly treated cryolite under contract to others as unavailable, and it imposed on defendant the burden of showing that the whole two thousand tons could be replaced. This allocation of the burden of proof is parallel to the rule that wrongdoers bear the risk of uncertainty in the measurement of damages.[92] It suggests a broader but sensible principle that adjudicated wrongdoers bear the risk of uncertainty on all questions related to remedy. Of most immediate relevance here, this allocation of the burden establishes a presumption in favor of the remedy preferred by plaintiff. If the court is uncertain whether the injury is irreparable, the equitable remedy is available.

The shortage cases rest on the ground that replacement is at least difficult and may be impossible. Occasionally, replacement is plainly possible and the unambiguous ground of decision is that a damage remedy would shift some significant difficulty from defendant to plaintiff. A contract example is *Thompson v. Commonwealth*,[93] specifically enforcing a contract to build roll-call voting machines. The evidence was that "any first class machine shop" could build the machines, but that only defendant was experienced at doing so. The court thought that in these circumstances the task of recruiting an alternate provider was sufficiently difficult to make the damage remedy inadequate. One way to explain the case is that part of what plaintiff had bought was defendant's expertise, and the expertise was not replaceable in the market. The court made the point a little differently: damages would force plaintiff to "assume the responsibility and risk which properly belong to defendants." It may have helped that plaintiff was the state, but the court did not say so. Other courts have applied similar reasoning to private plaintiffs.[94]

A well-known tort example is *Wheelock v. Noonan*,[95] where defendant covered plaintiff's land with huge boulders and refused to remove them. The court ordered defendant to remove the boulders, even though it was surely possible for plaintiff to have them removed and sue defendant for the expense. But the court thought that would "burden" plaintiff, "compelling him to do in advance for the trespasser what the latter is bound to do."[96]

This sounds more in moral indignation than in irreplaceability, but the two are linked. Labor to remove the boulders and land to dump them on was presumably available in the market and compensable in damages. But plaintiff would bear the inconvenience of hiring and supervising the workers and finding the alternate site, or of finding an independent contractor for this unusual chore. Defendant's persistent breach of his promise to remove the boulders suggests that he had not found it easy to dispose of them. Even if plaintiff could have been compensated for his time and trouble in 1888, he would still have spent the time and suffered the trouble. Damages could offset the loss but not replace it: it is no more possible to recover lost time and trouble than to replace the Mona Lisa.

Cases like *Thompson* and *Wheelock* stand for the proposition that significant inconvenience is irreparable injury, and that proposition follows from the general rule that damages are adequate only if they can be used to replace what plaintiff lost.

C. Damages That Are Hard to Measure

Damages are inadequate when they are hard to measure accurately.[97] Any case where the loss is irreplaceable on the market can also be described as a case where damages are hard to measure. The actual cost of cover is the most easily applied measure of damages. Value in an active market is nearly as easy. But value in an inactive or nonexistent market is difficult, and if plaintiff is unable to replace the item lost, there may be no actual transaction to support an assessment of value.[98] Consequential damages can also be difficult to measure, and they arise only when plaintiff cannot immediately replace what was lost. If the court in *Wheelock v. Noonan* had thought about compensating plaintiff for the time and trouble of removing the boulders, it might well have said that such damages were too difficult to measure.[99]

Whether courts think of these as uniqueness cases or difficult damages cases is partly a matter of habit, partly a matter of how the case is presented, and partly a matter of whether plaintiff's loss is commercial or personal. We tend to think of heirlooms as unique, although we could just as easily say that damages are hard to measure because heirlooms are difficult to value. Either explanation suffices to show the inadequacy of the legal remedy. But even if for some reason we had no doubt of the heirloom's value, those not committed to the economic dogma that all values are fungible would say that plaintiff is entitled to the heirloom itself and not just its value.[100] So in the heirloom context, to say that the thing is irreplaceable is to say something more than that its value is hard to measure.

Similarly, it is hard to value irreplaceable rights that never trade in any market. This is another way to explain the civil rights, environmental, personal injury, and emotional distress cases, and the opinions are occasionally written on the ground that damages would be too difficult to measure.[101] But these cases are also concerned with entitlements that many of us would not willingly sell for money even if we were confident of the valuation.

In commercial cases, where most parties are concerned primarily with the bottom line, there is less difference between saying that a thing is unique and saying that it is hard to value. A good example is *First National State Bank v. Commonwealth Federal Savings & Loan Association*.[102] Plaintiff was the construction lender on a shopping mall; defendant was the permanent lender who refused to honor its loan commitment when the mall turned out to be a loser. Plaintiff foreclosed on the mall and then sued for specific performance of the permanent loan commitment. Plaintiff's damages were the amount of the promised permanent loan less the value of the mall, and defendant thought that an adequate remedy. But the court found it impossible to accurately value the mall. Plaintiff could have sold the mall to determine its value, but no one suggested that. That would have shifted the burden of selling a half-occupied shopping mall from a defendant who had agreed to bear that risk to a plaintiff who had not. The court granted specific performance, holding that damages were inadequate because valuation was too difficult.

This is a case where plaintiff wanted to get rid of a unique property rather than acquire it, but that does not affect the analysis. The frustrated seller's desire to escape unique burdens is the mirror image of the frustrated buyer's desire to acquire unique benefits.[103] This is a better rationale than mutuality for the rule granting specific performance to sellers of real estate.[104]

The most common example of damages too difficult to measure is lost profits.[105] With equal accuracy but greater abstraction, we could say that the lost transaction that would have generated the profits was unique. It can perhaps be replaced with some other transaction, but that transaction will not be exactly the same; it may produce more profit or less, and the difference will be hard to estimate. Where plaintiff has available an alternative transaction that is identical or nearly so—where the cannery is able to buy the same quantity of tomatoes from the farmer down the road—lost profits are not so difficult to measure.

But a deal of any complexity cannot be replaced with an identical deal. Profits from such a deal are hard to measure, and the court will avoid measuring them if it can. As Pomeroy said of long-term contracts over a century ago, plaintiff should not be forced "to sell his possible profits at a price depending upon a mere guess."[106] It is, therefore, not surprising that output and requirements contracts are specifically enforced, whether or not there is a shortage.[107] Variations in the market price and in the quantity of goods produced or required make the damages too hard to measure.

Tortious interference with income-producing property produces similar questions about volume and profit margin: How much business was irreplaceably lost? After the fact the court will estimate such damages as best it can. But when there is time, the court will enjoin the interference on the ground that damages would be too hard to measure accurately.[108]

Similarly, damages from loss of intellectual property are notoriously difficult to measure. Injunctions are a routine remedy for misappropriation of trade secrets;[109] infringement of patents,[110] copyrights,[111] or trademarks;[112] violations of antitrust laws[113] or covenants not to compete;[114] interference with contract;[115] and other kinds of unfair competition.[116] The antitrust cases tend to assume that violations should be enjoined if they will cause future injury; the opinions are more likely to discuss whether injury is sufficiently threatened and the appropriate scope of the injunction.[117] In all these cases, damages or restitution of the wrongdoer's profits are generally reserved for past violations beyond the reach of injunctions.

D. Losses That Plaintiff Should Not Have to Suffer

Courts sometimes say that the loss is one plaintiff should not have to suffer even with compensation.[118] This is another label for a subset of unique and irreplaceable losses: cases where the tning lost is irreplaceable and the court is indignant or especially sympathetic. The pile of boulders in *Wheelock v. Noonan* is one example.[119]

Another example is *Fleischer v. James Drug Stores*,[120] where plaintiff was expelled from an association of independent druggists that provided cooperative purchasing, advertising, and other services. The court found that plaintiff would be forced out of business without the benefits of the co-op, and that damages would be hard to measure. The court went on to say that damages would be inadequate even if they could be accurately calculated, because the "subject matter of the contract has a peculiar and special value to the party demanding performance . . . Complainant has a right to his business."[121]

The court's statement presupposes that every small business is unique. That the plaintiff could use his damage judgment to buy a dry cleaner's, or even a different drugstore, is not the same as preserving his existing business in which he has presumably invested much time and effort. The "peculiar and special value" is like the *pretium affectionis* in the heirloom cases.[122] It is personal to plaintiff, and he should not have to give it up. Or as Judge

Friendly once put it, enjoining termination of a Ford dealership, plaintiffs "want to sell automobiles, not to live on the income from a damage award."[123]

Similar analysis is obviously applicable to environmental and personal injury cases, and especially to civil rights cases. Our political tradition speaks of "unalienable Rights."[124] If such rights are inalienable even voluntarily, certainly no court can permit their involuntary transfer on the ground that money damages will be an adequate remedy.

Notes on Irreplaceability

1. [land contracts] LaLonde v. Davis, 879 F.2d 665 (9th Cir. 1989) (granting specific performance without discussing irreparable injury); Curley v. Mobil Oil Corp., 860 F.2d 1129, 1134–37 (1st Cir. 1988) ("lower court's denial of specific performance will accordingly be reversed for abuse of discretion . . . 'in the absence of significant equitable reasons for refusing such relief'" (quoting Allen v. Rakes, 359 Mass. 1, 6, 267 N.E. 2d 628, 631 (1971))); Xanadu, Inc. v. Zetley, 822 F.2d 982, 985 (11th Cir. 1987) (granting specific performance without discussing irreparable injury); Henderson v. Fisher, 236 Cal. App. 2d 468, 473, 46 Cal. Rptr. 173, 177–78 (1965) (damages "presumed" inadequate and specific performance "a matter of course"); Atchison v. City of Englewood, 193 Colo. 367, 379, 568 P.2d 13, 22 (1977) (specific performance "generally granted even though the injury resulting from nonperformance is compensable in damages"); In re Frayser's Estate, 401 Ill. 364, 371–72, 82 N.E.2d 633, 637 (1948) (specific performance "a matter of right"); Donavan v. Ivy Knoll Apts. P'ship, 537 N.E.2d 47, 53–54 (Ind. App. 1989) (granting specific performance without discussing irreparable injury); Severson v. Elberon Elev., Inc., 250 N.W.2d 417, 423 (Iowa 1977) (courts "assume" that damages are inadequate); Forbes v. Wells Beach Casino, Inc., 307 A.2d 210, 220 (Me. 1973) ("generally accepted principle"); Gross v. J & L Camping & Sports Center, Inc., 270 Md. 539, 543, 312 A.2d 270, 273 (1973) ("matter of course"); Kent v. Bell, 374 Mich. 646, 651, 132 N.W.2d 601, 604 (1965) ("land, traditionally presumed to have a peculiar value, is subject to specific performance"); Gethsemane Lutheran Church v. Zacho, 258 Minn. 438, 443, 104 N.W.2d 645, 648 (1960) ("normally be granted as a matter of right"); Ide v. Leiser, 10 Mont. 5, 15, 24 P. 695, 697 (1890) ("presumption" that damages are inadequate); Meyer v. Reed, 91 N.J. Eq. 237, 239, 109 A. 733, 734 (1920) (too settled to require serious consideration); Hutchins v. Honeycutt, 286 N.C. 314, 318–19, 210 S.E.2d 254, 256–57 (1974) ("accepted doctrine"); Wittick v. Miles, 274 Or. 1, 6–7, 545 P.2d 121, 125 (Or. 1976) ("either party to a contract for the sale of land generally may have specific performance"); Payne v. Clark, 409 Pa. 557, 561–62, 187 A.2d 769, 771 (1963) (inadequate consideration does not defeat specific performance unless consideration is "grossly disproportionate"); Melrose Enterprises, Inc. v. Pawtucket Form Constr. Co., 550 A.2d 300 (R.I. 1988) (granting specific performance without

Irreplaceability

Irreplaceability 49

discussing irreparable injury); Arthur Linton Corbin, 5A *Corbin on Contracts* § 1143 at 126–27 (West, 2d ed. 1964) (legal remedies "inadequate, without regard to quality, quantity, or location"); John Norton Pomeroy, 3 *A Treatise on Equity Jurisprudence as Administered in the United States of America* § 1402 at 441–42 (Bancroft-Whitney Co. 1883) (when real estate contract is "unobjectionable . . . it is as much a matter of course for a court of equity to decree its specific performance as it is for a court of law to give damages for its breach"); Joseph Story, 2 *Commentaries on Equity Jurisprudence as Administered in England and America* § 750 at 53 (Little, Brown 1836) (same); Samuel Williston & Walter H.E. Jaeger, 11 *A Treatise on the Law of Contracts* § 1418A at 666–67 (Baker, Voorhis, 3d ed. 1968) ("ordinarily the specific performance of a contract to convey land is as much a matter of course as an action of damages for its breach"); Robert Bird & William Fanning, *Specific Performance of Contracts to Convey Real Estate*, 23 Ky. L.J. 380, 381–83 (1935) (collecting cases). See also Haisten v. Ziglar, 258 Ala. 554, 64 So.2d 592 (1953) (sale of growing timber treated as sale of land); Van Zandt v. Heilman, 54 N.M. 97, 110, 214 P.2d 864, 872 (1950) (contract to grant oil lease treated like "any other contract for the sale of land"); Herr Abstract Co. v. Vance, 284 Pa. Super. 111, 118, 425 A.2d 444, 447 (1980) (damages not an adequate remedy for defrauded seller of land who seeks to rescind transaction and retain land). But see Watkins v. Paul, 95 Idaho 499, 501, 511 P.2d 781, 783 (1973) (damages adequate and specific performance denied where buyer wanted land only for resale; court noted but did not rely on fact that rights of innocent third party had intervened); Bird & Fanning at 383–84 (collecting cases denying specific performance).

2. [all land unique] Henderson v. Fisher, 236 Cal. App. 2d 468, 473, 46 Cal. Rptr. 173, 177 (1965); Bauermeister v. Sullivan, 87 Ind. App. 628, 631, 160 N.E. 105, 107 (1928); Severson v. Elberon Elev., Inc., 250 N.W.2d 417, 423 (Iowa 1977); Thibbitts v. Crowley, 405 Mass. 222, —, 539 N.E.2d 1035, 1040 (1989); McCullough v. Newton, 348 S.W.2d 138, 144 (Mo. 1961); Greater Houston Bank v. Conte, 641 S.W.2d 407, 410 (Tex. App. 1982).

3. [uniqueness of land fictional] Suchan v. Rutherford, 90 Idaho 288, 295, 410 P.2d 434, 438 (1966); Edward Yorio, *Contract Enforcement: Specific Performance and Injunctions* § 10.1 at 263–64 (Little, Brown 1989); Bird & Fanning at 383–85; Ivan A. Elliott, *Specific Performance*, 1960 U. Ill. L.F. 72, 75; W. Page Keeton & Clarence Morris, *Notes on "Balancing the Equities,"* 18 Tex. L. Rev. 412, 414 & n.4 (1940); *Developments in the Law—Injunctions*, 78 Harv. L. Rev. 994, 1003 (1965).

4. [condos like personal property] Centex Homes Corp. v. Boag, 128 N.J. Super. 385, 393, 320 A.2d 194, 198 (1974). See also Jessen v. Keystone Sav. & Loan Ass'n, 142 Cal. App. 3d 454, 191 Cal. Rptr. 104 (1983) (damages are not adequate remedy for loss of two condominium units held for long-term investment, but are adequate for loss of two units listed for sale at stated price).

5. [key to social and political status] David Cohen, *The Relationship of Contractual Remedies to Political and Social Status: A Preliminary Inquiry*, 32 U. Toronto L.J. 31 (1982).

6. [encroachments] Storey v. Patterson, 437 So.2d 491, 495 (Ala. 1983) (driveway extending onto plaintiff's land); Rosenthal v. City of Crystal Lake, 171 Ill. App. 3d 428, 437–41, 525 N.E.2d 1176, 1182–83 (1988) (sewer line under plaintiff's land); Soergel v. Preston, 141 Mich. App. 585, 589–90, 367 N.W.2d 366, 368–69

(1985) (sewer line under plaintiff's land); Raposa v. Guay, 84 R.I. 436, 444, 125 A.2d 113, 117 (1956) (building on plaintiff's land).

7. [nuisance] Hart v. Wagner, 184 Md. 40, 40 A.2d 47 (1944) (trash fires); Schleissner v. Town of Provincetown, 27 Mass. App. 392,——, 538 N.E.2d 995, 998–99 (1989) (enjoining use of municipal storm sewers that flooded plaintiff's land; no discussion of irreparable injury); Borsvold v. United Dairies, 347 Mich. 672, 81 N.W.2d 378 (1957) (enjoining noisy dairy trucks without discussing irreparable injury); City of Aberdeen v. Wellman, 352 N.W.2d 204 (S.D. 1984) (enjoining noisy equipment without discussing irreparable injury); Jewett v. Deerhorn Enterprises, Inc., 281 Or. 469, 473, 575 P.2d 164, 169 (1978) (pig farm); Scott v. Jordan, 99 N.M. 567, 572, 661 P.2d 59, 64–65 (App. 1983) (feedlot); Pate v. City of Martin, 614 S.W.2d 46, 48 (Tenn. 1981) (sewage lagoon; "seldom if ever" are damages adequate where continuing nuisance could be corrected); Story, 2 *Equity Jurisprudence* §§ 924–26 (cited in note 1) (injunction available if nuisance is continuing or permanent).

8. [continuous or repeated trespass] Aoude v. Mobil Oil Corp., 862 F.2d 890, 892 (1st Cir. 1988) (ordering terminated operator of service station to give up possession and not to trespass); Harmon v. De Turk, 176 Cal. 758, 761, 169 P. 680, 681 (1917) (refusal to let plaintiff remove sand and gravel pursuant to contract, where contract might expire before plaintiff could get judgment in ejectment); Berin v. Olson, 183 Conn. 337, 340, 439 A.2d 357, 359–61 (1981) (diversion of water onto plaintiff's land); Cragg v. Levinson, 238 Ill. 69, 87 N.E. 121 (1909) (destruction of fence and threats to destroy any replacement fence); Terrebonne Parish Police Jury v. Matherne, 405 So.2d 314, 319 (La. 1981) (diversion of water onto plaintiff's land); Hall v. Nester, 122 Mich. 141, 80 N.W. 982 (1899) (seizure and use of stream that plaintiff dammed and improved for floating of logs); Chesarone v. Pinewood Builders, Inc., 345 Mass. 236, 240, 186 N.E.2d 712, 714–15 (1962) (diversion of water onto plaintiff's land); Petraborg v. Zontelli, 217 Minn. 536, 554, 15 N.W.2d 174, 183–84 (1944) (draining lake in violation of riparian rights); Whittaker v. Stangvick, 100 Minn. 386, 111 N.W. 295 (1907) (shooting birdshot over plaintiff's land); Czarnick v. Loup River Public Power Dist., 190 Neb. 521, 526, 209 N.W.2d 595, 598–99 (1973) (annual flooding of plaintiff's land); Thurston Enterprises, Inc. v. Baldi, 128 N.H. 760, 766, 519 A.2d 297, 302 (1986) (enjoining excessive use of easement); N.Y. Tel. Co. v. Town of N. Hempstead, 41 N.Y.2d 691, 695, 363 N.E.2d 694, 699, 395 N.Y.S.2d 143, 149 (1977) (attaching streetlights to plaintiff's telephone poles; injunction granted without discussing irreparable injury); Coatsworth v. Lehigh Valley Ry., 156 N.Y. 451, 453, 51 N.E. 301, 303 (1898) (railroad bridge on plaintiff's property); Tortolano v. Difilippo, 115 R.I. 496, 501–02, 349 A.2d 48, 51 (1975) (diversion of water and fill dirt onto plaintiff's land); Newport Yacht Club, Inc. v. Deomatares, 93 R.I. 60, 64, 171 A.2d 78, 80 (1961) (mooring boats on plaintiff's dock); Gregory v. Sanders, 635 P.2d 795, 801 (Wyo. 1981) (driving on private road on plaintiff's land); 2 Story, § 928 at 207 ("there is not the slightest hesitation, if the acts done, or threatened to the property would . . . impair the just enjoyment of the property in future"); Restatement (Second) of Torts, § 938 comment b, at 573 (1979) (injunction is obviously the better remedy for continuing trespass to land). See also Lloyd Corp. v. Whiffen, 307 Or. 674, 681, 773 P.2d 1294, 1297 (1989) ("injunction ordinarily issues against . . . continuing trespass," but trespass may be permitted where public

interest is served). But compare Wiles v. Wiles, 134 W. Va. 81, 58 S.E.2d 601 (1950) (refusing to enjoin one-time trespass to hold estate sale).
   9. [timber] Dean v. Coosa County Lumber Co., 232 Ala. 177, 167 So. 566, 572 (1936); Deer Slayers, Inc. v. La. Motel & Inv. Corp., 434 So.2d 1183, 1187–89 (La. App. 1983); Pardee v. Camden Lumber Co., 70 W. Va. 68, 69, 73 S.E. 82, 83–85 (1911); 2 Story § 929 at 208–09.
   10. [minerals] Erhardt v. Boaro, 113 U.S. 537 (1885) (gold and silver); Valero Transmission Co. v. Mitchell Energy Corp., 743 S.W.2d 658, 664 (Tex. App. 1987) (drainage of gas reserves); St. Louis Smelting & Rfg. Co. v. Hoban, 357 Mo. 436, 438, 209 S.W.2d 119, 122–23 (1948) (slag heap); Allegheny Dev. Corp. v. Barati, 273 S.E.2d 384, 387 (W. Va. 1980) (coal and overburden); 2 Story § 929 at 208–09.
   11. [lateral support] Gladin v. Von Engeln, 195 Colo. 88, 94, 575 P.2d 418, 422–23 (1978) (granting injunction without discussing irreparable injury); Gorton v. Schofield, 311 Mass. 352, 358–59, 41 N.E.2d 12, 15–16 (1942); Bradley v. Valicenti, 185 Pa. Super. 403, 407, 138 A.2d 238, 240 (1958) ("equity is the special forum for relief where there has been a trespass or nuisance of continuing and permanent character").
   12. [restrictive covenants] Taylor v. Kohler, 507 So.2d 426, 428 (Ala. 1987) ("mere breach of the covenant is a sufficient basis" for injunction, whether or not plaintiff is damaged); Smith v. Nelson, 149 Colo. 200, 368 P.2d 566 (1962) (enforcing covenant without discussing irreparable injury); Thomas v. Campbell, 107 Idaho 398, 410, 690 P.2d 333, 339–41 (1984) (enforcing "scenic easement"); Cashio v. Shoriak, 481 So.2d 1013 (La. 1986) (remedy is generally by injunction); Reed v. Williamson, 164 Neb. 99, 119, 82 N.W.2d 18, 29 (1957) ("injunction is in this class of cases an appropriate if not the only adequate remedy"); Hines Corp. v. City of Albuquerque, 95 N.M. 311, 621 P.2d 1116, 1118 (1980) (ordering quadraplexes converted to single-family homes); Vt. Nat'l Bank v. Chittenden Trust Co., 143 Vt. 257, 465 A.2d 284 (1983) (enforcing covenant without discussing irreparable injury); Remilong v. Crolla, 576 P.2d 461 (Wyo. 1978) (enforcing covenant without discussing irreparable injury).
   13. [zoning] IT Corp. v. County of Imperial, 35 Cal. 3d 63, 72–73, 672 P.2d 121, 127, 196 Cal. Rptr. 715, 721 (1983) (rebuttable presumption in favor of preliminary injunction where plaintiff shows probable violation of zoning law that authorizes permanent injunction); Johnson v. Murzyn, 1 Conn. App. 176, 180–81, 469 A.2d 1227, 1229–30 (1984) (municipality entitled to injunction against violation of statute without showing irreparable injury); Gray v. DeKalb County, 230 Ga. 95, 96, 195 S.E.2d 914, 916 (1973) (statute authorized injunction); City of Lewiston v. Knieriem, 107 Idaho 80, 685 P.2d 821 (1984) (granting injunction without discussing irreparable injury); De Schamps v. Bd. of Zoning Appeals, 241 Ind. 615, 620, 174 N.E.2d 581, 583 (1961) (any violation of zoning laws will be enjoined); Inc. City of Denison v. Clabaugh, 306 N.W.2d 748, 755–56 (Iowa 1981) ("injunction was the only effective remedy" for violation of setback requirement); Redfearn v. Creppel, 436 So.2d 1210, 1213 (La. App. 1983) (private plaintiff entitled to injunction if he is "materially and adversely affected in the enjoyment of his home"), rev'd on other grounds, 455 So.2d 1356 (La. 1984); Little Joseph Realty, Inc. v. Town of Babylon, 41 N.Y.2d 738, 744, 363 N.E.2d 1163, 1167 (1977) ("settled beyond doubt" that injunction is the "appropriate remedy"); Utah County v.

Baxter, 635 P.2d 61, 64–65 (Utah 1981) ("a showing that the zoning ordinance has been violated is tantamount to a showing of irreparable injury"); Jelinski v. Eggers, 34 Wis. 2d 85, 91, 148 N.W.2d 750, 753 (1967) (injunction to prevent interference with light, air, and view); Eugene McQuillin, 8A *The Law of Municipal Corporations* § 25.344 at 683–86 (Callaghan, 3d ed. rev. 1986) (collecting cases). See also Tierney v. Village of Schaumburg, 182 Ill. App. 3d 1055, 1060–61, 538 N.E.2d 904, 907–08 (1989) (enjoining construction of street in violation of ordinance requiring sidewalks and minimum width of eighty feet).

14. [condominium restrictions] Carroll v. El Dorado Estates Div. No. Two Ass'n, Inc., 680 P.2d 1158, 1160 (Alaska 1984) (statute authorized injunction); Constellation Condo. Ass'n, Inc. v. Harrington, 467 So.2d 378 (Fla. App. 1985) (granting injunction without discussing irreparable injury); Cobblestone II Homeowners Ass'n, Inc. v. Baird, 545 N.E.2d 1126, 1129–30 (Ind. App. 1989) (ordering removal of unapproved awning).

15. [leases] K-Mart Corp. v. Oriental Plaza, Inc., 875 F.2d 907, 914–16 (1st Cir. 1989) (covenant not to build additional structures that would block view of leased premises); Pantry Pride Enterprises, Inc. v. Stop & Shop Co., 806 F.2d 1227 (4th Cir. 1986) (specific performance of right of first refusal to take assignment of sublease of supermarket; irreparable injury not discussed); Ammerman v. City Stores Co., 394 F.2d 950, 955–56 (D.C. Cir. 1968) (contract to build and lease department store in shopping mall); F.B. Norman Co. v. E.I. du Pont de Nemours & Co., 12 Del. Ch. 155, 161, 108 A. 743, 746 (1920) (contract to improve and lease premises); Matlock v. Duncan, 220 Ga. 200, 137 S.E.2d 661 (1964) (contract to lease retail space); Read Drug & Chem. Co. v. Nattans, 130 Md. 465, 100 A. 736 (1917) (contract to extend lease of retail space); Rigs v. Sokol, 318 Mass. 337, 342, 61 N.E.2d 538, 541 (1945) ("well settled" that covenant in lease may be specifically enforced); Fred Gorder & Son v. Pankonin, 83 Neb. 204, 210, 119 N.W. 449, 451 (1909) (option to renew lease of retail space); Yorkville Restaurant, Inc. v. Perlbinder, 34 A.D.2d 14, 308 N.Y.S.2d 922 (1970) (option to lease restaurant and bar in any new building constructed on site of building where plaintiff originally leased space), judgment vacated and re-entered mem., 34 A.D.2d 637, 311 N.Y.S.2d 250 (1970), aff'd mem., 28 N.Y.2d 647, 269 N.E.2d 192, 320 N.Y.S.2d 521 (1971); Duckworth v. Michel, 172 Wash. 234, 241–43, 19 P.2d 914, 916 (1933) (lease of cropland); Story, 2 *Equity Jurisprudence* § 729 at 34 (cited in note 1). See also United Coin Meter Co. v. Lasala, 98 Mich. App. 238, 241, 296 N.W.2d 221, 223 (1980) (refusing injunction ordering landlord to readmit tenant to premises, because action for possession is adequate remedy at law).

16. [easements] Cont'l Baking Co. v. Katz, 68 Cal. 2d 512, 528, 439 P.2d 889, 899, 67 Cal. Rptr. 761, 771 (1968) (interference with access easement); Borrowman v. Howland, 119 Ill. App. 3d 493, 501, 457 N.E.2d 103, 108 (1983) (building on defendant's land, extending into plaintiff's easement); Crowley v. J.C. Ryan Constr. Co., 356 Mass. 31, 35, 247 N.E.2d 714, 717 (1969) (blocking drainage from plaintiff's land by raising grade of street); Dunnebacke v. Detroit, G.H. & M. Ry., 248 Mich. 450, 456, 227 N.W. 811, 813 (1929) (construction of railroad in land subject to plaintiff's easement); Bales v. Mich. State Highway Comm'n, 72 Mich. App. 50, 54–57, 249 N.W.2d 158, 161–62 (Mich. App. 1976) (same, highway); Graves v. Gerber, 208 Neb. 209, 302 N.W.2d 717 (1981) (fence blocking plaintiff's use of easement); Sievers v. Zenoff, 94 Nev. 53, 57, 573 P.2d 1190, 1192–93 (1978) (building on lot reserved for access easement); Kennedy v. Bond, 80 N.M. 734, 737, 460 P.2d 809, 813 (1969) (interference with access easement over private road); Mid-Continent Pipe Line Co. v. Emerson, 396 P.2d 734, 736 (Okla. 1964) (interference with plaintiff's pipeline under defendant's land); Haines v. Minnock Constr. Co., 289 Pa. Super. 209, 220, 433 A.2d 30, 35 (1981) (development of land dedicated as open space in plat of earlier development; granting injunction without discussing irreparable injury); Hall v. Weldon Foods Co., 500 S.W.2d 716, 718 (Tex. Civ. App. 1973) (fence blocking plaintiff's use of easement). See also Hailey v. Tex.-N.M. Power Co., 757 S.W.2d 833 (Tex. App. 1988) (interference with utility's statutory right to enter plaintiff's land to make survey).

  17. [foreclosures] Sundance Land Corp. v. Community First Fed. Sav. & Loan Ass'n, 840 F.2d 653, 661–62 (9th Cir. 1988); Johnson v. U.S. Dep't of Agric., 734 F.2d 774, 789 (11th Cir. 1984); Coleman v. Block, 580 F. Supp. 192, 210 (D.N.D. 1983); Weingand v. Atlantic Sav. & Loan Ass'n, 1 Cal. 3d 806, 819–20, 464 P.2d 106, 112–13, 83 Cal. Rptr. 650, 656–57 (1970); Greater Houston Bank v. Conte, 641 S.W.2d 407, 409–10 (Tex. App. 1982). See also United Church of the Medical Center v. Medical Center Comm'n, 689 F.2d 693, 701 (7th Cir. 1982) (enjoining wrongful attempt to enforce reversion); In re Stadium Management Corp., 95 Bankr. 264 (D. Mass. 1988) (enjoining lawful foreclosure on property owned by subsidiary of bankrupt debtor, where subsidiary's property was essential to debtor's reorganization); Nat'l Co. v. Bridgewater, 413 So.2d 230 (La. App. 1982) (injunction against entering premises to remove fixture); Harrington v. Harrington, 365 N.W.2d 552, 557 (N.D. 1985) (granting specific performance of contract to release mortgages); Sloane v. Clauss, 64 Ohio St. 125, 59 N.E. 884 (1901) (enjoining wrongful foreclosure on chattels); Carter v. Olsen, 660 S.W.2d 483 (Tenn. 1983) (enjoining foreclosure of disputed tax lien on timber lands).

  18. [variety of explanations] William Quinby de Funiak, *Equitable Protection Against Waste and Trespass*, 36 Ky. L.J. 255 (1948).

  19. [uniqueness of land] Sundance Land Corp. v. Community First Fed. Sav. & Loan Ass'n, 840 F.2d 653, 661 (9th Cir. 1988); (wrongful foreclosure); Ramirez de Arellano v. Weinberger, 745 F.2d 1500, 1527 (D.C. Cir. 1984) (trespass), vacated on other grounds mem., 471 U.S. 1113 (1985); United Church of the Medical Center v. Medical Center Comm'n, 689 F.2d 693, 701 (7th Cir. 1982) (wrongful reversion); Stockton v. Newman, 148 Cal. App. 2d 558, 563–65, 307 P.2d 56, 61 (1957) (wrongful foreclosure); F.B. Norman Co. v. E.I. du Pont de Nemours & Co., 12 Del. Ch. 155, 161, 108 A. 743, 746 (1920) (breach of lease); Thomas v. Campbell, 107 Idaho 398, 404, 690 P.2d 333, 340 (1984) (restrictive covenant); Pardee v. Camden Lumber Co., 70 W. Va. 68, 71–73, 73 S.E. 82, 84 (1911) (cutting of timber).

  20. [harm to substance of the estate] Erhardt v. Boaro, 113 U.S. 537, 539 (1885) (removal of minerals); Storey v. Patterson, 437 So.2d 491, 495 (Ala. 1983) (encroachment); Czarnick v. Loup River Public Power Dist., 190 Neb. 521, 526, 209 N.W.2d 595, 598–99 (1973) (annual flooding of plaintiff's land); Allegheny Dev. Corp. v. Barati, 166 W. Va. 218, 221–22, 273 S.E.2d 384, 387 (1980) (removal of minerals); Pomeroy, 3 *Equity Jurisprudence* § 1357 at 387 (cited in note 1) ("if the injury done or threatened is of such a nature that, when accomplished, the property can not be restored to its original condition").

  21. [damages hard to measure] Derwell Co. v. Apic, Inc., 278 A.2d 338, 343

(Del. Ch. 1971) (specific performance to seller of land); Valero Transmission Co. v. Mitchell Energy Corp., 743 S.W.2d 658, 664 (Tex. App. 1987) (drainage of gas reserves).

22. [multiplicity of suits] Berin v. Olson, 183 Conn. 337, 344, 439 A.2d 357, 360–61 (1981) (trespass); Cragg v. Levinson, 238 Ill. 69, 87 N.E. 121 (1909) (trespass); Gorton v. Schofield, 311 Mass. 352, 358–59, 41 N.E.2d 12, 15–16 (1942) (removal of lateral support); Colliton v. Oxborough, 86 Minn. 361, 363–64, 90 N.W. 793, 794 (1902) (trespass); Reed v. Williamson, 164 Neb. 99, 82 N.W.2d 18 (1957) (restrictive covenant); Kennedy v. Bond, 80 N.M. 734, 738, 460 P.2d 809, 813 (1969) (interference with easement); Coatsworth v. Lehigh Valley Ry., 156 N.Y. 451, 456, 51 N.E. 301, 303 (1898) (trespass); Gregory v. Sanders, 635 P.2d 795, 801 (Wyo. 1981) (trespass); 3 Pomeroy § 1357 at 387–88 (trespass).

23. [undue hardship] See ch. 7 part A.

24. [equity will not determine title] Anderson v. Turner, 133 Colo. 453, 457, 296 P.2d 1044, 1045 (1956) (refusing to enjoin alleged continuing trespass where surveys were confused and plaintiff's title was unclear); McRaven v. Culley, 324 Ill. 451, 155 N.E. 282 (1927) (refusing to enjoin use of alleged public way over plaintiff's land, where only dispute was whether plaintiff or public owned the way); St. Louis Smelting & Rfg. Co. v. Hoban, 357 Mo. 436, 444, 209 S.W.2d 119, 124 (1948) ("injunction is not the appropriate remedy to determine a disputed title"); Frame v. Frame, 227 Mont. 439, 442, 740 P.2d 655, 657–58 (1987) (title cannot be determined in suit for injunction, but court will issue injunction to protect possession where title is not at issue); Brown's Mills Land Co. v. Pemberton Township, 135 N.J. Eq. 203, 207–08, 37 A.2d 819, 821–22 (N.J. Ch. 1944) (many cases enjoin trespass, but few "determine a substantial dispute over a private legal right in land"); McDaniel v. Moyer, 662 P.2d 309, 313 n.13 (Okla. 1983) ("short of an emergency, an injunction suit cannot be used to litigate title to property"); Williamson v. Hall, 203 S.W.2d 265, 266 (Tex. Civ. App. 1947) ("well settled that the equitable remedy of injunction is not to be substituted for the legal remedy of trespass to try title"); de Funiak, 36 Ky. L.J. at 262–63 (cited in note 18).

25. [ejectment gives possession] Restatement (Second) of Torts § 945 comment a (1979); Dan B. Dobbs, *Handbook on the Law of Remedies* § 5.8 at 365 (West 1973); Douglas Laycock, *Modern American Remedies* 578–85 (Little, Brown 1985). For a typical statute, see Ill. Rev. Stat. ch. 110, ¶ 6–129 (1983). For an illustrative case, see Sun Oil Co. v. Fleming, 469 F.2d 211, 214 (10th Cir. 1972).

26. [policy here is jury trial] Sun Oil Co. v. Fleming, 469 F.2d 211, 214 (10th Cir. 1972); Tidwell v. H.H. Hitt Lumber Co., 198 Ala. 236, 238, 73 So. 486, 487 (1916); Teacher v. Kijurina, 365 Pa. 480, 485, 76 A.2d 197, 200 (1950); Hartman v. Pa. Water & Power Co., 317 Pa. 417, 420, 176 A. 437, 439 (1935) ("Plaintiff's argument that there is no adequate remedy at law for the injury alleged by her is entirely irrelevant to the present situation. She is not told that she has no remedy in equity, but simply that she must establish her right at law before she can have it protected in equity."); Freer v. Davis, 52 W. Va. 1, 7–8, 43 S.E. 164, 165–66 (1903). See also In re Markel, 254 A.2d 236, 239 (Del. 1969) (equity will not determine title to chattels, because defendant has constitutional right to jury trial in replevin).

27. [no jury if plaintiff in possession] Thomson v. Thomson, 7 Cal. 2d 671, 675, 62 P.2d 358, 362 (1936). See also Frank v. Coyle, 310 Mich. 14, 21, 16 N.W.2d

649, 650 (1944) (ordering defendant to specifically perform his promise to remove eight cabins from plaintiff's land; ejectment not an available remedy because plaintiff was in possession of land).

28. [injunctions pending trial of title] Erhardt v. Boaro, 113 U.S. 537, 538–39 (1885) ("it is now a common practice"); Wadsworth v. Goree, 96 Ala. 227, 229, 10 So. 848, 850 (1892) (enjoining cutting of timber, pending outcome of suit in ejectment); Haldas v. Comm'rs of Charlestown, 207 Md. 255, 261–62, 113 A.2d 886, 890 (1955) ("equity may grant a temporary injunction to preserve the disputed property from irreparable damage until the question of title is tried"); Gause v. Perkins, 56 N.C. (3 Jones Eq.) 177, 178–79 (1857) ("equity will exert its power of injunction in aid of the action at law by taking care of the subject-matter of the action, but without assuming jurisdiction to decide the question of title"); Mid-Continent Pipe Line Co. v. Emerson, 396 P.2d 734, 736 (Okla. 1964) (enjoining interference with pipeline, pending determination of plaintiff's right to maintain pipeline under defendant's land); Freer v. Davis, 52 W. Va. 1, 9–11, 43 S.E. 164, 166–68 (1903) ("great weight of authority"); de Funiak, 36 Ky. L.J. at 262–63 (cited in note 18).

29. [Chancellor Kent on enjoining trespass] Jerome v. Ross, 7 Johnson's Chancery 315 (N.Y. 1823).

30. [Kent opinion still in casebook] Owen M. Fiss & Doug Rendleman, *Injunctions* 63 (Foundation Press, 2d ed. 1984).

31. [Kent opinion repudiated] Pomeroy, 3 *Equity Jurisprudence* § 1357 at 388 n.1 (cited in note 1) (Jerome v. Ross "is opposed to the modern decisions of the highest ability and authority").

32. [Kent opinion repudiated] Tidwell v. H.H. Hitt Lumber Co., 198 Ala. 236, 242, 73 So. 486, 488–89 (1916); Cragg v. Levinson, 238 Ill. 60, 62, 87 N.E. 121, 122–23 (1909); Hall v. Nester, 122 Mich. 141, 144, 80 N.W. 982, 984 (1899); Whittaker v. Stangvick, 100 Minn. 386, 390, 111 N.W. 295, 297 (1907).

33. [Kent inconsistent] Livingston v. Livingston, 6 Johnson's Chancery 497 (N.Y. Ch. 1822) (enjoining cutting of timber to avoid multiplicity of suits).

34. [damages used to buy identical goods] Story, 2 *Equity Jurisprudence* § 717 at 24 (cited in note 1) ("damages at law, calculated on the market price of the stock or goods, are as complete a remedy for the purchaser, as the delivery of the goods contracted for; inasmuch as with the damages he may purchase the same quantity of the like stock or goods").

35. [heirlooms] Nakian v. Di Laurenti, 673 F. Supp. 699 (S.D.N.Y. 1987) (sculptures); Haydon v. Weltmer, 137 Fla. 130, 135–43, 187 So. 772, 773–77 (1939) (antique furniture); Redmond v. N.J. Historical Soc'y, 132 N.J. Eq. 464, 475, 28 A.2d 189, 191 (1942) (portrait of ancestor); Sloane v. Clauss, 64 Ohio St. 125, 59 N.E. 884 (1901) (miscellaneous heirlooms); UCC § 2–716, Official Comment 2; Pomeroy, 3 *Equity Jurisprudence* § 1402 at 443 n.1 (cited in note 1); 2 Story § 709 at 18–19.

36. [*pretium affectionis*] Haydon v. Weltmer, 137 Fla. 130, 139–43, 187 So. 772, 776–77 (1939); Redmond v. N.J. Historical Soc'y, 132 N.J. Eq. 464, 468, 28 A.2d 189, 191 (1942). See also *Black's Law Dictionary* 1069 (5th ed. 1979); Restatement (Second) of Torts § 944 comment b (1979) (money obviously inadequate for personal property with sentimental value); M.T. Van Hecke, *Equitable Replevin*, 33 N.C. L. Rev. 57, 57–60 (1954).

37. [unique commercial products] Copylease Corp. v. Memorex Corp., 408 F. Supp. 758 (S.D.N.Y. 1976) (toner for photocopier, allegedly unique because superior to all other brands); Colorado-Ute Elec. Ass'n, Inc. v. Envirotech Corp., 524 F. Supp. 1152, 1159 (D. Colo. 1981) (pollution-control equipment designed for plaintiff's plant); Gerwin v. Southeastern Cal. Ass'n of Seventh Day Adventists, 14 Cal. App. 3d 209, 212, 218, 92 Cal. Rptr. 111, 112, 116–17 (1971) (used fixtures and equipment for cocktail lounge, replaceable only with new equipment that plaintiff could not afford); Montgomery Enterprises v. Empire Theater Co., 204 Ala. 566, 574, 86 So. 880, 888 (1920) (first-run motion picture film); Ind. Shovel & Supply Co. v. Castillo, 142 Ind. App. 369, 373, 234 N.E.2d 867, 869–70 (1968) (crane); E. Rolling Mill Co. v. Michlovitz, 157 Md. 51, 66, 145 A. 378, 384 (1929) (steel scrap with "quality and concentrated weight which could not be secured anywhere within the extensive region"); Friend Bros., Inc. v. Seaboard Surety Co., 316 Mass. 639, 643, 56 N.E.2d 6, 9 (1944) (reinsurance policy in form unavailable elsewhere); Oreland Equip. Co. v. Copco Steel & Engineering Corp., 310 Mich. 6, 9, 16 N.W.2d 646, 648 (1944) (copper and brass from dismantled industrial plant); Stephan's Mach. & Tool, Inc. v. D & H Mach. Consultants, Inc., 65 Ohio App. 2d 197, 201, 417 N.E.2d 579, 583 (1979) (boring machine); McGowin v. Remington, 12 Pa. (2 Jones) 56, 62 (1849) (possibly irreplaceable maps and surveys of Pittsburgh); Ace Equip. Co. v. Aqua Chem., Inc., 73 Pa. D. & C. 2d 300, 20 UCC Rep. 392 (Pa. Com. Pl. 1975) (used transformer under contract for resale); Elk Rfg. Co. v. Falling Rock Cannel Coal Co., 92 W. Va. 479, 484, 115 S.E. 431, 433–34 (1922) (contract for uninterrupted supply of natural gas).

38. [customized cars] Tatum v. Richter, 280 Md. 332, 336, 373 A.2d 923, 926 (1977) (buyer recovers Ferrari in replevin, because cover impossible); Schweber v. Rallye Motors, Inc., 12 UCC Rep. 1154 (N.Y. Sup. 1973) (Rolls Royce). See also Sedmak v. Charlie's Chevrolet, Inc., 622 S.W.2d 694, 699–700 (Mo. App. 1981) (limited production Corvette, not "one of a kind," but "in short supply and great demand").

39. [customized boats] Fast v. S. Offshore Yachts, 587 F. Supp. 1354, 1357 (D. Conn. 1984) (customized yacht); Gay v. Seafarer Fiberglass Yachts, Inc., 14 UCC Rep. 1335 (N.Y. Sup. 1974) (custom-built yacht).

40. [custom stereo] Cumbest v. Harris, 363 So.2d 294 (Miss. 1978) (plaintiff's own creation, with irreplaceable parts).

41. [breeding stock] Price v. McConnell, 184 Cal. App. 2d 660, 666, 7 Cal. Rptr. 695, 698–99 (1960) (dwarf heifers); Harris v. Barcroft, 543 P.2d 656, 657 (Or. 1975) (champion dog; specific performance denied on other grounds).

42. [franchises] Triple-A Baseball Club Assoc. v. Northeastern Baseball, Inc., 832 F.2d 214, 222–25 (1st Cir. 1987) (minor league baseball franchise); ABA Distr., Inc. v. Adolph Coors Co., 542 F. Supp. 1272, 1293–94, 1297 (W.D. Mo. 1982) (beer distribution franchise); DeBauge Bros., Inc. v. Whitsitt, 512 P.2d 487, 489 (Kan. 1973) (bottling franchise; "franchises are by their very nature unique and exclusive"); Bidwell v. Long, 14 A.D.2d 168, 169–70, 218 N.Y.S.2d 108, 110 (1961) (bakery route franchise); Annotation, *Specific Performance of Agreement for Sale of Private Franchise*, 82 A.L.R.3d 1102 (1978). But see Thayer Plymouth Center, Inc. v. Chrysler Motors Corp., 255 Cal. App. 2d 300, 306–07, 63 Cal. Rptr. 148, 152 (1967) (automobile dealership too complex to supervise; damages hard to prove but adequate).

43. **[businesses]** Chamber of Commerce v. Barton, 195 Ark. 274, 286, 112 S.W.2d 619, 625 (1937) (goodwill of a radio station); Chariot Holdings, Ltd. v. Eastmet Corp., 153 Ill. App. 3d 50, 63, 505 N.E.2d 1076, 1085 (1987) (assets of five corporations); Potucek v. Blair, 176 Kan. 263, 267, 270 P.2d 240, 244–45 (1954) (half interest in joint venture to buy oil and gas leases); Cochrane v. Szpakowski, 355 Pa. 357, 361–62, 49 A.2d 692, 693–94 (1946) (restaurant with liquor license); Madariaga v. Morris, 639 S.W.2d 709, 711–12 (Tex. App. 1982) (company making "Albert's Famous Mexican Hot Sauce"); M.T. Van Hecke, *Changing Emphases in Specific Performance*, 40 N.C. L. Rev. 1, 3–4 (1961).

44. **[closely held stock]** Steinmeyer v. Warner Consol. Corp., 42 Cal. App. 3d 515, 520, 116 Cal. Rptr. 57, 60 (1974); Burns v. Gould, 172 Conn. 210, 214–15, 374 A.2d 193, 197 (1977); Smith v. Doctors' Serv. Bureau, Inc., 49 Ill. App. 2d 243, 247, 199 N.E.2d 831, 833–34 (1964) (mandamus to transfer stock); Northeast Inv. Co. v. Leisure Living Communities, Inc., 351 A.2d 845, 855–56 (Me. 1976); Peters v. Wallach, 366 Mass. 622, 628, 321 N.E.2d 806, 810 (1975); Evangelista v. Holland, 27 Mass. App. 244, —, 537 N.E.2d 589, 593 (1989) (granting specific performance without discussing irreparable injury); Chadwell v. English, 652 P.2d 310, 314 (Okla. App. 1982); Aldrich v. Geahry, 367 Pa. 252, 255, 80 A.2d 59, 61 (1951); Van Hecke, 40 N.C. L. Rev. at 1–3.

45. **[controlling stock]** Castle v. Cohen, 840 F.2d 173, 178–79 (3d Cir. 1988) (specific performance); Hyde Park Partners, L.P. v. Connolly, 839 F.2d 837, 853 (1st Cir. 1988) (unlawful resistance to tender offer); Heublein, Inc. v. Fed. Trade Comm'n, 539 F. Supp. 123, 127 (D. Conn. 1982) (unlawful resistance to tender offer); UV Indus., Inc. v. Posner, 466 F. Supp. 1251, 1256 (D. Me. 1979) (unlawful tender offer); Mills Acquisition Co. v. MacMillan, Inc., 559 A.2d 1261, 1278–79, 1288 (Del. 1989) (unlawful defensive tactics in response to tender offer).

46. **[monopoly]** Xenia Real-Estate Co. v. Macy, 147 Ind. 568, 572–73, 47 N.E. 147, 148–49 (1897) (natural gas); Graves v. Key City Gas Co., 83 Iowa 714, 718, 50 N.W. 283, 284 (1891) ("he could use candles, oils, or electricity; but he contracted for gaslight, and is entitled to it"); Gloucester Isinglass & Glue Co. v. Russia Cement Co., 154 Mass. 92, 95, 27 N.E. 1005, 1007 (1891) (fish skins); Adams v. Messenger, 147 Mass. 185, 190, 17 N.E. 491, 494–95 (1888) (patented machinery); Jaup v. Olmstead, 334 Mich. 614, 55 N.W.2d 119 (1952) (natural gas); Kann v. Wausau Abrasives Co., 81 N.H. 535, 541, 129 A. 374, 378–79 (1925) (crystalline garnet); John Norton Pomeroy, *A Treatise on the Specific Performance of Contracts as It Is Enforced by Courts of Equitable Jurisdiction in the United States of America* § 15 at 20 (Banks & Bros. 1879) ("contract for the sale and delivery of chattels which are essential in specie to the plaintiff, and which the defendant can supply, while no one else can, could be specifically enforced"). But see N. & L. Fur Co. v. Petkanas, 299 N.Y.S. 901 (A.D. 1937) (furcoat scraps).

47. **[shortage]** Laclede Gas Co. v. Amoco Oil Co., 522 F.2d 33, 39–40 (8th Cir. 1975) (propane); Iowa Elec. Light & Power Co. v. Atlas Corp., 467 F. Supp. 129, 135 (N.D. Iowa 1978) (uranium), rev'd on other grounds, 603 F.2d 1301 (8th Cir. 1979); Tenn. Valley Auth. v. Mason Coal, Inc., 384 F. Supp. 1107, 1111, 1116 (E.D. Tenn. 1974), aff'd mem., 513 F.2d 632 (6th Cir. 1975) (coal with specified characteristics; "the scarcity of raw fuel materials can make an otherwise common product assume a unique character"); Bomberger v. McKelvey, 35 Cal. 2d 607, 613–15, 220 P.2d 729, 734–35 (1950) (90-to-120-day wait for glass and skylights);

Sedmak v. Charlie's Chevrolet, Inc., 622 S.W.2d 694, 700 (Mo. App. 1981) (limited production Corvette, "in short supply and great demand"); Frame v. Frame, 227 Mont. 439, 441–42, 740 P.2d 655, 657 (1987) (plaintiff's only source of gravel for performance of roadwork contracts; no explanation of why gravel was not replaceable); Curtice Bros. v. Catts, 72 N.J. Eq. 831, 833, 66 A. 935, 936 (1907) ("inability to procure at any price at the time needed and of the quality needed, the necessary tomatoes to insure the successful operation of the plant"); Paullus v. Yarbrough, 219 Or. 611, 641–42, 347 P.2d 620, 635 (1959) (right to cut timber on small tract, where such rights on tracts within means of small loggers were scarce); Conemaugh Gas Co. v. Jackson Farm Gas Co., 186 Pa. 443, 445, 40 A. 1000, 1000–01, 1004–05 (1898) ("natural gas differs from an ordinary commodity which can be purchased in the open market"); UCC §2–716, Official Comment 2 ("inability to cover is strong evidence of 'other proper circumstances'" justifying specific performance); UCC § 2–713, Official Comment 3 ("when the unavailability of a market price is caused by a scarcity of goods of the type involved, a good case is normally made for specific performance under this Article"); Corbin, 5A *Contracts* § 1146 at 154 (cited in note 1) ("coal and gas, automobiles, tomatoes, garnets, fish skins, silver ores, slabs of lumber are common subjects of commerce ordinarily obtainable at a price; but scarcity might make the fact otherwise; and so might the inconvenience of getting a supply elsewhere"). See also Am. Mut. Liab. Ins. Co. v. Fisher, 58 Wis. 2d 299, 305, 206 N.W.2d 152, 156 (1973) (shortage of parking places).

48. [cotton] R.N. Kelly Cotton Merchant, Inc. v. York, 379 F. Supp. 1075, 1079 (M.D. Ga. 1973) ("price of cotton has nearly tripled;" breach by growers "would cause irreparable injury to plaintiff and to others in the stream of commerce"), aff'd, 494 F.2d 41 (5th Cir. 1974); Mitchell-Huntley Cotton Co. v. Waldrep, 377 F. Supp. 1215, 1219 (N.D. Ala. 1974) ("the cotton in question is unique and irreplaceable because of the scarcity of cotton"); R.L. Kimsey Cotton Co. v. Ferguson, 233 Ga. 962, 214 S.E.2d 360 (1975) (parties stipulated that cotton was unique); Austin v. Montgomery, 336 So.2d 745, 746 (Miss. 1976) (plaintiff alleged irreparable injury from sharp price increase; defendant apparently did not argue the point). See also Carolinas Cotton Growers Ass'n v. Arnette, 371 F. Supp. 65, 70–71 (D.S.C. 1974) (statute authorized specific performance); Bolin Farms v. Am. Cotton Shippers Ass'n, 370 F. Supp. 1353, 1360–65 (W.D. La. 1974) (specific performance preferred where possible under Louisiana law), aff'd mem. as Jones v. Allenberg Cotton Co., 505 F.2d 732 (5th Cir. 1974) and in five unpublished orders listed at 515 F.2d 508–09 (5th Cir. 1975); Staple Cotton Co-op Ass'n v. Pickett, 326 So.2d 337, 339 (La. 1976) (contract provided for specific performance; such clauses are given weight but are not controlling). But see Duval & Co. v. Malcom, 233 Ga. 784, 787–88, 214 S.E.2d 356, 359 (1975) (buyer alleged that it could not replace cotton, but court assumed it could if it paid "an unreasonable price"). Compare Weathersby v. Gore, 556 F.2d 1247, 1250–51, 1257–59 (5th Cir. 1977) (seller repudiated contract before shortage, and parties stipulated that buyer could have replaced cotton in open market at that time; specific performance denied).

49. [aviation fuel] E. Airlines v. Gulf Oil Corp., 415 F. Supp. 429, 442–43 (S.D. Fla. 1975).

50. [industrial chemicals] Kaiser Trading Co. v. Associated Metals & Minerals Corp., 321 F. Supp. 923, 930–34 (N.D. Cal. 1970), appeal dis'd, 443 F.2d 1364 (9th Cir. 1971).

51. [carrots] Campbell Soup Co. v. Wentz, 172 F.2d 80, 82–83 (3d Cir. 1948) ("virtually impossible to obtain") (specific performance denied on alternative ground that contract was unconscionable).

52. [automobiles] Heidner v. Hewitt Chevrolet Co., 166 Kan. 11, 14, 199 P.2d 481, 483 (1948); Boeving v. Vandover, 240 Mo. App. 117, 130, 218 S.W.2d 175, 177–78 (1949); De Moss v. Conart Motor Sales, 72 N.E.2d 158, 160 (Ohio Com. Pl. 1947), aff'd for want of proper record, 149 Ohio St.2d 299, 78 N.E.2d 675 (1948).

53. [shortage of cars less severe] McCallister v. Patton, 214 Ark. 293, 215 S.W.2d 701, 703–04 (1948) ("large numbers of cars of the type mentioned" have been produced and sold "in the open market"); Poltorak v. Jackson Chevrolet Co., 322 Mass. 699, 700–01, 79 N.E.2d 285, 285–86 (1948) ("settled" that buyer is entitled to specific performance if "substantially similar" article is unavailable, but here scarcity "went no farther than to occasion considerable delay in delivery," and plaintiff made no effort to buy elsewhere); Kirsch v. Zubalsky, 139 N.J. Eq. 22, 24–25, 49 A.2d 773, 775 (1946) (comes close to saying shortage does not matter without *pretium affectionis*, but finds only that cars "may be difficult to procure"); Fortner v. Wilson, 202 Okla. 563, 566, 216 P.2d 299, 301 (1950) (Chevrolets "could be obtained"); Hallobaugh v. Longnecker Motor Sales, 68 Pa. D. & C. 129, 131, 32 Erie Co. 130 (1949) (insufficient to allege that equivalent car cannot be purchased in the City of Erie); Welch v. Chippewa Sales Co., 252 Wis. 166, 169, 31 N.W.2d 170, 171 (1948) (cars "are being produced by the thousands").

54. [different car is adequate] Kirsch v. Zubalsky, 139 N.J. Eq. 22, 24, 49 A.2d 773, 775 (1946) (nothing "special or unique" about this car); Welch v. Chippewa Sales Co., 252 Wis. 166, 169, 31 N.W.2d 170, 171 (1948) (used cars are available and adequate, and any difference is compensable in damages).

55. [gray market is adequate] Fortner v. Wilson, 202 Okla. 563, 216 P.2d 299, 302–03 (1950) (car "could be obtained, by paying an additional amount of money").

56. [replevin and ejectment] For replevin, see Dobbs, *Remedies* § 5.13 at 399–402 (cited in note 25). For ejectment, see authorities cited in note 25.

57. [defendant cannot pay damages instead] Int'l Harvester Credit Corp. v. Hill, 496 F. Supp. 329, 337 (M.D. Tenn. 1980); Cent. Prod. Credit Ass'n v. Kruse, 156 Ill. App. 3d 526, 509 N.E.2d 136 (1987); Brook v. James A. Cullimore & Co., 436 P.2d 32 (Okla. 1967).

58. [less effective enforcement] See authorities cited in ch. 1 note 36.

59. [origins of ejectment and replevin] See Theodore F.T. Plucknett, *A Concise History of the Common Law* 357–75 (Little, Brown, 5th ed. 1956).

60. [property versus promises] See generally Guido Calabresi & A. Douglas Melamed, *Property Rules, Liability Rules, and Inalienability: One View of the Cathedral*, 85 Harv. L. Rev. 1089 (1972). For effective criticism of economic arguments for specifically enforcing property rights but not contract rights, see Ian R. Macneil, *Efficient Breach of Contract: Circles in the Sky*, 68 Va. L. Rev. 947, 961–68 (1982).

61. [destruction or conversion enjoined] Parks v. "Mr. Ford," 556 F.2d 132, 143 (3d Cir. 1977) (permanently enjoining sale of plaintiff's car); Parks v. "Mr. Ford," 386 F. Supp. 1251, 1269–70 (E.D. Pa. 1976) (enjoining sale of plaintiff's car pending appeal, to avoid "substantial injury" to plaintiff), rev'd in part, on other grounds, 556 F.2d 132 (3d Cir. 1977); Bass v. Alderman, 80 Fla. 345, 351, 86 So. 244, 246 (1920) (enjoining tax levy on cattle); Denny v. Denny, 113 Ind. 22, 25–26, 14 N.E. 593, 594–95 (1887) (enjoining sale of corn); Mitsubishi Int'l Corp. v. Century Moving & Warehouse Co.-Franklin Fireproof Warehouse Corp., 50 A.D.2d 788, 377 N.Y.S.2d 510 (1975) (enjoining defendant from interfering with plaintiff's efforts to remove its goods from leased space); Sumner v. Crawford, 91 Tex. 129, 41 S.W. 994 (1897) (injunction ordering converter to return stock of goods); Thomas v. Allis, 389 S.W.2d 109, 112 (Tex. Civ. App. 1965) (enjoining sale of plaintiff's cattle). Compare Weathersbee v. Wallace, 14 Ark. App. 174, 178–79, 686 S.W.2d 447, 449 (1985) (enjoining bank from paying funds to defendant); Perez v. Perez, 353 So.2d 1360, 1363 (La. App. 1978) (enjoining seizure of bank account).

62. [conversion permitted] Friedman v. Faser, 157 Ala. 191, 47 So. 320 (1908) (refusing to order defendant to return bonds to plaintiff); Kramer v. Slattery, 260 Pa. 234, 103 A. 610 (1918) (refusing to enjoin seizure of coal dirt or culm); Wiles v. Wiles, 134 W. Va. 81, 58 S.E.2d 601 (1950) (refusing to enjoin sale of farm equipment and livestock). See also Restatement (Second) of Torts § 938 comment b, at 573 (1979) (damages normally adequate remedy for conversion of wheat by solvent defendant).

63. [skepticism about merits] Kramer v. Slattery, 260 Pa. 234, 239, 103 A. 610, 611–12 (1918) (plaintiff failed to allege title to the land on which the culm lay, or any details of his possession, or of the seizure).

64. [environmental litigation] Amoco Prod. Co. v. Village of Gambell, 480 U.S. 531, 545 (1987) ("environmental injury, by its nature, can seldom be adequately remedied by money damages"); Nat'l Wildlife Fed'n v. Burford, 835 F.2d 305, 323–26 (D.C. Cir. 1987) (loss of wildlife habitat, air and water quality, and natural beauty); Hamilton v. Superior Court, 154 Ariz. 109, 110, 741 P.2d 242, 243 (1987) (development of golf course on desert park land).

65. [voting rights] Quinn v. Mo., 839 F.2d 425 (8th Cir. 1988) (exclusion of persons who do not own real property from participation on local governing board); Bell v. Southwell, 376 F.2d 659 (5th Cir. 1967) (racial segregation at polling place); Hamer v. Campbell, 358 F.2d 215 (5th Cir. 1966) (racial discrimination in voter registration); Schrenker v. Clifford, 270 Ind. 525, 387 N.E.2d 59 (1979) (mailing absentee ballots to addresses within the county). In each of these cases, the court granted injunctive relief without discussing irreparable injury. In the Indiana case, the court said that it could enjoin the violation of a statute despite "the nonexistence of provable damages." Id. at 528–29, 387 N.E.2d at 61.

66. [equal representation] Reynolds v. Sims, 377 U.S. 533, 585–87 (1964) (ordering injunction without discussing irreparable injury); O'Connors v. Helfgott, 481 A.2d 388, 394 (R.I. 1984) ("no amount of monetary damages can rectify this vote dilution").

67. [hearing] Gibson v. Berryhill, 411 U.S. 564, 571–75 (1973) (biased decision maker); United Church of the Medical Center v. Medical Center Comm'n, 689 F.2d 693, 701 (7th Cir. 1982) (biased decision maker); Coleman v. Block, 580 F. Supp. 192, 210 (D.N.D. 1983) (foreclosure of government-subsidized farm loans before hearing on factors affecting eligibility for deferral); Philadelphia Citizens in Action v. Schweiker, 527 F. Supp. 182, 194–95 (E.D. Pa. 1981) (loss of right to comment on proposed regulations), rev'd on other grounds, 669 F.2d 877 (3d Cir. 1982); Community Nutrition Inst. v. Butz, 420 F. Supp. 751, 757 (D.D.C. 1976) (loss of right to comment on proposed regulations); Oppenheimer Mendez v. Acevedo, 388 F. Supp. 326, 337–38 (D.P.R. 1974) (discharge of government attorney without pretermination hearing), aff'd, 512 F.2d 1373, 1375 (1st Cir. 1975); Orange County v. N.C. Dep't of Transp., 46 N.C. App. 350, 385, 265 S.E.2d 890, 910–11 (1980) (no hearing on location of proposed highway; court authorizes injunction without discussing irreparable injury); Hein v. Marts, 295 N.W.2d 167, 171–72 (S.D. 1980) (no notice of hearing on contested water permit). See also Goldberg v. Kelly, 397 U.S. 254 (1970) (due process requires hearing before, not after, termination of welfare benefits; remedy not explicitly discussed).

68. [integration] Brown v. Bd. of Educ., 349 U.S. 294 (1955) (ordering injunctions to desegregate public schools without discussing irreparable injury); U.S. v. Cent. Carolina Bank & Trust Co. 431 F.2d 972, 975 (4th Cir. 1970) (golf course); Everett v. Harron, 380 Pa. 123, 127–28, 110 A.2d 383, 386–88 (1955) (swimming pools).

69. [prison conditions] Hutto v. Finney, 437 U.S. 678 (1978) (affirming injunction restricting conditions of punitive isolation, without discussing irreparable injury).

70. [free speech] Elrod v. Burns, 427 U.S. 347, 373 (1976) ("loss of First Amendment freedoms, for even minimal periods of time, unquestionably constitutes irreparable injury") (plurality opinion; majority affirmed preliminary injunction); Allee v. Medrano, 416 U.S. 802, 814–15 (1974) (suppression of union organizing campaign); Miss. Women's Medical Clinic v. McMillan, 866 F.2d 788, 795 (5th Cir. 1989) (refusing to enjoin picketing at abortion clinic, because injunction would irreparably injure defendants); Mariani Giron v. Acevedo Ruiz, 834 F.2d 238, 239 (1st Cir. 1987) (politically motivated discharge from public employment); Jacobsen v. U.S. Postal Serv., 812 F.2d 1151, 1154 (9th Cir. 1987) (removing newspaper racks; "prevention of access to a public forum is, each day, an irreparable injury"); Citizens for a Better Environment v. City of Park Ridge, 567 F.2d 689, 691 (7th Cir. 1975) (ban on solicitation); Schnell v. City of Chicago, 407 F.2d 1084, 1086 (7th Cir. 1969) (physical interference with reporters gathering news); Hague v. Comm. for Indus. Org., 101 F.2d 774, 790–91 (3d Cir.) (exclusion of labor organizers from city streets), aff'd, 307 U.S. 496 (1939); Klein v. Baise, 708 F. Supp. 863, 865 (N.D. Ill. 1989) (prohibition of political advertising on bus stop shelters); Planned Parenthood Fed'n v. Bowen, 687 F. Supp. 540, 542 (D. Colo. 1988) ("plaintiffs have demonstrated irreparable injury as a matter of law because the regulations in question are unconstitutional"); Clean-Up '84 v. Heinrich, 590 F. Supp. 928, 933 (M.D. Fla. 1984) (ban on circulating petitions at polling places), aff'd, 759 F.2d 1511 (11th Cir. 1985); Ostrowski v. Local 1–2, Util. Workers Union, 530 F. Supp. 208, 215 (S.D.N.Y. 1980) (discipline of dissident union member); Collin v. O'Malley, 452 F. Supp. 577 (N.D. Ill. 1978) (denial of permit to assemble in park); Kenyon v. City of Chicopee, 320 Mass. 528, 533–34, 70 N.E.2d 241, 245–46 (1946) (ban on distribution of handbills).

71. [religious liberty] Deeper Life Christian Fellowship, Inc. v. Bd. of Educ., 852 F. 2d 676, 679 (2d Cir. 1988) (access to public forum); Islamic Center, Inc. v.

City of Starkville, 840 F.2d 293, 303 (5th Cir. 1988) (discriminatory zoning; injunction granted without discussing irreparable injury); Am. Civil Liberties Union v. City of St. Charles, 794 F.2d 265, 274–75 (7th Cir. 1986) (lighted cross on city firehouse); Fox v. City of Los Angeles, 22 Cal. 3d 792, 587 P.2d 663, 150 Cal. Rptr. 867 (1978) (lighted cross on city hall); Lily of the Valley Spiritual Church v. Sims, 169 Ill. App. 3d 624, 523 N.E.2d 999 (1988) (disruption of church services; injunction granted without discussing irreparable injury).

72. [education] Orozco v. Sobol, 674 F. Supp. 125, 128 (S.D.N.Y. 1987) (exclusion from public school); Ray v. School Dist., 666 F. Supp. 1524 (M.D. Fla 1987) (exclusion from public school); Clay v. Ariz. Interscholastic Ass'n, Inc., 161 Ariz. 474, 476, 779 P.2d 349, 351 (1989) (loss of athletic eligibility, reducing chances for college scholarship); Wilson v. Ill. Benedictine College, 112 Ill. App. 3d 932, 938–39, 445 N.E.2d 901, 907 (1983) (withholding college degree); Schank v. Hegele, 36 Ohio Misc. 2d 4, 7–8, 521 N.E.2d 9, 13 (Ohio Com. Pl. 1987) (expulsion from public school); Strank v. Mercy Hosp., 383 Pa. 54, 57, 117 A.2d 697, 698 (1955) (loss of academic credit).

73. [employment discrimination] Chalk v. U.S. Dist. Court, 840 F.2d 701, 709–10 (9th Cir. 1988) (AIDS discrimination); Gutierrez v. Mun. Court, 838 F.2d 1031, 1045 (9th Cir. 1988) (rule forbidding employees to speak Spanish); Equal Employment Opportunity Comm'n v. Cosmair, Inc., 821 F.2d 1085, 1090–91 (5th Cir. 1987) (age discrimination; irreparable injury presumed from violation of civil rights law, but not until administrative remedies have been exhausted); Equal Employment Opportunity Comm'n v. Chrysler Corp., 733 F.2d 1183, 1186 (6th Cir. 1984) (age discrimination); Middleton-Keirn v. Stone, 655 F.2d 609, 611 (5th Cir. 1981) (sex discrimination); Smallwood v. Nat'l Can Co., 583 F.2d 419, 420 (9th Cir. 1978) (retaliation against employee who opposed discrimination); U.S. v. Hayes Int'l Corp., 415 F.2d 1038, 1045 (5th Cir. 1969) (race discrimination; irreparable injury presumed from violation of civil rights law); Oshiver v. Court of Common Pleas, 469 F. Supp. 645, 653 (E.D. Pa. 1979) (sex discrimination).

74. [searches] Lewis v. Kugler, 446 F.2d 1343, 1350 (3d Cir. 1971) (police stops of cars driven by males with long hair); Lankford v. Gelston, 364 F.2d 197, 202 (4th Cir. 1966) (mass searches on anonymous tips); Hague v. Comm. for Indus. Org., 101 F.2d 774, 790–91 (3d Cir.) (arrest of labor organizers without probable cause), aff'd, 307 U.S. 496 (1939); Wong v. Nelson, 549 F. Supp. 895, 896 (D. Colo. 1982) (warrantless search of home and business). Compare Mapp v. Ohio, 367 U.S. 643, 648, 651–52 (1961) (remedies other than exclusionary rule are "worthless and futile," and reduce Fourth Amendment to "a form of words").

75. [other civil rights] N.Y. State Nat'l Org. for Women v. Terry, 886 F.2d 1339, 1362 (2d Cir. 1989) (physical interference with entrance to abortion clinic); Portland Feminist Women's Health Center v. Advocates for Life, Inc., 859 F.2d 681, 684 (9th Cir. 1988) (same); Mitchell v. Cuomo, 748 F.2d 804, 806 (2d Cir. 1984) (when deprivation of constitutional right is shown, "most courts hold that no further showing of irreparable injury is necessary"), quoting Charles Alan Wright & Arthur R. Miller, 11 *Federal Practice & Procedure* § 2948 at 440 (West 1973); Burrus v. Turnbo, 743 F.2d 693, 703 (9th Cir. 1984) (speedy trial rights under Interstate Agreement on Detainers), vacated on other grounds, 474 U.S. 1016 (1985); Gomez v. Layton, 394 F.2d 764, 766 (D.C. Cir. 1968) (enforcement of vagrancy ordinance, allegedly in violation of due process clause); Vietnamese Fisherman's Ass'n v.

Knights of the Ku Klux Klan, 543 F. Supp. 198, 218 (S.D. Tex. 1982) (paramilitary force threatening racial minorities; "victims of discrimination suffer irreparable injury, regardless of pecuniary damage"); Int'l Ass'n of Firefighters, Local 2069 v. City of Sylacauga, 436 F. Supp. 482, 492 (N.D. Ala. 1977) (promotion decisions without competitive examination; "deprivations of constitutional rights are usually held to constitute irreparable injury as a matter of law"); Am. Academy of Pediatrics v. Van de Kamp, 214 Cal. App. 3d 831, 263 Cal. Rptr. 46 (1989) (requirement that minors get parental or judicial consent for abortion); Murray v. Egan, 28 Conn. Supp. 204, 208, 256 A.2d 844, 847 (1969) (unlawful nonbinding referendum on school busing plan).

76. [clean air] U.S. v. City of Painesville, 644 F.2d 1186, 1193–94 (6th Cir. 1981) (no hearing required to determine presence of irreparable injury).

77. [clean water] Mayor of Morgan City v. Ascension Parish Police Jury, 468 So.2d 1291, 1300–01 (La. App. 1985) (pollution of lake); Att'y Gen'l v. Thomas Solvent Co., 146 Mich. App. 55, 380 N.W.2d 53, 58 (1985) (pollution of ground water); Petraborg v. Zontelli, 217 Minn. 536, 553–55, 15 N.W.2d 174, 183–84 (1944) (damming and draining lake). See also Miller & Lux v. Madera Canal & Irrigation Co., 155 Cal. 59, 99 P. 502 (1909) (enjoining misappropriation of water; irreparable injury not discussed); Reppun v. Bd. of Water Supply, 65 Hawaii 531, 537, 561, 656 P.2d 57, 62, 76 (1982) (injunction "normally remains a particularly appropriate remedy" for misappropriation of water).

78. [forest] Canal Auth. v. Callaway, 489 F.2d 567, 575–76 (5th Cir. 1974). See also the timber cases cited in note 9.

79. [species] Tenn. Valley Auth. v. Hill, 437 U.S. 153, 193–95 (1978) (affirming injunction without discussing irreparable injury); Fund for Animals v. Frizzell, 530 F.2d 982, 986–87 (D.C. Cir. 1975) (threat to species is irreparable injury to members of environmental group, but loss of single bird is not); Village of False Pass v. Watt, 565 F. Supp. 1123, 1163–65 (D. Alaska 1983), aff'd as Village of False Pass v. Clark, 733 F.2d 605 (9th Cir. 1984). See also Caney Hunting Club, Inc. v. Tolbert, 294 So.2d 894, 895 (La. App. 1974) (killing of game on hunting lease).

80. [environmental impact statement] Sierra Club v. Marsh, 872 F.2d 497, 499–504 (1st Cir. 1989) (partial construction of challenged project pending completion of proper environmental impact statement generates political momentum for project and "potentially irreparable . . . decisionmaking risk to the environment"); N. Cheyenne Tribe v. Hodel, 851 F.2d 1152, 1156–57 (9th Cir. 1988) (treating "bureaucratic rationalization and bureaucratic momentum" as irreparable harm); Friends of the Earth, Inc. v. Coleman, 518 F.2d 323, 330 (9th Cir. 1975) (irreparable injury "may be implied from the failure by responsible authorities to evaluate fully the environmental impact of the proposed project"); Environmental Defense Fund, Inc. v. Froehlke, 477 F.2d 1033, 1037 (8th Cir. 1973) ("violation of NEPA in itself may constitute a sufficient demonstration of irreparable harm"); Environmental Defense Fund v. Tenn. Valley Auth., 468 F.2d 1164, 1184 (6th Cir. 1972) (same); Scherr v. Volpe, 466 F.2d 1027, 1034 (7th Cir. 1972) (loss of "careful and informed decision-making process"); Orange County v. N.C. Dep't of Transp., 46 N.C. App. 350, 384–85, 265 S.E.2d 890, 911–13 (1980) (injunction authorized without discussing irreparable injury). See also Hanly v. Mitchell, 460 F.2d 640, 648 (2d Cir. 1972) (important to preserve integrity of environmental impact statement, even if agency adheres to original conclusion).

81. [domestic violence] Carpenter v. Carpenter, 252 So.2d 591 (Fla. App. 1971) (holding ex-husband in contempt of injunction ordering him not to "molest" ex-wife); Keller v. Keller, 158 N.W.2d 694 (N.D. 1968) (enjoining husband from "molesting or annoying" wife or children, without discussing irreparable injury); Marquette v. Marquette, 686 P.2d 990 (Okla. App. 1984) (enjoining ex-husband from "abusing, injuring, threatening, or harassing" ex-wife, rejecting challenges to statute authorizing such orders, and not discussing irreparable injury); see also Rosenbaum v. Rosenbaum, 184 Ill. App. 3d 987, —, 541 N.E.2d 872, 873 (1989) (enjoining mother from "verbally contacting" adult son or his wife). See also Beverly Balos & Katie Trotzky, *Enforcement of the Domestic Abuse Act in Minnesota: A Preliminary Study*, 6 L. & Inequality 83 (1988); Gary Richard Brown, *Battered Women and the Temporary Restraining Order*, 10 Women's Rights L. Rptr. 261 (1988).

82. [domestic violence statutes] Peter Finn, *Statutory Authority in the Use and Enforcement of Civil Protection Orders Against Domestic Abuse*, 23 Family L.Q. 43 (1989).

83. [violence against sharecropper] Bussell v. Bishop, 152 Ga. 428, 110 S.E. 174 (1921).

84. [risk of physical injury] Eng v. Smith, 849 F.2d 80 (2d Cir. 1988) (inadequate mental health care in prison, resulting in suicide of one inmate); Todd v. Sorrell, 841 F.2d 87, 88 (4th Cir. 1988) (refusal to pay for liver transplant); L.J. v. Massinga, 838 F.2d 118, 120–21 (4th Cir. 1988) (failure to prevent physical abuse of foster children); Ramirez de Arellano v. Weinberger, 745 F.2d 1500, 1528 (D.C. Cir. 1984) (military activities on private property), vacated on other grounds mem., 471 U.S. 1113 (1985); Friends for All Children, Inc. v. Lockheed Aircraft Corp., 746 F.2d 816, 831 (D.C. Cir. 1984) (ordering defendant to pay for tests to diagnose minimal brain dysfunction before age at which it became irreversible); Johnson v. U.S. Dep't of Agric., 734 F.2d 774 (11th Cir. 1984) (damage to health); United Steelworkers v. Fort Pitt Steel Casting, 598 F.2d 1273, 1280 (3d Cir. 1979) (lapse of medical insurance); Lakeshore Hills, Inc. v. Adcox, 90 Ill. App. 3d 609, 413 N.E.2d 548 (1980) (bear in residential neighborhood); S. Cent. Bell Tel. Co. v. F. Miller & Sons, 382 So.2d 264, 265 (La. App. 1980) (disruption of telephone service, creating inability to call for police, fire, or ambulance protection); O'Sullivan v. Secretary of Human Serv., 402 Mass. 190, —, 521 N.E.2d 997, 1002 (1988) (failure to supervise mental patient in physical restraint or seclusion); Att'y Gen'l v. Thomas Solvent Co., 146 Mich. App. 55, 380 N.W.2d 53, 58 (1985) (toxic chemicals in municipal wells); Whittaker v. Stangvick, 100 Minn. 386, 392, 111 N.W. 295, 297 (1907) (reckless hunters); Smith v. W. Elec. Co., 643 S.W.2d 10, 13 (Mo. App. 1982) (cigarette smoke in workplace); Armintor v. Community Hosp., 659 S.W.2d 86, 89 (Tex. App. 1983) (damage to quality of care in hospital). See also Monmouth County Correctional Inst'l Inmates v. Lanzaro, 834 F.2d 326, 329 (3d Cir. 1987) (refusal to provide abortions for female prisoners). For a collection of older cases, see Joseph Moscovitz, *Civil Liberties and Injunctive Protection*, 39 Ill. L. Rev. 144, 153 n.58 (1944).

85. [emotional distress] Bowen v. City of N.Y., 476 U.S. 467, 483–84 (1986) (termination of disability benefits to mental patients); Ray v. School Dist., 666 F. Supp. 1524, 1534–35 (M.D. Fla. 1987) (exclusion of AIDS patients from public school); Mooney v. Cooledge, 30 Ark. 640, 642–43 (1875) (removing bodies of ancestors from family cemetery); Mental Health Info. Serv. v. Schenectady County Dep't of Social Serv., 128 Misc. 2d 282, 290, 488 N.Y.S.2d 335, 340 (1985) (service of process on mental patient). For additional cases enjoining interference with dead bodies, see Moscovitz, at 153 n.60.

86. [difficulty not enough] Klein v. PepsiCo, Inc., 845 F.2d 76, 80 (4th Cir. 1988) (contract to sell jet plane; only a few similar models available); Duval & Co. v. Malcom, 233 Ga. 784, 787–88, 214 S.E.2d 356, 359 (1975) (cotton in shortage; court assumed buyer could cover if it paid "an unreasonable price"); Beckman v. Vassall-Dillworth Lincoln-Mercury, Inc., 321 Pa. Super. 428, 468 A.2d 784 (1983) (automobile); Scholl v. Hartzell, 20 Pa. D. & C. 3d 304, 309 (Pa. Com. Pl. 1981) (1962 Corvette); cases cited in notes 53–55 (shortage of automobiles following World War II). See also Kaiser v. Wolf, 18 Pa. D. & C. 3d 555 (Pa. Com. Pl. 1981) (timber; plaintiff did not argue difficulty of replacement, but only that he would have to count the trees to prove his damages, and that would be inconvenient).

87. [difficulty enough] Laclede Gas Co. v. Amoco Oil Co., 522 F.2d 33, 40 (8th Cir. 1975) (propane "readily available," but long-term contract for propane "probably" not available); Campbell Soup Co. v. Wentz, 172 F.2d 80, 82–83 (3d Cir. 1948) ("virtually impossible"); Bomberger v. McKelvey, 35 Cal. 2d 607, 613–15, 220 P.2d 729, 734–35 (1950) (90-to-120-day wait); Heidner v. Hewitt Chevrolet Co., 166 Kan. 11, 13, 199 P.2d 481, 483 (1948) (not "readily purchased"); Sedmak v. Charlie's Chevrolet, Inc., 622 S.W.2d 694, 700 (Mo. App. 1981) ("in short supply and great demand"); Boeving v. Vandover, 240 Mo. App. 117, 121, 218 S.W.2d 175, 177 (1949) (not "readily purchased"); De Moss v. Conart Motor Sales, 72 N.E.2d 158, 160 (Ohio Com. Pl. 1947) ("hard to get"), aff'd for want of proper record, 149 Ohio St.2d 299, 78 N.E.2d 675 (1948); Paullus v. Yarbrough, 219 Or. 611, 641–42, 347 P.2d 620, 635 (1959) ("increasingly difficult"); Corbin, 5A *Contracts* § 1146 at 154 (cited in note 1) ("inconvenience of getting a supply elsewhere").

88. [tomato crop essential to cannery] Curtice Bros. Co. v. Catts, 72 N.J. Eq. 831, 833, 66 A. 935, 936 (1907).

89. [chaos in market for aviation fuel] E. Airlines v. Gulf Oil Corp., 415 F. Supp. 429, 442 (S.D. Fla. 1975).

90. [defendant must show replaceability] Kaiser Trading Co. v. Associated Metals & Minerals Corp., 321 F. Supp. 923, 933 (N.D. Cal. 1970), appeal dis'd, 443 F.2d 1364 (9th Cir. 1971).

91. [efficient breach theory] See Richard A. Posner, *Economic Analysis of Law* § 4.8 at 107 (Little, Brown, 3d ed. 1986).

92. [defendant bears risk of uncertainty] Bigelow v. RKO Radio Pictures, 327 U.S. 251, 265 (1946); Brink's Inc. v. City of N.Y., 717 F.2d 700, 710–12 (2d Cir. 1983).

93. [difficulty shifted to plaintiff] Thompson v. Commonwealth, 197 Va. 208, 212–14, 89 S.E.2d 64, 67–68 (1955).

94. [same reasoning for private plaintiffs] First Nat'l State Bank v. Commonwealth Fed. Sav. & Loan Ass'n, 610 F.2d 164, 173–74 (3d Cir. 1979) (specifically enforcing contract to permanently finance failed shopping mall, placing hardship on party that agreed to bear it); Laclede Gas Co. v. Amoco Oil Co., 522 F.2d 33, 40 (8th Cir. 1975) (even if plaintiff could replace propane, "it would still face considerable expense and trouble which cannot be estimated in advance"); Leasco

Corp. v. Taussig, 473 F.2d 777, 786 (2d Cir. 1972) (specifically enforcing promise to buy subsidiary, where sale to anyone else would be "difficult if not impossible," and defendant was better situated than plaintiff to manage the subsidiary); Southwest Pipe Line Co. v. Empire Natural Gas Co., 33 F.2d 248, 258 (8th Cir. 1929) (sale of natural gas at wellhead, where replacement would require new pipeline to other wells); Sedmak v. Charlie's Chevrolet, Inc., 622 S.W.2d 694, 700 (Mo. App. 1981) (limited production Corvette; "difficult, if not impossible, to obtain its replication without considerable expense, delay and inconvenience"). But see Fortner v. Wilson, 202 Okla. 563, 566, 216 P.2d 299, 301 (1950) ("new Chevrolet automobiles were not available on the open market at that time, and could only be obtained at great expense and inconvenience from used-car dealers; but the fact remains that they could be obtained").

95. [removing boulders] Wheelock v. Noonan, 108 N.Y. 179, 15 N.E. 67 (1888).

96. [doing what trespasser is bound to do] Id. at 185, 15 N.E. at 68. See also Frank v. Coyle, 310 Mich. 14, 16 N.W.2d 649 (1944) (ordering specific performance of defendant's promise to remove eight tourist cabins from plaintiff's land).

97. [damages hard to measure] Youngstown Sheet & Tube Co. v. Sawyer, 343 U.S. 579, 585 (1952) (seizure of steel mills); Walla Walla City v. Walla Walla Water Co., 172 U.S. 1, 11–13 (1898) (competing water works); Vogel v. Am. Soc'y of Appraisers, 744 F.2d 598, 599–600 (7th Cir. 1984) (expulsion from professional society); Phillips v. Crown Cent. Petroleum Corp., 602 F.2d 616, 629–30 (4th Cir. 1979) (antitrust; "future injury of uncertain date and magnitude is irreparable"); Ammerman v. City Stores Co., 394 F.2d 950, 955–56 (D.C. Cir. 1968) (lease in new shopping mall); Roof v. Conway, 133 F.2d 819, 826–27 (6th Cir. 1943) (threat to certificate of public convenience and necessity); Southwest Pipe Line Co. v. Empire Natural Gas Co., 33 F.2d 248, 258 (8th Cir. 1929) (sale of natural gas at wellhead, where future flows were unpredictable); Travellers Int'l AG v. Trans World Airlines, Inc., 684 F. Supp. 1206, 1216 (S.D.N.Y. 1988) (loss of goodwill); Nakian v. Di Laurenti, 673 F. Supp. 699, 701 (S.D.N.Y. 1987) (loss of opportunity to exhibit sculptures); Buckwalter Motors, Inc. v. Gen'l Motors Corp., 593 F. Supp. 628, 633 (S.D. Iowa 1984) (threats to automobile dealership); Southwest Village Water Co. v. Fleming, 442 So.2d 89, 92 (Ala. 1983) (failure to keep leased premises in good repair); De Ritis v. AHZ Corp., 444 So.2d 93, 94–95 (Fla. App. 1984) (disparaging condominiums to potential buyers); Edgecomb v. Edmonston, 257 Mass. 12, 18, 153 N.E. 99, 101 (1926) (covenant not to compete); Hines Corp. v. City of Albuquerque, 95 N.M. 311, 313, 621 P.2d 1116, 1118 (1980) (restrictive covenant); Strank v. Mercy Hosp., 383 Pa. 54, 57, 117 A.2d 697, 698 (1955) (loss of academic credit); Valero Transmission Co. v. Mitchell Energy Corp., 743 S.W.2d 658, 664 (Tex. App. 1987) (drainage of gas reserves); Story, 2 *Equity Jurisprudence* § 718 at 27, id. § 722 at 29 (cited in note 1); Restatement (Second) of Torts § 944 comments c, d (1979). See also W. Airlines, Inc. v. Int'l Bhd. of Teamsters, 480 U.S. 1301, 1308–10 (1987) (O'Connor in chambers) (staying order of court of appeals, and permitting consummation of airline merger, because of extraordinarily complex chain of consequences if merger were delayed).

98. [uniqueness means uncertain value] For an argument equating uniqueness with valuation difficulties, see Anthony T. Kronman, *Specific Performance*, 45 U. Chi. L. Rev. 351, 355–65 (1978).

99. [value of time and trouble] See text at notes 95–97.

100. **[all values fungible]** For a defense of the irreparable injury rule explicitly based on the universal substitutability of goods, see Kronman at 359 ("all goods are ultimately commensurable").

101. **[nonmarket rights hard to value]** Galella v. Onassis, 353 F. Supp. 196, 235 (S.D.N.Y. 1972) (harassment by photographer), aff'd in relevant part, 487 F.2d 986, 998–99 (2d Cir. 1973); Mooney v. Cooledge, 30 Ark. 640, 642–43 (1875) (removing bodies of ancestors from family cemetery); Hart v. Wagner, 184 Md. 40, 47, 40 A.2d 47, 50–51 (1944) (trash fires); Block v. Mayor of Baltimore, 149 Md. 39, 59, 129 A. 887, 894 (1925) (open garbage scows; damages for "loss of sleep, nausea, or . . . impairment of health . . . hard to prove and harder to measure").

102. **[half-empty shopping mall]** First Nat'l State Bank v. Commonwealth Fed. Sav. & Loan Ass'n, 610 F.2d 164 (3d Cir. 1979).

103. **[unique burdens of unsold property]** For more explicit examples, see Leasco Corp. v. Taussig, 473 F.2d 777, 785–86 (2d Cir. 1972) (specifically enforcing buyer's promise to buy subsidiary, where subsidiary was hard to sell and damages "would have burdened Leasco with a company it did not want (and could not handle)"); Derwell Co. v. Apic, Inc., 278 A.2d 338, 343–44 (Del. Ch. 1971) (specifically enforcing buyer's promise to buy land; damages inadequate where denial of zoning change might have rendered land unsalable); Trachtenburg v. Sibarco Stations, Inc., 477 Pa. 517, 524–25, 384 A.2d 1209, 1213 (1978) (contract-market damages are inadequate where land is in depressed neighborhood and seller wants to be "relieved of the burden of land ownership"). See also David Co. v. Jim W. Miller Constr., Inc., 444 N.W.2d 836, 839 (Minn. 1989) (arbitration award ordering builder to buy back defective building and buy the land on which it sat, where units were "unmarketable absent extensive and costly repairs"); UCC § 2–709(1)(b) (seller may recover the price "of goods identified to the contract if the seller is unable after reasonable effort to resell them at a reasonable price or the circumstances reasonably indicate that such effort will be unavailing").

104. **[mutual remedy for sellers]** For the mutuality rationale, see ch. 1 at note 79.

105. **[lost profits]** Triple-A Baseball Club Assoc. v. Northeastern Baseball, Inc., 832 F.2d 214, 225 (1st Cir. 1987) (breach of contract to sell minor league baseball franchise); Humana, Inc. v. Avram A. Jacobson, M.D., P.A., 804 F.2d 1390, 1394 (5th Cir. 1986) (billing practices that jeopardized plaintiff's Medicare funding); Molex, Inc. v. Nolen, 759 F.2d 474, 478 (5th Cir. 1985) (scheme to steal customer); Dino de Laurentiis Cinematografica, S.p.A. v. D-150, Inc., 366 F.2d 373, 375–76 (2d Cir. 1966) (breach of contract to use new product); Long Island R.R. v. Int'l Ass'n of Machinists, 709 F. Supp. 376, 388–89 (S.D.N.Y. 1989) (shutdown of railroad by unlawful strike), aff'd, 874 F.2d 901, 911 (2d Cir. 1989), cert. denied, 110 S. Ct. 836 (1990); Gulf & W. Corp. v. Craftique Prod., Inc., 523 F. Supp. 603, 607–08 (S.D.N.Y. 1981) (breach of contract to market books; future sales impossible to predict, so damages impossible to measure); Hogan v. Norfleet, 113 So.2d 437, 439–40 (Fla. App. 1959) (breach of contract to sell bottled-gas franchise); Bio-Medical Labs., Inc. v. Trainor, 68 Ill. 2d 540, 549, 370 N.E.2d 223, 227 (1977) (suspension of medical provider from eligibility for Medicaid reimbursement); Agrimerica, Inc. v. Mathes, 170 Ill. App. 3d 1025, 1034, 524 N.E.2d 947, 953 (1988) (covenant not to compete, threatening loss of plaintiff's competitive position); Niedzialek v. Journey-

68 THE DEATH OF THE IRREPARABLE INJURY RULE

men Barbers Local No. 552, 331 Mich. 296, 300, 49 N.W.2d 273, 275 (1951) (picketing barbershop); Callanan v. Powers, 199 N.Y. 268, 285, 92 N.E. 747, 752 (1910) (breach of contract to build railroad); Am. Mut. Liab. Ins. Co. v. Fisher, 58 Wis. 2d 299, 304–05, 206 N.W.2d 152, 156 (1973) (landlord's failure to provide parking for tenant's customers); Restatement (Second) of Torts § 944 comment c (1979) (compensation often inadequate for loss of commercial profits, because they cannot be proved with reasonable certainty). See also cases cited in note 97. But see City Centre One Assoc. v. Teachers Ins. & Annuity Ass'n, 656 F. Supp. 658 (D. Utah 1987) (refusing to specifically enforce equity participation loan) (discussed in ch. 4 at notes 16–18); Spielman v. Sigrist, 72 N.Y.S.2d 861 (Sup. 1947) (refusing to specifically enforce contract for placement of cigarette vending machine).

106. [sell profits for a mere guess] Pomeroy, *Specific Performance* § 15 at 20 (cited in note 46). See also Story, 2 *Equity Jurisprudence* § 718 at 26–27 (cited in note 1) ("the profit upon the contract, being to depend on future events, could not be correctly estimated in damages, where the calculation must proceed upon conjecture").

107. [output and requirement contracts] Southwest Pipe Line Co. v. Empire Natural Gas Co., 33 F.2d 248, 258 (8th Cir. 1929) (natural gas); Hunt Foods, Inc. v. O'Disho, 98 F. Supp. 267, 269–70 (N.D. Cal. 1951) (peaches); Fraser v. Cohen, 159 Fla. 253, 31 So.2d 463, 465, 468 (1947) (bananas); E. Rolling Mill Co. v. Michlovitz, 157 Md. 51, 67, 145 A. 378, 383–84 (1929) (steel scrap; "By what method would a jury determine the future quarterly tonnage, the quarterly contract price, and quarterly market price during these coming years?"); Ebsary Fireproofing & Gypsum Co. v. Empire Gypsum Co., 110 Misc. 272, 277, 181 N.Y.S. 270, 273 (1920) (plaster; other sources uneconomical); Fuchs v. United Motor Stage Co., 135 Ohio St. 509, 523, 21 N.E.2d 669, 675–76 (1939) (gasoline); Schipper Bros. Coal Mining Co. v. Economy Domestic Coal Co., 277 Pa. 356, 361, 121 A. 193, 194–95 (1923) (coal; other sources uneconomical); Mo. Public Serv. Co. v. Peabody Coal Co., 583 S.W.2d 721, 724 (Mo. App. 1979) (coal; "UCC gives the party injured by the breach a clear option to sue in specific performance"); UCC § 2–716, Official Comment 2; Williston & Jaeger, 11 *Contracts* § 1419B at 695–97 (cited in note 1); Van Hecke, 40 N.C. L. Rev. at 4–9 (cited in note 43); But see Cappetta v. Atlantic Rfg. Co., 74 F.2d 53, 55 (2d Cir. 1934) (gasoline); N. & L. Fur Co. v. Petkanas, 299 N.Y.S. 901 (A.D. 1937) (furcoat scraps).

108. [interference with commercial property] Danielson v. Local 275, Laborers Int'l Union, 479 F.2d 1033, 1036–37 (2d Cir. 1973) (construction delays caused by unlawful picketing); Sambo's, Inc. v. City Council of Toledo, 466 F. Supp. 177, 181 (N.D. Ohio 1979) (city refused to let defendant open business under its tradename); Justices of the Inferior Court v. Griffin & W. Point Plank Road Co., 11 Ga. 246, 250–51 (1852) (destruction of tollgates on private road); Eagle Books, Inc. v. Jones, 130 Ill. App. 3d 407, 411, 474 N.E.2d 444, 447–48 (1985) (picketing plaintiff's business); McDaniel v. Moyer, 662 P.2d 309, 313 n.13 (Okla. 1983) (interfering with plaintiff's right to drill oil well on defendant's land); McGowin v. Remington, 12 Pa. (2 Jones) 56, 62 (1849) (withholding papers essential to surveying business).

109. [trade secrets] Winston Research Corp. v. Minn. Mining & Mfg. Co., 350 F.2d 134, 143 (9th Cir. 1965) (expressly finding irreparable injury without explanation); Webcraft Technology, Inc. v. McCaw, 674 F. Supp. 1039, 1048 (S.D.N.Y.

1987) (expressly finding irreparable injury without explanation); Herold v. Herold China & Pottery, 257 F. 911, 913 (6th Cir. 1919) ("well settled that secret formulas and processes" will be protected by injunction); Unistar Corp. v. Child, 415 So.2d 733, 735 (Fla. App. 1982) (irreparable injury "presumed"); Lane v. Commonwealth, 401 Mass. 549, 517 N.E.2d 1281 (1988) (injunction issued without discussing irreparable injury); Valco Cincinnati, Inc. v. N & D Mach. Serv., Inc., 24 Ohio St. 3d 41, 47, 492 N.E.2d 814, 819 (1986) ("injunctions are, of course, the appropriate remedy"); Loveall v. Am. Honda Motor Co., 694 S.W.2d 937, 939–40 (Tenn. 1985) (forbidding plaintiff to disclose trade secrets obtained in discovery from defendant); Jeter v. Associated Rack Corp., 607 S.W.2d 272, 278 (Tex. Civ. App. 1980) ("future damages would have been difficult if not impossible to ascertain"); Unif. Trade Secrets Act § 2(a), 14 Unif. Laws Ann. 541, 544 (1980) ("actual or threatened misappropriation may be enjoined"); id. § 2(b) ("in exceptional circumstances, an injunction may condition future use upon payment of a reasonable royalty") (Supp. 1985).

110. [patents] Hybritech Inc. v. Abbott Labs., 849 F.2d 1446, 1456–57 (Fed. Cir. 1988) ("may have market effects never fully compensable in money"); H.H. Robertson, Co. v. United Steel Deck, Inc., 820 F.2d 384, 390 (Fed. Cir. 1987) (irreparable injury "presumed" when clear infringement shown); Atlas Powder Co. v. Ireco Chem., 773 F.2d 1230, 1233 (Fed. Cir. 1985) (same); Smith Int'l, Inc. v. Hughes Tool Co., 718 F.2d 1573, 1581 (Fed. Cir. 1983) (same; "very nature of the patent right is the right to exclude others"); Donald S. Chisum, 5 Patents § 20.04 at p. 20–267 (1987) (permanent injunction "will normally be granted unless the public interest otherwise dictates"); id. § 20.04[1][e] at p. 20–291 (at preliminary injunction stage, finding of irreparable injury or lack thereof appears to be parasitic on plaintiff's showing of validity and infringement); Story, 2 Equity Jurisprudence §§ 930–34 (cited in note 1) (damage remedy is wholly inadequate, and injunction is routine, but validity of contested patent must be determined at law); Craig S. Summers, *Remedies for Patent Infringement in the Federal Circuit—A Survey of the First Six Years*, 29 Idea 333, 334–39 (1989) ("once infringement has been established, an injunction normally follows").

111. [copyrights] Allied Mktg. Group, Inc. v. CDL Mktg., Inc., 878 F.2d 806, 810 n.1 (5th Cir. 1989) ("damage to the goodwill of [plaintiff's] customers—as a result of confusion between [plaintiff's products] and those of [defendant]—might be incapable of calculation"); Apple Computer, Inc. v. Formula Int'l, Inc., 725 F.2d 521, 525 (9th Cir. 1984) (irreparable injury presumed); Atari, Inc. v. N. Am. Philips Consumer Elec. Corp., 672 F.2d 607, 620 (7th Cir. 1982) (same); Wainwright Securities, Inc. v. Wall Street Transcript Corp., 558 F.2d 91, 94 (2d Cir. 1977) (same); Albert E. Price, Inc. v. Metzner, 574 F. Supp. 281, 288–90 (E.D. Pa. 1983) (damages incalculable); 2 Story §§ 930–35 (damage remedy is wholly inadequate, and injunction is routine, but validity of contested copyright must be determined at law); Melville Nimmer & David Nimmer, 3 *Nimmer on Copyright*, § 14.06[B] at p. 14–56.1 (Matthew Bender 1988) ("it would appear to be an abuse of discretion to deny a permanent injunction where liability has been established and there is a threat of continuing infringement"); id. § 14.06[A] at pp. 14–54.1 to 14–54.3 (at preliminary injunction stage, "prima facie case of copyright infringement or reasonable likelihood of success on the merits raises a presumption of irreparable harm").

112. [trademarks] Am. Cyanamid Co. v. Campagna per le Farmacie in Italia S.p.A., 847 F.2d 53, 55 (2d Cir. 1988) (likelihood of confusion is sufficient to show irreparable harm); Hartford House, Ltd. v. Hallmark Cards, Inc., 846 F.2d 1268, 1271 (10th Cir. 1988) (trade dress; defendant conceded irreparable injury); Int'l Kennel Club, Inc. v. Mighty Star, Inc., 846 F.2d 1079, 1091–92 (7th Cir. 1988) (trademark damages "are by their very nature irreparable and not susceptible of adequate measurement"); Artemide SpA v. Grandlite Design & Mfg. Co., 672 F. Supp. 698, 712 (S.D.N.Y. 1987) (trade dress; "finding of irreparable harm almost inevitably follows a finding of likelihood of confusion"); Miller Brewing Co. v. Carling O'Keefe Breweries, Ltd., 452 F. Supp. 429, 437–38 (W.D.N.Y. 1978) (damages hard to measure; loss of business reputation); Restatement (Second) of Torts § 938 comment b, at 574 (1979) (injunctions routine). See also Southeast Bank, N.A. v. Lawrence, 104 A.D.2d 213, 216, 483 N.Y.S.2d 218, 220 (1984) (unauthorized use of name of plaintiff's decedent), rev'd on other grounds, 66 N.Y.2d 910, 489 N.E.2d 744, 498 N.Y.S.2d 775 (1985).

113. [antitrust] Cal. v. Am. Stores Co., 110 S. Ct. 1853, 1859 (1990) ("divestiture is the preferred remedy"); Fed. Trade Comm'n v. Elders Grain, Inc., 868 F.2d 901 (7th Cir. 1989) (preliminary injunction requiring rescission of one competitor's acquisition of another); U.S. v. BNS Inc., 848 F.2d 945, 947 (9th Cir. 1988) (preliminary injunction against completing acquisition); Roland Mach. Co. v. Dresser Indus., Inc., 749 F.2d 380, 386, 391 (7th Cir. 1984) (plaintiff's business may be destroyed, or lost profits may be hard to calculate); Phillips v. Crown Cent. Petroleum Corp., 602 F.2d 616, 629–30 (4th Cir. 1979) ("future injury of uncertain date and incalculable magnitude"); Schwartz v. Laundry & Linen Supply Drivers' Union, Local 187, 339 Pa. 353, 357, 14 A.2d 438, 440 (1940) (tendency to impair or destroy plaintiff's business).

114. [covenants not to compete] Molex, Inc. v. Nolen, 759 F.2d 474, 478 (5th Cir. 1985) (theft of customer); Churchill Communications Corp. v. Demyanovich, 668 F. Supp. 207, 214 (S.D.N.Y. 1987) (loss of customers); Hoppe v. Preferred Risk Mut. Ins. Co., 470 So.2d 1161, 1164 (Ala. 1985) (expressly finds irreparable injury without explaining why); Monogram Indus., Inc. v. Sar Indus., Inc., 64 Cal. App. 3d 692, 134 Cal. Rptr. 714 (1976) (affirming preliminary injunction without discussing irreparable injury); Capraro v. Lanier Business Prod., Inc., 466 So.2d 212, 213 (Fla. 1985) (irreparable injury "presumed"); Canfield v. Spear, 44 Ill. 2d 49, 51, 254 N.E.2d 433, 434 (1969) (injunction is "customary and proper"); Retina Serv., Ltd. v. Garoon, 182 Ill. App. 3d 851, 854, 859, 538 N.E.2d 651, 652, 655 (1989) (ordering trial court to grant preliminary injunction); R.M. Sedrose, Inc. v. Mazmanian, 326 Mass. 578, 582–83, 95 N.E.2d 677, 679 (1950) (plaintiff entitled to elect injunction or damages; irreparable injury not discussed); Webb Pub. Co. v. Fosshage, 426 N.W.2d 445, 448–49 (Minn. App. 1988) (loss of revenue and damage to business reputation); Winrock Enterprises, Inc. v. House of Fabrics, Inc., 91 N.M. 661, 664, 579 P.2d 787, 790 (1978) (multiplicity of suits); A.E.P. Indus., Inc. v. McClure, 308 N.C. 393, 406, 302 S.E.2d 754, 761–64 (1983) (damages hard to measure, and plaintiff entitled to his rights); John G. Bryant Co. v. Sling Testing & Repair, Inc., 471 Pa. 1, 7–10, 369 A.2d 1164, 1167–68 (1977) ("incalculable damage;" "where a covenant of this type meets the test of reasonableness, it is prima facie enforceable in equity"); Martin v. Linen Systems for Hosp., Inc., 671 S.W.2d 706, 710 (Tex. App. 1984) ("dollar value cannot easily be assigned to a company's loss of clientele, goodwill, marketing techniques, office stability, etc."); System Concepts, Inc. v. Dixon, 669 P.2d 421, 427–28 (Utah 1983) (damages conjectural); Lakeside Oil Co. v. Slutsky, 8 Wis. 2d 157, 165, 98 N.W.2d 415, 421–22 (1959) (damages hard to measure). See also Merrill Lynch, Pierce, Fenner & Smith, Inc. v. Dutton, 844 F.2d 726 (10th Cir. 1988) (enforcing contractual agreement to preliminary injunction); Indep. Bankers Ass'n v. Smith, 534 F.2d 921, 950 (D.C. Cir. 1976) (networks of automatic teller machines would irreparably harm state banks); Weatherford Oil Tool Co. v. Campbell, 161 Tex. 310, 314–15, 340 S.W.2d 950, 952–53 (1960) (overbroad covenant not to compete may be reformed and enforced by injunction, but not by damages).

115. [interference with contract] Paul L. Pratt, P.C. v. Blunt, 140 Ill. App. 3d 512, 519, 488 N.E.2d 1062, 1067 (1986) (solicitation of former employer's clients); Pure Milk Prod. Coop. v. Nat'l Farmers Org., 64 Wis. 2d 241, 262, 219 N.W.2d 564, 575 (1974) (expressly finding irreparable injury without explaining why).

116. [unfair competition] McNeilab, Inc. v. Am. Home Prod. Corp., 848 F.2d 34 (2d Cir. 1988) (misleading comparative advertising; irreparable injury presumed); Quabaug Rubber Co. v. Fabiano Shoe Co., 567 F.2d 154, 160–61 (1st Cir. 1977) (mislabeled goods; consumer confusion is irreparable injury); U-Haul Int'l, Inc. v. Jartran, Inc., 522 F. Supp. 1238, 1255–56 (D. Ariz. 1981) (misleading comparative advertising; damages unmeasurable), aff'd, 681 F.2d 1159 (9th Cir. 1982); People v. Black's Food Store, 16 Cal. 2d 59, 105 P.2d 361 (1940) (selling goods below cost; preliminary injunction affirmed without discussion of irreparable injury); Restatement (Second) of Torts § 938 comment b, at 574 (1979) (injunctions routine). See also People v. Pacific Land Research Co., 20 Cal. 3d 10, 141 Cal. Rptr. 20, 569 P.2d 125 (1977) (misrepresentations in sale of land); State ex rel. Danforth v. Independence Dodge, Inc., 494 S.W.2d 362, 370 (Mo. App. 1973) (consumer fraud).

117. [antitrust cases assume inadequacy] See Zenith Radio Corp. v. Hazeltine Research, Inc., 395 U.S. 100, 129–33 (1969); U.S. v. Parke, Davis & Co. 362 U.S. 29, 48 (1960); U.S. v. Borden Co., 347 U.S. 514, 518–20 (1954); Standard Oil Co. v. U.S., 221 U.S. 1, 77–82 (1911); U.S. v. Am. Tobacco Co., 221 U.S. 106, 184–88 (1911); Addyston Pipe & Steel Co. v. U.S., 175 U.S. 211, 247–48 (1899). For an opinion that makes this assumption explicit, see Cal. v. Am. Stores Co., 872 F.2d 837, 844 (9th Cir. 1989) ("the district court's determination of irreparable harm follows naturally from its holding of likelihood of success on the merits"), rev'd on other grounds, 110 S. Ct. 1853 (1990).

118. [loss that should not be suffered] Cross Word Prod., Inc. v. Suter, 97 Ill. App. 3d 282, 286, 422 N.E.2d 953, 957 (1981) (breach of fiduciary duty; irreparable injury is "that species of injury that ought not to be submitted to on the one hand or inflicted on the other"); A.E.P. Indus., Inc. v. McClure, 308 N.C. 393, 407, 302 S.E.2d 754, 763 (1983) (covenant not to compete; irreparable injury is injury "to which the complainant should not be required to submit or the other party permitted to inflict").

119. [burden of removing boulders] See text at note 95.

120. [loss of drugstore] Fleischer v. James Drug Stores, 1 N.J. 138, 62 A.2d 383 (1948).

121. [right to business] Id. at 148, 62 A.2d at 388. For other cases holding loss of a business to be irreparable injury, see Tri-State Generation & Transmission

Ass'n, Inc. v. Shoshone River Power, Inc., 805 F.2d 351, 355 (10th Cir. 1986) (breach of contract); Roso-Lino Beverage Distr. v. Coca-Cola Bottling Co., 749 F.2d 124, 125–26 (2d Cir. 1984) (franchise termination); Ramirez de Arellano v. Weinberger, 745 F.2d 1500, 1528 (D.C. Cir. 1984) (military activity threatened to destroy plaintiff's ranch), vacated on other grounds mem., 471 U.S. 1113 (1985); Travellers Int'l AG v. Trans World Airlines, Inc., 684 F. Supp. 1206, 1216 (S.D.N.Y. 1988) (breach of contract); Rosenbalm Aviation, Inc. v. Port Auth., 636 F. Supp. 212, 215 (S.D.N.Y. 1986) (cancellation of airplane landing rights); Janmort Leasing, Inc. v. Econo-Car Int'l, Inc., 475 F. Supp. 1282, 1294 (E.D.N.Y. 1979) (antitrust); Keller Oil Co. v. Ind. Dep't of Revenue, 512 N.E.2d 501, 503 (Ind. Tax 1987) (liquidation of business may be irreparable injury, but injunction denied on other grounds); Schwartz v. Laundry & Linen Supply Drivers' Union, Local 187, 339 Pa. 353, 358, 14 A.2d 438, 440 (1940) (antitrust).

122. [*pretium affectionis*] See text and notes at note 36.

123. [**Ford dealer does not want investments**] Semmes Motors Inc. v. Ford Motor Co., 429 F.2d 1197, 1205 (2d Cir. 1970).

124. [**unalienable rights**] The Declaration of Independence ¶ 2 (U.S. 1776).

3

Other Means of Escaping the Rule

The replaceability requirement is the most important doctrine for eliminating the irreparable injury rule as a significant obstacle to equitable relief. But other doctrines serve the same goal. There are several other important sources of irreparable injury. And sometimes courts simply ignore the rule, or hold it inapplicable. This chapter reviews these other means of escaping the irreparable injury rule.

A. Other Sources of Irreparable Injury

1. Preventing a *"Multiplicity of Suits"*

The legal remedy is inadequate if it would require a "multiplicity of suits."[1] The most common reason why the legal remedy would require multiple litigation is that damages might not deter repeated violations. This rationale has been applied in many contexts, including trespass,[2] temporary nuisance,[3] and contracts for child support[4] and spouse support.[5]

Hart v. Wagner[6] is a good example. Defendant "habitually" burned trash in the alley, with the result that smoke and ashes blew into plaintiff's house. In a damage action, plaintiff could recover only damages accrued to date, because there would be no way to know whether defendant would continue to burn trash in the future. The court said the damages were too hard to measure, and that in any one case they would be small, so that plaintiff would have to sue continuously. The unstated connection between small damages and continuous litigation is that small damages might not deter the burning, and that mounting litigation costs might deter plaintiff from suing before they deterred defendant from burning.

The court said that inability to prove any actual damages "often furnishes the very best reason why a court of equity should interfere in cases where the nuisance is a continuous one."[7] This[8] and similar[9] comments appear frequently in the cases, and they clarify an important point. Irreparability has to do with the nature of the injury, not its seriousness or extent.[10] An irreparable injury is one that cannot be cured with money. That an injury has little monetary value is often a cause of irreparability, not an antidote.

Injunctions against torts that cause small damages have a parallel in injunctions against crimes that carry small penalties. A dying corollary of the irreparable injury rule is the rule that equity will not enjoin a crime.[11] One of this rule's many exceptions is that criminal prosecution is inadequate where the penalty is too small to deter repeated violations. An example is *City of Chicago v. Cecola*,[12] where the court predicted that the maximum statutory fine of two hundred dollars per day would not force a massage parlor to close. Finding the criminal remedy inadequate, the court enjoined continued operation of the business.

The traditional understanding sometimes suggests that injury is not irreparable unless it is especially great or serious.[13] But these statements usually appear in cases where minor harm to plaintiff would be outweighed by great hardship to defendant if the injunction issues. Such comparison of hardships makes sense,[14] but the dictum that plaintiff's injury must pass some threshold of seriousness, more than de minimis, makes no sense at all.

It may well make sense to say that the law will not take notice of trifles. But that maxim[15] and its exceptions[16] apply to both common law and equity. If the injury is big enough for courts to take notice of at all, there is no reason to say that damages are available but injunctions are not. To the contrary, courts often grant injunctions where plaintiff suffered no provable damages whatever.[17]

Preventing a multiplicity of suits is also the rationale in a quite different context, the use of injunctions to consolidate scattered litigation. Modern joinder rules have greatly reduced this problem, and its most important modern manifestations are now addressed by specific procedures such as the automatic stay in bankruptcy[18] and the Judicial Panel on Multi-District Litigation.[19] But occasional cases still arise where equity courts act ad hoc to avoid multiple litigation.[20] A recent example is a securities fraud suit by limited partners against their general partner. The federal court hearing the case enjoined the general partner from suing each limited partner separately, in different state courts, for unpaid partnership contributions.[21]

2. Insolvent Defendants

Damages are no remedy at all if they cannot be collected, and most courts sensibly conclude that a damage judgment against an insolvent defendant is an inadequate remedy.[22] But it is essential to distinguish threatened injuries from injuries already suffered. Courts sometimes say that an uncollectible judgment is an adequate remedy for injuries already suffered.[23] These decisions have nothing to do with the irreparable injury rule; they are based on the policy of equality among creditors.

Where a tort is completed, or where plaintiff has paid or performed under a contract and defendant has not yet performed in return, plaintiff has already suffered her loss. Now she is simply a creditor. If a court orders defendant to repair the harm or perform the contract, plaintiff will be preferred over other creditors as effectively as if she and only she collected her damages in full.[24]

Thus, a bankruptcy court will not order the bankrupt estate to specifically perform a prebankruptcy contract,[25] and it will not order the estate to undo the effects of a prebankruptcy tort, except in extraordinary circumstances involving danger to public safety.[26] But these rules merely protect the bankrupt estate and the policy of treating all creditors equally.[27] There is no plausible claim that they defer to an adequate legal remedy; the point of bankruptcy is to give all general creditors equally inadequate remedies. But courts occasionally explain such results on the misleading ground that an uncollectible damage judgment is an adequate remedy.[28]

When a creditor seeks specific relief against an insolvent debtor, the only serious question is whether the nonbankruptcy court should enforce bankruptcy policies. If the same creditor seeks damages, nonbankruptcy courts will award them and help collect them, until and unless someone files a bankruptcy petition. That is, our collections policy creates a race of diligence in nonbankruptcy courts, subject to a power in the debtor or a coalition of other creditors to end the race by filing in the bankruptcy court. Arguably, the same policy should apply to a creditor's suit for specific performance, but courts have reached the opposite result without considering the choice.

The traditional practice probably makes sense. The bankrupt estate may recover any payments that prefer particular creditors in the last ninety days before bankruptcy. It is easy to determine the amount paid in the last ninety days on a money judgment. It might be very much harder to determine the value of specific performance, or the value of work performed pursuant to an injunction ordering repair of damage from a tort. Whether or not that argument is persuasive, it is clear that the reason for denying specific relief to creditors of insolvents is fairness to other creditors, and not the adequacy of uncollectible judgments.

Threatened injuries are very different from injuries already inflicted. There is no reason for a court to stand aside while an insolvent inflicts harm he can never pay for. An insolvent can obey an order not to commit a threatened tort, and such an injunction will not prefer plaintiff over other creditors. Even a bankruptcy court should enjoin the estate from committing new torts.[29]

Similarly, insolvent defendants can often specifically perform a contract in exchange for the unpaid price, even though they could not pay plaintiffs' damages from the breach. Debtors in bankruptcy are given a choice of performing or repudiating such contracts, but again this rule serves bankruptcy policies and has nothing to do with the adequacy of bankruptcy damages. If performance of the contract is unprofitable for the bankrupt, then the other party is like a creditor with a claim to the expected value of her side of the contract. The bankrupt is entitled to breach the contract, pay a pro rata share of the expectancy damages, and discharge the unpaid portion of the claim.[30]

Defendant's solvency is also at issue in a third class of cases, where plaintiff seeks prejudgment equitable relief to secure collection of an anticipated judgment. Plaintiff may seek such relief merely because defendant is insolvent, or because defendant is actively concealing or disposing of assets. In some of these cases, the court says that uncollectible damages are an inadequate remedy and grants relief;[31] in others, the court says uncollectible damages are adequate and denies relief.[32] Either rationale misses the point, reflecting a confusion engendered by too much talk of irreparable injury.

These cases present no choice between preventing harm or letting it happen. The harm will happen, and damages will be the remedy. The issue is how aggressively the court will act to make the damages collectible. A preliminary injunction to secure a later damage judgment interferes with defendant's property before trial,[33] bypasses more restricted prejudgment remedies such as attachment,[34] and may prefer plaintiff over other creditors.[35] The proper balance of these competing interests must come from collections law, not the irreparable injury rule. The obvious inadequacy of an uncollectible damage judgment goes into the balance, but cannot resolve it.

The cases are mixed, in part because so many courts have failed to ask the right questions. Those that do ask the right questions tend to require a strong showing of defendant's propensity to conceal or dissipate her assets.[36] And a plaintiff with a property right in the proceeds of a specific asset has a much better chance of getting a preliminary order securing his interest than an ordinary tort or contract creditor has of getting an order securing his unsecured claim.[37]

3. Immune Defendants

Government defendants are often immune from suits for damages but not from injunctions. This distinction is central to the Supreme Court's interpretation of the Eleventh Amendment[38] and of federal sovereign immunity.[39] Many states have similar rules.[40] These rules flatly reverse the traditional relationship between legal and equitable remedies. Courts have reasoned that damage judgments for violating the law are a greater judicial intrusion into the running of government than injunctions requiring government to comply with the law henceforth.

The nonexistent damage remedy against an immune defendant is plainly inadequate, and the cases so hold.[41] The immune defendant is just like an insolvent defendant, except that there is no concern about preferring plaintiff over other creditors. Thus, unlike a bankrupt estate, government defendants who are immune from damages are subject to reparative and structural injunctions[42] ordering them to undo the consequences of past wrongs.[43]

The leading case on the inadequacy of damage remedies against immune defendants is *Toomer v. Witsell.*[44] The Supreme Court enjoined the enforcement of unconstitutional state shrimping regulations, where compliance would have resulted in expenses or lost business "for which South Carolina provides no means of recovery." The point is highlighted by the Court's simultaneous dismissal of a challenge to the state's income tax. The state had waived its immunity to tax-refund suits; a tax refund would restore exactly what was lost to the tax; and deference to tax authorities is one of the remaining reasons that make courts genuinely reluctant to interfere, whether by injunction or otherwise.[45]

4. Harms from Interim Uncertainty

A common form of irreparable injury arises from uncertainty about legal rights. One familiar example is in suits to enjoin enforcement of unconstitutional statutes, such as *Toomer v. Witsell.*[46] If plaintiffs complied with the state law, they would forfeit their asserted constitutional rights and also suffer substantial monetary losses that could not be recovered from the state in a damage action. They could avoid these losses by violating the law, but only at the risk of substantial penalties if the court rejected their constitutional theory and upheld the statute.[47] The legal "remedy" was to violate the law, wait to be prosecuted, and then defend on the ground that the law was unconstitutional. This was a remedy in the sense that it would sooner or later produce a ruling on the constitutional claim, but it would not avoid the risk of penalties if the constitutional claim were rejected.[48]

The Supreme Court first clearly articulated this form of irreparable injury in *Ex parte Young,*[49] and in earlier work I have called it the *Young* dilemma.[50] The Court has since granted relief from the *Young* dilemma in scores of cases,[51] including some where the penalty for violation was nominal.[52] The Court created some confusion about this form of irreparable injury in the 1940s and again in the 1970s; the best known of these cases are *Douglas v. City of*

Jeannette[53] and *Younger v. Harris*.[54] *Douglas* generally forbids federal injunctions against enforcement of state laws after the constitutional issue has been resolved, and *Younger* generally forbids federal injunctions if state court proceedings are already pending. Each opinion was written in broad terms that cast doubt on whether the risk of prosecution was a form of irreparable injury that justified federal injunctions against enforcement of state law.

But each time, the Court soon reaffirmed the need to grant relief from the *Young* dilemma. In *Steffel v. Thompson*, the Court again described the *Young* dilemma, this time calling it a Scylla and Charybdis.[55] The Court made clear that lower courts had general authority to grant relief from the dilemma where no state prosecution was pending, cautioning only that there is no need to enjoin enforcement if a declaratory judgment of invalidity will suffice. Both declaratory judgment and injunction give specific relief; they differ in the means of enforcement and in the visibility of the threat to personally coerce defendant.[56] The basic insight of *Ex parte Young* remains unchanged: a remedy that does not relieve from the dilemma of risking penalties or forfeiting constitutional rights is not an adequate remedy.

It is only because of arguments over federalism that recognition of the *Young* dilemma has been controversial in federal suits to enjoin enforcement of state laws. The same principle has been applied with less controversy to ordinary civil litigation. Suppose *A* claims that *B*'s plans are illegal, and that if *B* goes through with them, *A* will sue for large damages. *B* would often prefer to find out whether his plans are illegal without incurring the risk of damage liability. Today *B* is likely to sue for a declaratory judgment.[57] But even before the advent of declaratory judgment acts, *B* could sue to enjoin *A* from suing him.[58]

A variation on this pattern produced the dissent quoted at the beginning of chapter 1. Massachusetts and the United States disagreed over details of the state's right to reimbursement for Medicaid expenditures. The dissenters thought it adequate that Massachusetts could sue to recover the sums it claimed after the United States refused to pay them.[59] But the majority was "not willing to assume, categorically, that a naked money judgment against the United States" would be an adequate remedy. The Medicaid program was continuing and complex, and the state's "interest in planning future programs . . . may be more pressing than the monetary amount in dispute."[60] The state needed the flexibility of an injunction or declaratory judgment to settle the dispute for the future as well as the past.

One effect of this holding was to create jurisdiction in the United States District Court for Massachusetts, instead of in the Claims Court. That collateral consequence appears to have motivated the dissent.[61] Thus, Justice Scalia's enthusiastic invocation of the irreparable injury rule nicely illustrates my general thesis: he had a strong preference about the allocation of jurisdiction, and the irreparable injury rule was a prop for that preference.

Legal uncertainty can result in irreparable harm even where the victim is not required to act at peril of penalties, liabilities, or unreimbursable expenses. If A asserts a claim against B but refuses to sue on it, or if a fraudulent or mistaken document seems to create rights in A and cast doubt on corresponding rights in B, B may suffer anxiety, loss of credit rating, or inability to sell property affected by the claim. B may fear that A will sue after evidence has been lost,[62] or after B's defense is time-barred.[63] Declaratory judgment acts solve these problems too. But long before declaratory judgment acts, equity had developed specialized declaratory remedies to deal with some of the most important cases. These included the bill to remove a cloud on title,[64] and its statutory descendant, the bill to quiet title;[65] cancellation or rescission of instruments or contracts,[66] re-execution of lost instruments,[67] and some uses of reformation.[68] (Notes 67 and 68 contain additional explanation.) Some potential defendants simply sued for an injunction against suing or making claims.[69]

In each of these cases, B was a potential defendant at law, but unable to sue at law to resolve the uncertainty. Thus, there was no legal remedy for the harm that might be suffered while waiting for A to sue. The equitable remedy allowed potential defendants at law to become plaintiffs in equity, thus forcing a decision that would eliminate the uncertainty. There was a time when some American jurisdictions limited such relief to protect the potential plaintiff's right to jury trial,[70] but the solicitude for jury trial is considerably less today.[71] In any event, jury trial in a declaratory judgment proceeding,[72] or jury trial of a counterclaim asserting the underlying claim,[73] largely avoids the problem.

5. *Loss of Legitimate Tactical Advantage*

Courts occasionally grant injunctions on the ground that any other remedy would be procedurally or tactically disadvantageous for the plaintiff. This is one explanation for the rules that courts will specifically enforce agreements to arbitrate[74] or to settle litigation.[75] If plaintiff bargained for arbitration or for compromise, he is entitled to those procedures if he wants them.

More idiosyncratic examples sometimes produce more express statements of the rationale. For example, Justice Kennedy enjoined a local election pending clearance under the Voting Rights Act.[76] The election could have been set aside and rerun if plaintiffs ultimately prevailed. But "permitting the election to go forward would place the burdens of inertia and litigation delay on those whom the statute was intended to protect," and this was irreparable injury.

Another express example arose in the context of collective bargaining.[77] Mack Trucks changed the health insurer that covered its employees, and the Auto Workers objected. The terms of the two policies were identical, and the new insurers were financially sound, so the workers lost nothing from the change itself. But the union was entitled to bargain over the identity of the insurer. The court found that the union had lost a bargaining chip: the union could withhold consent to the change to extract concessions on some other issue. Obviously unable to predict the course of such bargaining, the court found it "manifest" that specific performance was the only possible remedy.

The principal issue in these and similar cases[78] is the legitimacy of the tactical advantage plaintiff seeks to preserve. *Defendant* may be irreparably harmed if a court shifts tactical advantage without sufficient justification.[79] Litigants and negotiators will always maneuver for tactical advantage; they will always seek to shift burdens of inertia and delay to the other side. For a court to allocate such burdens with an injunction, it must be quite confident that it knows where the burdens belong. In the arbitration, settlement, and collective bargaining examples, the entitlements come from contract and from public policy supporting such contracts. In the voting rights example, Justice Kennedy had already found that plaintiffs were likely to prevail, and the whole point of the statute was to overcome a century of inertia with remedies that would really work. These are substantive issues, and they are often unclear. But when one side is entitled to a procedural or tactical advantage, loss of that advantage is plainly irreparable harm.

6. *Procedural Restrictions on Legal Remedies*

Before the merger of law and equity, equity had a number of useful procedural devices that were not available at law. These included discovery,[80] more liberal joinder rules,[81] interpleader,[82] bills of peace,[83] class actions,[84] and shareholders' derivative suits.[85] These have generally been absorbed into merged procedure,[86] so that their absence is no longer thought of as a source of irreparable injury. Indeed, the federal courts have held that actions invoking these procedures are legal if the underlying claim is legal, so that the parties are entitled to jury trial.[87] The bill of peace has been revived to cope with repetitive pro se litigation,[88] and unsuccessfully urged as a means of handling large numbers of parallel claims in disaster and products liability cases.[89] But these cases are argued in modern procedural terms; there is no longer any sense of the bill of peace as a separate remedy. These remedies have passed into the law of civil procedure, and we rarely think of irreparable injury as a prerequisite to their use.

B. Cases Refusing to Apply the Rule

When a judge believes that the irreparable injury rule requires a wrong result, he may do what he thinks is right whether or not he can explain it. He may escape the rule by giving a declaratory judgment instead of an injunction.[90] Or he may simply say that this is a case to which the irreparable injury rule should not apply.[91] The most common example of this practice has grown to the status of a rule: where a statute provides for injunctions against violations, courts say the irreparable injury rule does not apply.[92]

Sometimes this is explained on the ground that the legislature presumed that any violation would cause irreparable injury.[93] Some cases go further, asserting inherent equitable power to enforce legislative policy.[94] A few cases actually say that plaintiff need not show irreparable injury if he shows a violation of law.[95] This would expressly abolish the irreparable injury rule if taken literally. These statements may well reflect the courts' sense of natural justice, but they appear to result from sloppy language rather than conscious intent to eliminate the rule.

When courts desire for some reason not to enjoin a statutory violation, they find that the statute only authorizes injunctions but does not mandate them. Usually, the ground for withholding injunctive relief is identifiable and has nothing to do with the irreparable injury rule, even if the opinion is shrouded in irreparable injury talk.[96] These cases have been criticized by scholars who urge that the judicial duty to enforce statutes by injunctions should be absolute or nearly so.[97]

An occasional court will get entangled in these precedents, knowing that an injunction should issue but finding neither irreparable injury nor sufficient statutory mandate. An example is *Board of Education v. Warren Township High School Federation of Teachers.*[98] The trial court preliminarily enjoined a union and a state labor relations board from arbitrating a teacher's discharge. Thinking that this injunction reflected the appropriate relation between court and agency, the intermediate appellate court affirmed. That court interpreted a statute to say that arbitration could be stayed while the court decided whether the dispute was arbitrable. But plaintiff's request was labeled preliminary injunction rather than stay, and that label seemed to invoke the irreparable injury rule. What to do? The court explained that this preliminary injunction "need not strictly meet the traditional criteria." It also noted that the injunction avoided "unnecessary litigation." But apparently it did not see that the uncompensated expense of that litigation would be irreparable injury. Arbitration when the state's policy favored litigation would be as irreparable as litigation when the state's policy favors arbitration.

The state supreme court reversed, but not for lack of irreparable injury. The appellate court had misread the statute, and therefore, the state's policy. The issue of arbitrability was committed to the administrative agency, and not to the court. The supreme court opinion focuses on the only important issue in the case, the respective jurisdictions of court, agency, and arbitrator.[99] Whether to enjoin arbitration depended on that issue. The supposed lack of irreparable injury and the supposed distinction between stays and preliminary injunctions were irrelevant distractions.

Notes on Other Means of Escape

1. [multiplicity of suits] Lee v. Bickell, 292 U.S. 415, 421 (1934) (collection of tax on every memoranda of transfer of corporate securities); Wilson v. Ill. S. Ry., 263 U.S. 574, 576–77 (1924) (tax assessment by five separate counties); Reed Enterprises v. Corcoran, 354 F.2d 519, 522–23 (D.C. Cir. 1965) (multiple criminal prosecutions); U.S. v. Savoie, 594 F. Supp. 678, 681–83 (W.D. La. 1984) (tax-return preparer giving fraudulent advice to many taxpayers); Buckwalter Motors, Inc. v. Gen'l Motors Corp., 593 F. Supp. 628, 633 (S.D. Iowa 1984) (threats to automobile franchise); Johnson v. Mansfield Hardwood Lumber Co., 143 F. Supp. 826, 834 (W.D. La. 1956) (enjoining liquidation of corporation, to avoid subsequent suit against each shareholder for pro rata share of judgment), aff'd, 242 F.2d 45 (5th Cir. 1957); Howell Pipeline Co. v. Terra Resources, Inc., 454 So.2d 1353, 1357–58 (Ala. 1984) (failure to pay for natural gas as pumped); Dotolo v. Schouten, 426 So.2d 1013 (Fla. App. 1983) (misappropriation of trade secret); Witter v. Buchanan, 132 Ill. App. 3d 273, 291, 476 N.E.2d 1123, 1137 (1985) (numerous transfers to bona fide purchasers of disputed interests in oil leases), rev'd on other grounds as Daleiden v. Wiggins Oil Co., 118 Ill. 2d 528, 517 N.E.2d 1059 (1987); Potucek v. Blair, 176 Kan. 263, 267, 270 P.2d 240, 244 (1954) (accounting for interest in joint venture to buy oil and gas leases avoids separate suits for value of interest in each lease); Smith v. W. Elec. Co., 643 S.W.2d 10, 13 (Mo. App. 1982) (cigarette smoke in workplace); Winrock Enterprises, Inc. v. House of Fabrics, Inc., 91 N.M. 661, 664, 579 P.2d 787, 790 (1978) (covenant not to compete); Ansonia Assoc. v. Ansonia Residents' Ass'n, 78 A.D.2d 211, 219, 434 N.Y.S.2d 370, 376 (1980) (concerted refusal to pay rent); Everett v. Harron, 380 Pa. 123, 129, 110 A.2d 383, 386–87 (1955) (exclusion of blacks from swimming pools); Restatement (Second) of Torts § 944 comments g, h (1979); John Norton Pomeroy, 1 *A Treatise on Equity Jurisprudence as Administered in the United States of America* §§ 243–75 at 254–300 (Bancroft-Whitney Co. 1881). Compare Repka v. Am. Nat'l Ins. Co., 143 Tex. 542, 546–51, 186 S.W.2d 977, 979–82 (1945) (refusing to enjoin parallel suit where first judgment would be res judicata in the other case). The phrase is also used in cases where the legal remedy would require more than one suit because of inadequate procedures at law. See this ch. part A.6.

2. [trespass] Donovan v. Pa. Co., 199 U.S. 279, 304–05 (1905) (many hackmen crowding plaintiff's railroad station to solicit passengers); cases cited ch. 2 note 22.

3. [temporary nuisance] Hart v. Wagner, 184 Md. 40, 40 A.2d 47 (1944) (trash fires); Scott v. Jordan, 99 N.M. 567, 571, 661 P.2d 59, 64–65 (App. 1983) (feedlot); Pate v. City of Martin, 614 S.W.2d 46, 48 (Tenn. 1981) (sewage lagoon; damages "seldom if ever" adequate).

4. [child support] Tuttle v. Palmer, 117 N.H. 477, 478, 374 A.2d 661, 662 (1977) ($10 per week until child reached age eighteen).

5. [spouse support] Moore v. Moore, 297 N.C. 14, 17, 252 S.E.2d 735, 737–38 (1979) ($250 per month until wife reached age sixty-five or remarried).

6. [trash fires] Hart v. Wagner, 184 Md. 40, 40 A.2d 47 (1944).

7. [inability to prove damages] Id. at 48, 40 A.2d at 51, quoting Byron K. Elliott & William F. Elliott, *Roads and Streets* 497 (Bowen-Merrill Co. 1890).

8. [inability to prove damages] Newell v. Sass, 142 Ill. 104, 116, 31 N.E. 176, 180 (1892) (quoting the same passage from Elliott & Elliott); Mut. Life Ins. Co. v. Executive Plaza, Inc., 99 Ill. App. 3d 190, 195, 425 N.E.2d 503, 507–08 (1981) (same, issuing injunction to avoid inconvenience in finding parking spaces).

9. [inability to prove damages] Cragg v. Levinson, 238 Ill. 69, 86, 87 N.E. 121, 127 (1909) ("if plaintiff's legal remedy may be vexatious, harassing, and hence inadequate, when he recovers substantial damages, still more would it seem to be so when his recovery is only nominal" (quoting Pomeroy, 1 *Equity Jurisprudence* § 496 (cited in note 1)); A.E.P. Indus., Inc. v. McClure, 308 N.C. 393, 407, 302 S.E.2d 754, 763 (1983) (where plaintiff has shown no damage, reparable or irreparable, preliminary injunction is only way to protect its right).

10. [irreparable not same as serious] Enterprise Int'l, Inc. v. Corporacion Estatal Petrolera Ecuatoriana, 762 F.2d 464, 472 (5th Cir. 1985) ("when 'the threatened harm is more than de minimis, it is not so much the magnitude but the irreparability that counts for purposes of a preliminary injunction"); Berin v. Olson, 183 Conn. 337, 341, 439 A.2d 357, 360 (1981) (whether injury is irreparable "depends more upon the nature of the right which is injuriously affected than upon the pecuniary loss suffered"); Bd. of Educ. v. Bd. of Educ., 112 Ill. App. 3d 212, 217, 445 N.E.2d 464, 469 (1983) ("Irreparable injury does not mean that the harm inflicted . . . is great. Rather, it denotes transgressions of a continuing nature, of such constant and frequent recurrence that redress cannot be had at law.").

11. [equity will not enjoin crime] See ch. 9, part A.2.

12. [enjoining massage parlor] City of Chicago v. Cecola, 75 Ill. 2d 423, 427, 389 N.E.2d 526, 528 (1979).

13. [irreparable means serious] Weinberger v. Romero-Barcelo, 456 U.S. 305, 311 (1982) (injunction will not "restrain an act the injurious consequences of which are merely trifling"); Consol. Canal Co. v. Mesa Canal Co., 177 U.S. 296, 302 (1900) (same); Caribbean Marine Serv. Co. v. Baldrige, 844 F.2d 668, 676 (9th Cir. 1988) (same); Albert E. Price, Inc. v. Metzner, 574 F. Supp. 281, 289 (E.D. Pa. 1983) ("substantial" and "material" injury); Tully v. Mott Supermarkets, Inc., 337 F. Supp. 834, 850 (D.N.J. 1972) (same); Myers v. Caple, 258 N.W.2d 301, 305 (Iowa 1977); Colliton v. Oxborough, 86 Minn. 361, 364, 90 N.W. 793, 794 (1902) (injunction should not issue for "slight causes"); Brown v. Voss, 105 Wash.2d 366, 373, 715 P.2d 514, 517 (1986) ("actual and substantial injury"); Gene R. Shreve, *Federal Injunctions and the Public Interest*, 51 Geo. Wash. L. Rev. 382, 385, 390–92 (1983) ("immediate and substantial," but noting "apparent reluctance of equity courts to characterize imminent wrongs as insubstantial").

14. [undue hardship] See ch. 7 part A.

15. [law will not take notice of trifles] Christian v. Fry, 108 Colo. 394, 396, 118 P.2d 459, 460 (1941) (one-day delay in paying fifty-cent filing fee does not bar appeal); Smith Oil & Rfg. Co. v. Dep't of Fin., 371 Ill. 405, 408, 21 N.E.2d 292, 294 (1939) (oil was consumed and not resold, even though minute portions seeped into finished product); Bristol-Myers Co. v. Lit Bros., 336 Pa. 81, 89, 6 A.2d 843,

848 (1939) (maxim applied in equity; court refuses to treat trading stamps as unlawful price cutting); 1 Am. Jur. 2d, *Actions* § 67 at 596 (1962); Annotation, *"De minimis non curat lex,"* 44 A.L.R. 168, 169–74 (1926).

16. [exceptions] Reeves v. Jackson, 207 Ark. 1089, 1093, 184 S.W.2d 256, 258 (1944) (maxim does not apply to trespass); Whittaker v. Stangvick, 100 Minn. 386, 389, 111 N.W. 295, 296 (1907) (maxim does not apply to trespass in either law or equity); Mosley v. Nat'l Fin. Co., 36 N.C. App. 109, 113, 243 S.E.2d 145, 148 (1978) (maxim does not apply where construction of statute is at issue); Dan B. Dobbs, *Handbook on the Law of Remedies* § 3.8 at 191–94 (West 1973) (discussing nominal damages).

17. [injunctions without provable damage] Quabaug Rubber Co. v. Fabiano Shoe Co., 567 F.2d 154, 160–63 (1st Cir. 1977) (unfair competition); Strike It Rich, Inc. v. Joseph Schlitz Brewing Co., 505 F. Supp. 89, 91 (D.D.C. 1980) (trademark infringement); Taylor v. Kohler, 507 So.2d 426, 428 (Ala. 1987) (restrictive covenant); Schrenker v. Clifford, 270 Ind. 525, 528–29, 387 N.E.2d 59, 61 (1979) (enjoining mailing of absentee ballots to addresses within the county); Dunlap v. Foss, 82 N.H. 449, 136 A. 257 (1926) (contract to sell land). See also Edgecomb v. Edmonston, 257 Mass. 12, 18, 153 N.E. 99, 101 (1926) (covenant not to compete; provable damages would be "inadequate and unsubstantial").

18. [automatic stay] 11 U.S.C. § 362 (1988).

19. [Panel on Multi-District Litigation] 14 U.S.C. § 1407 (1988).

20. [multiple litigation] Talbert & Mallon, P.C. v. Carlson, 170 Ill. App. 3d 698, 703–05, 525 N.E.2d 141, 144–45 (1988) (former law partners disputed division of contingent fees in some 250 cases handled by their firm; court ordered attorneys not to assert liens in the underlying cases, and to resolve all fee disputes in one litigation among the attorneys).

21. [suits against limited partners] Bruce v. Martin, 680 F. Supp. 616, 622 (S.D.N.Y. 1988).

22. [insolvent defendant] Tri-State Generation & Transmission Ass'n v. Shoshone River Power, Inc., 805 F.2d 351, 355 (10th Cir. 1986) (breach of executory contract); Molex, Inc. v. Nolen, 759 F.2d 474, 477–78 (5th Cir. 1985) (continuing theft of customer); Roland Mach. Co. v. Dresser Indus., Inc., 749 F.2d 380, 386 (7th Cir. 1984) (continuing antitrust violation); Lankford v. Gelston, 364 F.2d 197, 202 (4th Cir. 1966) (unconstitutional searches); Interpoint Corp. v. Truck World, Inc., 656 F. Supp. 114, 116–18 (N.D. Ind. 1986) (threatened interference with leasehold); Proyectos Electronicos, S.A. v. Alper, 37 Bankr. 931 (E.D. Pa. 1983) (specific performance of contract to sell goods; usual policy against preferring single creditor held not to apply, because goods had been constructively delivered and were no longer property of the bankrupt estate); State ex rel. Meredith v. Bd. of Trustees of Salvation Army, 102 Fla. 219, 224, 135 So. 781, 783 (1931) (threatened conversion of furniture); Potucek v. Blair, 176 Kan. 263, 267, 270 P.2d 240, 244 (1954) (refusal to recognize half interest in joint venture to buy oil and gas leases); Gause v. Perkins, 56 N.C. (3 Jones Eq.) 177, 179–80, 182 (1857) (trespass; injunction denied because no allegation of insolvency); R.H. Sanders Corp. v. Haves, 541 S.W.2d 262, 265 (Tex. Civ. App. 1976) (threatened violation of corporate voting agreement); Restatement (Second) of Torts § 944 comment i (1979). See also Black Ass'n of New Orleans Firefighters v. City of New Orleans, 853 F.2d 347, 353 (5th Cir. 1988) (finding sufficient risk of irreparable injury to support interlocutory appeal, where appellee's failure to post bond made it unlikely that appellant intervenors could ever recover damages for harm done by preliminary injunction); Edward Yorio, *Contract Enforcement: Specific Performance and Injunctions* § 7.4.1 at 154–55 (Little, Brown 1989). But see Willing v. Mazzocone, 482 Pa. 377, 383, 393 A.2d 1155, 1158 (1978) (refusing to enjoin defamation by insolvent); Heilman v. Union Canal Co., 37 Pa. 100, 104 (1860) (refusing to enjoin continued diversion of water by insolvent canal company; canal had diverted water for decades).

23. [injuries already suffered] See cases cited in note 28.

24. [plaintiff as preferred creditor] Express Co. v. R.R. Co., 99 U.S. 191, 200–01 (1878) ("as well might he be decreed to satisfy the appellant's demand by money, as by the service sought to be enforced"); Jamison Coal & Coke Co. v. Goltra, 143 F.2d 889, 894 (8th Cir. 1944) ("specific performance would enable plaintiff to obtain a preference over Goltra's other creditors"); George E. Warren Co. v. A.L. Black Coal Co., 85 W. Va. 684, 102 S.E. 672, 673 (1920) ("performance of his contract by an insolvent would enable a plaintiff to obtain a preference over the defendant's other creditors").

25. [no specific performance in bankruptcy] Jay Lawrence Westbrook, *A Functional Analysis of Executory Contracts*, 74 Minn. L. Rev. 227, 255–57 (1989). But compare Proyectos Electronicos, S.A. v. Alper, 37 Bankr. 931 (E.D. Pa. 1983) (where goods had been paid for, crated, and set aside on delivery dock with buyer's order number before seller's bankruptcy, goods were constructively delivered and no longer belonged to bankrupt; specific performance granted).

26. [danger to public safety] Compare Midlantic Nat'l Bank v. N.J. Dep't of Environmental Protection, 474 U.S. 494, 505–06 & n.9 (1986) (bankrupt estate may not abandon toxic waste dump without adequately protecting public health and safety from "imminent and identifiable harm"); with In re Smith-Douglass, Inc., 856 F.2d 12, 16–17 (4th Cir. 1988) (bankrupt estate may abandon fertilizer plant despite extant violations of environmental laws, where there is no "serious" and "immediate" danger to "public health or safety" and bankrupt has no unencumbered assets).

27. [treat all creditors equally] See Arthur Linton Corbin, 5A *Corbin on Contracts* § 1156 at 172–77 (West, 2d ed. 1964); E. Allan Farnsworth, *Contracts* § 12.6 at 831 (Little, Brown 1982); Yorio, *Contract Enforcement* § 7.4.3 at 157–60 (cited in note 22); H.C. Horack, *Insolvency and Specific Performance*, 31 Harv. L. Rev. 702 (1918); Henry L. McClintock, *Adequacy of Ineffective Remedy at Law*, 16 Minn. L. Rev. 233, 253–54 (1932). Professor McClintock concluded from a survey of 284 cases that courts held uncollectible damages adequate only where the issue first arose in a case where there were "ample" other reasons to deny equitable relief.

28. [uncollectible damages adequate] Derry Township School Dist. v. Barnett Coal Co., 332 Pa. 174, 177, 2 A.2d 758, 760 (1938) (unpaid taxes; legal remedies are adequate even if they fail to collect anything); George E. Warren Co. v. A.L. Black Coal Co., 85 W. Va. 684, 102 S.E. 672, 673 (1920) ("if the contract is not of that class which equity will enforce, defendant's insolvency will not aid the jurisdiction"); Note, *Specific Performance and Insolvency—A Reappraisal*, 41 St. John's L. Rev. 577 (1967) (stating that most cases hold contract damages adequate, but tort damages inadequate, when defendant is insolvent, and failing to recognize that most tort plaintiffs seek to enjoin future tort, while more contract plaintiffs

have already paid for undelivered goods or services). Cf. Bryan v. Luhning, 106
S.W.2d 403, 404 (Tex. Civ. App. 1937) ("the right to file a supersedeas bond . . .
is an adequate remedy at law, even though an appellant is financially unable to do
so").

29. [bankruptcy court will enjoin torts] See Ohio v. Kovacs, 469 U.S. 274, 285
(1985) (anyone in possession of land, including bankrupt and trustee in bankruptcy,
must comply with environmental laws) (dictum).

30. [rejection of contracts] See Westbrook, 74 Minn. L. Rev. at 252–55 (cited
in note 25).

31. [injunction to preserve assets] Deckert v. Independence Shares Corp., 311
U.S. 282, 288–89 (1940); Airlines Reporting Corp. v. Barry, 825 F.2d 1220, 1226–
27 (8th Cir. 1987); Unisys Corp. v. Dataware Prod., Inc., 848 F.2d 311, 314–15
(1st Cir. 1988); Teradyne, Inc. v. Mostek Corp., 797 F.2d 43, 52–53 (1st Cir. 1986);
Philipp Bros. Div. of Englehard Minerals & Chem. Corp. v. El Salto, S.A., 487
F. Supp. 91, 95 (S.D.N.Y. 1980); Anderson Foreign Motors v. New England Toyota
Distr., Inc., 475 F. Supp. 973, 978–79 (D. Mass. 1979); Boston Athletic Ass'n v.
Int'l Marathons, Inc., 392 Mass. 356, 362, 467 N.E.2d 58, 62 (1984). See also
Middlebrooks v. Lonas, 246 Ga. 720, 721, 272 S.E.2d 687, 698 (1980) (damage
judgment inadequate where equitable lien would give priority over mortgagee with
notice of claim).

32. [refusing injunction to preserve assets] Hiles v. Auto Bahn Fed'n, Inc., 498
So.2d 997 (Fla. App. 1986).

33. [interfering with defendant's property] Martin v. James B. Berry Sons' Co.,
83 F.2d 857, 861 (1st Cir. 1936); Diamond Sav. & Loan Co. v. Royal Glen Condo.
Ass'n, 173 Ill. App. 3d 431, 435 526 N.E.2d 372, 375–76 (1988).

34. [bypassing attachment] See In re Rare Coin Galleries, Inc., 862 F.2d 896,
903–04 (1st Cir. 1988) (reversing preliminary injunction to reach and apply insurance proceeds, because plaintiff could not satisfy specific requirements of state-law
reach-and-apply remedies); Dorfman v. Boozer, 414 F.2d 1168, 1171–74 (D.C.
Cir. 1969) (reversing preliminary injunction against rent strike, forcing plaintiff to
use normal landlord/tenant remedies); Wahlgren v. Bausch & Lomb Optical Co.,
77 F.2d 121, 123 (7th Cir. 1935) (standards for preliminary injunction freezing
assets should be same as standards for attachment, "unless there are adduced
specific facts which would indicate [that an injunction is] indispensable to the doing
of equity between the parties"); Taunton Mun. Lighting Plant v. Dep't of Energy,
472 F. Supp. 1231, 1233 (D. Mass. 1979) (attachment is proper remedy); St. Lawrence Co., N.V. v. Alkow Realty, Inc., 453 So.2d 514, 515 (Fla. App. 1984)
("prejudgment" attachment or garnishment, with attendant safeguards, may be
available," but not preliminary injunction); Carriage Way Apts. v. Pojman, 172
Ill. App. 3d 827, 836–39, 527 N.E.2d 89, 95–97 (1988) (injunction is never allowed
to substitute for attachment); Alger v. Davis, 345 Mich. 635, 76 N.W.2d 847 (1956)
(denying constructive trust and receiver because replevin would be adequate remedy to recover personal property); Derry Township School Dist. v. Barnett Coal
Co., 332 Pa. 174, 177, 2 A.2d 758, 760 (1938); (statutory remedies for collection
of taxes are exclusive); Minexa Ariz., Inc. v. Staubach, 667 S.W.2d 563, 567–68
(Tex. App. 1984) (order granted; attachment and garnishment inadequate to reach
unknown or fraudulently conveyed assets).

35. [plaintiff as preferred creditor] SECI, Inc. v. Chafitz, Inc., 493 A.2d 1100,

1104 (Md. App. 1985) (rule against preliminary injunction freezing assets "is a necessary complement to the more basic system we have of establishing the priorities among general creditors in the property of a debtor in terms of the entry and recording of judgments"). See also In re Rare Coin Galleries, Inc., 862 F.2d 896, 901–03 (1st Cir. 1988) (preliminary injunction against use of liability insurance fund to pay defense costs would interfere with insured defendant's priority over injured plaintiff).

36. [propensity to conceal assets] Republic of the Philippines v. Marcos, 862 F.2d 1355, 1361–64 (9th Cir. 1988) (written as an ordinary preliminary injunction opinion, but emphasizing concealment of assets in analysis of facts); EBSCO Indus. v. Lilly, 840 F.2d 333 (6th Cir. 1988) (order granted; defendant invoked privilege against self-incrimination when asked about his assets); Fed. Sav. & Loan Ins. Corp. v. Dixon, 835 F.2d 554, 560–66 (5th Cir. 1987) (order granted against officers whose self-dealing allegedly bankrupted savings and loan association); Productos Carnic, S.A. v. Cent. Am. Beef & Seafood Trading Co., 621 F.2d 683, 686 (5th Cir. 1980) (order granted; defendants had altered documents, closed bank accounts, attempted to transfer disputed goods to fictitious company, and intended to frustrate any judgment on merits); Wahlgren v. Bausch & Lomb Optical Co., 77 F.2d 121, 123 (7th Cir. 1935) ("unless there is made to appear some definite manifestation that [defendant will secrete or dispose of his property,] the mere likelihood, though coupled with animosity, is not sufficient to invoke the court's injunctive process"); 790247 Ontario, Ltd. v. Winston Frost Securities, Inc., 708 F. Supp. 610, 611 (S.D.N.Y. 1989) (inadequate records are not enough where plaintiff had access to records and failed to offer in evidence detailed analysis of defendant's financial condition); Ramil v. Keller, 68 Hawaii 608, 618, 726 P.2d 254, 261 (1986) (order granted after nine days of evidence that defendants misappropriated substantial sums from insurance company); Maas v. Cohen Assoc., Inc., 112 Ill. App. 3d 191, 196, 445 N.E.2d 517, 520–21 (1983) (allegations on information and belief are insufficient); Minexa Ariz., Inc. v. Staubach, 667 S.W.2d 563, 567–68 (Tex. App. 1984) (order granted; strong and specific allegations of disappearing assets, but apparently no hearing yet).

37. [plaintiff with property right] See De Beers Consol. Mines v. U.S., 325 U.S. 212, 220 (1945) (reversing preliminary injunction against removing property from the United States, where property affected could not be "dealt with in any final injunction that might be entered"); Fed. Sav. & Loan Ins. Corp. v. Dixon, 835 F.2d 554, 560–65 (5th Cir. 1987) (affirming preliminary injunction with respect to assets subject to specific restitution, but reversing with respect to other assets); USACO Coal Co. v. Carbomin Energy, Inc., 689 F.2d 94, 96–99 (6th Cir. 1982) (arguments "concerning the court's power to sequester assets as security for a potential damage award are inapposite. The injunction here preserves assets for which the defendants may be accountable under a constructive trust"); Martin v. James B. Berry Sons' Co., 83 F.2d 857, 861 (1st Cir. 1936) ("simple contract creditor cannot . . . sustain an action to enjoin a threatened fraudulent transfer of his debtor's property until he has obtained a specific lien upon such property"); In re Steffan, 97 B.R. 741 (Bankr. N.D.N.Y. 1989) (enjoining distribution of money in marital trust); Carriage Way Apts. v. Pojman, 172 Ill. App. 3d 827, 836–39, 527 N.E.2d 89, 95–97 (1988) (preliminary injunction can reach specific assets that are subject of dispute, but can never reach general assets for purpose of anticipating judgment).

38. [Eleventh Amendment] Edelman v. Jordan, 415 U.S. 651, 660–71 (1974); Ex parte Young, 209 U.S. 123, 149–61 (1908).

39. [federal sovereign immunity] Larson v. Domestic & Foreign Commerce Corp., 337 U.S. 682, 688–90 (1949).

40. [state sovereign immunity] See Beck v. Kan. Adult Auth., 241 Kan. 13, 21, 735 P.2d 222, 229 (1987) ("while the State of Kansas is a person for purposes of Section 1983 actions wherein injunctive relief is sought, the State has not waived its sovereign immunity from suits seeking damages under that section"). For examples of state court suits to prevent enforcement of state law, see Cohen v. Bd. of Supervisors, 40 Cal. 3d 277, 285–90, 707 P.2d 840, 844–47, 219 Cal. Rptr. 467, 471–74 (1985) (reviewing California decisions); Am. Academy of Pediatrics v. Van de Kamp, 214 Cal. App. 3d 831, 214 Cal. Rptr. 46 (1989) (enjoining enforcement of law restricting abortions); Bellanca v. N.Y. State Liquor Auth., 50 N.Y.2d 524, 407 N.E.2d 460, 429 N.Y.S.2d 616 (1980) (declaring unconstitutional state law restricting topless dancing in premises with liquor licenses), rev'd on other grounds, 452 U.S. 714 (1981); Bio-Medical Labs., Inc. v. Trainor, 68 Ill. 2d 540, 370 N.E.2d 223 (1977) (enjoining enforcement); Wise v. McCanless, 183 Tenn. 107, 191 S.W.2d 169 (1945) (enjoining enforcement of regulation forbidding retail sale of alcoholic beverages within one hundred feet of public place in which alcoholic beverges were consumed). I do not believe that any state would allow a damage suit against the state to recover the losses resulting from compliance with an invalid statute.

41. [immune defendants] Am. Trucking Ass'ns Inc. v. Gray, 483 U.S. 1306, 1309 (1987) (payment of disputed tax where state asserted immunity from refund suit) (Blackmun in chambers); Grosjean v. Am. Press Co., 297 U.S. 233, 242 (1936) (payment of disputed tax where state had no refund procedure); Ohio Oil Co. v. Conway, 279 U.S. 813, 815 (1929) (same); Johnson v. U.S. Dep't of Agric., 734 F.2d 774, 789 (11th Cir. 1984) (enjoining wrongful foreclosures by possibly immune federal agency); U.S. v. N.Y., 708 F.2d 92 (2d Cir. 1983) (enjoining airport curfew, where state would be immune from suit for consequential damages to plaintiff airline); U.S. v. Nev. Tax Comm'n, 439 F.2d 435, 441 (9th Cir. 1971) (suit to declare disputed tax uncollectible, where no clear state remedy was available); U.S. v. Bd. of Educ., 610 F. Supp. 702, 705 (N.D. Ill. 1985) (restraining expenditure of earmarked funds, pending determination of plaintiff's entitlement to them, where plaintiff had no claim against funds in the general treasury); S. Packaging & Storage Co. v. U.S., 588 F. Supp. 532, 550 (D.S.C. 1984) (government illegally rejected plaintiff's bid for government contract; damages limited by law to cost of bid preparation); Conoco, Inc. v. Watt, 559 F. Supp. 627, 630 (E.D. La. 1982) (allowing plaintiff to pay civil penalties into registry of the court, pending refund action, so that plaintiff could recover interest on eventual refund); Bass v. Alderman, 80 Fla. 345, 350–51, 86 So. 244, 246 (1920) (enjoining improper tax levy); Bio-Medical Labs., Inc. v. Trainor, 68 Ill. 2d 540, 548–49, 370 N.E.2d 223, 227 (1977) (enjoining suspension of medical provider from eligibility for Medicaid reimbursement); Am. Trucking Ass'ns Inc. v. State, 512 N.E.2d 920, 923–25 (Ind. Tax 1987) (payment of disputed tax where refund procedure might not apply); Long v. Kistler, 72 Pa. Commw. 547, 552, 457 A.2d 591, 593 (1983) (no provision in state tax assessment law for challenging discriminatory assessments). See also

Bates v. City of Hastings, 145 Mich. 574, 581–85, 108 N.W. 1005, 1008–09 (1906) (scheme to issue municipal bonds and spend money for private purposes threatens irreparable harm, because once bonds are negotiated they must be paid). But see Black United Fund, Inc. v. Kean, 763 F.2d 156, 161 (3d Cir. 1985) (Eleventh Amendment immunity does not make injury irreparable; mootness, hardship to defendant, preliminary stage of proceedings, and doubt whether plaintiff was entitled to remedy requested also contributed to decision); New Club Carlin, Inc., v. City of Billings, 237 Mont. 194, 196–97, 772 P.2d 303, 305 (1989) (refusing to enjoin enforcement of ban on nude dancing, stating that money damages would be adequate remedy for business losses; no indication in opinion that city would be liable in damages).

42. [reparative and structural injunctions] The labels are developed in Owen M. Fiss, *The Civil Rights Injunction* 7 (Ind. Univ. Press 1978). For further analysis, see Douglas Laycock, *Injunctions and the Irreparable Injury Rule* (Book Review), 57 Tex. L. Rev. 1065, 1073–76 (1979).

43. [no immunity] Milliken v. Bradley, 433 U.S. 267, 288–90 (1977) (compensatory education is prospective remedy for school segregation, and not compensation barred by Eleventh Amendment).

44. [leading case] Toomer v. Witsell, 334 U.S. 385, 391–92 (1948).

45. [deference to tax collection] See ch. 6 notes 7, 30.

46. [enjoining unconstitutional statutes] Toomer v. Witsell, 334 U.S. 385, 391–92 (1948).

47. [risk of penalties] Doran v. Salem Inn, Inc., 422 U.S. 922, 932 (1975).

48. [criminal defense inadequate] The defects in the legal remedy are fully explored in Douglas Laycock, *Federal Interference with State Prosecutions: The Need for Prospective Relief*, 1977 Sup. Ct. Rev. 193.

49. [first articulation] Ex parte Young, 209 U.S. 123, 161–67 (1908).

50. [*Young* dilemma] Douglas Laycock, *Federal Interference with State Prosecutions: The Cases Dombrowski Forgot*, 46 U. Chi. L. Rev. 636, 641–42 (1979).

51. [relief from *Young* dilemma] The then-extant cases are collected id. at 641–59, 664–65.

52. [nominal penalties] Two Guys, Inc. v. McGinley, 366 U.S. 582, 585–86, 589 (1961) (Sunday closing law; $100 fine for violating one section; $4 fine for violating another section).

53. [after constitutional issue resolved] Douglas v. City of Jeannette, 319 U.S. 157 (1943).

54. [while prosecution pending] Younger v. Harris, 401 U.S. 37 (1971).

55. [if no prosecution pending] Steffel v. Thompson, 415 U.S. 452, 462 (1974).

56. [declaratory judgments] See Douglas Laycock, *Modern American Remedies* 3 (Little, Brown 1985) ("It is somewhat misleading to describe declaratory remedies as noncoercive. It is more accurate to say that the coercive threat is implicit rather than explicit.")

57. [declaring no civil liability] Grain Processing Corp. v. Am. Maize-Prod. Co., 840 F.2d 902, 905–06 (Fed. Cir. 1988) (seeking declaration that plaintiff had not infringed defendant's patents; relief denied on ripeness grounds); Pain Prevention Lab, Inc. v. Elec. Waveform Labs, Inc., 657 F. Supp. 1486, 1491–92 (N.D. Ill.

1987) (seeking declaration that plaintiff had not infringed defendant's patents or trade secrets).

58. **[enjoining civil suits]** Beacon Theatres, Inc. v. Westover, 359 U.S. 500, 502–03 (1959) (seeking injunction against defendant's threatened antitrust suit, and declaration that plaintiff had not violated antitrust laws).

59. **[Medicaid reimbursement adequate]** Bowen v. Mass., 487 U.S. 879, 925–28 (1988) (Scalia dissenting).

60. **[reimbursement inadequate for planning]** Id. at 905–07 (opinion of the Court).

61. **[jurisdictional consequences]** See id. at 930 (Scalia dissenting) ("the jurisdiction of the Claims Court has been thrown into chaos"). For analysis of the jurisdictional issue and why it mattered, see Cynthia Grant Bowman, *Bowen v. Massachusetts: The "Money Damages Exception" to the Administrative Procedure Act and Grant-in-Aid Litigation*, 21 Urban Law. 557 (1989).

62. **[risk of losing evidence]** Aetna Life Ins. Co. v. Haworth, 300 U.S. 227, 239 (1937) (seeking declaration that life insurance policy lapsed for failure to pay premiums, where insured claimed policy remained in effect because his disability triggered premium waiver); Newman Mach. Co. v. Newman, 275 N.C. 189, 193, 198, 166 S.E.2d 63, 66, 69 (1969) (seeking declaration that plaintiff did not defraud defendant in purchase of his business, where key witness was seventy years old).

63. **[defenses time-barred]** Am. Life Ins. Co. v. Stewart, 300 U.S. 203, 210–13 (1937) (suit to cancel life insurance policy for fraud, where policy would become incontestable in two years).

64. **[cloud on title]** Suplee v. Eckert, 35 Del. Ch. 428, 120 A.2d 718 (1956) (bill to remove cloud created to reach cases not reached by ejectment); Estate of Gilbert Smith, Inc. v. Cohen, 123 N.J. Eq. 419, 196 A. 361 (1938) (reviewing similar history); Pomeroy, 3 *Equity Jurisprudence* §§ 1398–99 at 435–39 (1883) (cited in note 1).

65. **[quiet title]** Sharon v. Tucker, 144 U.S. 533 (1892) (bill to quiet title acquired by adverse possession); Holland v. Challen, 110 U.S. 15 (1884) (reviewing history of ejectment, bill to remove cloud, and bill to quiet title); Newman Mach. Co. v. Newman, 275 N.C. 189, 196–98, 166 S.E.2d 63, 68–69 (1969) (reviewing creation of bill to quiet title to cover cases not reached by bill to remove cloud); 3 Pomeroy §§ 1396–97 at 431–35.

66. **[cancellation]** Am. Life Ins. Co. v. Stewart, 300 U.S. 203, 210–13 (1937) (suit to cancel life insurance policy for fraud); U.S. v. Am. Bell Tel. Co., 128 U.S. 315, 356–73 (1888) (cancelling patents procured by fraud); Jones v. Bolles, 76 U.S. (8 Wall.) 364, 369 (1869) (rescinding perpetual mining contract procured by fraud); Boyce's Executors v. Grundy, 28 U.S. (3 Pet.) 210, 215 (1830) (rescinding land-sale contract procured by fraud); Miller v. San Sebastian Gold Mines, Inc., 540 F.2d 807, 809 (5th Cir. 1976) (cancelling common stock issued without consideration); Dumas v. Dumas, 261 Ark. 178, 547 S.W.2d 417 (1977) (cancelling deeds motivated by fraud and insane delusion); Parks v. Quintana, 86 Nev. 847, 477 P.2d 869 (1970) (equity suit to set aside deed for fraud may lie where statutory suit to quiet title does not); 3 Pomeroy § 1377 at 415–17; Joseph Story, 2 *Commentaries on Equity Jurisprudence as Administered in England and America* § 649 at 5–6 (Little, Brown 1836).

67. [lost instruments] Smith v. Lujan, 588 F.2d 1304, 1305–06 (9th Cir. 1979) (re-execution of lost lease); 3 Pomeroy § 1376 at 413 n.3. Equity would also grant relief on the lost instrument without a prior re-execution. See 2 Pomeroy §§ 831– 32 at 289–91 (1882); 1 Story §§ 78–88 at 94–105 (1835).

68. [reformation] Wasatch Mining Co. v. Crescent Mining Co., 148 U.S. 293 (1893) (reforming deed to correct misdescription of land conveyed); Walden v. Skinner, 101 U.S. 577 (1879) (reforming deed to trustee to properly describe plaintiff's beneficial interest); 3 Pomeroy §§ 1375–76 at 413–15; George E. Palmer, 4 *The Law of Restitution* § 13.13 at 87–88 (Little, Brown 1978). Despite reformation's declaratory potential, parties often fail to discover the mistake or seek reformation until a more conventional dispute arises. For examples, see Highlands Underwriters Ins. Co. v. Elegante Inns, Inc., 361 So.2d 1060 (Ala. 1978) (reforming fire insurance policy after fire); Cherokee Water Co. v. Forderhause, 741 S.W.2d 377 (Tex. 1987) (defendant counterclaims to reform option contract after plaintiff sues for specific performance).

69. [enjoining civil suits] Beacon Theatres, Inc. v. Westover, 359 U.S. 500, 502– 03 (1959) (seeking injunction against threatened antitrust suit); Jones v. Bolles, 76 U.S. (8 Wall.) 364, 369 (1869) (injunction against suit on contract procured by fraud); 3 Pomeroy §§ 1360–65 at 393–402.

70. [jury trial formerly] Johnson v. Swanke, 128 Wis. 68, 107 N.W. 481 (1906).

71. [jury trial now] See ch. 9 part A.1.

72. [jury trial in declaratory judgment] See Simler v. Conner, 372 U.S. 221, 223 (1963) (declaratory judgment suit raising legal issues is legal, so that jury trial is available).

73. [jury trial of counterclaim] See Beacon Theatres, Inc. v. Westover, 359 U.S. 500 (1959) (where plaintiff sues to enjoin filing of antitrust suit, and defendant files antitrust suit as counterclaim, counterclaim must be tried first and to a jury).

74. [arbitration] United Steelworkers v. Warrior & Gulf Navigation Co., 363 U.S. 574 (1960) ("In the commercial case, arbitration is the substitute for litigation. Here [in a labor case] arbitration is the substitute for industrial strife."); United Steelworkers v. Am. Mfg. Co., 363 U.S. 564 (1960) (ordering arbitration of labor grievance without discussing irreparable injury); Textile Workers Union v. Lincoln Mills, 353 U.S. 448 (1957) (authorizing specific performance of arbitration clauses in collective bargaining agreements, without discussing irreparable injury); ABA Distr., Inc. v. Adolph Coors Co., 542 F. Supp. 1272, 1297 (W.D. Mo. 1982) (plaintiff's "loss of its potential right to arbitration under the Agreement left [plaintiff] without an adequate remedy at law and has irreparably injured" plaintiff); Daigre Engineers, Inc. v. City of Winnfield, 385 So.2d 866, 872 (La. App. 1980) (ordering arbitration); Martino v. Transp. Workers' Union, Local 234, 505 Pa. 391, 396–97, 480 A.2d 242, 244–45 (1984) (same); Wylie Indep. School Dist. v. TMC Found., Inc., 770 S.W.2d 19, 23 (Tex. App. 1989) (same). See also Securities Indus. Ass'n v. Connolly, 883 F.2d 1114, 1117, 1125 (1st Cir. 1989) (enjoining enforcement of state law that made certain arbitration agreements unenforceable).

75. [settlement agreements] Peters v. Wallach, 366 Mass. 622, 628–29, 321 N.E.2d 806, 810 (1975); Landau v. St. Louis Public Serv. Co., 364 Mo. 1134, 1138, 273 S.W.2d 255, 257 (1954); Restatement (Second) of Contracts § 281(3) (1981) (accord is specifically enforceable); Samuel Williston & Walter H.E. Jaeger, 15 *A Treatise on the Law of Contracts* § 1845 at 526–27 (Baker, Voorhis, 3d ed. 1972) (same). See also Carson v. Am. Brands, Inc., 450 U.S. 79, 86–88 (1981) (trial court's disapproval of consent decree is immediately appealable, because disapproval of settlements inflicts serious and irreparable injury).

76. [Voting Rights Act] Lucas v. Townsend, 486 U.S. 1301, 1305 (1988) (Kennedy in chambers).

77. [bargaining chip] Int'l Union, United Auto. Workers v. Mack Trucks, Inc., 820 F.2d 91, 95–96 (3d Cir. 1987).

78. [loss of tactical advantage] Porter v. Lee, 328 U.S. 246, 250–51 (1946) (enjoining eviction in violation of rent control, at request of Price Administrator, where it would be inconvenient and sometimes impossible for Price Administrator to intervene in state eviction proceedings); Valentine v. Beyer, 850 F.2d 951, 957 (3d Cir. 1988) (reduction in quality of legal assistance to prison inmates); Miller v. Rich, 845 F.2d 190, 192 (9th Cir. 1988) (injunction ordering National Transportation Safety Board to allow owner to observe testing of his jet engine; irreparable injury not discussed); Johnson v. U.S. Dep't of Agric., 734 F.2d 774, 789 (11th Cir. 1984) ("additional delays" in recovering property); Itek Corp. v. First Nat'l Bank, 730 F.2d 19, 22 (1st Cir. 1984) (litigation in revolutionary Iran); Long Island R.R. v. Int'l Ass'n of Machinists, 709 F. Supp. 376, 386 (S.D.N.Y. 1989) (injunction "is the only practical, effective means of enforcing the duty to exert every reasonable effort to make and maintain [collective bargaining] agreements," quoting Chicago & N.W. Ry. v. United Transp. Union, 402 U.S. 570, 583 (1971)), aff'd, 874 F.2d 901, 911 (2d Cir. 1989), cert. denied, 110 S. Ct. 836 (1990); Nat'l Ass'n of Radiation Survivors v. Walters, 589 F. Supp. 1302, 1327–28 (N.D. Cal. 1984) (administrative adjudication without counsel), rev'd on other grounds, 473 U.S. 305 (1985); Douglas v. Thrasher, 489 A.2d 422 (Del. 1985) (retaining jurisdiction over claim for reformation of ex-wife's defective deed, where Family Court proceeding between former spouses might not provide adequate remedy for buyer); James v. Grand Trunk W. R.R., 14 Ill.2d 356, 152 N.E.2d 858 (1958) (litigation in undesirable forum with resulting pressure for unjust settlement); Sanford v. Boston Edison Co., 316 Mass. 631, 633–34, 56 N.E.2d 1, 3 (1944) (specific performance of contract to check off union dues, avoiding "continuous litigation or long delay"); Murphy v. McQuade Realty, Inc., 122 N.H. 314, 316–17, 444 A.2d 530, 532 (1982) (affirming, *dubitante*, preliminary injunction to prevent financing seller from foreclosing mortgage before hearing on buyer-debtor's suit to rescind purchase and return land to seller); Meyer v. Reed, 91 N.J. Eq. 237, 239–40, 109 A. 733, 734–35 (N.J. Ch. 1920) (litigation in distant forum); Blum v. Mott, 664 S.W.2d 741 (Tex. App. 1983) (allowing plaintiff to pursue remedy with lower burden of proof than statutory remedy that defendant urged was adequate); Dodson v. Seymour, 664 S.W.2d 158, 162 (Tex. App. 1983) (forcible entry and detainer not adequate remedy where probate court's injunction ordering devisee to stay away from premises would help assure orderly administration). But see Lewis v. S.S. Baune, 534 F.2d 1115 (5th Cir. 1976) (denying injunction against settling without consent of plaintiff's attorney, because settlement could be set aside and injunction was wrong on merits); Kaiser v. Wolf, 18 Pa. D. & C. 3d 555 (Pa. Com. Pl. 1981) (refusing to specifically enforce contract for cutting of timber, where plaintiff's only theory of irreparable injury was that he would have to count the trees to prove his damages).

79. [irreparable harm to defendant] See Foxboro Co. v. Arabian Am. Oil Co., 805 F.2d 34, 36–37 (1st Cir. 1986) (refusing to preliminarily enjoin payment of letter of credit; refusal forced plaintiff to arbitrate in Saudi Arabia as it agreed); Powell v. Nat'l Football League, 690 F. Supp. 812, 817 (D. Minn. 1988) (preliminary injunction permitting football players to change teams without restriction "would wholly subvert the collective bargaining process").

80. [discovery] See Pomeroy, 1 *Equity Jurisprudence* §§ 190–215, at 179–215, §§ 223–30 at 228–38 (cited in note 1); Story, 2 *Equity Jurisprudence* §§ 689–91 at 1–4, §§ 1480–1516 at 699–731 (cited in note 66).

81. [joinder] See 1 Pomeroy §§ 113–14 at 96–99.

82. [interpleader] See 28 U.S.C. §§ 1335, 2361 (1988); Avant Petroleum, Inc. v. Banque Paribas, BP, 853 F.2d 140 (2d Cir. 1988); 1 Pomeroy §§ 1319–29 at 343–56; 2 Story §§ 800–24 at 110–28.

83. [bills of peace] See Zechariah Chafee, *Some Problems of Equity* 149–98 (Univ. Mich. 1950); 1 Pomeroy §§ 246–48 at 257–59; 2 Story §§ 852–60 at 147–53.

84. [class actions] See Chafee at 200–13; Stephen C. Yeazell, *From Medieval Group Litigation to the Modern Class Action* 125–96 (Yale Univ. Press 1987). Yeazell's account is considerably more sophisticated.

85. [derivative suits] See 3 Pomeroy §§ 1088–95 at 1–13.

86. [merged procedure] Fed. R. Civ. Proc. 20 (permissive joinder), 22 (interpleader), 23 (class actions), 23.1 (shareholders' derivative suits), 26–37 (discovery). See Stephen N. Subrin, *How Equity Conquered Common Law: The Federal Rules of Civil Procedure in Historical Perspective*, 135 U. Pa. L. Rev. 909 (1987).

87. [jury trial] Ross v. Bernhard, 396 U.S. 531 (1970) (shareholder's derivative suit). For cases and commentary applying *Ross* to other equitable procedures, *see* Charles Alan Wright, Arthur R. Miller, & Mary Kay Kane, 7 *Federal Practice & Procedure* § 1718 at 622–29 (West, 2d ed. 1986) (interpleader); 7B id. § 1801 at 458–59 (class actions).

88. [repetitive pro se litigation] See In Matter of Packer Ave. Assoc., 884 F.2d 745 (3d Cir. 1989); Tripati v. Beaman, 878 F.2d 351 (10th Cir. 1989); In re Davis, 878 F.2d 211 (7th Cir. 1989); Maxberry v. Securities & Exchange Comm'n, 879 F.2d 222 (6th Cir. 1989); Urban v. United Nations, 768 F.2d 1497 (D.C. Cir. 1985); In re Martin-Trigona, 763 F.2d 140 (2d Cir. 1985); Pavilonis v. King, 626 F.2d 1075 (1st Cir. 1980).

89. [disaster and products liability cases] In re Federal Skywalk Cases, 93 F.R.D. 415 (W.D. Mo.), rev'd, 680 F.2d 1175 (8th Cir. 1982); In re N. Dist. of Cal. "Dalkon Shield" IUD Prod. Liab. Litig., 526 F. Supp. 887 (N.D. Cal. 1981), rev'd, 693 F.2d 847 (9th Cir. 1982).

90. [declaratory judgments] Steffel v. Thompson, 415 U.S. 452, 462–75 (1974) (authorizing federal courts to declare that it would be unconstitutional to enforce state statutes); Exxon Corp. v. Fed. Trade Comm'n, 411 F. Supp. 1362, 1376 (D. Del. 1976) (declaring that administrative agency's discovery order violated plaintiff's rights).

91. [rule inapplicable] In re Martin-Trigona, 737 F.2d 1254, 1262 (2d Cir. 1984) (injunction against repeated frivolous litigation); Gillette v. Pepper Tank Co., 694 P.2d 369, 373 (Colo. App. 1984) (equitable relief will be granted despite adequate remedy at law, where equity is more consistent with "right, justice, and morality"); Petraborg v. Zontelli, 217 Minn. 536, 555, 15 N.W.2d 174, 184 (1944) (irreparable injury rule has been modified in cases of violation of riparian rights); Lauderback v. Multnomah County, 111 Or. 681, 226 P. 697 (1924) (court will enjoin misuse of eminent domain power without showing of irreparable injury, because of tendency to abuse).

92. [injunctions authorized by statute] Porter v. Dicken, 328 U.S. 252, 255 (1946) (enjoining pending state judicial proceedings without discussing irreparable injury, where statute authorized enforcement by injunction); U.S. v. Odessa Union Warehouse Co-op, 833 F.2d 172, 175-76 (9th Cir. 1987) ("where an injunction is authorized by statute . . . the agency to whom the enforcement of the right has been entrusted is not required to show irreparable injury"); Equal Employment Opportunity Comm'n v. Cosmair, Inc., 821 F.2d 1085, 1090–91 (5th Cir. 1987) ("when an injunction is expressly authorized by statute and the statutory conditions are satisfied, the movant need not establish specific irreparable injury to obtain a preliminary injunction"); Ill. Bell Tel. Co. v. Ill. Commerce Comm'n, 740 F.2d 566, 571 (7th Cir. 1984) ("where the plaintiff seeks an injunction to prevent the violation of a federal statute that specifically provides for injunctive relief, it need not show irreparable harm"); Southwestern Bell Tel. Co. v. Ark. Public Serv. Comm'n, 738 F.2d 901, 907–08 (8th Cir. 1984) (statute provides that any party injured by violation may apply for injunction; "traditional equitable criterion of irreparable injury is thus inapplicable"), vacated on other grounds, 476 U.S. 1167 (1986); Gov't of the Virgin Islands v. Virgin Islands Paving, Inc., 714 F.2d 283, 286 (3d Cir. 1983) ("when a statute contains, either explicitly or implicitly, a finding that violations will harm the public, the courts may grant preliminary equitable relief on a showing of a statutory violation without requiring any additional showing of irreparable harm"); Environmental Defense Fund, Inc. v. Lamphier, 714 F.2d 331, 338 (4th Cir. 1983) ("where a statute authorizes injunctive relief for its enforcement, plaintiffs need not plead and prove irreparable injury"); Atchison, Topeka, & Santa Fe Ry. v. Lennen, 640 F.2d 255, 259–61 (10th Cir. 1981) (when defendant is about to violate statute that "provides for injunctive relief to prevent such violations, irreparable harm to the plaintiffs need not be shown"); Carroll v. El Dorado Estates Div. No. Two Ass'n Inc., 680 P.2d 1158, 1160 (Alaska 1984) ("where a statute specifically authorizes injunctive relief, the plaintiff need not show either irreparable injury or lack of an adequate remedy at law"); In re Marriage of Van Hook, 147 Cal. App. 3d 970, 985, 195 Cal. Rptr. 541, 550–51 (1983) ("irreparable injury need not be shown in cases involving a preliminary injunction, where the injunction is authorized by statute, and the statutory conditions are satisfied"); People ex rel. Carpentier v. Goers, 20 Ill. 2d 272, 276, 170 N.E.2d 159, 161 (1960) (defendant's arguments "that the complaint fails to allege facts showing that irreparable injury is threatened in the absence of an injunction, and that the remedy at law is adequate . . . are negatived by the statute which expressly authorizes issuance of an injunction"); Kliebert Educ. Trust v. Watson Marines Serv., Inc., 454 So.2d 855, 860 (La. App. 1984) ("injunction granted pursuant to [statute authorizing injunction against interference with possession of real property] may be granted without any showing of irreparable injury"); Nev. Real Estate Comm'n v. Ressel, 72 Nev. 79, 294 P.2d 1115 (1956) ("overwhelming weight of authority"); Va. Beach S.P.C.A., Inc. v. S. Hampton Roads Veterinary Ass'n, 329 S.E.2d 10, 13 (Va. 1985) ("when a statute empowers a court to grant injunctive relief, the party seeking an injunction is not required to establish the traditional prerequisites, i.e., irreparable harm and lack of an adequate remedy at law"). See also the zoning cases cited in ch. 2 note 13.

93. [presumption of irreparable injury] Heublein, Inc. v. Fed. Trade Comm'n, 539 F. Supp. 123, 128 (D. Conn. 1982) ("irreparable harm to the public and to Heublein is presumed in this case because equitable requirements are satisfied *per se* when a violation of federal law is shown since, in enacting the statute, Congress declared that violations of the statute are contrary to the public interest and, therefore, cause irreparable harm"); Ariz. State Bd. of Dental Examiners v. Hyder, 114 Ariz. 544, 546, 562 P.2d 717, 719 (1977) ("harm is conclusively presumed from the legislative declaration"); Johnson v. Murzyn, 1 Conn. App. 176, 179–80, 469 A.2d 1227, 1230 (1984) ("enactment of the statute by implication assumes there was not an adequate remedy at law and that the injury was irreparable, i.e., the legislation was needed or else it would not have been enacted") (quoting Conway v. Miss. State Bd. of Health, 252 Miss. 315, 324–25, 173 So.2d 412, 416 (1965)); State v. Andrews, 65 Hawaii 289, 290, 651 P.2d 473, 474 (1982) ("continuing operation of such a school without a license is *per se* an irreparable injury to the public policy of the State"); Business & Prof. People for the Public Interest v. Ill. Commerce Comm'n, 171 Ill. App. 3d 948, 969–70, 525 N.E.2d 1053, 1066 (1988) ("the logic behind the rule is that since the legislature has seen fit to enact legislation, it may be presumed that there is a need for injunctive remedy"); Union Ins. Co. v. State ex rel. Ind. Dep't of Ins., 401 N.E.2d 1372, 1375 (Ind. App. 1980) ("legislature has declared that . . . there is no adequate legal remedy and irreparable injury exists as a matter of law").

94. [inherent power to enforce statutes] Mitchell v. Robert de Mario Jewelry, Inc., 361 U.S. 288, 292 (1960) ("there is inherent in the Courts of Equity a jurisdiction to . . . give effect to the policy of the legislature," quoting Clark v. Smith, 38 U.S (13 Pet.) 195, 203 (1839) (ellipsis in original)); U.S. v. City of San Francisco, 310 U.S. 16, 30–31 (1940) ("equitable doctrines relied on do not militate against the capacity of a court of equity as a proper forum in which to make a declared policy of Congress effective"); Environmental Defense Fund, Inc. v. Lamphier, 714 F.2d 331, 337–38 (4th Cir. 1983) ("it is familiar doctrine that an injunction is an appropriate means for the enforcement of an Act of Congress when it is in the public interest"); Carson v. Ross, 509 N.E.2d 239, 241 (Ind. App. 1987) ("when the acts sought to be enjoined are declared unlawful by the legislature the plaintiff does not have to show either irreparable injury or a balance of hardship in his favor," but preliminary injunction denied on merits).

95. [any violation of law] Heublein, Inc. v. Fed. Trade Comm'n, 539 F. Supp. 123, 128 (D. Conn. 1982) (irreparable harm is presumed "when a violation of federal law is shown"); Mayor of Morgan City v. Ascension Parish Police Jury, 468 So.2d 1291, 1300–01 (La. App. 1985) ("when the plaintiff in an injunction proceeding alleges the defendant is acting in violation of the law, there is no need to prove irreparable harm") (citing two other Louisiana cases).

96. [statutory injunctions denied] Amoco Prod. Co. v. Village of Gambell, 480 U.S. 531 (1987) (balance of hardship, with some irreparable injury talk); Weinberger v. Romero-Barcelo, 456 U.S. 305 (1982) (deference and undue hardship, with irreparable injury talk); Rondeau v. Mosinee Paper Corp., 422 U.S. 49 (1975) (mootness, with irreparable injury talk); Pyrodyne Corp. v. Pyrotronics Corp., 847 F.2d 1398 (9th Cir. 1988) (laches and estoppel); U.S. Jaycees v. Cedar Rapids

Jaycees, 794 F.2d 379, 382–83 (8th Cir. 1986) (unclean hands); Sadat v. Am. Motors Corp., 104 Ill. 2d 105, 470 N.E.2d 997 (1984) (failure to plead irreparable injury only apparent ground for decision) (discussed in text at 102–103).

97. [duty to enforce statutes] Daniel A. Farber, *Equitable Discretion, Legal Duties, and Environmental Injunctions*, 45 U. Pitt. L. Rev. 513 (1984); Zygmunt J.B. Plater, *Statutory Violations and Equitable Discretion*, 70 Cal. L. Rev. 524 (1982).

98. [court entangled in precedents] Bd. of Educ. v. Warren Township High School Fed'n of Teachers, 162 Ill. App. 3d 676, 681–84, 515 N.E.2d 1331, 1335–36 (1987), rev'd on other grounds, 128 Ill. 2d 155, 538 N.E.2d 524 (1989).

99. [rule was irrelevant] 128 Ill. 2d at 166, 538 N.E.2d at 529 ("we therefore conclude that the circuit court lacked jurisdiction to enjoin arbitration and to decide questions of arbitrability").

4

Why Courts Invoke the Rule

Chapters 2 and 3 reviewed a sweeping range of doctrines for holding legal remedies inadequate or irrelevant. There are very few cases not subject to at least one of these doctrines. If plaintiff has any plausible need for specific relief, he can describe that need as irreparable injury and find ample precedent to support his claim. Yet there are cases denying specific relief and invoking the irreparable injury rule as the reason.

These cases can be divided into two very unequal groups. One group consists of all those cases in which the irreparable injury rule appears to be the actual ground of decision. This group is small, and in most of these cases, the choice between legal and equitable remedies appears to be of little practical consequence.

The second group is vastly larger. The cases in this group are better explained on other grounds, and have nothing to do with a preference for legal remedies. The irreparable injury rule is invoked in the opinion, but it does not explain the result.

A third group of cases deserves passing mention. Often the irreparable injury rule appears in a formulaic recitation that does not even purport to affect the result. Courts regularly recite the prerequisites to preliminary injunctions,[1] or to equitable relief generally,[2] and then deny the remedy on some other ground, such as lack of probable success on the merits. Reciting the legal background is a common approach to opinion writing; there is nothing unusual about this example of it. Occasionally, the review of the rule is more thoughtful than formulaic.[3] But whether formulaic or thoughtful, these frequent recitations of the rule help sustain the illusion that it is still a viable part of our law.

99

A. Cases Actually Applying the Rule

A handful of cases can be explained on no ground other than the traditional understanding of the irreparable injury rule. These are cases in which plaintiff seeks some equitable remedy, and is remitted to a legal remedy instead, on the ground that the legal remedy would be adequate. The opinion does not reveal any special difficulty with the equitable remedy or any judicial hostility to the merits of plaintiff's case. There are remarkably few of these cases—fewer than I expected to find when I began this research. But they do occur. They do not make the irreparable injury rule look good.

In a few of these cases, plaintiff is remitted to some legal form of specific relief that will accomplish exactly what equity could have accomplished. What is at issue is not the choice between specific and substitutionary relief, but the choice between personal commands and impersonal judgments.[4] Some of these are miscellaneous applications of lis pendens[5] or res judicata.[6] The largest set of cases in this category holds that replevin is an adequate remedy to recover personal property, and thus refuses equitable remedies that would recover the same property.[7] Some of these cases can be explained on grounds analogous to the policy against imprisonment for debt.[8] But when there is no prospect of enforcement difficulties in a particular case, the preference for replevin over injunction seems to be a real application of the irreparable injury rule.

In most of the remaining cases, plaintiff seeks specific performance of contracts to deliver goods. In some, it appears that the goods are fungible and the market is orderly; so far as the opinion reveals, plaintiff can easily and immediately exchange money damages for identical goods.[9] Where that is true, the distinction between specific and substitutionary relief disappears.[10] Either way, plaintiff gets identical goods. With damages for any difference in price, she gets the goods at the same effective cost. If she measures damages by the difference between the contract price and the replacement price, the amount of damages does not even depend on anyone's estimate of value.

In the fungible goods cases, the irreparable injury rule survives as a tiebreaker.[11] Each remedy appears to be equally complete, practical, and efficient; the remedies produce identical final results; and the rule says to grant only the legal remedy in that situation.

Unless some critical fact is omitted from the opinion, it is hard to see why plaintiff seeks specific performance in such a case, why defendant resists it, or why we have a rule that encourages the parties to litigate the choice of remedy. In these cases, the legal remedy really is just as good as the equitable remedy. These cases arise either from bad lawyering, or from critical undisclosed facts that make the choice of remedy significant. If the critical facts that drive the litigation are omitted from the opinion, it can only be because the irreparable injury rule has diverted the court's attention from the real issue.

There are very few of these cases in which the goods appear entirely fungible and plaintiff seeks specific performance anyway. These cases shade into those where the goods are replaceable only with difficulty, or only with similar but not identical goods. Plaintiff argues that replacement is difficult or impossible; the court finds that replacement is possible and damages are adequate. Where replacement is difficult, a majority of cases grant specific relief, but a substantial minority do not.[12] So long as the rule persists that damages are an adequate remedy for loss of goods that are available elsewhere, some cases will fall near the line and some cases near the line will be decided each way. We can argue whether this line is worth drawing and litigating over, but for now it survives. It is the principal remnant of the irreparable injury rule.

A similar group of cases involves simple construction services that can easily be purchased in the market. These cases arise both in contract[13] and in tort.[14] Again, if the services are in fact readily available, legal and equitable remedies are equivalent, and it is hard to see what drives the litigation. If the services are not readily available, or if plaintiff for some reason cares that the services be performed only by defendant, an essential fact is missing from the opinion. It is probably fair to count the simple construction cases as true applications of the irreparable injury rule, but they can also be explained on the ground of avoiding direct judicial supervision of the construction.[15]

There remain a very few cases in which damages are plainly not as good for plaintiff as specific relief, but the court fails to recognize the inadequacy or considers it insufficient to satisfy the irreparable injury rule. Plaintiff is worse off for being remitted to damages, and the opinion does not indicate any way in which defendant or the judicial system is better off. Unless there are countervailing considerations that do not appear in the opinions, the irreparable injury rule leads the court to a bad result in these cases. Remarkably, I have found only one such case in the original sample of four hundred cases, and only three in the larger sample of fourteen hundred cases. Surely there are more, but I have not found them.

The most recent of these cases is *City Centre One Associates v. Teachers Insurance & Annuity Association*.[16] The court refused to specifically enforce a contract to borrow money, reasoning that the lender wanted only interest and that damages were wholly adequate. But the lender's expected return included a share of the profits in the real estate that would have secured the loan, a sum that depended on long-term developments and could only be estimated in a damage award. There is ample authority for holding that long-term profits are too difficult to measure.[17] The lender's fears of a low estimate apparently exceeded its hopes of a high estimate, because it sought specific performance instead of damages. The court forced the lender to bear that risk, for reasons that are not apparent but that it explained in terms of the irreparable injury rule.

An economically identical transaction could have been structured as a loan, plus a purchase of a fractional interest in the building, plus a right to sell back the fractional interest at the original price. This contract would have been subject to the rule that contracts to buy real estate are specifically enforceable.[18] It makes no sense to deny specific performance when the same deal is structured as a participating loan.

The second example is *Sadat v. American Motors Corp.*,[19] a suit in state court under the federal Magnuson-Moss Warranty Act.[20] Defendant's dealer had failed in seven attempts to repair serious defects in plaintiff's fully warranted new car. On these facts, the statute required that defendant either refund plaintiff's money or replace the car without charge, at plaintiff's election.[21] Defendant refused plaintiff's request for a new car. Plaintiff sued for an injunction ordering defendant to deliver a new car or its cash equivalent. The court dismissed the complaint for failure to plead irreparable injury. The court refused to read the statute to authorize an injunction, because the statute merely authorized "equitable relief" and did not use the word "injunction."

Plaintiff's legal remedy was to recover the value of the car if it had been as warranted less the value of the car on the date of purchase.[22] She could also recover incidental and consequential damages and attorneys' fees, but that would be true with or without the injunction.[23]

The legal remedy is adequate in theory, but the problem is to prove the value of the defective car. That should not be an insuperable obstacle, but neither is it easy.[24] It adds a substantial additional issue to every case, it makes some otherwise undefendable cases worth defending, and it may require plaintiff to hire an expert witness whose fees are often not recoverable.[25] The risk of erroneous valuation bears heavily on plaintiff with a single case, but not on the manufacturer who can expect errors to balance out over many cases.[26] This unequal ability to bear risk will hold down settlement values. These defects of damage remedies led to a nationwide wave of consumer protection legislation,[27] including the federal refund-or-replace remedy. To remit plaintiff to the damage remedy is to *pro tanto* repeal the statute.

Sadat may have been a misguided test case; plaintiff refused to plead irreparable injury and may have failed to argue that the legal remedy was inadequate. Perhaps subsequent Illinois consumers plead irreparable injury and got their injunction, although there is no hint of that in more recent articles on Illinois law.[28] The dissenting judge believed that plaintiff could never show irreparable injury, because there were millions of mass-produced substitutes on the market.[29] He noted some of the problems with the legal remedy, but he did not suggest that these problems made the legal remedy inadequate. Despite his own analysis of the legal remedy, he was captured by the traditional view that damages are adequate unless the goods are unique.

Whatever the subsequent course of Illinois law, it is clear that the irreparable injury rule led to an erroneous result in *Sadat*. The majority insisted on applying the rule; the usual formulation of the rule led the dissenter, and perhaps the plaintiff, to think the rule was not satisfied; and the result was to eviscerate an act of Congress.

The final example, *Wiles v. Wiles*,[30] is forty years old. Defendant advertised an estate sale, including several items of live-stock and farm equipment belonging to plaintiff. Some of these items were on defendant's land, some on plaintiff's. Plaintiff sought an injunction against the sale of his goods and against the trespass required to sell the items that were on his own land. The court dismissed. With respect to the goods, it held that detinue would be an adequate remedy.[31] With respect to the trespass, it held that damages would be adequate, and that because defendant would trespass only once, there was no danger of a multiplicity of suits.[32]

The case unambiguously holds that damages are an adequate remedy for the trespass. Plaintiff might have recovered the goods themselves in detinue, but not necessarily. The court considered the possibility that the goods might be damaged or destroyed, and held that damages would be adequate if that happened.[33] The court did not note the risk that the goods might pass into the hands of a bona fide purchaser; presumably, it would have said that damages would be adequate in that event as well. The court did not consider whether plaintiff could use his damage recovery, based on depreciated value, to replace the items.

Plaintiff alleged that "physical combat" was the only way to save his goods, and that he had neither the desire nor the capacity for that.[34] The court appeared unconcerned about the risk of physical confrontation. It acknowledged that plaintiff could not recover for mental suffering, but said that equity could not remedy that either.[35] It failed to see that preventing the sale would prevent most of the mental suffering.

Wiles is the classic case contemplated by the quotation that opened this book. The law stood by and let a wrong be committed, remitting plaintiff to compensation after the fact. Plaintiff is hurt, and it is hard to see who is helped. Perhaps the court wanted a jury trial on the issue of ownership, but it did not say that. It wrote the opinion solely on the ground of the irreparable injury rule.

These three cases—*City Centre*, *Sadat*, and *Wiles*—are consistent with the formal statement of the irreparable injury rule, but inconsistent with the great mass of cases. They are aberrational results of the misleading "rule" and the traditional understanding.

B. Cases Purporting to Apply the Rule

Sometimes courts have real reasons for denying plaintiff's choice of remedy. Specific relief may be more burdensome to defendant or the court, or it may infringe some other legitimate interest of the defendant. In these cases, something like the traditional understanding of the irreparable injury rule might serve a real purpose: plaintiff should not be entitled to a burdensome remedy if some other adequate remedy is less burdensome. But the actual irreparable injury rule is little help in such cases, because the legal remedy is so rarely adequate.

One approach to this problem is to redefine irreparable injury. Damages may be less complete, less practical, and less efficient, but good enough where there is real reason to avoid the remedy plaintiff seeks. This is done in the preliminary injunction cases, where the courts prefer relief after full trial to relief after preliminary hearing.

Another approach is to directly state the reasons for sometimes denying plaintiff's choice of remedy. A clear example is the rule that equity will not specifically enforce a promise to perform personal services. Such rules are not derived from the adequacy of the legal remedy, even if the opinions sometimes add as an alternate ground that plaintiff's injury is not irreparable anyway.

Courts often combine these two approaches. Courts balance the cost to defendant or the court from a fully adequate remedy against the cost to plaintiff of a less than adequate remedy. Such balancing is sometimes explicit, as in the preliminary injunction and balance of hardship cases, and sometimes implicit, as in the difficulty-of-supervision cases.

Sometimes the reason for denying relief goes to the substantive claim rather than the remedy, and the court would be equally unwilling to award damages. Occasionally, as in many speech and personal service cases, courts prefer the less adequate remedy precisely because it is less adequate; they fear over enforcement from the more effective remedy. But whenever a court denies plaintiff's request for an equitable remedy, the irreparable injury rule may be offered as a ground of decision.

Virtually all the modern cases purporting to deny relief because of the irreparable injury rule fall into one of these patterns. That is, there is a real reason for denying the remedy sought in the particular case, but the reason is not applicable to all or even most cases and has nothing to do with a general preference for law over equity or for substitutionary over specific relief. The irreparable injury rule is used to explain or prop up the opinion, even though the legal remedy is not as complete, practical, and efficient as the equitable remedy.

Several of the real reasons for denying specific relief are embodied in familiar doctrines. I obviously do not claim to have discovered that these doctrines are often reasons for denying specific relief. What I have discovered is that these are virtually the only occasions on which courts say that plaintiff's legal remedy is adequate, and that the rhetorical role of irreparable injury talk varies with each real reason for denying specific relief. The one constant is that courts do not deny specific relief because of the irreparable injury rule alone. There is always another reason.

I have already explored two of the real reasons for denying equitable remedies. Except for certain privileged claims, courts do not order defendants to pay money and enforce such orders with the contempt power.[36] And courts do not grant specific relief against insolvents where the effect would be to prefer plaintiff over other creditors.[37] These are two important rules for choosing among remedies, but neither can be derived from the irreparable injury rule. In the chapters that follow, I identify more of the real reasons for denying plaintiff's choice of remedy. These are the operative rules that actually govern the choice of remedy in American courts.

Notes on Invoking the Rule

1. [recitations re preliminary injunctions] Pyrodyne Corp. v. Pyrotronics Corp., 847 F.2d 1398, 1403 (9th Cir. 1988); Hartford House, Ltd. v. Hallmark Cards, Inc., 846 F.2d 1268, 1270 (10th Cir. 1988); Faheem-El v. Klincar, 841 F.2d 712, 716 (7th Cir. 1988); Gaston Drugs, Inc. v. Metro. Life Ins. Co., 823 F.2d 984, 988 (6th Cir. 1987); Garza v. Tex. Educ. Found., Inc., 565 F.2d 909, 910–11 (5th Cir. 1978); Jessen v. Keystone Sav. & Loan Ass'n, 142 Cal. App. 3d 454, 459, 191 Cal. Rptr. 104, 108 (1983); Lambert v. State, 468 N.E.2d 1384, 1390 (Ind. App. 1984).

2. [recitations re equitable relief] Porter v. Warner Holding Co., 328 U.S. 395, 399 (1946) (explaining that equity could decide all relevant matters in dispute once

it assumed jurisdiction, even though money recovery "could not be obtained through an independent suit in equity if an adequate legal remedy were available"); Buzz Barton & Assoc., Inc. v. Giannone, 108 Ill. 2d 373, 387, 483 N.E.2d 1271, 1278 (1985) (directing award of damages for wrongful preliminary injunction); McNulty v. Heitman, 600 S.W.2d 168, 172 (Mo. App. 1980) (explaining plaintiff's choice between legal and equitable remedies in paternity suit).

3. **[thoughtful recitation]** Del. & Hudson Ry. v. United Transp. Union, 450 F.2d 603, 619–20 (D.C. Cir. 1971) (discussing relationship between irreparable injury and probability of success on motion for preliminary injunction).

4. **[personal command v. impersonal judgment]** See ch. 1 part B.1 at 14–15.

5. **[lis pendens adequate]** Schwartz v. Coldwell Banker Title Serv., Inc., 178 Ill. App. 3d 971, 975–76, 533 N.E.2d 1161, 1163 (1989) (no preliminary injunction against transfer of land where lis pendens would be equally effective); Oxequip Health Indus., Inc. v. Canalmar, Inc., 94 Ill. App. 3d 955, 419 N.E.2d 625 (1981) (same).

6. **[res judicata adequate]** Repka v. Am. Nat'l Ins. Co., 143 Tex. 542, 550, 186 S.W.2d 977, 981–82 (1945) (refusing to enjoin one of two parallel suits, where first judgment would be res judicata in the other case, so that with or without injunction, one and only one suit would be litigated). For cases contra, see ch. 6 note 72.

7. **[replevin adequate]** Charles Simkin & Sons, Inc. v. Massiah, 289 F.2d 26, 29 n.1 (3d Cir. 1961) (refusing preliminary injunction ordering defendant to return plaintiff's tools; "equitable jurisdiction in these cases really rests upon the fact that the only relief which the plaintiff can have is possession of the *identical* thing, and this remedy cannot *with certainty* be obtained by any common law action," quoting John Norton Pomeroy, 1 *A Treatise on Equity Jurisprudence as Administered in the United States of America* § 185 at 265–66 (Bancroft-Whitney Co., 5th ed. 1941) (emphasis in Pomeroy's original)); Haavik v. Farnell, 264 Ala. 326, 329, 87 So.2d 629, 631 (1956) (refusing injunction ordering defendant to return plaintiff's personal property, "which we consider to be nothing more than a substitute for an action in detinue"); Alger v. Davis, 345 Mich. 635, 76 N.W.2d 847 (1956) (denying constructive trust and receiver because replevin would be adequate remedy to recover personal property). For analysis, see M.T. Van Hecke, *Equitable Replevin*, 33 N.C. L. Rev. 57 (1954).

8. **[sometimes like imprisonment for debt]** See ch. 1 part B.2 at 18.

9. **[damages adequate where goods replaceable]** Pierce-Odom, Inc. v. Evenson, 5 Ark. App. 67, 70, 632 S.W.2d 247, 249 (1982) (mobile home, not alleged to be unique); Le Moyne Ranch v. Agajanian, 121 Cal. App. 423, 8 P.2d 1055 (1932) (garbage for hog feed; more expensive feed readily available); Hilmor Sales Co. v. Helen Neushaefer Div. of Supronics Corp., 6 UCC Rep. 325 (N.Y. Sup. 1969) (lipstick, not unique in any way, but acquired at bargain price); Tower City Grain Co. v. Richman, 232 N.W.2d 61, 65–67 (N.D. 1975) (wheat). In *Tower City*, plaintiff's claim for damages was later rejected on the merits. 262 N.W.2d 22 (1978). Compare Weathersby v. Gore, 556 F.2d 1247 (5th Cir. 1977) (cotton; seller repudiated contract before shortage and sharp price increase; parties stipulated that buyer could have replaced cotton at that time).

10. **[substitutionary equal to specific]** See Marion Mfg. Co. v. Long, 588 F.2d 538, 542 (6th Cir. 1978) ("where, as here, the product or good in question is not unique and no shortage exists; (sic) there is no difference between an award of 'specific performance' and an award of the difference between the market price and the contract price"); Joseph Story, 2 *Commentaries on Equity Jurisprudence as Administered in England and America* §§ 717 at 24 (Little, Brown 1836).

11. **[earlier treatment of rule as tiebreaker]** I first characterized the rule as a tiebreaker in Douglas Laycock, *Injunctions and the Irreparable Injury Rule* (Book Review), 57 Tex. L. Rev. 1065, 1071 (1979). For analysis of that characterization, see ch. 1 part B.4.

12. **[specific relief where cover is difficult]** See ch. 2 part B.

13. **[breach of contract for routine services]** Ryan v. Ocean Twelve, Inc., 316 A.2d 573, 575 (Del. Ch. 1973) (plaintiffs could hire another contractor to repair their condominium units, and recover cost from defendant); McCormick v. Proprietors, Cemetery of Mt. Auburn, 285 Mass. 548, 550–51, 189 N.E. 585, 586 (1934) (plaintiff could hire another contractor to raise grade of cemetery monument, and recover cost from defendant); Gerety v. Poitras, 126 Vt. 153, 155, 224 A.2d 919, 921 (1966) (defendant refused to honor warranty on house sold to plaintiff; plaintiff had already retained contractor who had itemized the necessary work).

14. **[tort requiring routine services]** M & A Farms, Ltd. v. Town of Ville Platte, 422 So.2d 708, 712 (La. App. 1982) (refusing to order defendant to rebuild plaintiff's levee; no indication plaintiff would have difficulty finding a contractor); Thurston Enterprises, Inc. v. Baldi, 128 N.H. 760, 764, 519 A.2d 297, 300 (1986) (refusing to order defendant to repave easement across plaintiff's land). See also Cont'l & Vogue Health Studios, Inc. v. Abra Corp., 369 Mich. 561, 564–67, 120 N.W.2d 835, 837–38 (1963) (damages from refusal to reconstruct destroyed building was difference between rent plaintiff paid and rent plaintiff charged sublessees).

15. **[avoidance of judicial supervision]** See ch. 9 part C.

16. **[real application of rule]** City Centre One Assoc. v. Teachers Ins. & Annuity Ass'n, 656 F. Supp. 658 (D. Utah 1987).

17. **[long-term profits unmeasurable]** See ch. 2 part C.

18. **[damages inadequate for real estate]** See ch. 2 part A.1.

19. **[real application of rule]** Sadat v. Am. Motors Corp., 104 Ill. 2d 105, 112–14, 470 N.E.2d 997, 1001 (1984).

20. **[Magnuson-Moss Warranty Act]** 15 U.S.C. § 2301 *et seq.* (1988).

21. **[refund-or-replace remedy]** Id. § 2304(a).

22. **[measure of damages]** Compare UCC 2–714(2) (contract damages for breach of warranty). The federal statute simply authorizes "damages," without specifying the measure. 15 U.S.C. §2310(d)(1) (1988).

23. **[additional damages and fees]** 15 U.S.C. § 2310(d) (1988) (damages and fees); UCC § 2–714(3) (incidental and consequential damages).

24. **[proof of value of defective product]** See Timothy J. Muris, *Comment: The Costs of Freely Granting Specific Performance*, 1982 Duke L.J. 1053, 1064 (arguing against specific performance where damages are easy to measure, but conceding that this condition may not be met where expert appraisal is required).

25. **[expert witness fees not recoverable]** See Crawford Fitting Co. v. J.T. Gibbons, Inc., 482 U.S. 437 (1987).

26. **[effect of risk of error in valuation]** See Marc Galanter, *Why the "Haves" Come Out Ahead: Speculation on the Limits of Legal Change*, 9 L. & Soc'y Rev. 95, 99–100 (1974).

27. **[defects in damage remedy led to statutes]** See State ex rel. Danforth v. Independence Dodge, Inc., 494 S.W.2d 362, 370 (Mo. App. 1973) (legislatures throughout the country enacted consumer fraud statutes, because "private causes of action had proved largely ineffective"); William A. Lovett, *State Deceptive Trade Practice Legislation*, 46 Tulane L. Rev. 724, 724–31 (1972).

28. **[subsequent Illinois law]** See Comment, *Illinois Lemon Car Buyer's Options in a Breach of Warranty Action*, 20 John Marshall L. Rev. 483 (1987); Casenote, *Sadat v. American Motors Corporation: Limiting Consumer Remedies Under Magnuson-Moss and the New Car Buyer Protection Act*, 19 John Marshall L. Rev. 163 (1985).

29. **[substitutes preclude irreparable injury]** Sadat, 104 Ill. 2d at 118–19, 470 N.E.2d at 1003–04 (Simon dissenting).

30. **[real application of rule]** Wiles v. Wiles, 134 W. Va. 81, 58 S.E.2d 601 (1950).

31. **[detinue adequate for goods]** Id. at 88–89, 58 S.E.2d at 605.

32. **[damages adequate for trespass]** Id. at 92–93, 58 S.E.2d at 607.

33. **[damages adequate for goods]** Id. at 88–89, 58 S.E.2d at 605.

34. **[risk of physical combat]** Id. at 84, 58 S.E.2d at 603.

35. **[no remedy for mental suffering]** Id. at 89, 58 S.E.2d at 605.

36. **[no personal orders to pay money]** See ch. 1 part B.2 at 17–18.

37. **[no preference over other creditors]** See ch. 3 part A.2.

5

Preliminary Relief

Far and away the most common occasions for irreparable injury opinions are motions for preliminary relief: temporary restraining orders,[1] preliminary injunctions,[2] receivers,[3] and the like.[4] These cases have almost nothing in common with the choice of remedy at final judgment. If they are thought of as a completely separate category, with a completely different meaning for "irreparable," the phrase "irreparable injury" can actually do some good here.

A. The Dominance of Preliminary Relief Cases

Opinions on motions for preliminary relief account for a large majority of the headnotes reciting the irreparable injury rule and its corollaries, but the headnote writers do not always note the distinction.[5] The frequency of such headnotes contributes to a misleading sense of the viability of the irreparable injury rule.

The West Key Number system gives a crude sense of the numerical dominance of opinions on preliminary relief. In choosing the ten Key Numbers used to draw the initial sample of cases for this book, I excluded the Key Numbers for preliminary injunctions. I excluded them because I did not want to be swamped with preliminary injunction cases. The ten numbers assigned to general statements of the irreparable injury rule contain only 661 entries from January 1980 to December 1989.[6] The two most precise subdivisions of Key Numbers on the irreparable injury rule as applied to preliminary injunctions contain 1,166 entries in the same decade.[7] Thus, there are nearly twice as many irreparable injury

110

headnotes under preliminary injunctions as under the irreparable injury rule generally.

This ratio actually understates the dominance of headnotes on preliminary relief. The preliminary relief entries are all from preliminary relief cases, save only for the possibility of occasional blunders by the digesters. But the general entries are not all from final judgments; many of these are also from preliminary relief cases. In our initial sample of 212 cases denying equitable relief, 54% of the federal cases and 30% of the state cases denied motions for preliminary injunctions or temporary restraining orders.[8] Thus it appears that in cases denying equitable relief—the only cases in which the irreparable injury rule might actually be applied—some 79% of all irreparable injury headnotes are from opinions denying motions for preliminary injunctions or temporary restraining orders. The calculation is explained in the note.[9]

These comparisons of Key Number entries are too crude to support precise calculations, and the number of headnotes is only a crude proxy for the number of cases. If it were feasible to actually count and classify all the cases, the proportion of preliminary injunction cases might be somewhat higher or lower than 79%. But 79% is indicative of the range. I am confident that a substantial majority of cases that deny injunctions and discuss the irreparable injury rule are preliminary relief cases.

B. Contrasting Permanent and Preliminary Relief

Something called the irreparable injury rule is thus very much alive at the stage of preliminary relief. But the rule that is alive here is very different from the rule that I claim is dead at final judgment.

The reasons for being cautious with preliminary relief are clear. The court must act without a full trial, sometimes on sketchy motion papers and affidavits. A preliminary order may inflict serious costs on a defendant who had little time to prepare a defense or to present all that he could have prepared.[10] Plaintiff faces similar procedural handicaps; that makes the proceeding more equal but not more reliable. Acting without a full presentation from either side and without time for reflection, the court is more likely to err.

Thus, the reason for sometimes refusing preliminary injunctions is neither reluctance to grant specific relief nor reluctance to grant equitable relief. The relevant policy is reluctance to grant preliminary relief. This point is most clearly demonstrated by contrasting the rule permitting preliminary injunctions with the rule forbidding preliminary substitutionary relief. The rule against preliminary damage awards is usually said to be absolute or nearly so.[11] This rule is sometimes explained as a corollary of the irreparable injury rule: if plaintiff seeks only money, damages after final judgment will be an adequate remedy.[12] That will sometimes be true, but not if plaintiff suffers severe financial hardship in the meantime.[13] In fact, the rule seems to be an unjustified artifact of the law-equity distinction. But whatever the reasons for the rule, and whatever the merits of those reasons, the fact is that courts often grant preliminary specific relief and almost never grant preliminary substitutionary relief. This pattern belies any general preference for substitutionary relief.

There is an important and little-recognized exception to the rule against preliminary awards of money. The exception consists of cases enjoining termination of a series of periodic payments.[14] Courts appear to think of these orders as true injunctions, and not as disguised damages. There is good reason for that characterization, although in this context the distinction is formal. The formal distinction does not seem to justify relieving irreparable injury in one set of cases and not the other. But the formal distinction may be sufficient to solve the problem of defendant's right to jury trial.

The formal distinction is this: an order to continue a stream of payments is specific relief that happens to be monetary. The payments are not compensation for some legal wrong done to plaintiff; they are not a substitute for some other entitlement now irretrievably lost. A monthly payment is the specific thing to which plaintiff claims entitlement. On a sufficient showing of probable entitlement and immediate need, courts will order defendants to continue the payments pending trial. In some contexts, such as welfare payments, recipients are entitled to a hearing before their benefits are terminated,[15] and preliminary injunctions are the only effective way to protect that right. But these cases have so far had little effect on the judicial unwillingness to order preliminary payments of damages pending trial.

In all contexts, reluctance to grant preliminary relief reduces the risk of error resulting from inadequate hearings and preliminary decisions. With respect to substitutionary relief, courts entirely avoid the risk by simply barring preliminary relief. With respect to specific relief, that solution is thought to impose intolerable costs on plaintiffs. But courts reduce the risk by granting preliminary relief cautiously. The flexible requirement that plaintiff post a bond further reduces the risk of error, but can not eliminate it.[16] Money from the bond may be an inadequate remedy for a wrongfully enjoined defendant, just as money damages are inadequate for plaintiff. Moreover, the bond requirement is often waived or reduced, because a serious bond requirement would be a substantial burden on most plaintiffs and an insuperable obstacle for many.[17]

The inevitable solution is a balancing test that takes account of the irreparable injury to plaintiff if preliminary relief is erroneously denied and the irreparable injury to defendant if preliminary relief is erroneously granted. I will consider disputes over the precise formulation of this test in part C of this chapter. But first, I want to consider in general terms the role of irreparable injury in motions for preliminary relief.

Irreparable injury figures prominently in the various formulations of the test for preliminary relief, but the term does not mean what it means at the permanent injunction stage. First, there is a temporal limitation that is obvious and uncontroversial: the only injury that counts is injury that cannot be prevented after a more complete hearing at the next stage of the litigation. There is no need to issue a temporary restraining order if the injury can be prevented by a preliminary injunction,[18] and no need to issue a preliminary injunction if the injury can be prevented by a permanent injunction.[19] This does not limit the meaning of irreparable injury; it specifies that only some irreparable injury counts.

More to the point, courts at the preliminary relief stage routinely find that damages will be an adequate remedy for injuries they would consider irreparable after a full trial.[20] Pending trial, plaintiff must sometimes accept damages even though he cannot use them to replace the specific thing he has lost,[21] and he must accept estimates of damage that would be considered too difficult to measure if a permanent injunction could avoid the need to measure them.[22]

A good example is the injunction ordering the National Football

League not to interfere with the transfer of the Raiders from Oakland to Los Angeles. The Ninth Circuit reversed a preliminary injunction for lack of irreparable injury.[23] It affirmed a permanent injunction without even discussing irreparable injury.[24] Both results are correct, although the preliminary injunction opinion does not fully state the arguments that make it correct.

The Los Angeles Coliseum Commission requested a preliminary injunction that would let the Raiders play in Los Angeles pending trial. There is no doubt that the injury shown at the preliminary injunction hearing would have been considered irreparable under the standards described in chapter 2. In the first place, damages could not be used to replace the specific thing the Coliseum was about to lose. If the preliminary injunction were denied, no professional football team would play in the Coliseum during the next two seasons, and no amount of damages would ever change that. The Ninth Circuit noted that the Coliseum had college football, that it would not go broke without the Raiders, and that it had not proved its allegation that delay would kill the deal permanently.[25]

These observations go to the severity and duration of the injury, and it is reasonable to balance them against defendants' interest in a full trial. But there is no pretense that the Coliseum would ever be fully restored to the position it would have occupied but for the wrong. But for the NFL's antitrust violation, the Coliseum would have had college football plus the Raiders, and it would have had the Raiders immediately instead of later. It is true that these losses were short-term, but for that period they were irreplaceable, and therefore irreparable.[26] An accurate explanation of the result would have been that doing without the Raiders for two seasons is an irreparable injury, but that this injury is not severe enough to justify a preliminary injunction in light of the costs to defendants, the uncertain probability of success on the merits, and the procedural values of a full trial.

The Coliseum also alleged financial losses that would be difficult to measure. The Coliseum alleged lost profits from ticket sales and concessions, lost market value and good will, and lost financing for stadium renovations. The court casually said that all of these were monetary injuries that could be remedied by damages.[27] The court did not explain how it planned to measure the damages.

If the court had thought about the problem, it could have argued that lost profits to a football stadium might be more easily measurable than lost profits to other kinds of businesses. Seating capacity and the number of games were known, and this provided a relatively certain starting point for calculation. Ticket prices, unsold seats, no-show rates, concession sales, and expenses could be estimated from the experience of other teams. The temporary loss of good will and market value would be irrelevant unless the Coliseum sold or refinanced before trial. The cost of delaying renovations would be harder to figure: construction costs could rise, interest rates could change, and renovations could change the seating capacity and support higher ticket prices for all events at the stadium. But none of these numbers would be wholly speculative; the court could measure these damages if it had to, and it eventually did.

But if liability were established, any court would issue the permanent injunction and let the Raiders move rather than litigate all these damage issues. If the issue were raised, a court would surely say the injury was irreparable because damages were too hard to measure. Temporary damages would be easier to estimate than permanent damages, but as events showed, even temporary damages gave lawyers plenty to argue over.

After liability was established, the court conducted a nine-month jury trial devoted solely to the damages suffered by the Coliseum and the Raiders during the two years the Raiders were prevented from moving to Los Angeles. The jury brought in a $4.9 million verdict for the Coliseum, which was trebled by the court and affirmed on appeal.[28] A separate verdict of $11.6 million for the Raiders was also trebled and affirmed, subject to remand for trial of an offsetting benefit issue. The published opinions do not indicate how much trial time was devoted to the separate claims of the Raiders and the Coliseum, but that allocation does not affect the analysis here. A preliminary injunction for the Coliseum would have eliminated most of the Raiders' damage trial as well, and even if analysis is limited to the Coliseum, the trial of its damages was plainly lengthy and burdensome.

The sheer burden of conducting this trial should be considered irreparable injury, although courts do not view it that way.[29] Moreover, in this case the Coliseum could recover its attorneys' fees under the antitrust laws.[30] But these damages were also hard to measure in the doctrinally relevant sense of accuracy. A jury can have only a hazy impression of the calculations presented in a nine-month damage trial, and the court would surely have upheld a wide range of verdicts.

The court did not inquire into the difficulty of proving damages when it ruled that there was no irreparable injury. The losses were financial, and at the preliminary injunction stage, that is generally enough to make damages seem adequate. Courts are, and should be, much more ambitious about measuring damages when the alternative is a preliminary injunction than when the alternative is a permanent injunction.

The Raiders' case is a clear illustration because the stakes were high enough to support separate appeals of the preliminary injunction, the permanent injunction, and the damage award. But there is nothing unusual about the two meanings of irreparable injury in the case.[31] It is almost universally true that courts are more willing to grant permanent injunctions than preliminary injunctions, and a common way to explain the results is to find no or insufficient irreparable injury at the preliminary injunction stage. Preliminary injunctions are hotly contested and often denied in substantive areas where all injury is irreparable and permanent injunctions are routine, such as intellectual property,[32] civil rights and civil liberties,[33] and environmental law.[34]

This pattern is so widespread that it is difficult to find recent permanent injunction cases that seriously discuss irreparable injury. The principal cases on the issue in my casebook date from 1911 and 1944,[35] because I did not find a more recent case with an opinion I considered adequate for teaching purposes.

It is not just courts, but also defendants, that tend to ignore the irreparable injury rule at the permanent injunction stage. At the preliminary injunction stage, many defendants still expect to win. They expect never to pay the damages that will accrue pending trial, and the benefits of defeating the preliminary injunction motion outweigh the risk of letting the damages accrue. But if defendant loses on the merits and defeats the permanent injunction only on irreparable injury grounds, she will have to pay permanent damages. Some defendants may prefer to pay the damages and continue with profitable or spiteful violations of the law, but most will not. So most defendants have no reason to raise the irreparable injury rule at the permanent injunction stage. Those who do raise it have little prospect of success unless the court sees some substantial and legitimate advantage to letting defendant continue its conduct and pay for the privilege.

In the Raiders case, defendants pressed a venue objection in their appeal from the permanent injunction.[36] They did not argue irreparable injury or the choice between damages and injunction. Consider the minuscule chances that a complex antitrust case would be retried because of a venue objection; consider that in this very case, defendants had won their appeal from the preliminary injunction by arguing irreparable injury; and then consider the implications of the decision to argue venue instead of irreparable injury in the appeal from the permanent injunction. Defendants had no interest in winning on irreparable injury grounds, and no chance of doing so.

The irreparable injury rule has largely died at the permanent injunction stage because it serves no purpose there; it has teeth at the preliminary injunction stage because it does serve a purpose there. At the preliminary injunction stage, the merits are unresolved, plaintiff may be undeserving, and no remedy at all remains a possible outcome. Defendant has legitimate interests in a full hearing and in freedom to act in ways not yet shown to be unlawful. These interests coincide with the court's interest in avoiding error and being fair to both sides. These interests may also coincide with less savory interests, such as defendant's desire to use delay and litigation costs to force a cheap settlement. But the court may not be able to screen out such interests until it hears the merits.

At the permanent injunction stage, the merits are resolved, defendant is a known wrongdoer, and the court has eliminated the option of no remedy at all. Now the choice is between damages and injunction, and in most cases, neither the court nor defendant has any interest in damages. Moreover, the court has heard the merits and is now in position to assess the legitimacy of any reasons defendant does offer for preferring damages. Where damages are a better remedy, the court can usually explain why. But as we shall see in later chapters, it may also invoke the irreparable injury rule.

C. The Standard for Preliminary Injunctions

It is plain that courts are balancing interests in the preliminary injunction cases, and there is broad agreement on the basic elements that weigh in the balance. But neither courts nor commentators have been able to agree on a single formulation of a balancing test. Minor variations in the statement of the rule, if subjected to careful and literal analysis, turn out to have surprising implications.[37] I explore the problem here because it is important and controversial in itself, and because it further reveals the implicit judicial conception of irreparable injury.

Some formulations of the standard for preliminary injunctions simply list the factors to be considered without specifying the relationship among them.[38] A larger number of cases state the unrealistic standard that plaintiff must prove each factor separately.[39] The traditional list of factors is plaintiff's probability of success on the merits, the threat of irreparable injury to plaintiff, the balance of hardships between the parties, and the public interest. More sophisticated courts have refined these factors into "a sliding scale in which the required degree of irreparable harm increases as the probability of success decreases."[40] The implicit logic of this standard is that the risk of harm to each side is discounted by the probability that that harm is legally justified—by the probability that that side will eventually lose on the merits.

That approach leads directly to John Leubsdorf's formulation: that courts "should aim to minimize the probable irreparable loss of rights caused by errors incident to hasty decision."[41] Three courts adopted Leubsdorf's proposal in the first five years after its appearance.[42] But Leubsdorf drew little reaction until Judge Posner adopted his standard and reduced it to a mathematical formula:[43]

Grant the preliminary injunction if but only if

$$P \times H_p > (1 - P) \times H_d$$

where P is the probability that plaintiff will succeed on the merits, H_p is the irreparable harm that plaintiff will suffer if the preliminary injunction is denied, and H_d is the irreparable harm that defendant will suffer if the preliminary injunction is granted. Despite the algebraic notation, the math involved is simple arithmetic. One does not solve this equation for an unknown variable; instead, one assigns values to each variable, performs two multiplications, and compares the products. All the intellectual or judicial work is in the assignment of values.

Perhaps because it was Posner, perhaps because of the math, this opinion produced a strong hostile reaction.[44] Some of the same critics have schizophrenically claimed both that Posner's formula is a "wholesale revision"[45] or "bold rewriting of preliminary injunction law,"[46] and that it is merely a distillation that changed nothing.[47] The attack seems addressed more to the illusion of quantification, or to the scope of appellate review,[48] than to the substance of the standard.

None of the critics has offered a clear hypothetical in which she thinks a judge would err by minimizing the risk of erroneous irreparable harm. Linda Silberman's thoughtful article suggests an abstract category of such cases: where plaintiff has only a tiny chance of success, but the balance of harms is so overwhelming that a preliminary injunction would minimize the risk of erroneous harm even though the injunction is very likely erroneous. She notes that a literal reading of traditional formulations would deny preliminary relief in such cases.[49]

It is hard to decide whether a preliminary injunction should issue in such cases without a set of facts that actually present the issue. What kind of case might present such an overwhelming balance of harms? I assume that in death penalty litigation, she would stay the execution pending the first appeal even if the appeal were frivolous. It is hard to imagine a plausible civil case with similar stakes and little probability of success; the whole category may be empty. But if there were such a case, it is hard to see why such devastating harm should be inflicted before judgment.

Both Posner and Leubsdorf offered their approach as an analytic framework; neither expected courts to actually quantify the variables.[50] Some critics dismissed these disclaimers as "disingenuous" or ineffectual;[51] one went on to insist that the inevitable truth of the disclaimers rendered the whole approach "fraudulent."[52]

My own judgment is that the Leubsdorf–Posner formula is what they said it was: a distillation of the cases intended to guide analysis. It is a helpful distillation in one important way: it focuses attention on the point of the balancing process and specifies the relationship among the factors to be balanced.

It is a misleading distillation in another way. It greatly oversimplifies the variables that go into the balance, including the variable of irreparable injury. The problem is not just that the variables cannot be quantified in fact. The problem is more fundamental: these variables cannot be conceptualized even in theory as having discrete values that could be represented by points on a graph or by single numbers in an equation. Rather, these variables stand for ranges of possible developments, with the probabilities changing at every point in the range.

Thus, the court may not face a simple binary choice of preliminary injunction or no preliminary injunction. There is often a range of plausible preliminary injunctions, more or less protective of plaintiff and more or less harmful to defendant. Each of these possible injunctions could be subjected to a range of possible conditions and a range of bond requirements.[53]

Similarly, the outcome of the lawsuit is not a simple binary event, such that plaintiff's probability of success is P and defendant's probability of success is $1 - P$. Plaintiff often succeeds in part. The real question is not probability of success on some abstraction called "the merits," or the probability that plaintiff will prevail on some issue of ultimate liability. What matters is the probability that the preliminary relief to be granted will be a part of the relief to be awarded at final judgment, or at least not inconsistent with the rights to be determined by the final judgment.

The two variables for irreparable harm are even more complicated. The irreparable harm that is feared if the injunction is granted or denied is not a simple binary event. That is, the court often cannot say that a certain harm will happen and then try to quantify its value. Rather, the magnitude of possible harms varies over a range, with a probability distribution that also varies over the range, and different preliminary injunctions will reduce that probability by different amounts.

Finally, and most important to the larger thesis of this book, the characterization of possible harms as reparable or irreparable is not a simple binary classification. The Leubsdorf–Posner formula implicitly assumes that all harm can be characterized as either reparable or irreparable, and that only irreparable harm counts. Thus, judges should identify the irreparable harms and consider only those. I suspect that most remedies scholars have shared these implicit assumptions; I confess that I shared them. I recognized that "irreparable" meant something quite different at the preliminary injunction stage than at the permanent injunction stage, but I did not think to question the assumption that each discrete harm either counted or did not count under the appropriate definition.

But when I tried to list the harms that count as irreparable in a motion for preliminary injunction, I realized that no such list is possible, and that this approach to the problem cannot explain the cases. Harms vary over a range of irreparability, and this range is partly independent of their variation over a range of severity and over a range of likelihoods. Stated in terms of adequacy, the remedy at final judgment may be slightly inadequate (only a little bit worse than preliminary relief), seriously inadequate, nearly worthless, or something in between. Implicitly, the degree of irreparability is a separate variable in the balancing test for preliminary injunctions.

Consider loss of money, or temporary loss of opportunities to make money. These harms are generally not a ground for preliminary relief, even if the damages will be difficult to measure. Even if large sums are at stake, as in the Raiders' case, the difficulties of measurement are not generally thought to justify a preliminary injunction.

But this generalization about most cases is not a rule in all cases. Courts do not simply say that the difficulty of measuring temporary loss of income does not count at the preliminary injunction stage. We could not entirely omit such harm from Posner's equation without overruling many cases. Consider preliminary injunctions in intellectual property cases. Preliminary injunctions are certainly less available than permanent injunctions in such cases, but they are common when plaintiff shows sufficient likelihood of success on the merits.[54] The harm to be avoided is lost income, and this harm is irreparable because the damages will be hard to measure. So if the difficulties of measurement are great enough, and the probability of success is high enough, courts will grant preliminary injunctions to avoid the necessity of measuring temporary damages. The difficulty of measuring commercial damages counts, even at the preliminary injunction stage. But it counts for less than other kinds of irreparable harm.

Other kinds of harm are more irreparable. If a loss of property or a loss of business or employment opportunities will become irretrievable before final judgment, damages will not be even an approximate remedy. We therefore find Judge Posner distinguishing between a business that might be destroyed before trial and a business that will lose most of its profits pending trial.[55] Damages from either would be hard to measure, but the permanent loss of the business is a qualitatively greater deviation from full specific relief than the loss of interim profits. If the business can be saved with permanent specific relief, and if the interim losses can be approximately compensated with damages, then the problem reduces to the difficulty of measuring commercial damages, and the plaintiff's interest in preliminary rather than permanent relief is much weaker.

Even temporary loss of civil liberties is irretrievable, and thus a common ground for preliminary relief. The right to speak or vote or worship after trial does not replace the right to speak or vote or worship pending trial, and damages for temporary loss of such rights are not even approximate compensation. Courts express this view in the statement that even temporary loss of First Amendment rights is irreparable.[56] I take such statements to mean that the degree of irreparability is very high, so that the risk of such a loss weighs heavily in favor of preliminary relief, even though the severity of the loss is not great because the loss is of short duration.

All of these complexities can be incorporated into the Leubs-dorf–Posner formulation if it is considered merely as an analytic framework. Courts deciding whether to grant preliminary relief should try to minimize the risk of legally unjustified irreparable harm, considering the probability that the preliminary relief will be consistent with the ultimate rights of the parties, and considering the likelihood, severity, and degree of irreparability of the harm that plaintiff may suffer if preliminary relief is erroneously denied and of the harm that defendant may suffer if preliminary relief is erroneously granted, recognizing that each of these variables extends over a range of possibilities.

This rewriting of the Leubsdorf–Posner formulation still focuses attention on the ultimate goal—to minimize the risk of legally unjustified irreparable harm. But my reformulation dispels any illusions of simplicity. I assume that my reformulation could still be modeled in an equation, but it could not be done in the simple arithmetic of Posner's opinion. The probability, severity, and degree of irreparability of harm are continuous variables, partly interdependent. An equation to model them would require at least calculus, and so would be of little help to most judges even as an analytic framework or a guide to intuitive balancing. And assigning numerical values to these complex variables would be even more arbitrary than assigning numerical values to the seemingly simple variables in Posner's original equation.

What judges can do is what they do in any balancing test: they balance the relevant factors in qualitative terms. It helps to clearly identify the relevant factors and to specify the relationship among the factors and the criteria for balancing. Judges can think in terms of strong case, weak case, wholly uncertain case; severe harm, some harm, no harm; harm that can be fixed in-kind after judgment and harm that can never be fixed in-kind; harm for which substitutionary relief is imperfect, seriously inadequate, or grossly inadequate; and so on.

Recognizing degrees of irreparability or inadequacy could reunite the preliminary and permanent relief cases, but only with a sharp change in judicial rhetoric. Courts could recognize that even in preliminary injunction cases nearly all injury is irreparable, citing the precedents from permanent injunction cases. This would require them also to recognize that a bare finding of irreparable injury helps the plaintiff little. The real variable is the degree of irreparability, and that goes into a balancing test along with the severity and likelihood of injury and the likelihood of success on the merits.

Notes on Preliminary Relief

1. [temporary restraining orders] See Fed. R. Civ. Proc. 65(b) (temporary restraining order without notice may be granted only to prevent immediate irreparable harm and efforts to give notice have failed); Carroll v. President of Princess Anne, 393 U.S. 175, 180–85 (1968) (constitution requires notice, if notice is possible, before temporary restraining order against speech, whether or not speech would be substantively protected by First Amendment); Bd. of Educ. v. Parlor, 85 Ill. 2d 397, 401, 424 N.E.2d 1152, 1153 (1981) ("injunction is extraordinary remedy requiring urgent and extreme circumstances before it may be issued without notice").

2. [preliminary injunctions] See Fed. R. Civ. Proc. 65(a)(1) (no preliminary injunction without notice); Sampson v. Murray, 415 U.S. 61, 88–92 (1974) (refusing a preliminary injunction to reinstate a probationary civil service employee, holding that temporary loss of income and financial hardship is not irreparable injury in that context); Bell v. Olson, 424 N.W.2d 829, 833 (Minn. App. 1988) (no preliminary injunction against cancellation of land-sale contract, where plaintiff could avoid cancellation by paying $750); Barnstone v. Robinson, 678 S.W.2d 562, 563 (Tex. App. 1984) (no preliminary injunction against eviction pending construction of lease, where plaintiffs could avoid eviction by paying higher rent demanded by defendants).

3. [receivers] See Fed. R. Civ. Proc. 66 (providing for appointment of receivers in federal court); Sires v. Luke, 544 F. Supp. 1155, 1161–62 (S.D. Ga. 1982) (receiver is "one of the harshest remedies" known to the law, "allowable only in extreme cases"); Dixie-Land Iron & Metal Co. v. Piedmont Iron & Metal Co., 235 Ga. 503, 220 S.E.2d 130 (1975) (affirming appointment of receiver to manage assets of deadlocked partnership); Douglas Laycock, *Modern American Remedies* 738–54 (Little, Brown 1985).

4. [other preliminary orders] See Unisys Corp. v. Dataware Prod., Inc., 848 F.2d 311, 314 (1st Cir. 1988) (order forbidding transfer of assets except in ordinary course of business, and requiring that audited financial statements be supplied to court, described by plaintiff as "equitable attachment," treated by court as preliminary injunction).

5. [misleading headnotes] See Lewis v. S.S. Baune, 534 F.2d 1115 (5th Cir. 1976) (headnote 15); Citizens Comm. v. Volpe, 297 F. Supp. 804 (S.D.N.Y. 1969) (headnote 8); Carson v. Ross, 509 N.E.2d 239 (Ind. App. 1987) (headnote 2); Lambert v. State, 468 N.E.2d 1384 (Ind. App. 1984) (headnote 10); Barnstone v. Robinson, 678 S.W.2d 562 (Tex. App. 1984) (headnote 4); System Concepts, Inc. v. Dixon, 669 P.2d 421 (Utah 1983) (headnote 1).

6. [general Key Numbers] These Key Numbers were Injunctions §§ 14–19, Equity §§ 43, 45–46, and Specific Performance § 5. The count was made on Westlaw in April 1990, with the search restricted to dates after 1979 and before 1990.

7. [preliminary relief Key Numbers] These Key Numbers are Injunctions §§ 138.6 and 138.9 since early 1985, and Injunctions §§ 136(3) and 137(2) before then.

8. [preliminary relief in sample] The sample is described in ch. 1 part B.5. Karen Patton Bogle classified the cases into denials of permanent relief and denials of preliminary relief.

9. [calculation] This calculation, shown in the table at 125, applies the proportion of preliminary relief cases in our original sample of state and federal cases to the universe of cases digested under the same Key Numbers in the 1980s.

This calculation makes several assumptions that are not a source of scholarly pride. The justification for the assumptions is that the resulting number is offered

	State Cases	Federal Cases	All Cases
(1) Headnotes in Preliminary Relief Key Numbers, 1980–1989	367	799	1166
(2) Headnotes in General Key Numbers, 1980–1989	463	198	661
(3) Percentage of preliminary relief cases in sample from General Key Numbers	30%	54%	37%
(4) Estimated preliminary relief headnotes under General Key Numbers (line 2 × line 3)	139	107	278
(5) Estimated headnotes from preliminary relief cases, 1980–1989 (line 1 + line 4)	506	906	1444
(6) Total headnotes, 1980–1989 (line 1 + line 2)	830	997	1827
(7) Estimated percentage of headnotes from preliminary relief cases, 1980–1989 (line 5 divided by line 6)	61%	91%	79%

only to suggest a general order of magnitude; nothing in my argument turns on any claim of precision. Some of these assumptions could be eliminated by counting more cases, but the marginal increase in precision is not worth the large increase in labor. An analysis of the assumptions and their likely effect follows.

This calculation assumes that the cases denying injunctions among the 661 cases from 1980–1989 (line 2) are similar to the original sample of 212 denials drawn from the same Key Numbers. The sample of state cases was drawn from 1980–1985; the sample of federal cases was drawn from 1968–1985. This difference arose because there are many more state cases than federal cases.

Thus, the calculation assumes that the error introduced by the difference in time periods is not substantial. Even if the flow of litigation did not change, digesting practices at the West Publishing Company might have changed. The number of cases digested under the Key Numbers for preliminary injunctions decreased sharply beginning in about 1985. This may reflect greater accuracy in classification and a reduction in the number of preliminary relief cases turning on other issues but digested under the Key Numbers for irreparable injury. It may reflect a reduction in duplicative digesting in both the general and preliminary Key Numbers. Or it may reflect an actual decline in the proportion of reported preliminary litigation. The first two explanations, which seem more likely, would mean that the calculation tends to overestimate the proportion of preliminary relief cases. The third explanation would not affect the accuracy of the calculation for the decade, but it would mean that a calculation confined to data since 1985 would more accurately reflect the current situation. Even with analysis restricted to the smaller proportion of preliminary injunction headnotes after 1985, it remains the case that a majority of irreparable injury headnotes come from preliminary injunction cases.

This calculation also assumes that the proportion of opinions denying injunctions is similar in both the general and preliminary relief Key Numbers. If, as seems likely, the proportion of denials is higher in the cases digested under preliminary relief Key Numbers, then the calculation tends to underestimate the proportion of preliminary relief cases among denials. This error would tend to offset the error described in the previous paragraph.

Finally, because each case in the original sample was examined individually, multiple headnotes from the same case were discarded, and the case was counted only once. The 1,827 cases from 1980 to 1989 were not examined individually for this purpose, so multiple headnotes from the same case are included. This calculation necessarily assumes that this source of error does not sharply change the result.

10. [short notice and compressed hearing] Thornburgh v. Am. College of Obstetricians, 476 U.S. 747, 755–56 (1986) (preliminary injunction is "issued on a procedure less stringent than that which prevails at the subsequent trial on the merits"); Univ. of Tex. v. Camenisch, 451 U.S. 390, 395 (1981) (preliminary injunctions are granted in "haste," "on the basis of procedures that are less formal and evidence that is less complete than in a trial"); Am. Civil Liberties Union v. City of St. Charles, 794 F.2d 265, 269 (7th Cir. 1986) (preliminary injunction requires decision "on an incomplete, because hastily compiled, record"); Enercons Va., Inc. v. Am. Security Bank, 720 F.2d 28, 28 (D.C. Cir. 1983) (hearing held two hours after notice to defendant); IT Corp. v. County of Imperial, 35 Cal. 3d 63, 73 n.6, 672 P.2d 121, 128 n.6, 196 Cal. Rptr. 715, 722, n.6 (1983) (preliminary injunction standard must protect "defendants who may ultimately succeed at trial from the severe or irreparable harm which a preliminary injunction may cause"); Packaging Indus. Group, Inc. v. Cheney, 380 Mass. 609, 617, 405 N.E.2d 106, 111 (1980) ("preliminary injunction must be granted or denied after an abbreviated presentation of the facts and the law"); New Castle Orthopedic Assoc. v. Burns, 481 Pa. 460, 463, 392 A.2d 1383, 1384–85 (1978) ("preliminary injunction is somewhat like a judgment and execution before trial").

11. [no preliminary damage awards] See Enercons Va., Inc. v. Am. Security Bank, 720 F.2d 28 (D.C. Cir. 1983) (reversing tro ordering defendant to pay check); In re Arthur Treacher's Franchisee Litig., 689 F.2d 1137, 1144–45 (3d Cir. 1982) (reversing a preliminary award of past due royalties, and finding no authority to support such an award); Schlosser v. Commonwealth Edison Co., 250 F.2d 478, 480–81 (7th Cir. 1958) (refusing preliminary injunction ordering defendant to pay retirement annuity); Sims v. Stuart, 291 F. 707, 707–08 (S.D.N.Y. 1922) (opinion by Learned Hand) (refusing preliminary injunction ordering return of converted money); Compute-A-Call, Inc. v. Tolleson, 285 Ark. 355, 687 S.W.2d 129 (1985) (reversing temporary injunction ordering payment of money); Conway v. Stratton, 434 So.2d 1197, 1198–99 (La. App. 1983) (refusing preliminary injunction to pay plaintiff's share of partnership assets). Compare Friends for All Children, Inc. v. Lockheed Aircraft Corp., 746 F.2d 816, 830–31 (D.C. Cir. 1984) (preliminary injunction ordering payment of money after final determination of liability but before final determination of amount).

12. [if damages only, later is adequate] In re Arthur Treacher's Franchisee Litig., 689 F.2d 1137, 1145–46 (3d Cir. 1982); Conway v. Stratton, 434 So.2d 1197, 1198–99 (La. App. 1983).

13. [irreparable harm while awaiting damages] See Rhonda S. Wasserman, *Eq-*

uity Transformed: Preliminary Injunctions to Require the Payment of Money, 70
B.U. L. Rev. — (forthcoming 1990) (arguing that personal injury plaintiffs who
need money for medical care suffer irreparable injury).
   14. **[enjoining termination of payments]** See cases cited in ch. 1 note 56. Each
of those cases granted a preliminary injunction.
   15. **[right to pretermination hearing]** Goldberg v. Kelly, 397 U.S. 254 (1970).
   16. **[bonds a partial solution]** Bond is required by Fed. R. Civ. Proc. 65(c) and
similar state rules. See generally Dan B. Dobbs, *Should Security Be Required as
a Pre-Condition to Provisional Injunctive Relief?* 52 N.C. L. Rev. 1091 (1974).
   17. **[bonds burden plaintiffs]** See City of Atlanta v. Metro. Atlanta Rapid Transit
Auth., 636 F.2d 1084, 1094 (5th Cir. 1981) (waiving bond in public interest litigation); Laycock, *Remedies* at 431 (cited in note 3) ("a truly mandatory bonding
rule would make preliminary relief generally unavailable in civil rights, environmental, and consumer litigation, to workers in labor litigation, and, in general, to
nonwealthy plaintiffs").
   18. **[temporal limitation on relevant injury]** G & J Parking Co. v. City of Chicago, 168 Ill. App. 3d 382, 387, 522 N.E.2d 774, 777 (1988) (to justify temporary
restraining order without notice, it must appear that immediate and irreparable
injury will result before notice can be served and a hearing had).
   19. **[temporal limitation on relevant injury]** Public Serv. Co. v. Town of W.
Newbury, 835 F.2d 380, 382–83 (1st Cir. 1987) (no need to consider effect of
defendant's wrong on plaintiff's licensing proceeding, where claim for permanent
injunction against defendant can be decided before licensing proceeding will be
decided); Roland Mach. Co. v. Dresser Indus., Inc., 749 F.2d 380, 386 (7th Cir.
1984) ("only if he will suffer irreparable harm in the interim—that is, harm that
cannot be prevented or fully rectified by the final judgment after trial—can he get
a preliminary injunction"); Canal Auth. v. Callaway, 489 F.2d 567, 574, 577 (5th
Cir. 1974) (draining of lake not irreparable injury where it can be refilled after
judgment); Cohen v. Bd. of Supervisors, 40 Cal. 3d 277, 286, 707 P.2d 840, 844,
219 Cal. Rptr. 467, 471 (1985) (second factor in decision on preliminary injunction
is "interim harm"); Sun Oil Co. v. Whitaker, 424 S.W.2d 216, 218 (Tex. 1968)
(plaintiff seeking preliminary injunction must show "probable right on final trial
to the relief he seeks and probable injury in the interim"). See also Packaging
Indus. Group, Inc. v. Cheney, 380 Mass. 609, 617 n.10, 405 N.E.2d 106, 111 n.10
(1980) ("risk that a party will suffer irreparable harm during the time between the
hearing on the preliminary injunction and final adjudication on the merits may be
minimized by consolidating" the two hearings).
   20. **[more stringent meaning of irreparable]** Loretangeli v. Critelli, 853 F.2d 186,
196 n.17 (3d Cir. 1988) (defendant's insolvency makes monetary damages irreparable at final judgment, but not at preliminary injunction); Public Serv. Co. v.
Town of W. Newbury, 835 F.2d 380, 381–83 (1st Cir. 1987) (removal of utility
poles, treated as interference with easement; court emphasizes difference between
preliminary and permanent injunctions); Williams v. State Univ., 635 F. Supp.
1243, 1247–48 (E.D.N.Y. 1986) (mental anguish and economic hardship from race
discrimination in employment); Columbia Gas Transmission Corp. v. Larry H.
Wright, Inc., 443 F. Supp. 14, 24–25 (S.D. Ohio 1977) (UCC's liberal standard
for specific performance should not be applied at preliminary injunction stage);
Miller v. Am. Tel. & Tel. Corp., 344 F. Supp. 344, 347–49 (E.D. Pa. 1972) (refusing

to control conduct of corporate officers by preliminary injunction, on ground that internal corporate mechanisms and derivative suit for breach of duty would be "clearly adequate" remedies); Gonzalez v. Benoit, 424 So.2d 957, 959 (Fla. App. 1983) (eviction from apartment); Bd. of Educ. v. Bd. of Educ., 112 Ill. App. 3d 212, 217–19, 445 N.E.2d 464, 469–71 (1983) (transfer of students to another school district, resulting in loss of state education aid); Levitt Homes Inc. v. Old Farm Homeowner's Ass'n, 111 Ill. App. 3d 300, 307–08, 444 N.E.2d 194, 204–05 (1982) (violation of restrictive covenant); Mich. Council 25, AFSCME v. County of Wayne, 136 Mich. App. 21, 26–27, 355 N.W.2d 624, 627 (1984) (loss of cost of living adjustment to plaintiffs' pay); Doster v. Estes, 126 Mich. App. 497, 501, 507–10, 337 N.W.2d 549, 551, 554–55 (1983) (race discrimination in employment).

21. [money adequate for irreplaceable losses] Chisom v. Roemer, 853 F.2d 1186, 1188–89 (5th Cir. 1988) (judicial election in alleged violation of Voting Rights Act); James A. Merrit & Sons v. Marsh, 791 F.2d 328, 331 (4th Cir. 1986) (temporary suspension of eligibility to bid on government contracts); Moteles v. Univ. of Pa., 730 F.2d 913, 919 (3d Cir. 1984) (sleep disruption and inability to attend Spanish class); Canal Auth. v. Callaway, 489 F.2d 567, 574, 577 (5th Cir. 1974) (draining of lake); Shodeen v. Chicago Title & Trust Co., 162 Ill. App. 3d 667, 672–75, 515 N.E.2d 1339, 1343–45 (1987) (breach of alleged duty to convey title to real estate); In re Marriage of Sherwin, 123 Ill. App. 3d 748, 752–55, 463 N.E.2d 755, 758–60 (1984) (removal of art objects, paintings, crystal, sterling silver place settings, and other marital property); Arbour v. Total CATV, Inc., 400 So.2d 1155, 1156 (La. App. 1981) (buried cable on plaintiff's land); Charter Medical Corp. v. Miller, 554 S.W.2d 220, 222–23 (Tex. Civ. App. 1977) (temporary suspension of right to practice podiatry in defendant's hospital; other hospitals were available).

22. [hard to measure damages are adequate] Modern Computer Systems, Inc. v. Modern Banking Systems, Inc., 871 F.2d 734, 737–38 (8th Cir. 1989) (lost profits; termination of franchise); Frank's GMC Truck Center, Inc. v. Gen'l Motors Corp., 847 F.2d 100 (3d Cir. 1988) (lost profits; termination of franchise; permanent injunction might also have been denied to avoid forcing GM to stay in a business it wanted to abandon); Baker's Aid, A Div. of M. Raubvogel Co. v. Hussmann Foodservice Co., 830 F.2d 13 (2d Cir. 1987) (lost profits; covenant not to compete); Proimos v. Fair Auto. Repair, Inc. 808 F.2d 1273, 1277 (7th Cir. 1987) (lost profits; competition by former franchisees); Design Pak, Inc. v. Secretary of the Treasury, 801 F.2d 525 (1st Cir. 1985) (lost profits; award of government contract to competitor); Fox Valley Harvestore, Inc. v. A.O. Smith Harvestore Prod., Inc., 545 F.2d 1096 (7th Cir. 1976) (lost profits; termination of franchise); Samjens Partners I v. Burlington Indus., Inc., 663 F. Supp. 614, 621 (S.D.N.Y. 1987) (proceeds to shareholders from fraudulent tender offer); Envirogas Inc. v. Walker Energy Partners, 641 F. Supp. 1339, 1342–44 (W.D.N.Y. 1986) (termination of contract to operate 940 oil and gas wells); Kamakazi Music Corp. v. Robbins Music Corp., 534 F. Supp. 57, 68 (S.D.N.Y. 1981) (copyright infringement; plaintiff argued that damages would be impossible to measure); Fuller v. Highway Truck Drivers & Helpers Local 107, 228 F. Supp. 287, 290 (E.D. Pa. 1964) ("The inconvenience entailed by earlier rising and less desirable trip assignments . . . has never been regarded as a type of damage immeasurable in dollars. Courts daily award damages for pain, suffering and far more serious inconveniences."), aff'd on other grounds, 428 F.2d 503 (3d Cir. 1970); Delcon Group, Inc. v. N. Trust Corp., 159 Ill. App.

3d 275, 280, 512 N.E.2d 378, 381–82 (1987) (foreclosure on accounts receivable, cutting off cash flow to business); Allstate Amusement Co. v. Pasinato, 96 Ill. App. 3d 306, 308–10, 421 N.E.2d 374, 375–76 (1981) (lost profits from diversion of employer's business opportunity).

23. **[preliminary injunction reversed]** Los Angeles Memorial Coliseum Comm'n v. Nat'l Football League, 634 F.2d 1197, 1202–03 (9th Cir. 1980).

24. **[permanent injunction affirmed]** Los Angeles Memorial Coliseum Comm'n v. Nat'l Football League, 726 F.2d 1381 (9th Cir. 1984).

25. **[minimizing Coliseum's injury]** 634 F.2d 1197, 1202–03 (9th Cir. 1980).

26. **[short-term losses]** Carson v. Am. Brands, Inc., 450 U.S. 79, 88–89 (1981) (delay in receiving promised transfer or promotion to better job might cause "serious, perhaps, irreparable harm"); Elrod v. Burns, 427 U.S. 347, 373 (1976) ("loss of First Amendment freedoms, for even minimal periods of time, unquestionably constitutes irreparable injury") (plurality opinion); Jacobsen v. U.S. Postal Serv., 812 F.2d 1151, 1155 (9th Cir. 1987) (removing newspaper racks from public sidewalk); Vogel v. Am. Soc'y of Appraisers, 744 F.2d 598, 600 (7th Cir. 1984) (suspension from professional society); Heublein, Inc. v. Fed. Trade Comm'n, 539 F. Supp. 123, 127 (D. Conn. 1982) (delay of tender offer); Hatcher v. Graddick, 509 N.E.2d 258, 260 (Ind. App. 1987) (unauthorized reduction in court's budget; legal remedy would be delayed and therefore ineffective); Van Buren Public School Dist. v. Wayne County Circuit Judge, 61 Mich. App. 6, 17, 232 N.W.2d 278, 284 (1975) (administrative remedy was inadequate because it "was not *immediately available*, a primary consideration in passing on the adequacy of any legal remedy" (emphasis in original)).

27. **[monetary losses are reparable]** *Los Angeles Coliseum*, 634 F.2d 1197, 1202 (9th Cir. 1980).

28. **[Coliseum's damages]** Los Angeles Memorial Coliseum Comm'n v. Nat'l Football League, 791 F.2d 1356, 1359 (9th Cir. 1986).

29. **[litigation costs not irreparable]** Renegotiation Bd. v. Bannercraft Clothing Co., 415 U.S. 1, 24 (1974) ("mere litigation expense, even substantial and unrecoupable cost, does not constitute irreparable injury"); Kaiser v. Wolf, 18 Pa. D. & C. 3d 555 (Pa. Com. Pl. 1981) (burden of counting trees to establish damages is not irreparable injury justifying specific performance of contract to sell standing timber); cases cited in ch. 6 note 65. But see Restatement (Second) of Torts § 944 comment f (1979) (courts should consider cost of litigating damages in considering adequacy of damage remedy).

30. **[attorneys' fees for antitrust plaintiffs]** 15 U.S.C. § 15 (1988).

31. **[two meanings of irreparable]** For another one-case example, compare ABA Distr., Inc. v. Adolph Coors Co., 661 F.2d 712 (8th Cir. 1981) (reversing preliminary injunction against termination of beer distributorship); with ABA Distr., Inc. v. Adolph Coors Co., 542 F. Supp. 1272, 1293 (W.D. Mo. 1982) (granting permanent injunction, and interpreting court of appeals' opinion to require that result if plaintiff succeeded on the merits).

32. **[intellectual property]** Capital Tool & Mfg. Co. v. Maschinenfabrik Herkules, 837 F.2d 171, 172–73 (4th Cir. 1988) (trade secrets; court emphasizes difference between preliminary and permanent injunction); Calvin Klein Cosmetics Corp. v. Lenox Labs., Inc., 815 F.2d 500, 505 (8th Cir. 1987) (trademark infringement; irreparable injury presumed, but only if plaintiff shows probable success on the merits); Citibank, N.A. v. Citytrust, 756 F.2d 273, 276 (2d Cir. 1985) (trademark infringement; delay in seeking relief may "indicate an absence of the kind of irreparable harm required to support a preliminary injunction," even though it does "not rise to the level of laches and thereby bar a permanent injunction"); Interox Am. v. PPG Indus., Inc., 736 F.2d 194, 202 (5th Cir. 1984) (trade secrets); GTE Corp. v. Williams, 731 F.2d 676, 678–79 (10th Cir. 1984) (trademark infringement; court emphasizes difference between preliminary and permanent relief); Signode Corp. v. Weld-Loc Systems, Inc., 700 F.2d 1108, 1111–15 (7th Cir. 1983) (patent infringement); Am. Metro. Enterprises, Inc. v. Warner Bros. Records, Inc., 389 F.2d 903, 905 (2d Cir. 1968) (copyright of musical compositions); Ecologix, Inc. v. Fansteel, Inc., 676 F. Supp. 1374, 1383–84 (N.D. Ill. 1988) (misuse of confidential information); Long Island-Airports Limousine Serv. Corp. v. N.Y. Airport Serv. Corp., 641 F. Supp. 1005, 1008–10 (E.D.N.Y. 1986) (trademark infringement); Kamakazi Music Corp. v. Robbins Music Corp., 534 F. Supp. 57, 68 (S.D.N.Y. 1981) (copyright); Packaging Indus. Group, Inc. v. Cheney, 380 Mass. 609, 617, 405 N.E.2d 106, 114 (1980) (trade secrets); Tephguard Corp. v. Great N. Am. Indus., Inc., 571 S.W.2d 554 (Tex. Civ. App. 1978) (trademark infringement).

33. [civil rights and civil liberties] Marxe v. Jackson, 833 F.2d 1121, 1125–28 (3d Cir. 1987) (retaliation against plaintiff in employment discrimination case); Holt v. Cont'l Group, Inc., 708 F.2d 87, 90–92 (2d Cir. 1983) (retaliation against plaintiff in employment discrimination case); Rushia v. Town of Ashburnham, 701 F.2d 7 (1st Cir. 1983) (freedom of speech); Gleaves v. Waters, 175 Cal. App. 3d 413, 421, 220 Cal. Rptr. 621, 626 (1985) (warrantless search); Meerbrey v. Marshall Field & Co., 169 Ill. App. 3d 1014, 524 N.E.2d 228 (1988) (right to enter department store).

34. [environmental law] Amoco Prod. Co. v. Village of Gambell, 480 U.S. 531, 545 (1987) (reversing preliminary injunction against oil and gas wells in Alaskan waters, on ground that plaintiffs had shown insufficient risk of environmental injury to justify preliminary relief, but noting that "environmental injury, by its nature, can seldom be adequately remedied by money damages"); Citizens Comm. v. Volpe, 297 F. Supp. 804, 807 (S.D.N.Y. 1969) (highway construction; loss of homes, businesses, and schools can be compensated in damages).

35. [teaching cases] These were Pardee v. Camden Lumber Co., 70 W. Va. 68, 73 S.E. 82 (1911); Hart v. Wagner, 184 Md. 40, 40 A.2d 47 (1944). The cases are excerpted in Laycock, *Remedies* at 325 and 342 (cited in note 3).

36. [venue objection] See *Los Angeles Coliseum*, 726 F.2d 1381, 1399–1401 (9th Cir. 1984). The argument appears in Opening Brief of NFL Appellants at 4 n.1 (No. 82–5572).

37. [minor variations in formulation] For a summary of the various standards, see John Leubsdorf, *The Standard for Preliminary Injunctions*, 91 Harv. L. Rev. 525, 525–26 (1978). For a more detailed analysis, see Lea Vaughn, *A Need for Clarity: Toward a New Standard for Preliminary Injunctions,* 68 Or. L. Rev. 839 (1990).

38. [unstructured list of factors] See Calvin Klein Cosmetics Corp. v. Lenox Labs., Inc., 815 F.2d 500, 503 (8th Cir. 1987).

39. [each factor to be proved separately] Miss. Women's Medical Clinic v. McMillan, 866 F.2d 788, 790–91 (5th Cir. 1989); Zenith Radio Corp. v. U.S., 710

Preliminary Relief

131

F.2d 806, 809 (Fed. Cir. 1983); Planned Parenthood League v. Bellotti, 641 F.2d 1006, 1009 (1st Cir. 1981); Lakeshore Hills, Inc. v. Adcox, 90 Ill. App. 3d 609, 611, 413 N.E.2d 548, 549–50 (1980). See also Doran v. Salem Inn, Inc., 422 U.S. 922, 931 (1975) (casual dictum); Sampson v. Murray, 415 U.S. 61, 90 n.63 (1974) (same).

40. **[sliding scale]** U.S. v. Odessa Union Warehouse Co-op, 833 F.2d 172, 174 (9th Cir. 1987). For similar formulations, see Ohio Oil Co. v. Conway, 279 U.S. 813, 815 (1929); L.J. v. Massinga, 838 F.2d 118, 120 (4th Cir. 1988), cert. denied, 109 S. Ct. 816 (1989); Charles of the Ritz Group Ltd. v. Quality King Distr., Inc., 832 F.2d 1317, 1320 (2d Cir. 1987); Blackwelder Furniture Co. v. Seilig Mfg. Co., 550 F.2d 189, 194–95 (4th Cir. 1977); King v. Meese, 43 Cal. 3d 1217, 1227, 743 P.2d 889, 895, 240 Cal. Rptr. 829, 835 (1987). See also Kuflom v. D.C. Bureau of Motor Vehicle Serv., 543 A.2d 340, 344 (D.C. 1988) (holding that probability of success was so great that preliminary injunction should have issued even though plaintiff failed to show irreparable injury).

41. **[minimize risk of irreparable injury]** Leubsdorf, 91 Harv. L. Rev. at 540–42 (cited in note 37).

42. **[courts adopting Leubsdorf]** IT Corp. v. County of Imperial, 35 Cal. 3d 63, 73, 672 P.2d 121, 127, 196 Cal. Rptr. 715, 721 (1983); Packaging Indus. Group, Inc. v. Cheney, 380 Mass. 609, 617, 405 N.E.2d 106, 111–12 (1980); Pickering & Co., Inc. v. E.V. Game, Inc., 482 F. Supp. 1111, 1112–13 (E.D.N.Y. 1980).

43. **[Posner's equation]** Am. Hosp. Supply Corp. v. Hosp. Prod. Ltd., 780 F.2d 589, 593 (7th Cir. 1986).

44. **[critics of Leubsdorf-Posner]** Id. at 608–09 (Swygert dissenting); Linda S. Mullenix, *Burying (With Kindness) the Felicific Calculus of Civil Procedure*, 40 Vand. L. Rev. 541 (1987); Linda J. Silberman, *Injunctions by the Numbers: Less Than the Sum of Its Parts*, 63 Chi.-Kent L. Rev. 279 (1987); Vaughn, 68 Or. L. Rev. 839 (cited in note 37). But see Linz Audain, *Of Posner, and Newton, and Twenty-First Century Law: An Economic and Statistical Analysis of the Posner Rule for Granting Preliminary Injunctions*, 23 Loyola L.A. L. Rev. 1215 (1990) (extravagantly praising the equation and comparing Posner to Sir Isaac Newton).

45. **[Posner as wholesale revision]** Am. Hosp. Supply Corp. v. Hosp. Prod. Ltd., 780 F.2d 589, 602 (7th Cir. 1986) (Swygert dissenting).

46. **[Posner as bold rewriting]** Mullenix at 547.

47. **[Posner as distillation]** Mullenix at 556 ("except for the fact that Judge Posner's formula has added an appearance of scientism to injunction decisions, nothing has changed"); Schultz v. Frisby, 807 F.2d 1339, 1343 (7th Cir. 1986) (opinion by Swygert) ("the law remains unchanged"), vacated, 818 F.2d 1284 (7th Cir. en banc), result reinstated by equally divided court, 822 F.2d 642 (7th Cir. 1987) (en banc), rev'd on other grounds, 487 U.S. 474 (1988).

48. **[scope of appellate review]** See Silberman, 63 Chi.-Kent L. Rev. at 285–303 (cited in note 44).

48. **[scope of appellate review]** See Silberman, 63 Chi.-Kent L. Rev. at 285–303 (cited in note 44).

49. **[tiny chance of success]** Id. at 305.

50. **[Leubsdorf-Posner not to be quantified]** Am. Hosp. Supply Corp. v. Hosp. Prod. Ltd., 780 F.2d 589, 593 (7th Cir. 1986) (the formula "is intended not to force analysis into a quantitative straitjacket but to assist analysis by presenting succinctly the factors that the court must consider . . . and by articulating the relationship among the factors"); Leubsdorf, 91 Harv. L. Rev. at 542 (cited in note 37) ("reducing this model to hard figures is usually impractical").

51. [disclaimers disingenuous] Mullenix, 40 Vand. L. Rev. at 547 (cited in note 44) ("Judge Posner's caveats, however, are disingenuous"); Vaughn, 68 Or. L. Rev. at 873 n. 156 (cited in note 37) ("he does not call for forcing decisions into mathematical strait-jackets, and at no time in his opinion does he reduce the outcome to hard numbers. His approach, however, does encourage that type of behavior by jurists and lawyers.").

52. [disclaimers make approach fraudulent] Mullenix at 572 ("the final objection to a calculus of civil procedure is simply that it is fraudulent").

53. [range of possible injunctions] For a good example, see Johnson v. Kay, 860 F.2d 529, 540–41 (2d Cir. 1988) (distinguishing injunction prohibiting union referendum from injunction regulating the campaign process, and distinguishing injunction granting plaintiff all relief available at final judgment from injunction granting part of that relief).

54. [intellectual property cases] See Am. Cyanamid Co. v. Campagna per le Farmacie in Italia S.p.A., 847 F.2d 53, 55 (2d Cir. 1988) (on motion for preliminary injunction against trademark infringement, "'likelihood of confusion as to source or sponsorship establishes the requisite likelihood of success on the merits as well as risk of irreparable harm'"); Melville Nimmer & David Nimmer, 3 *Nimmer on Copyright*, § 14.06[A] at pp. 14–54.1 to 14–54.3 (Matthew Bender 1988) (at preliminary injunction stage, "prima facie case of copyright infringement or reasonable likelihood of success on the merits raises a presumption of irreparable harm").

55. [permanent commercial losses] See Roland Mach. Co. v. Dresser Indus., Inc., 749 F.2d 380, 391–93 (7th Cir. 1984).

56. [temporary loss of civil liberties] Elrod v. Burns, 427 U.S. 347, 373 (1976) ("loss of First Amendment freedoms, for even minimal periods of time, unquestionably constitutes irreparable injury") (plurality opinion; majority affirmed preliminary injunction).

6

Deference to Other Authority

The irreparable injury rule is often invoked to serve its original purpose of allocating jurisdiction among decision makers. Litigants frequently seek to move disputes from the forum their adversary selected to the forum they would have selected. They ask courts to enjoin administrative agencies[1] and arbitrators;[2] they ask federal courts to enjoin proceedings in state courts;[3] they ask state courts to enjoin proceedings in other states;[4] they ask courts with equity powers to prevent proceedings in courts without equity powers, even in the same court system;[5] they ask appellate courts to prevent proceedings in trial courts;[6] and they ask courts to prevent the collection of taxes[7] and enjoin improper conduct by the executive branch.[8]

Sometimes these litigants seek to prevent irreparable injury that cannot be prevented by any procedure available in the other forum; sometimes they seek a quicker resolution than the other forum can provide; sometimes they hope to move the dispute to a friendlier forum. These motivations overlap and the same litigant may act on all of them, but for obvious tactical reasons she will emphasize the inadequacy of the other forum's remedy. Often the request is for a preliminary injunction, and the hazards of premature decision reinforce the court's tendency to deference.

The results in these cases depend largely on the relationship between the court and the other decision maker. When that relationship is unsettled, the cases are often argued in terms of irreparable injury. But if necessary to achieve the desired degree of deference, the court will distort its analysis of irreparable injury. Eventually the relationship between the tribunals will become set-

133

tled by a new set of rules. Subsequent cases can be decided by reference to these rules, with or without mentioning irreparable injury. Sometimes the rules that emerge require case-by-case balancing of the adequacy of plaintiff's remedy against the costs of intervention.[9] But often they are simply flat rules for or against intervention in various situations.

A. Federal Courts and State Courts

Federal suits to enjoin enforcement of unconstitutional state laws have been through this cycle three times.[10] The need for such injunctions first received sustained attention as a result of judicial interference with economic regulation in the *Lochner*[11] era. The Court resolved the question the first time in *Ex parte Young*,[12] finding state remedies inadequate and clearing the way for routine federal injunctions against threatened enforcement of state laws.

The issue was reopened in the wake of the New Deal. Judges appointed to overrule the economic due process cases also attacked the remedy associated with those cases. But the injunction against state enforcement was not just a tool of laissez faire; it was equally important to the emerging civil and political constitutional rights. There were a series of inconsistent cases in the 1940s,[13] but the reasoning of *Ex parte Young* was re-established by 1948.[14] That resolution lasted until the 1960s, when the expansion of § 1983 liability[15] and the pressures of civil unrest reopened the issue just in time for the arrival of the Burger Court.[16]

From 1971 to 1977 the Supreme Court decided at least thirty-four cases on federal interference with state law enforcement.[17] These cases relied on the irreparable injury rule to reinforce the majority's view of federalism, and the irreparable injury argument was most prominent in the early cases in the series, when the law was most unsettled.[18] None of the justices questioned the assumption that defense of a pending prosecution is an adequate remedy for most constitutional claims.[19] That assumption is incorrect, and inconsistent with the Court's reasoning in cases where no prosecution is pending, as I have argued elsewhere.[20] But the rhetoric of irreparable injury served the Court's purposes. The rules became settled again, litigants learned to play by the new rules, and the flood of litigation slowed. The more recent cases deal with marginal issues and details of implementation.[21]

The new rules are known as the *Younger* rules, after the most famous case in the series.[22] The basic *Younger* rules are now clearly settled. Litigants who avoid being prosecuted can challenge state laws in federal court,[23] and they can get preliminary injunctions against threatened state prosecutions.[24] Litigants who violate state law before obtaining such an injunction may be prosecuted in state criminal court, and if that happens, federal declaratory and injunctive remedies are barred.[25] These rules do not require balancing; they flatly bar specific relief in certain situations.

The *Younger* rules apply to declaratory judgments as well as to injunctions,[26] even though the irreparable injury rule historically applied only to injunctions. In *Steffel v. Thompson*, the Court expressed a preference for declaratory relief as less confrontational,[27] but that distinction has been of no practical significance.[28] The *Younger* rules may eventually apply to damage actions;[29] the Court has already made that extension with respect to federal challenges to state taxation.[30] These extensions make sense to the extent the underlying rules do, because these are rules about relations between state and federal court. They are not about relations between law and equity, and the historical scope of the irreparable injury rule is wholly irrelevant.

The *Younger* rules have only a tenuous relationship to irreparable injury: usually, but not always,[31] and eventually, but often not promptly,[32] the criminal prosecution will resolve the constitutional claim. In the meantime, prosecuted litigants are under just as much pressure to forfeit their constitutional rights as unprosecuted litigants. These rules reflect not the absence of irreparable injury, but rather the Court's sense of impropriety about interference with state court litigation, and a hint that those who violate the law without first getting a court order deserve whatever happens to them.[33]

As the rules became settled again, federalism arguments came to dominate the opinions, and irreparable injury rhetoric faded to an undeveloped factor in the litany of "equity, comity, and federalism."[34] Sometimes equity disappeared altogether, and the litany was shortened to "comity and federalism."[35] The majority had used the irreparable injury rule as a prop in its attempt to change the law. When the major fight was over, and settled rules were no longer under active attack, the prop was not needed. The emphasis in the opinions shifted to the real grounds for decision, with their greater explanatory power.

B. Courts and Administrative Agencies

Litigants file similar suits to bypass administrative agencies, seeking to enjoin proceedings before the agency or simply to present their claim to a court instead of to the agency. Courts generally refuse such relief, and the rules are mature enough to be stated independently of the irreparable injury rule. Courts say that litigants must first exhaust administrative remedies,[36] or that they must invoke the primary jurisdiction of the agency.[37]

A common explanation of the distinction between the exhaustion and primary jurisdiction rules is that pending administrative proceedings must be exhausted, and that primary jurisdiction must be invoked when no administrative proceeding is pending.[38] A similar but more sophisticated explanation is that administrative remedies must be exhausted when a claim is "cognizable in the first instance by an administrative agency alone," and that primary jurisdiction must be invoked when a claim that "is originally cognizable in the courts" requires the resolution of issues committed to the special competence of an administrative agency.[39] The two rules serve closely related policies, and I will use the plural, "exhaustion rules," to refer to them together.

The exhaustion rules began as an application of the irreparable injury rule: courts would issue an injunction only if the administrative remedy would be inadequate.[40] But the exhaustion rules soon took on a life of their own. Precedents that governed the relationship between law and equity would not produce the right results if applied directly to the relationship between courts and agencies. For starters, the exhaustion rules have a broader scope; they apply at law as well as in equity,[41] and to declaratory judgments as well as injunctions.[42] Second, they rarely pose a choice between specific and substitutionary relief. Rather, they usually pose a choice between immediate judicial relief on a de novo judicial record and much later judicial relief on review of an administrative record. The same permanent remedial options are usually available at either stage, but exhaustion rules often foreclose important possibilities for preliminary relief.

Most important, the exhaustion rules must take account of the relative responsibility and expertise of court and agency. When Kenneth Culp Davis attempted to reconcile the conflicting decisions on exhaustion by a litigant who challenges the agency's jurisdiction, he concluded that the "key factors are three: extent of injury from pursuit of administrative remedy, degree of apparent clarity or doubt about administrative jurisdiction, and involvement of specialized administrative understanding in the question of jurisdiction."[43] Louis Jaffe emphasized a fourth factor in primary jurisdiction cases, the pervasiveness of the agency's regulation.[44]

Davis's first two factors bear some resemblance to the irreparable injury and probability of success inquiries from the preliminary injunction cases. But there are important differences. In the preliminary injunction cases, the inquiry into probability of success goes to the merits. Here, it goes not so much to the probability of ultimate success on the merits as to the probability that the agency is exceeding its jurisdiction.

Davis's third factor, and Jaffe's fourth, have no analogue in the preliminary injunction cases. The emphasis on the specialized expertise and policy responsibility of the agency, and on the superior legal expertise and responsibility of the court, is a special feature of judicial review of agencies.[45] It has only the most attenuated resemblance to the relationship between trial courts and appellate courts, and no resemblance to the relationship between law courts and equity courts.

The exhaustion rules also differ from the *Younger* rules, because the relationship between court and agency differs from the relationship between state and federal courts. The primary jurisdiction rule is more stringent than *Younger*, which never requires federal litigants to initiate state proceedings if none are pending.[46] On the other hand, courts have created far more exceptions to the exhaustion rules than to *Younger*.[47]

Courts have not distilled the exhaustion rules and their exceptions into any standard test. The Supreme Court's best formulation came in the related context of whether an administrative decision is ripe for judicial review: "The problem is best seen in a twofold aspect, requiring us to evaluate both the fitness of the issues for judicial decision and the hardship to the parties of withholding court consideration."[48] Fitness for judicial decision may include Davis's factors of the clarity of jurisdiction and the relevance of administrative expertise, as well as the need for an administrative record.[49]

These factors help make sense of judicial debate over a variety of alleged exceptions to the exhaustion rules: issues of law,[50] constitutional challenges to the statute enforced by the agency,[51] challenges to the agency's jurisdiction,[52] cases where the agency cannot grant the relief sought,[53] and cases that are "inherently judicial" in nature.[54] Exhaustion rules vary with the substantive law context,[55] most obviously in the rule that plaintiffs alleging state violations of federal law need not exhaust state administrative remedies.[56] Federal exhaustion rules tend to be more stringent than state exhaustion rules.[57] Hardship to the litigant is usually relevant, but no version of the irreparable injury rule can capture the variations.

Courts are generally far more deferential to agency remedies than equity courts are to legal remedies. In ordinary litigation over permanent injunctions, most injuries are irreparable and injunctions are routinely available. But if administrative agencies are to function, exhaustion must be the norm rather than the exception. If the test is stated in terms of irreparable injury, most injuries must be reparable, and most injunctions must be denied. An early article by Raoul Berger found the equity analogy "misleading" in exhaustion cases; he thought the standard was not "comparative inadequacy," but rather the "almost complete absence of the administrative remedy."[58]

Even so, many statements of the exhaustion rule recognize an exception for irreparable injury,[59] or for inadequate[60] or futile[61] administrative remedies. At least some courts continue to equate the exhaustion and irreparable injury rules.[62] And attempts to create exceptions to exhaustion rules are often argued in terms of irreparable injury.[63]

As in the cases on preliminary injunctions and deference to state courts, judges often deny the existence of plainly irreparable injury to help justify deference to the other tribunal.[64] For example, defendants often seek to avoid spending thousands or millions of dollars litigating the agency proceeding on the merits before presenting some potentially dispositive claim in the ordinary course of judicial review; sometimes they also argue that unnecessarily protracting the proceeding will harm their reputation through adverse publicity. Courts generally hold that such harms are not irreparable injury.[65] But the only legal remedy for such harms would be to recover damages or attorneys' fees from the agency, and courts have no intention of permitting that. Unrecoverable litigation expenses are in fact irreparable injury, just like any other losses inflicted by an immune defendant.[66]

The real reason for not recognizing the irreparable harm of unrecoverable litigation expenses is that this harm occurs in every case. If the expense of exhausting administrative remedies were sufficient to excuse exhaustion, nothing would be left of the exhaustion rules or of the legislative decision to commit a wide range of questions to administrative agencies.[67] It is not that litigation expenses are reparable, but that this irreparable loss is outweighed by the policies supporting deference to the agency. Litigation expenses are *insufficient* injury to justify an injunction against a pending administrative proceeding. Courts too often say instead that litigation expenses are not irreparable injury at all.

Courts do recognize that litigation expenses are irreparable injury when that is consistent with other relevant policies. Wasted litigation expense is a principal reason for not requiring litigants to exhaust futile administrative remedies.[68] For similar reasons, Illinois has developed a rule that where an agency requires repeated hearings before the same decision maker, litigants need exhaust only one of these "remedies."[69]

Outside the administrative law context, courts will enjoin breach of settlement agreements, arbitration agreements, or other wrongs that deprive an opposing litigant of legitimate procedural advantage.[70] Courts will enjoin harassing repetitive litigation, and any other wrong for which the legal remedy might require a multiplicity of suits.[71] Courts will often enjoin relitigation of issues already decided.[72] When the Supreme Court refused to enjoin state court relitigation of issues decided in federal court,[73] Congress intervened to authorize such injunctions,[74] and said that it was restoring the law to what had formerly been "generally understood."[75] Avoidance of unnecessary litigation expenses is an obvious part of the explanation for each of these rules. The reason for refusing to enjoin agency proceedings is not lack of irreparable injury, but the countervailing value of deference to the agency.

Sometimes courts are clear about the varying content of the irreparable injury rule. For example, the Fifth Circuit has recognized that it has two lines of cases on preliminary injunctions against employment discrimination.[76] After administrative remedies are exhausted, irreparable injury is "presumed."[77] Before that point, plaintiff must show irreparable injury sufficient to justify disruption of the administrative proceeding.[78]

C. Courts and the Executive

Courts are generally more willing to enjoin misconduct by executive officers than to enjoin litigation before another tribunal. These categories are not wholly distinct; in the modern administrative state, executive action blurs into administrative adjudication. I do not claim any sharp distinction, but only that courts are less deferential at the nonadjudicatory end of this continuum.

Courts do defer when they believe that the costs of interference with the executive outweigh the benefits of the injunction. Usually the court explicitly states the need for deference, and sometimes the opinion stops there.[79] But courts are often tempted to add some version of the irreparable injury rule as an additional ground of decision.[80]

A dramatic example arose from the Reagan administration's effort to prevent American technology from being used to build the Siberian gas pipeline.[81] An American company that had sold goods to a French firm working on the pipeline found itself caught between an American Executive Order forbidding it to deliver and French regulations requiring it to deliver. The American court refused to enjoin enforcement of the Executive Order, for obvious reasons related to executive control over foreign affairs, and also for the much less plausible reason that plaintiff had not shown it would suffer irreparable injury. The court bolstered the irreparable injury holding by pointing to unexhausted administrative remedies. These remedies were highly unpromising, but they were enough to save the irreparable injury holding from utter absurdity.

Another clear example is *Sampson v. Murray*,[82] where a discharged federal employee sought reinstatement pending Civil Service review. The Court said that "insufficiency of savings or difficulties in immediately obtaining other employment . . . will not support a finding of irreparable injury, however severely they may affect a particular individual."[83] The Court's other formulation of the point was not so dissembling: assuming financial distress and harm to reputation, plaintiff had not shown "the *type* of irreparable injury . . . necessary . . . in this type of case."[84]

Plainly the injury from financial distress would often be irreparable. [85] The government would not be liable for the value of home or goods lost to creditors, or even for interest paid on borrowed funds. The Back Pay Act authorizes recovery of lost salary, seniority, and attorneys' fees; the government is not liable for additional damages unless it expressly creates the liability and consents to be sued.[86] Even for private defendants, the traditional rule is that there is no liability for consequential damages resulting from failure to pay money. Exceptions are emerging but the rule retains considerable force.[87] Even if the government would pay the financial losses from a mortgage foreclosure, the loss of real estate is commonly said to always be irreparable. Similarly, the Court has correctly held that bankruptcy is an irreparable injury even at the preliminary injunction stage.[88]

In the Court's view, these irreparable injuries did not justify judicial interference with the government's control over its own work force. These injuries could not suffice because they were "common to most discharged employees," and recognizing them as irreparable would undermine the policy that the Back Pay Act be "the usual, if not the exclusive, remedy for wrongful discharge." Quite possibly the Court will never issue such injunctions and no form of irreparable injury is sufficient, but that issue was left open.[89] At least one state supreme court has rejected *Sampson*'s reasoning.[90]

One cost of explaining the result in terms of irreparable injury is that the holding has been applied to similar suits against private employers,[91] where the argument for deference may be considerably weaker. Other courts have recognized that the Court created a separate standard for government personnel cases, much more stringent than the usual standard for preliminary injunc-

142   THE DEATH OF THE IRREPARABLE INJURY RULE

tions.[92] In any event, the debate is limited to preliminary relief. At the final judgment stage, reinstatement is routine unless there is some clear reason to deny it, such as personal friction with supervisors or co-workers.[93]

The policy of deference has almost nothing to do with a preference for law over equity; it applies with equal force to legal remedies. Government officials[94] and government itself[95] get broad immunities from damage liability. Occasionally courts will withhold specific relief but make the government pay; the most important example is the common immunity from specific performance of government contracts.[96] But it is far more common for courts to deny damages and grant specific relief requiring government to comply with the law in the future.[97] When deference is considered especially important, courts will not grant either form of remedy.[98] Despite the frequent talk of irreparable injury in suits to enjoin other government agencies, the rule has little power to explain the patterns of deference between courts and other agencies.

Notes on Deference

1. **[requests to enjoin agency proceedings]** Renegotiation Bd. v. Bannercraft Clothing Co., 415 U.S. 1, 3–7, 23–24 (1974) (reversing preliminary injunction that ordered agency to produce documents and staying agency proceedings until the documents were produced); Myers v. Bethlehem Shipbuilding Corp., 303 U.S. 41, 43, 50–51 (1938) (reversing preliminary injunction against agency hearing on alleged unfair labor practice); Bio-Medical Labs., Inc. v. Trainor, 68 Ill. 2d 540, 548, 370 N.E.2d 223, 227 (1977) (enjoining suspension of medical provider from eligibility for Medicaid reimbursement); Forrest House Apts. v. La. Tax Comm'n, 433 So.2d 824, 826–27 (La. App. 1983) (refusing, on grounds of irreparable injury rule, to order Tax Commission to publicly reprimand a local tax assessor); Highland Tap, Inc. v. City of Boston, 26 Mass. App. 239, 526 N.E.2d 253 (1988) (enjoining city from revoking plaintiff's liquor license); Klump v. Cybulski, 274 Wis. 604, 609–10, 81 N.W.2d 42, 46 (1957) (refusing to enjoin eminent domain proceeding).

2. **[requests to enjoin arbitrations]** Bd. of Educ. v. Warren Township High School Fed'n of Teachers, 162 Ill. App. 3d 676, 678–79, 683–84, 515 N.E.2d 1331, 1332, 1335–36 (1987) (enjoining arbitration of grievance, expressly holding irreparable injury rule inapplicable), rev'd, 128 Ill. 2d 155, 538 N.E.2d 524 (1989) (holding that court lacked jurisdiction and not discussing irreparable injury rule). See also Int'l Ass'n of Machinists v. Soo Line R.R., 850 F.2d 368, 380–82 (8th Cir. 1988) (reversing injunction against employer, on ground that dispute was arbitrable and courts lacked jurisdiction).

3. [requests to enjoin state proceedings] Thornburgh v. Am. College of Obstetricians, 476 U.S. 747, 750, 772 (1986) (enjoining enforcement of state law restricting abortion); Bellotti v. Baird, 443 U.S. 622, 651 (1979) (same); Younger v. Harris, 401 U.S. 37, 38–39, 43–54 (1971) (refusing to enjoin enforcement of California Criminal Syndicalism Act, where prosecution was pending against federal plaintiffs); Cavanaugh v. Looney, 248 U.S. 453 (1919) (refusing to enjoin civil enforcement of state eminent domain law); Ex parte Young, 209 U.S. 123, 133–34, 163–67 (1908) (enforcing injunction against enforcement of railroad rate regulation); Mershon v. Kyser, 852 F.2d 335 (8th Cir. 1988) (refusing to enjoin prosecution allegedly brought in bad faith); Gloucester Marine Rys. v. Charles Parisi, Inc., 848 F.2d 12, 13 (1st Cir. 1988) (reversing injunction against attempts to collect state court judgment); Kerr-McGee Chem. Corp. v. Hartigan, 816 F.2d 1177 (7th Cir. 1987) (refusing to enjoin enforcement of state environmental laws); Birch v. Mazander, 678 F.2d 754, 756 (8th Cir. 1982) (refusing federal injunctive relief from judgment in state municipal court, where plaintiff failed to allege unavailability of new trial, appeal, or collateral attack in state court); U.S. v. Navarro, 429 F.2d 928 (5th Cir. 1970) (refusing to enjoin admission of illegally seized heroin in state criminal trial, but enjoining federal officers from testifying in that trial).

4. [requests to enjoin trial in sister states] Crawley v. Bauchens, 57 Ill.2d 360, 366–67, 312 N.E.2d 236, 239 (1974) (reversing injunction against adoption proceeding in Canal Zone); James v. Grand Trunk W. R.R., 14 Ill.2d 356, 366–72, 152 N.E.2d 858, 864–67 (1958) (directing trial court to enjoin defendant from enforcing Michigan injunction ordering plaintiff not to pursue litigation in Illinois); State ex rel. Gen'l Dynamics Corp. v. Luten, 566 S.W.2d 452, 458–62 (Mo. 1978) (vacating injunction against duplicative litigation in California, because balance of litigation convenience lay with California and remedy in its courts would be adequate); Gurvich v. Tyree, 694 S.W.2d 39, 41–47 (Tex. App. 1985) (reversing injunction against parallel litigation in Louisiana).

5. [requests to enjoin in same court system] U.S. Postal Serv. v. Council of Greenburgh Civic Ass'ns, 453 U.S. 114, 116 (1981) (suit in federal court to enjoin enforcement of federal criminal statute; statute upheld on merits); Bellanca v. N.Y. State Liquor Auth., 50 N.Y.2d 524, 407 N.E.2d 460, 429 N.Y.S.2d 616 (1980) (declaring state statute unconstitutional), rev'd on other grounds, 452 U.S. 714 (1981); W. Allis Memorial Hosp., Inc. v. Bowen, 852 F.2d 251, 256 (7th Cir. 1988) (refusing to enjoin prosecution of proposed Medicare billing scheme); Blalock v. U.S., 844 F.2d 1546, 1549–50 (11th Cir. 1988) (refusing to enjoin alleged prosecutorial misconduct before federal grand jury); 7978 Corp. v. Pitchess, 41 Cal. App. 3d 42, 46, 115 Cal. Rptr. 746, 748 (1974) (refusing to enjoin enforcement of dancehall curfew); Gorham v. City of New Haven, 82 Conn. 153, 156–57, 72 A. 1012, 1014 (1909) (refusing to enjoin condemnation proceeding); West v. Town of Winnsboro, 252 La. 605, 211 So.2d 665 (1967) (enjoining enforcement of Sunday closing ordinance); Ingraham v. Univ. of Maine, 441 A.2d 691, 692–93 (Me. 1982) (refusing to enjoin enforcement of probation condition and refusing to order "reversal and rescission" of criminal conviction); Kenyon v. City of Chicopee, 320 Mass. 528, 534–36, 70 N.E.2d 241, 245–46 (1946) (enjoining enforcement of ordinance forbidding distribution of handbills); Ferrante v. City of N.Y., 17 N.Y.2d 616, 216 N.E.2d 27, 268 N.Y.S.2d 931 (1966) (declaratory judgment upholding constitutionality of city Hospital Code); Sloane v. Clauss, 64 Ohio St. 125, 59 N.E.

884 (1901) (enjoining foreclosure of chattel mortgage in justice of the peace court); Martin v. Baldy, 249 Pa. 253, 258–59, 94 A. 1091, 1093 (1915) (enjoining enforcement of law restricting practice of optometry); S. Coventry Township v. Philadelphia Elec. Co., 94 Pa. Commw. 289, 504 A.2d 368, 373 (1986) (enjoining enforcement of zoning laws); Orwick v. City of Seattle, 103 Wash. 2d 249, 692 P.2d 793 (1984) (suit to enjoin mishandling of speeding prosecutions in municipal court, dismissed as moot).

6. [requests to enjoin trial courts] In the Matter of Lipari v. Owens, 70 N.Y.2d 731, 732–33, 514 N.E.2d 378, 379 (1987) (no writ of prohibition to correct pretrial error where appeal is adequate remedy); State ex rel. P.O.B., Inc. v. Hair, 23 Ohio St. 3d 50, 491 N.E.2d 306 (1986) (no mandamus to prevent trial judge from exceeding jurisdiction, where appeal is adequate remedy). See also City of Lincoln v. Cather & Sons Constr., Inc., 206 Neb. 10, 13–16, 290 N.W.2d 798, 801–02 (1980) (dismissing action in district court to enjoin action in county court).

7. [requests to prevent tax collection] Cal. v. Grace Brethren Church, 457 U.S. 393, 407–17 (1982) (refusing to enjoin enforcement of unemployment tax or declare its constitutionality as applied to churches); Fair Assessment in Real Estate Ass'n v. McNary, 454 U.S. 100, 113–17 (1981) (refusing to entertain suit for damages from unconstitutional administration of state tax laws); Rosewell v. LaSalle Nat'l Bank, 450 U.S. 503, 512–28 (1981) (holding that suit for refund would be adequate remedy, even though refund would be without interest and after two-year delay); Tully v. Griffin, Inc., 429 U.S. 68, 73–77 (1976) (refusing to enjoin collection of state sales tax from out-of-state seller); U.S. v. Am. Friends Serv. Comm., 419 U.S. 7, 11 (1974) (irreparable injury is necessary but not sufficient condition for enjoining collection of federal taxes); Enochs v. Williams Packing Co., 370 U.S. 1, 6–7 (1962) (same); Great Lakes Dredge & Dock Co. v. Huffman, 319 U.S. 293, 297–302 (1943) (refusing to declare constitutionality of state unemployment tax); Dows v. City of Chicago, 78 U.S. (11 Wall.) 108, 109–12 (1870) (refusing to enjoin collection of tax where payment and refund would be adequate remedy); In re Heritage Village Church & Missionary Fellowship, Inc., 851 F.2d 104 (4th Cir. 1988) (reversing injunction against revoking tax-exempt status of debtor in bankruptcy); In re Gillis, 836 F.2d 1001 (6th Cir. 1988) (refusing to declare that plaintiffs, owners of real property subject to property tax, were denied equal protection by systematic underassessment of mineral rights owned by other taxpayers); Smith v. Booth, 823 F.2d 94 (5th Cir. 1987) (refusing to entertain challenge to government's interpretation of right to pay estate tax in installments); U.S. v. Augspurger, 452 F. Supp. 659, 666–67 (W.D.N.Y. 1978) (refusing to enjoin assessment and levy); Am. Trucking Ass'ns v. Gray, 280 Ark. 258, 259–60, 657 S.W.2d 207, 208 (1983) (refusing to enjoin distribution of state motor fuel tax from state treasury to local governments); Modern Barber Colleges, Inc. v. Cal. Employment Stabilization Comm'n, 31 Cal. 2d 720, 192 P.2d 916 (1948) (refusing to enjoin collection of unemployment compensation tax); Hoffman v. Colo. State Bd. of Assessment Appeals, 683 P.2d 783 (Colo. 1984) (refusing to enjoin erroneous tax assessment where administrative review of assessment provided plain, speedy, and efficient remedy); Barry v. Am. Tel. & Tel. Co., 563 A.2d 1069, 1073–76 (D.C. 1989) (refusing to enjoin enforcement of tax on telecommunications services, or declare its constitutionality); Chicago Health Clubs, Inc. v. Picur, 124 Ill. 2d 1, 528 N.E.2d 978 (1988) (enjoining collection of unconstitutional tax on health-club membership fees); La Salle Nat'l Bank v. County of Cook, 57 Ill. 2d 318, 322, 312 N.E.2d 252, 254 (1974) (refusing to declare constitutionality of local tax assessment procedures); Impact Promotions, Inc. v. State, 104 Mich. App. 520, 523–27, 305 N.W.2d 253, 255–57 (1981) (administrative remedy adequate, despite unlawful three-year delay); Ganser v. County of Lancaster, 215 Neb. 313, 315–18, 338 N.W.2d 609, 611–12 (1983) (suit for refund is adequate remedy); Carter v. Olsen, 660 S.W.2d 483 (Tenn. 1983) (enjoining foreclosure of disputed tax lien); Tyler Pipe Indus., Inc. v. State Dep't of Revenue, 96 Wash. 2d 785, 794–97, 638 P.2d 1213, 1218–19 (1982) (holding suit for refund to be an adequate remedy, even though state paid only three percent interest on refund). For an unusual statute authorizing injunctions against tax collection, pending appeal of the tax liability, see Ind. Code § 33–3–5–11(c) (Supp. 1989). For a case granting an injunction under the statute, see Keller v. Ind. Dep't of State Revenue, 530 N.E.2d 787, 790–91 (Ind. Tax 1988).

8. [requests to enjoin executive branch] Rizzo v. Goode, 423 U.S. 362, 378–81 (1976) (refusing to enjoin pattern of police brutality); Deaver v. Seymour, 822 F.2d 66 (D.C. Cir. 1987) (refusing to enjoin prosecutor from seeking indictment, where prospective criminal defendant sought to avoid harm to reputation and anxiety of prosecution); Arnold v. Engelbrecht, 164 Ill. App. 3d 704, 708–10, 518 N.E.2d 237, 240–41 (1987) (refusing to order supervisor to change performance review of police officers, deferring to supervisor's discretion and finding that rating of "Performance Far Below Standard" inflicted no injury); Lutheran Serv. Ass'n, Inc. v. Metro. Dist. Comm'n, 397 Mass. 341, 344–45, 491 N.E.2d 255, 257–58 (1986) (refusing to control exercise of eminent domain power by mandamus); Bales v. Mich. State Highway Comm'n, 72 Mich. App. 50, 54–56, 249 N.W.2d 158, 161–62 (1976) (enjoining construction of highway before acquisition of plaintiff's easement); Pelham Realty Corp. v. Bd. of Transp., 303 N.C. 424, 431–33, 279 S.E.2d 826, 831–32 (1981) (refusing to control exercise of eminent domain power by injunction); Garono v. State, 37 Ohio St. 3d 171, 173–76, 524 N.E.2d 496, 498–501 (1988) (reversing injunction that forbad prosecutors to publicly denounce plaintiff's machines as gambling devices, but ordering prosecutors to return the machines); Earhart v. Young, 174 Tenn. 198, 124 S.W.2d 693 (1939) (refusing to enjoin seizure of pinball machine).

9. [case-by-case balancing] McKart v. U.S., 395 U.S. 185, 192–201 (1969) (excusing failure to exhaust administrative remedies where benefits of exhaustion would have been limited and consequence of requiring exhaustion would be loss of only defense to criminal prosecution); Public Util. Comm'n v. Pedernales Elec. Coop., Inc., 678 S.W.2d 214, 220 (Tex. App. 1984) ("correct application of the *exhaustion* doctrine in specific circumstances depends upon a balancing of the underlying purposes of the doctrine against the injury claimed by the applicant for relief in equity" (emphasis in original)).

10. [enjoining enforcement of state law] For a detailed review of the cases, see Douglas Laycock, *Federal Interference with State Prosecutions: The Cases Dombrowski Forgot*, 46 U. Chi. L. Rev. 636, 641–64 (1979).

11. [*Lochner* era] Lochner v. N.Y., 198 U.S. 45 (1905).

12. [issue first resolved] Ex parte Young, 209 U.S. 123, 161–68 (1908). For subsequent cases, see Laycock, 46 U. Chi. L. Rev. at 641–42 (cited in note 10).

13. [conflicting cases in 1940s] Compare Ryan v. Thompson, 324 U.S. 821 (1945) (mem.); Yakus v. U.S., 321 U.S. 414, 444 (1944); Meredith v. Winter Haven, 320

U.S. 228, 235 (1943); Burford v. Sun Oil Co., 319 U.S. 315, 333 n.29 (1943); Douglas v. City of Jeannette, 319 U.S. 157 (1943); Watson v. Buck, 313 U.S. 387 (1941); and Beal v. Mo. Pacific R.R., 312 U.S. 45 (1941) (all holding or stating that federal courts may not consider suits to enjoin enforcement of state laws); with Toomer v. Witsell, 334 U.S. 385 (1948); Am. Fed'n of Labor v. Watson, 327 U.S. 582 (1946); Switchmen's Union v. Nat'l Mediation Bd., 320 U.S. 297, 306 (1943); W. Va. State Bd. of Educ. v. Barnette, 319 U.S. 624 (1943); Parker v. Brown, 317 U.S. 341, 349–50 (1943); Reitz v. Mealey, 314 U.S. 33 (1941); Hines v. Davidowitz, 312 U.S. 52 (1941) (all considering suits to enjoin enforcement of state law or stating that federal courts may do so).

   14. [original solution re-established] Toomer v. Witsell, 334 U.S. 385, 391–92 (1948) (enjoining enforcement of law discriminating against out-of-state shrimpers). For subsequent cases, see Laycock, 46 U. Chi. L. Rev. at 649–59 (cited in note 10).

   15. [expansion of § 1983] 42 U.S.C. § 1983 (1982). See Monroe v. Pape, 365 U.S. 167, 171–87 (1961) (victims of official misconduct that violates both state and federal law may sue in federal court without exhausting state remedies); Louise Weinberg, *The New Judicial Federalism*, 29 Stan. L. Rev. 1191, 1209–11 (1977) (modern scope of § 1983 would be unworkable if that statute authorized injunctions against any pending state judicial proceeding that raised an issue cognizable under the statute).

   16. [issue reopened] Younger v. Harris, 401 U.S. 37, 43–54 (1971) (except in extraordinary circumstances, federal court may not enjoin enforcement of state law at request of litigant against whom state prosecution is pending); Dombrowski v. Pfister, 380 U.S. 479, 483–89 (1965) (injunction against enforcement of state law is exceptional, but is available where risk of prosecution would chill first amendment rights).

   17. [34 cases in six years] The cases are collected in Douglas Laycock, *Federal Interference with State Prosecutions: The Need for Prospective Relief*, 1977 S. Ct. Rev. 193, 193–94 nn.1–3.

   18. [rule most prominent in early cases] See New Orleans Public Serv., Inc. v. Council of New Orleans, 109 S. Ct. 2506, 2515–16 (1989) (*Younger* "was based partly on traditional principles of equity, but rested primarily on the 'even more vital consideration' of comity," quoting *Younger*, 401 U.S. at 43–44). Compare Pennzoil Co. v. Texaco, Inc., 481 U.S. 1, 10–14 (1987) (explaining applicability of *Younger* rule with one sentence on adequate remedy at law and two pages on federalism); Juidice v. Vail, 430 U.S. 327, 333–34 (1977) (explaining *Younger* rule on basis of "comity and federalism," and not mentioning irreparable injury); with Younger v. Harris, 401 U.S. 37, 43–46 (1971) (explaining refusal to enjoin pending state proceeding in terms of irreparable injury rule, comity, and "Our Federalism," giving substantial attention to each). See Aviam Soifer & H.C. Macgill, *The Younger Doctrine: Reconstructing Reconstruction*, 55 Tex. L. Rev. 1141, 1169–91 (1977) (arguing that equity strand of *Younger*'s holding had disappeared by 1975).

   19. [assumed adequacy of criminal defense] See Laycock, 46 U. Chi. L. Rev. at 684–85 (cited in note 10) (concluding, after detailed review of cases, that only Chief Justice Stone had ever acknowledged that refusal to enjoin enforcement of state law remitted federal plaintiff to state remedy that could not fully protect alleged constitutional rights).

20. [inadequacy of criminal defense] Laycock, 1977 S. Ct. Rev. at 199–222 (cited in note 17).

21. [recent cases marginal] See New Orleans Public Serv., Inc. v. Council of New Orleans, 109 S. Ct. 2506, 2515–20 (1989) (*Younger* rules do not require that federal pre-emption challenge to city council's rate order be brought in state court); Pennzoil Co. v. Texaco, Inc., 481 U.S. 1 (1987) (refusing to enjoin enforcement of state civil judgment pending appeal in state court); Ohio Civil Rights Comm'n v. Dayton Christian Schools, Inc., 477 U.S. 619, 626–29 (1986) (refusing to enjoin state administrative proceedings against religious school that asserted First Amendment right to be wholly free from agency's jurisdiction); In re Special March 1981 Grand Jury, 753 F.2d 575, 581 (7th Cir. 1985) (refusing to enjoin use in state enforcement proceedings of business records supplied to federal grand jury and then turned over to state); W.C.M. Window Co. v. Bernardi, 730 F.2d 486, 490–93 (7th Cir. 1984) (preliminary injunction against enforcement of state law, despite civil enforcement proceeding pending in state court, where not all federal plaintiffs were state defendants and adverse state precedent appeared controlling).

22. [most famous case] Younger v. Harris, 401 U.S. 37 (1971).

23. [unprosecuted can sue in federal court] Steffel v. Thompson, 415 U.S. 452, 460–75 (1974) (federal declaratory judgment is available even if injunction is not).

24. [can get preliminary injunction] Doran v. Salem Inn, Inc., 422 U.S. 922, 930–31 (1975).

25. [prosecuted cannot sue] Hicks v. Miranda, 422 U.S. 332, 348–50 (1975) (federal relief barred by subsequent state prosecution filed before substantial proceedings on the merits in federal court); Roe v. Wade, 410 U.S. 113, 125–27 (1973) (pending state prosecution for one past violation bars federal injunction against enforcement of statute with respect to contemplated future violations); Samuels v. Mackell, 401 U.S. 66, 68–74 (1971) (pending state prosecution bars federal declaratory judgment on constitutionality); Younger v. Harris, 401 U.S. 37, 43–54 (1971) (federal court cannot enjoin pending state prosecution).

26. [rules apply to declaratory relief] Doran v. Salem Inn, Inc., 422 U.S. 922, 929 (1975) (federal declaratory judgment barred by state prosecution filed while federal case was in "embryonic stage"); Samuels v. Mackell, 401 U.S. 66, 73 (1971) (denying declaratory judgment under rules applicable to injunctions, because "ordinarily . . . the practical effect of the two forms of relief will be virtually identical"). See also U.S. Steel Corp. Plan for Employee Ins. Benefits v. Musisko, 885 F.2d 1170, 1175 (3d Cir. 1989) (Anti-Injunction Act, barring federal injunctions against pending state litigation, also bars declaratory judgment that would have same effect as injunction).

27. [declaratory relief preferred] Steffel v. Thompson, 415 U.S. 452, 462 (1974).

28. [preference insignificant] See Laycock, 46 U. Chi. L. Rev. at 665–66 (cited in note 10).

29. [rules may apply to damages] See Deakins v. Monaghan, 484 U.S. 193, 201 (1988) (staying federal suit for damages from illegal search, until conclusion of pending state criminal prosecution, and reserving issue whether *Younger* doctrine applies to damage actions).

30. [no federal damages for state taxation] Fair Assessment in Real Estate Ass'n v. McNary, 454 U.S. 100, 113–17 (1981) (refusing to entertain suit for damages from unconstitutional administration of state tax laws).

31. [prosecution may not resolve issue] See Zwickler v. Koota, 261 F. Supp. 985, 987 (E.D.N.Y. 1966) (federal plaintiff had already litigated criminal conviction for distributing anonymous political leaflets to highest state court, where he was acquitted "on the facts," without decision of the constitutional issue), rev'd on other grounds, 389 U.S. 241 (1967); Laycock, 1977 S. Ct. Rev. at 200–02 (cited in note 17) (collecting cases where authorities continued to enforce invalidated statute); id. at 214–19 (permanent injunction against enforcement is needed because of doubts about preclusive effect of criminal acquittal on constitutional issue).

32. [may not resolve it promptly] See Laycock, 1977 S. Ct. Rev. at 202–14 (cited in note 17) (preliminary injunction is needed because of risk of prosecution for offenses committed during pendency of criminal prosecution for past offense).

33. [violators undeserving] Doran v. Salem Inn, Inc., 422 U.S. 922, 929 (1975) ("having violated the ordinance, rather than awaiting the normal development of its federal lawsuit, [plaintiff] cannot now be heard to complain . . . ").

34. [equity, comity, and federalism] See note 18. For the litany, see Parsons Steel, Inc. v. First Ala. Bank, 474 U.S. 518, 526 (1986); Trainor v. Hernandez, 431 U.S. 434, 439 (1977); Ohio Bureau of Employment Serv. v. Hodory, 431 U.S. 471, 478 n.8 (1977); Rizzo v. Goode, 423 U.S. 362, 379 (1976); Ellis v. Dyson, 421 U.S. 426, 432 (1975); Huffman v. Pursue, Ltd., 420 U.S. 592, 595 n.1 (1975); Steffel v. Thompson, 415 U.S. 452, 454, 462 (1974); Gibson v. Berryhill, 411 U.S. 564, 573, 575 (1973); Mitchum v. Foster, 407 U.S. 225, 243 (1972).

35. [comity and federalism] New Orleans Public Serv., Inc. v. Council of New Orleans, 109 S. Ct. 2506, 2517 (1989); Ohio Civil Rights Comm'n v. Dayton Christian Schools, Inc., 477 U.S. 619, 627 (1986); Hawaii Housing Auth. v. Midkiff, 467 U.S. 229, 237 (1984); Pennhurst State School & Hosp. v. Halderman, 465 U.S. 89, 104 n.13 (1984); Middlesex County Ethics Comm. v. Garden State Bar Ass'n, 457 U.S. 423, 429 (1982); Juidice v. Vail, 430 U.S. 327, 334 (1977); Town of Lockport v. Citizens for Community Action at the Local Level, Inc., 430 U.S. 259, 264 n.8 (1977); Huffman v. Pursue, Ltd., 420 U.S. 592, 606, 607 (1975).

36. [exhaustion] McKart v. U.S., 395 U.S. 185, 193 (1969) ("doctrine of exhaustion of administrative remedies is well established in the jurisprudence of administrative law"); Ill. Commerce Comm'n v. Thomson, 318 U.S. 675, 686 (1943) (injunction against railroad rate order should have been denied because of "failure first to pursue the administrative remedy"); Myers v. Bethlehem Shipbuilding Corp. 303 U.S. 41, 51 (1938) ("long settled rule of judicial administration that no one is entitled to judicial relief for a supposed or threatened injury until the prescribed administrative remedy has been exhausted"); Facchiano v. U.S. Dep't of Labor, 859 F.2d 1163, 1166 (3d Cir. 1988) ("doctrine of exhaustion of remedies requires that parties first use all prescribed administrative measures for resolving a conflict before they seek judicial remedies"); Andrade v. Lauer, 729 F.2d 1475, 1484 (D.C. Cir. 1984) ("exhaustion of available administrative remedies is in general a prerequisite to obtaining judicial relief for an actual or threatened injury"); Liberman v. Dep't of Justice, 714 F. Supp. 639, 641 (E.D.N.Y. 1989) ("exhaustion of remedies with the agency is a precondition to filing suit"); Graham v. Ill. Racing Bd., 76 Ill. 2d 566, 573, 394 N.E.2d 1148, 1151 (1979) ("administrative remedies must be exhausted prior to seeking equitable relief," subject to certain exceptions); Abbott v. Burke, 100 N.J. 269, 296–303, 495 A.2d 376, 390–94 (1985) (plaintiffs challenging constitutionality of school finance scheme must exhaust administrative remedies before Commissioner of Education and Office of Administrative Law); Pechner v. Pa. Ins. Dep't, 499 Pa. 139, 145, 452 A.2d 230, 232–33 (1982) (refusing to review insurance rates, "because appellants had not exhausted their administrative remedies before the Commissioner prior to seeking equity"). For surveys and criticism of the doctrine, see Kenneth Culp Davis, *Administrative Law Treatise* ch. 26 (K.C. Davis Pub. Co., 2d ed. 1978); Robert C. Power, *Help Is Sometimes Close at Hand: The Exhaustion Problem and the Ripeness Solution*, 1987 U. Ill. L. Rev. 547.

37. [primary jurisdiction] Ricci v. Chicago Mercantile Exchange, 409 U.S. 289, 298–306 (1973) (defendant allegedly violated both antitrust laws and Commodity Exchange Act; court stayed adjudication of antitrust claim pending presentation of Commodity Act claim to Commodity Exchange Commission); Arrow Transp. Co. v. S. Ry., 372 U.S. 658, 668 (1963) (refusing to suspend freight rates pending decision of Interstate Commerce Commission); U.S. v. W. Pacific R.R., 352 U.S. 59, 62–70 (1956) (interpretation of railroad tariff is within primary jurisdiction of Interstate Commerce Commission); Far East Conf. v. U.S., 342 U.S. 570, 573–76 (1952) (suit to enjoin shipping rates under antitrust laws is within primary jurisdiction of Federal Maritime Board); Bar Harbor Banking & Trust Co. v. Alexander, 411 A.2d 74, 77–78 (Me. 1980) (refusing to enjoin agency from holding hearing to determine whether bank had violated consumer credit law); Television Cable Serv. v. Bryant, 684 S.W.2d 196, 198–99 (Tex. App. 1984) (refusing to order cable television service to plaintiff's home, where city council had primary jurisdiction). For a survey of the doctrine, see Davis, *Treatise* ch. 22 (cited in note 36); Louis Jaffe, *Primary Jurisdiction*, 77 Harv. L. Rev. 1037 (1964).

38. [distinguishing doctrines] Sharkey v. City of Stamford, 196 Conn. 253, 255–57, 492 A.2d 171, 172–73 (1985); Murphy v. Admin'r of Div. of Personnel Admin., 377 Mass. 217, 220–21, 386 N.E.2d 211, 213–14 (1979); Kenneth Culp Davis, *Administrative Remedies Often Need Not Be Exhausted*, 19 F.R.D. 437, 438 (1958).

39. [more sophisticated distinction] U.S. v. W. Pacific R.R., 352 U.S. 59, 63–64 (1956).

40. [exhaustion as application of rule] See Raoul Berger, *Exhaustion of Administrative Remedies*, 48 Yale L.J. 981, 985–88, 1006 (1939) ("from the beginning, the exhaustion rule was formulated in terms of *equity jurisdiction*" (emphasis in original)).

41. [applies to law and equity] McGee v. U.S., 402 U.S. 479, 483–91 (1971) (barring defense to criminal prosecution because defendant failed to exhaust administrative remedies); Myers v. Bethlehem Shipbuilding Corp., 303 U.S. 41, 51 n.9 (1938) ("because the rule is one of judicial administration—not merely a rule governing the exercise of discretion—it is applicable to proceedings at law as well as suits in equity"); First Nat'l Bank v. Bd. of County Comm'rs, 264 U.S. 450, 450, 453–55 (1924) (dismissing suit for tax refund because plaintiff failed to exhaust administrative remedies); J. & J. Enterprises, Inc. v. Martignetti, 369 Mass. 535, 539, 341 N.E.2d 645, 648 (1976) (where agency cannot award damages, suit for damages should be stayed rather than dismissed, pending resort to agency).

42. [applies to declaratory relief] Abbott Labs. v. Gardner, 387 U.S. 136, 146 (1967) ("a court would not grant injunctive or declaratory judgment relief unless the appropriate administrative procedure is exhausted"); Jojan Corp. v. Kusper, 173 Ill. App. 3d 622, 528 N.E.2d 989 (1987) (refusing to determine constitutionality of tax statute in suit for declaratory judgment, where proper remedy was to pay taxes under protest and sue for refund); E. Chop Tennis Club v. Mass. Comm'n Against Discrimination, 364 Mass. 444, 450, 305 N.E.2d 507, 510–12 (1973) ("a proceeding for declaratory relief in itself does not operate to suspend the ordinary requirement that a plaintiff exhaust his administrative remedies before seeking judicial relief"); Roadway Express, Inc. v. Kingsley, 37 N.J. 136, 139, 179 A.2d 729, 731 (1962) ("strong policy in favor of exhaustion of administrative remedies applies equally" to declaratory judgment and prerogative writ).

43. [three key factors in exhaustion] Davis, 19 F.R.D. at 450 (cited in note 38).

44. [fourth factor] Jaffe, 77 Harv. L. Rev. at 1040–41 (cited in note 37) ("it is not merely the presence of expertness, but the wide-reaching and systematic character of agency regulation which tends to choke out the normal jurisdiction of the courts").

45. [factor unique to agencies] See McKart v. U.S., 395 U.S. 185, 194 (1969) (exhaustion requirement is justified by "a notion peculiar to administrative law," which is "particularly pertinent" in cases that "involve exercise of discretionary powers granted the agency by Congress, or require application of special expertise").

46. [primary jurisdiction and *Younger*] Steffel v. Thompson, 415 U.S. 452, 462 (1974) ("relevant principles of equity, comity, and federalism 'have little force in the absence of a pending state proceeding'"); Laycock, 1977 S. Ct. Rev. at 235 (cited in note 17) ("the Court has not wavered from the rule that, when the citizen is free to become a civil rights plaintiff, he has a right to file in federal court"). See also Douglas v. Seacoast Prod., Inc., 431 U.S. 265, 271 n.4 (1977) ("it is the 'solemn responsibility' of 'all levels of the federal judiciary to give due respect to a suitor's choice of a federal forum for the hearing and decision of his federal constitutional claims,'" quoting Zwickler v. Koota, 389 U.S. 241, 248 (1967); Monroe v. Pape, 365 U.S. 167, 171–87 (1961) (victims of official misconduct that violates both state and federal law may sue in federal court without exhausting state remedies).

47. [exceptions] Compare text at notes 50–56 (exceptions to exhaustion rules); with Charles Alan Wright, Arthur R. Miller, & Edward H. Cooper, 17A *Federal Practice & Procedure* § 4255 at 252–67 (West, 2d ed. 1988) (*Younger* exceptions are almost never successfully invoked).

48. [Supreme Court's formulation] Abbott Labs. v. Gardner, 387 U.S. 136, 149 (1967). See also Nader v. Allegheny Airlines, Inc., 426 U.S. 290, 304 (1976) (resort to primary jurisdiction of agency is particularly important "when the issue involves technical questions of fact uniquely within the expertise and experience of an agency"); Ezratty v. Puerto Rico, 648 F.2d 770, 774 (1st Cir. 1981) (exhaustion is not always required, because the "issue may be a pure matter of law as to which specialized administrative understanding plays little role," and exhaustion may "work severe harm upon a litigant"). For a proposal to make the Abbott Labs. test the universal standard for exhaustion claims, see Power, 1987 U. Ill. L. Rev. 547 (cited in note 36).

49. [agency expertise and record] See Weinberger v. Salfi, 422 U.S. 749, 765 (1975) (exhaustion give agency opportunity "to afford the parties and the courts the benefit of its experience and expertise, and to compile a record which is adequate for judicial review").

50. [issues of law] McKart v. U.S., 395 U.S. 185, 197–99 (1969) (issue of statutory interpretation requiring neither expertise nor discretion, where it was too late to exhaust administrative remedies and consequence of failure to exhaust would be criminal conviction); Great N. Ry. v. Merchants Elev. Co., 259 U.S. 285, 294 (1922) (meaning of railroad tariff where question was purely one of "construction," involving no dispute over facts or administrative discretion); Bethlehem Steel Corp. v. Environmental Protection Agency, 669 F.2d 903, 907 (3d Cir. 1982) (exhaustion not required "where a dispute centers on legal questions such as constitutional or statutory interpretation, and the facts are uncontested"); Murphy v. Admin'r of Div. of Personnel Admin., 377 Mass. 217, 221, 386 N.E.2d 211, 213–14 (1979) ("questions of law which have not been committed to agency discretion"); Nolan v. Fitzpatrick, 9 N.J. 477, 487, 89 A.2d 13, 17 (1952) (on "judicial review of a question of law the opinions of these administrative tribunals would not be persuasive as they would be on questions of fact within their purview").

51. [constitutional challenges] Mathews v. Eldridge, 424 U.S. 319, 329–30 (1976) ("it is unrealistic to expect that the Secretary would consider substantial changes in the current administrative review system at the behest of a single aid recipient raising a constitutional challenge in an adjudicatory context"); Weinberger v. Salfi, 422 U.S. 749, 767 (1975) (constitutional challenge to eligibility requirement in social security statute is beyond the competence of the Secretary, so that exhaustion would be "futile and wasteful"); State v. Superior Court, 12 Cal. 3d 237, 251, 524 P.2d 1281, 1290, 115 Cal. Rptr. 497, 506 (1974) ("it would be heroic indeed to compel a party to appear before an administrative body to challenge its very existence and to expect a dispassionate hearing . . . on the constitutionality of the statute establishing its status and functions"); Northwestern Univ. v. City of Evanston, 74 Ill. 2d 80, 86, 383 N.E.2d 964, 967–68 (1978) (exhaustion not required where litigant plausibly attacks statute as unconstitutional "as a whole or in its terms" or "on its face"); Bare v. Gorton, 84 Wash. 2d 380, 383, 526 P.2d 379, 381 (1974) ("administrative body does not have authority to determine the constitutionality of the law it administers"). See Davis, 19 F.R.D. at 454–60 (cited in note 38) (distinguishing constitutional challenge to the statute from constitutional challenge to agency's application of the statute in a particular case).

52. [challenges to jurisdiction] Compare McKart v. U.S., 395 U.S. 185, 194 (1969) ("courts ordinarily should not interfere with an agency until it has completed its action, or else has clearly exceeded its jurisdiction"); Public Util. Comm'n v. U.S., 355 U.S. 534, 539–40 (1958) (litigant was constitutionally immune from the agency's jurisdiction); Landfill, Inc. v. Pollution Control Bd., 74 Ill. 2d 541, 551, 387 N.E.2d 258, 261 (1978) ("where an administrative body's assertion of jurisdiction is attacked on its face and in its entirety on the ground that it is not authorized by statute," exhaustion is not required); and Ward v. Keenan, 3 N.J. 298, 308–09, 70 A.2d 77, 82 (1949) ("persuasive" reasons to doubt the agency's jurisdiction); with Myers v. Bethlehem Shipbuilding Corp., 303 U.S. 41, 50–51 (1938) (exhaustion has "repeatedly" been required where "contention is made that the administrative body lacked power over the subject matter"). See Davis, 19 F.R.D. at 440–48 (cited in note 38) (analyzing fourteen Supreme Court decisions on the issue, seven of which required exhaustion).

53. [limitations on agency relief] Myers v. Caple, 258 N.W.2d 301, 304 (Iowa 1977) (administrative remedy inadequate and exhaustion not required where agency, charged with protecting state's interest in water resources, lacks power to remedy wrongs to individuals); Foree v. Crown Cent. Petroleum Corp., 431 S.W.2d 312, 316 (Tex. 1968) (agency has no power either to grant relief sought or make findings essential to that relief); Moore v. Pacific Northwest Bell, 662 P.2d 398, 400–02 (Wash. App. 1983) (agency has no power to grant relief sought and no special competence to adjudicate claim). But see Ricci v. Chicago Mercantile Exchange, 409 U.S. 289 (1973) (defendant allegedly violated both antitrust laws and Commodities Exchange Act; court stayed adjudication of antitrust claim pending claim to Commodity Exchange Commission).

54. **[matters inherently judicial]** Gregg v. Delhi-Taylor Oil Corp., 344 S.W.2d 411, 415–16 (Tex. 1961) (trespass).

55. **[exhaustion varies with substance]** Weinberger v. Salfi, 422 U.S. 749, 765 (1975) ("the doctrine of administrative exhaustion should be applied with a regard for the particular administrative scheme at issue"); McKart v. U.S., 395 U.S. 185, 195 (1969) ("the exhaustion doctrine must be tailored to fit the peculiarities of the administrative system Congress has created"); In re MCorp, 101 Bankr. 483 (S.D. Tex. 1989) (enjoining regulatory proceedings against bank holding company and its nonbank subsidiaries, so that all proceedings could be consolidated in bankruptcy court); Myers v. Caple, 258 N.W.2d 301, 303 (Iowa 1977) ("much depends upon the legislative intent in establishing the particular administrative remedy").

56. **[no exhaustion in § 1983 cases]** Patsy v. Bd. of Regents, 457 U.S. 496 (1982); Gibson v. Berryhill, 411 U.S. 564, 574 (1973); McNeese v. Bd. of Educ., 373 U.S. 668, 671–73 (1963).

57. **[federal exhaustion rules more stringent]** Compare Myers v. Bethlehem Shipbuilding Corp., 303 U.S. 41, 50–51 (1938) (challenge to agency's jurisdiction does not excuse failure to exhaust administrative remedies); with Ward v. Keenan, 3 N.J. 298, 308–09, 70 A.2d 77, 82 (1949) (explicitly rejecting *Myers* and excusing exhaustion where there are "persuasive" reasons to doubt the agency's jurisdiction). For a comparison of state and federal exhaustion rules, see Davis, 19 F.R.D. at 485–92 (cited in note 38).

58. **[comparative inadequacy and exhaustion]** Berger, 48 Yale L.J. at 987 (cited in note 40).

59. **[exception for irreparable injury]** Mathews v. Eldridge, 424 U.S. 319, 331 n.11 (1976) (even statutory "finality requirements should, if possible, be construed so as not to cause crucial collateral claims to be lost and potentially irreparable injuries to be suffered"); Renegotiation Bd. v. Bannercraft Clothing Co., 415 U.S. 1, 24 (1974) ("without a clear showing of irreparable injury, failure to exhaust administrative remedies serves as a bar to judicial intervention in the agency process"); Facchiano v. U.S. Dep't of Labor, 859 F.2d 1163, 1168 (3d Cir. 1988) (exhaustion not required where administrative procedures are "clearly shown to be inadequate to prevent irreparable injury"); Roadway Express, Inc. v. Kingsley, 37 N.J. 136, 142, 179 A.2d 729, 732 (1962) (exhaustion required where "nothing before us in anywise suggests that pursuit of the administrative remedies will entail any undue delay or expense or any irreparable harm to the plaintiff"); Clark v. Hansen, 631 P.2d 914, 916 (Utah 1981) ("no court requires exhaustion when exhaustion will involve irreparable injury and when the agency is palpably without jurisdiction" (quoting Davis, *Treatise* § 20.08 (1958) (current edition cited in note 36). For sharp and insightful criticism of irreparable injury talk in exhaustion cases, see Power, 1987 U. Ill. L. Rev. at 587–98, 624–28 (cited in note 36).

60. [inadequate administrative remedies] Gibson v. Berryhill, 411 U.S. 564, 574–75, 578–79 (1973) (administrative remedy is not adequate where agency is biased by prejudgment and pecuniary interest); U.S. v. Anthony Grace & Sons, Inc., 384 U.S. 424, 429–30 (1966) ("parties will not be required to exhaust the administrative procedure if it is shown by clear evidence that such procedure is 'inadequate or unavailable'"); McNeese v. Bd. of Educ., 373 U.S. 668, 674–76 (1963) (administrative remedy is inadequate where it lacks enforcement mechanisms); U.S. v. Blair, 321 U.S. 730, 736–37 (1944) ("if it were shown that the [administrative] appeal procedure provided in the contract was in fact inadequate . . . we would have quite a different case"); Smith v. Ill. Bell Tel. Co., 270 U.S. 587, 590–92 (1926) (administrative remedy is not adequate where for two years agency takes no action on pending claim); Mercy Hosp. v. Pa. Human Relations Comm'n, 499 Pa. 132, 136–37, 451 A.2d 1357, 1359 (1982) ("equitable intervention is appropriate where the administrative process is for some reason inadequate to resolve the dispute"). See also Union Pacific R.R. v. Bd. of County Comm'rs, 247 U.S. 282, 283–87 (1918) (state judicial remedy is inadequate where it is unclear whether one or many actions would be required).

61. [futile administrative remedies] Bowen v. City of N.Y., 476 U.S. 467, 485 (1986) (futile to exhaust remedies where federal agency is pressuring state agency to follow undisclosed policy inconsistent with published regulations); Andrade v. Lauer, 729 F.2d 1475, 1487–88 (D.C. Cir. 1984) (futile to appeal to official whose authority is challenged, but other stages of the administrative remedy must still be exhausted); Wolff v. Selective Serv. Local Bd. No. 16, 372 F.2d 817, 825 (2d Cir. 1967) (futile to exhaust remedies where agency has already decided identical cases); Standard Alaska Prod. Co. v. State Dep't of Revenue, 773 P.2d 201, 208–09 (Alaska 1989) (exhaustion not required where it "will be futile because of the certainty of an adverse decision," but adverse precedent not sufficient where agency indicates willingness to consider argument for an exception); Northwestern Univ. v. City of Evanston, 74 Ill. 2d 80, 87–89, 383 N.E.2d 964, 968–69 (1978) (exhaustion not required "when it would be patently useless," but it is not enough that "relief may be, or even probably will be, denied"); Karches v. City of Cincinnati, 38 Ohio St. 3d 12, 17–18, 526 N.E.2d 1350, 1355–57 (1988) ("neither repeated applications and denials nor patently fruitless measures to obtain relief are required"); Orion Corp. v. State, 103 Wash. 2d 441, 456–60, 693 P.2d 1369, 1378–80 (1985) (futile to exhaust remedies where plaintiff's claim would require state to abandon policy to which it was firmly committed). Compare Glover v. St. Louis-San Francisco Ry., 393 U.S. 324, 330–31 (1969) (futile for black employees in segregated job classification to exhaust remedies under collective bargaining agreement); Naylor v. Harkins, 11 N.J. 435, 444, 94 A.2d 825, 829 (1953) (exhaustion of internal union remedies not required where appellate body would not convene for two years).

62. [equating rules] Criterion Ins. Co. v. State Dep't of Ins., 458 So.2d 22, 27 (Fla. App. 1984) ("The test to determine whether injunctive relief should be granted to relieve a party from administrative action is the same as that which courts have otherwise used in determining whether to grant injunctive relief: The party applying for same must make a showing of the likelihood of irreparable harm; such a showing depends upon the unavailability of an adequate remedy at law, or, as here, the absence of an adequate administrative remedy to cure allegedly egregious agency error"); Ill. Bell Tel. Co. v. Allphin, 60 Ill. 2d 350, 358, 326 N.E.2d 737, 742

(1975) ("exceptions to the exhaustion doctrine have been fashioned in recognition of the time-honored rule that equitable relief will be available if the remedy at law is inadequate"); Anzelmo v. La. Comm'n on Ethics for Public Employees, 435 So.2d 1082, 1087–88 (La. App. 1983) (refusing to enjoin administrative proceedings because of irreparable injury rule, without mentioning exhaustion rules); School Dist. v. Mich. State Tenure Comm'n, 367 Mich. 689, 692–93, 117 N.W.2d 181, 183 (1962) (plaintiff "has an adequate legal remedy and has failed to exhaust the administrative remedy" and "there is no proof that complainant would suffer irreparable injury").

   63. [exceptions argued as irreparable injury] Bowen v. City of N.Y., 476 U.S. 467, 483–84 (1986) (exhaustion would inflict irreparable injury where mental patients might suffer severe medical harm from "ordeal" of administrative appeal process); Renegotiation Bd. v. Bannercraft Clothing Co., 415 U.S. 1, 23–24 (1974) (rejecting claim that administrative litigation without adequate discovery would inflict irreparable injury); Flowers Indus. v. Fed. Trade Comm'n, 849 F.2d 551, 552–53 (11th Cir. 1988) (divestiture of two bakeries would be irreparable injury, but agency had no power to unilaterally cause divestiture); Thorbus v. Bowen, 848 F.2d 901, 904 (8th Cir. 1988) (refusing to enjoin exclusion of physician from eligibility for Medicare and Medicaid reimbursement, where irreparable injury to physician was outweighed by danger to patients and physician's low probability of success); United Church of the Medical Center v. Medical Center Comm'n, 689 F.2d 693, 701 (7th Cir. 1982) (enjoining proceeding before biased agency, to avoid irreparable loss of neutral adjudicator and possible irreparable loss of real estate); Graham v. Ill. Racing Bd., 76 Ill. 2d 566, 574–75, 394 N.E.2d 1148, 1151 (1979) (injury to reputation from commencement of license revocation proceeding is not irreparable injury justifying injunction against proceeding); Pechner v. Pa. Ins. Dep't, 499 Pa. 139, 144 n.8, 452 A.2d 230, 232 n.8 (1982) (rejecting argument that administrative remedy could not result in refund of money claimed, and that inability to litigate on behalf of class made administrative remedy inadequate); Brown v. Amaral, 460 A.2d 7, 10 (R.I. 1983) (chief of police, discharged for misconduct, failed to show irreparable injury where proper remedy was arbitration); State v. Associated Metals & Minerals Corp., 635 S.W.2d 407, 410–11 (Tex. 1982) (chemical plant seeking permission to increase sulfur dioxide emissions alleged that administrative delay would inflict irreparable harm; court rejected claim, equating irreparable harm with violation of due process).

   64. [judges deny irreparable injury] Sears, Roebuck & Co. v. Nat'l Labor Relations Bd., 473 F.2d 91, 93 (D.C. Cir. 1972) (litigating administrative charge without access to evidence will not result in irreparable injury); Smith v. Dep't of Registration & Educ., 170 Ill. App. 3d 40, 47, 523 N.E.2d 1271, 1275 (1988) (rejecting claim that revocation of medical license would inflict irreparable injury by destroying plaintiff's practice). For a more accurate explanation of such a result, see Standard Alaska Prod. Co. v. State Dep't of Revenue, 773 P.2d 201, 209–10 (Alaska 1989) ("the 'irreparable harm' alleged by Standard is not serious enough to justify an exception to the requirements of the exhaustion doctrine").

   65. [litigation expense not irreparable] Fed. Trade Comm'n v. Standard Oil Co., 449 U.S. 232, 244 (1980) ("mere litigation expense, even substantial and unrecoupable cost, does not constitute irreparable injury"); Renegotiation Bd. v. Bannercraft Clothing Co., 415 U.S. 1, 23–24 (1974) (same); Matsushita Elec. Indus.

Co. v. U.S., 823 F.2d 505, 509 (Fed. Cir. 1987) (litigation and discovery expenses are not irreparable injury, even though they will not be compensated); Kuflom v. D.C. Bureau of Motor Vehicle Serv., 543 A.2d 340, 344 (D.C. 1988) ("mere injuries, however substantial, in terms of money, time and energy necessarily expended in the absence of a stay, are not enough"); Ind. State Dep't of Public Welfare v. Nucleopath, Inc., 526 N.E.2d 1032, 1035 (Ind. App. 1988) ("expense and annoyance of compliance with administrative procedures are part of the social burden of living under government" and are not irreparable injury); Bar Harbor Banking & Trust Co. v. Alexander, 411 A.2d 74, 79 (Me. 1980) (cost and reputational injury are not irreparable harm, but "unavoidable consequence of regulation"). See also City of Lincoln v. Cather & Sons Constr., Inc., 206 Neb. 10, 13–14, 290 N.W.2d 798, 801 (1980) (litigation expenses are not irreparable injury that justify injunction against lawsuit). For an opinion that comes closer to stating the real reason, see Petroleum Exploration, Inc. v. Public Serv. Comm'n, 304 U.S. 209, 221 (1938) (unrecoverable litigation expense "is not the sort of irreparable injury against which equity protects," treating issue as "the weight to be given complaints of irrecoverable and irreparable cost and damage").

66. [unrecoverable expense is irreparable] See ch. 3 part A.3.

67. [litigation expense universal] See Myers v. Bethlehem Shipbuilding Corp., 303 U.S. 41, 50–51 (1938) ("the contention is at war with the long settled rule" of exhaustion); Nat'l Gypsum Co. v. Corns, 736 S.W.2d 325, 327–28 (Ky. 1987) (treating litigation expense as universal, and refusing to make exception for massive antitrust case allegedly barred by limitations).

68. [futile administrative remedies] See cases cited in note 61.

69. [multiple administrative remedies] Graham v. Ill. Racing Bd., 76 Ill. 2d 566, 573, 394 N.E.2d 1148, 1151 (1979) (exception "where multiple remedies exist before the same administrative agency and at least one has been exhausted"); Herman v. Village of Hillside, 15 Ill. 2d 396, 407–08, 155 N.E.2d 47, 53 (1959) (useless to request zoning variance from same board that denied rezoning); Nat'l Account Systems, Inc. v. Anderson, 82 Ill. App. 3d 233, 236–38, 402 N.E.2d 656, 658–59 (1980) (multiple rehearings before agency). See also Cont'l Can Co. v. Marshall, 603 F.2d 590, 596–97 (7th Cir. 1979) (enjoining repeated administrative litigation of same issue at each of defendant's eighty plants).

70. [loss of procedural advantage] See ch. 3 part A.5.

71. [multiplicity of suits] See id. part A.1.

72. [relitigation] Amalgamated Sugar Co. v. NL Indus., Inc., 667 F. Supp. 87, 92 (S.D.N.Y. 1987) (expense of relitigation is irreparable injury); Brazos River Conservation & Reclamation Dist. v. Allen, 141 Tex. 208, 216–17, 171 S.W.2d 842, 846–47 (1943) (enjoining relitigation before commissioners who could not hear plea of res judicata); Browning v. Ryan, 756 S.W.2d 379 (Tex. App. 1988) (state court injunction against relitigation). But see Repka v. Am. Nat'l Ins. Co., 143 Tex. 542, 550, 186 S.W.2d 977, 981–82 (1945) (refusing to enjoin one of two parallel suits, where first judgment would be res judicata in the other case, so that with or without the injunction, one and only one suit would be litigated).

73. [no enjoining state relitigation] Toucey v. N.Y. Life Ins. Co., 314 U.S. 118 (1941) (interpreting the Anti-Injunction Act, then 28 U.S.C. § 379 (1940)).

74. [overruled by statute] 28 U.S.C. § 2283 (1988) (authorizing federal court to enjoin state litigation where necessary "to protect or effectuate its judgments").

For recent applications, see Zagano v. Fordham Univ., 720 F. Supp. 266 (S.D.N.Y. 1989) (enjoining state administrative hearing on claim of employment discrimination previously dismissed with prejudice in federal court); Amalgamated Sugar Co. v. NL Indus., Inc., 667 F. Supp. 87, 96 (S.D.N.Y. 1987) (enjoining litigation in state court demanding performance of stock purchase plan previously enjoined by federal court).

75. [statute restored earlier law] Historical and Revision Notes to § 2283.

76. [two lines of cases] Middleton-Keirn v. Stone, 655 F.2d 609, 612 (5th Cir. 1981) ("two distinct lines of cases are involved").

77. [after exhaustion] Equal Employment Opportunity Comm'n v. Cosmair, Inc., 821 F.2d 1085, 1090–91 (5th Cir. 1987) (age discrimination); Middleton-Keirn v. Stone, 655 F.2d 609, 612 (5th Cir. 1981) (sex discrimination); Murry v. Am. Standard, Inc., 488 F.2d 529, 530 (5th Cir. 1973) (unspecified Title VII claim); Culpepper v. Reynolds Metal Co., 421 F.2d 888, 894–95 (5th Cir. 1970) (race discrimination); U.S. v. Hayes Int'l Corp., 415 F.2d 1038, 1045 (5th Cir. 1969) (race discrimination).

78. [before exhaustion] Morgan v. Fletcher, 518 F.2d 236, 239–40 (5th Cir. 1975) (financial hardship, emotional distress, and loss of job, home, and medical insurance are not irreparable injury). For a similar case in another circuit, see Soldevila v. Secretary of Agric., 512 F.2d 427, 430 (1st Cir. 1975) ("the strong policy against enjoining incomplete agency actions, which is reinforced by the equity policy against enforcing personal service contracts and the disruptive effect of granting temporary relief in such cases, requires an extraordinarily strong showing of irreparable harm to warrant a preliminary injunction").

79. [deference to executive] Yakus v. U.S., 321 U.S. 414, 437–43 (1944) (upholding statutory ban on preliminary injunctions against price controls); Rental Equip. Co. v. Meridian Engineering Co., 374 F. Supp. 892, 896–97 (D.V.I. 1974) (refusing to enjoin award of government contract).

80. [deference plus rule] Weinberger v. Romero-Barcelo, 456 U.S. 305, 311–12 (1982) (refusing to enjoin Navy artillery practice, reciting irreparable injury rule but emphasizing deference and balance of hardship); Rizzo v. Goode, 423 U.S. 362, 378–79 (1976) (refusing to order program to reduce police brutality, emphasizing federalism and interference with executive branch, but also stating generally that "principles of equity nonetheless militate heavily against the grant of an injunction except in the most extraordinary circumstances"); Chisom v. Roemer, 853 F.2d 1186, 1188–89 (5th Cir. 1988) (refusing preliminary injunction against judicial election, emphasizing deference and hardship, but refusing to presume that violation of voting rights causes irreparable injury); Ghandi v. Police Dep't, 747 F.2d 338, 343–44 (6th Cir. 1984) (refusing to enjoin police surveillance, stating that permanent injunction is "an extraordinary remedy" granted "only for compelling reasons," and that "standard is particularly high" when defendant is a law enforcement agency); Evenson v. Ortega, 605 F. Supp. 1115, 1120–21 (D. Ariz. 1985) (refusing to enjoin sheriff from placing false ads for escort service, finding no evidence that legal remedies were inadequate, and stating that "an injunction is an extraordinary remedy and is never lightly dispensed," and that "this is even more the case when" the injunction would interfere with law enforcement); Clements v. Bd. of Educ., 133 Ill. App. 3d 531, 536, 478 N.E.2d 1209, 1212–13 (1985) (refusing to order reinstatement of student suspended from softball team for being present at party where beer was served to minors, stating that courts are reluctant to interfere with public schools and injunctions are an extraordinary remedy); Freeman v. Treen, 442 So.2d 757 (La. App. 1983) (refusing to preliminarily enjoin governor's exercise of line-item veto); Christoffel v. Shaler Area School Dist., 60 Pa. Commw. 17, 19, 430 A.2d 726, 728 (1981) (refusing parents' request to order school board to amend budget to provide for five principal's aides).

81. **[Siberian gas pipeline]** Dresser Indus., Inc. v. Baldridge, 549 F. Supp. 108 (D.D.C. 1982).

82. **[loss of job not irreparable]** Sampson v. Murray, 415 U.S. 61, 91–92 & n.68 (1974).

83. **[loss of job not irreparable]** For similar holdings, see Morton v. Beyer, 822 F.2d 364, 371–73 (3d Cir. 1987) (no irreparable injury from loss of income and reputation to discharged prison guard with debts and a son attending out-of-state university); Gilley v. U.S., 649 F.2d 449, 452–56 (6th Cir. 1981) (no irreparable injury from transfer to distant city, which would cause loss of favorable interest rate on home mortgage, disrupt medical care for plaintiff's wife, and make it difficult and expensive to pursue administrative appeal); Morgan v. Fletcher, 518 F.2d 236, 238–40 (5th Cir. 1975) (loss of medical insurance and probable foreclosure of mortgage on home are not irreparable injury).

84. **[wrong type of irreparable injury]** *Sampson*, 415 U.S. at 91–92 (emphasis added).

85. **[financial distress is irreparable]** Sheehan v. Purolator Courier Corp., 676 F.2d 877, 886 (2d Cir. 1981) (discharge from job); Philadelphia Citizens in Action v. Schweiker, 527 F. Supp. 182, 194 (E.D. Pa. 1981) (loss of welfare benefits), rev'd on other grounds, 669 F.2d 877 (3d Cir. 1982); Perez v. Perez, 353 So.2d 1360, 1363 (La. App. 1978) (seizure of only funds under plaintiff's control, when her share of debt could be paid with her community interest in much larger sums under husband's control); Van Buren Public School Dist. v. Wayne County Circuit Judge, 61 Mich. App. 6, 16–17, 232 N.W.2d 278, 283–84 (1975) (loss of opportunity to bargain collectively over threatened loss of jobs); Ansonia Assoc. v. Ansonia Residents' Ass'n, 78 A.D.2d 211, 218–20, 434 N.Y.S.2d 370, 376–77 (1980) (concerted refusal to pay rent). Compare Cleveland Bd. of Educ. v. Loudermill, 470 U.S. 532, 543–44 (1985) (requiring hearing before discharge of employee with property interest in his job, because of financial hardship resulting from discharge); Goldberg v. Kelly, 397 U.S. 254, 261 (1970) (requiring preliminary hearing before termination of welfare benefits, because of financial hardship resulting from termination).

86. **[Back Pay Act]** See 5 U.S.C. § 5596(b)(1) (1988); U.S. v. Testan, 424 U.S. 392, 400–02 (1976) (no back pay for federal employee whose job was misclassified at improperly low salary, because Back Pay Act does not authorize recovery).

87. **[consequential loss from delay of money]** See Douglas Laycock, *Modern American Remedies* 125–31 (Little, Brown 1985).

88. **[bankruptcy is irreparable]** Doran v. Salem Inn, Inc., 422 U.S. 922, 932 (1975) (risk of bankruptcy from compliance with ordinance restricting topless dancing); Enochs v. Williams Packing & Navigation Co., 370 U.S. 1, 6 (1962) ("ruination of taxpayer's enterprise" would be irreparable injury, but would not by itself justify injunction against collection of taxes). For similar cases in other courts, see Atwood Turnkey Drilling, Inc. v. Petroleo Brasileiro, S.A., 875 F.2d 1174, 1179 (5th Cir.

1989) (ordering defendant to reinstate letter of credit for benefit of plaintiff), cert. denied, 110 S. Ct. 1124 (1990); Tri-State Generation & Transmission Ass'n, Inc. v. Shoshone River Power, Inc., 805 F.2d 351, 356 (10th Cir. 1986) (utility cooperative threatened with bankruptcy by members withdrawing from the system); Hull Mun. Lighting Plant v. Mass. Mun. Wholesale Elec. Co., 399 Mass. 640, 643–45, 506 N.E.2d 140, 141–42 (1987) (utility threatened with bankruptcy by defendant's refusal to make payments on nuclear plant).

89. [not yet an absolute rule] Sampson, 415 U.S. at 92 n.68.

90. [contrary state law] State Employees Ass'n v. Dep't of Mental Health, 421 Mich. 152, 163–68, 365 N.W.2d 93, 99–101 (1984) (requiring very detailed showing of serious irreparable injury, but rejecting federal rule "to the extent that Sampson appears to have been understood as a preclusion per se to a finding of irreparable injury in civil servant discharge cases").

91. [applied to private employers] Holt v. Cont'l Group, Inc., 708 F.2d 87, 90–91 (2d Cir. 1983) ("the requisite irreparable harm is not established in employee discharge cases by financial distress or inability to find other employment, unless truly extraordinary circumstances are shown"); Charles A. Sullivan, Michael J. Zimmer, & Richard F. Richards, Federal Statutory Law of Employment Discrimination § 4.2 at 366–70 (Michie-Bobbs-Merrill 1980) ("the Murray decision provides authoritative guidance as to the meaning of 'irreparable injury' in the employment context").

92. [special rule for government] Sebra v. Neville, 801 F.2d 1135, 1139 (9th Cir. 1986) (refusing to enjoin transfer of national guard employee to another base).

93. [reinstatement at final judgment] See ch. 7 part C at 172–73.

94. [official immunity] Harlow v. Fitzgerald, 457 U.S. 800, 813–19 (1982) (public officials are immune from suits for damages inflicted by their official acts, unless they violated clearly settled law); Nixon v. Fitzgerald, 457 U.S. 731, 744–58 (1982) (President is absolutely immune from suits for damages); Stump v. Sparkman, 435 U.S. 349 (1978) (judges are absolutely immune from suit for damages inflicted by their judicial acts, unless they act in "clear absence of all jurisdiction"); Imbler v. Pachtman, 424 U.S. 409, 420–31 (1976) (prosecutors are absolutely immune from suit for damages inflicted by their prosecutorial acts); Yerardi's Moody Street Restaurant & Lounge, Inc. v. Bd. of Selectmen, 878 F.2d 16 (1st Cir. 1989) (applying immunity rules to suit for damages against officials who voted to restrict liquor license to 1:00 A.M. closing time).

95. [sovereign immunity] Pa. v. Union Gas Co., 109 S. Ct. 2273, 2277, 2281–86 (1989) (state is immune from suit for damages for violation of federal law, unless Congress overrides state immunity with unmistakable clarity); Atascadero State Hosp. v. Scanlon, 473 U.S. 234, 237–47 (1985) (state is immune from suit for damages for violation of federal law); Dalehite v. U.S., 346 U.S. 15, 30–45 (1953) (United States is immune from suit for damages caused by discretionary decisions of federal officials, even if those decisions are at operational level); Hans v. La., 134 U.S. 1 (1890) (states are immune from suit in federal court); Riss v. City of N.Y., 22 N.Y.2d 579, 240 N.E.2d 860, 293 N.Y.S.2d 897 (1968) (victim of crime cannot sue city for failing to provide reasonable police protection). For analysis see Peter H. Schuck, Suing Government (Yale Univ. Press 1983); Laycock, Remedies at 1096–1172 (cited in note 87).

96. **[no specific performance]** See 28 U.S.C. § 1491(a)(3) (1988) (authorizing declaratory and injunctive relief only in contract claims "brought before the contract is awarded," thus excluding specific performance claims); Larson v. Domestic & Foreign Commerce Corp., 337 U.S. 682 (1949) (court cannot order federal official to specifically perform a government contract); Chemung County v. Dole, 781 F.2d 963, 967–71 (2d Cir. 1986) (court can grant pre-award equitable relief but cannot grant "disguised specific performance"); Clark v. Pa. State Police, 496 Pa. 310, 313–14, 436 A.2d 1383, 1385 (1981) (state's waiver of sovereign immunity for breach of contract limited remedy to arbitration and damages). The current version of 28 U.S.C. § 1491 was a response to U.S. v. King, 395 U.S. 1 (1969), which held that the jurisdiction of the Court of Claims was limited to money claims and did not extend to claims for any form of equitable remedy or declaratory judgment.

97. **[injunctions but not damages]** See Edelman v. Jordan, 415 U.S. 651, 660–71 (1974) (federal court can order state official to comply with federal law in future, but cannot order him to use state funds to compensate for past violations); U.S. v. Testan, 424 U.S. 392, 403 (1976) (civil service employee who was underpaid because his job was misclassified can seek administrative or judicial order reclassifying the job for the future, but cannot sue for back pay). Compare Pulliam v. Allen, 466 U.S. 522, 528–43 (1984) (judges are not immune from injunction against misconduct); with Stump v. Sparkman, 435 U.S. 349 (1978) (judicial immunity from damages). Compare Ex parte Young, 209 U.S. 123, 149–61 (1908) (prosecutors may be enjoined from enforcing unconstitutional law); with Imbler v. Pachtman, 424 U.S. 409, 420–31 (1976) (prosecutorial immunity from damages).

98. **[neither remedy allowed]** Eastland v. U.S. Servicemen's Fund, 421 U.S. 491, 503 (1975) (speech and debate clause bars criminal prosecution, suit for damages, and suit for injunction against member of Congress for legislative acts).

7

Avoiding Over Enforcement

Sometimes courts refuse specific relief for fear of over enforcement. In the largest group of such cases, the specific remedy seems unduly expensive, and the argument is whether the remedy is worth the cost.

In other cases, defendant relies on a countervailing substantive policy, such as freedom of speech or freedom to choose employment. Seeking remedies for plaintiffs that do not destroy the rights of defendants, courts are drawn to half measures. In these cases, courts prefer legal remedies because they are less effective—not because they are adequate, but because they are inadequate.

A. Hardship to Defendant or Others

Specific relief sometimes costs more than it is worth. Courts take account of that danger under a long-standing but poorly defined defense: if specific relief would impose serious hardship disproportionate to the benefit to plaintiff, then specific relief may be denied and plaintiff remitted to damages.[1] Some commentators would abolish or at least sharply restrict the doctrine,[2] but it is well entrenched in the cases. It is regularly applied in tort,[3] contract,[4] and property[5] cases—in all substantive areas of law.

The doctrine is commonly called "balancing" the "equities" or "hardships."[6] "Hardship" is a better label for the countervailing consideration that leads courts to withhold specific relief. But once a plausible showing of hardship is made, courts inquire into all sorts of things, including defendant's culpability,[7] the public interest,[8] plaintiff's delay or other conduct that aggravated the risk of hardship,[9] and the disadvantage to plaintiff of getting damages instead of specific relief. "Balancing the equities" may be a better label for that whole process.

Undue hardship matters doctrinally only when damages are inadequate.[10] That is, if plaintiff has an adequate remedy at law, he is not entitled to an equitable remedy, and any hardship caused by such a remedy is not at issue. In fact a claim of hardship is almost always relevant, because the legal remedy is almost never adequate. The important point is that to deny equitable relief on grounds of undue hardship is to remit plaintiff to an inadequate remedy.

Not surprisingly, courts balance the hardship to defendant from specific relief against any hardship to plaintiff from a less-than-adequate remedy. Inevitably, courts that deny specific relief often add irreparable injury talk as well.[11] A similar pattern appears in cases that deny specific relief because of hardship to innocent parties.[12]

An excellent example is *Van Wagner Advertising Corp. v. S & M Enterprises.*[13] Van Wagner held a ten-year lease on advertising space on the side of a building facing an exit from the Midtown Tunnel into Manhattan. S & M bought the building and others on the block, planning to tear them down and erect a large new building. S & M terminated the advertising lease, and Van Wagner sued for specific performance.

There was nothing fictional about the uniqueness of this real estate; no other building faced the tunnel exit in the same way. But to give Van Wagner the specific thing it was promised would certainly limit, and perhaps prevent, the plan to redevelop the block. Not surprisingly, the court denied specific performance on the ground that it "would disproportionately harm S & M."[14] A major real estate development trumps a billboard.

The court also held that damages were an adequate remedy, even though the subject matter of the contract was unique real estate. This required considerable modification of the irreparable injury rule. The court distinguished leases from sales, noting that leases of real estate are not specifically enforced "as a matter of course," citing one trial court decision and dropping a "but see" citation to Corbin, Williston, Pomeroy, and the Restatement (Second) of Contracts.[15] The court conceived uniqueness solely in terms of the difficulty of measuring damages and the consequent risk of undercompensation;[16] the site's unique location did not "entitle" Van Wagner to specific performance. Van Wagner had subleased the space at a profit for three of the ten years, and the rental in the sublease was used to measure damages for the whole ten-year period.

These damages are imperfect at best, and may be seriously defective. Van Wagner lost any chance to charge a higher rent for years four through ten, and the court made no effort to compensate that loss. More important is the sublessee, the advertiser who bargained for three years of exposure to the tunnel exit. His damages seem entirely unmeasurable. Either he loses his expectancy entirely, receiving no compensation other than release of his obligation to pay rent, or Van Wagner is liable for the speculative value of the advertiser's lost expectancy. Van Wagner got no compensation for that liability, and the court did not venture an opinion on how to measure the advertiser's damages.

The court did not explicitly link its irreparable injury holding to its undue hardship holding. But the opinion makes no sense unless such a link is implied. If there were no reason to withhold specific performance, there would be no need to guess about profits from the last seven years of the lease, no need to make plaintiff do without the unique exposure to the tunnel for which it bargained, no need to override the received rules on real estate transactions, and no need to ignore the rights of the sublessee. It was perfectly sound to say that damages were good enough in light of the cost of specific performance; it is not true that the damage remedy was adequate in the usual sense of equally complete, practical, and efficient.

Undue hardship in the guise of no irreparable injury produced an even more astonishing pair of opinions in a freight forwarder's suit against a competing company organized by plaintiff's disloyal employees. A court wound up saying that injury was irreparable at the motion for preliminary injunction, but not irreparable at final judgment. This absurdity arose because the trial court erroneously refused a preliminary injunction. On the first appeal, the appellate court said that this refusal had been an abuse of discretion.[17] On remand, the trial court still refused a preliminary injunction. Eventually, it refused a permanent injunction and awarded damages instead.

The second appeal was decided nearly four years after the separation of the two companies. The appellate court affirmed, because an injunction at that time might "greatly disrupt" defendant's business "while not substantially benefitting plaintiff."[18] This perfectly plausible undue hardship holding is tucked into one clause of a three-clause sentence, in the middle of a paragraph, in the middle of a long passage about lack of irreparable injury and the difference between preliminary and permanent injunctions. At one point the court implies that a lesser showing of irreparable injury should be required for preliminary injunctions, which merely preserve the status quo.[19]

The case is a powerful example of a court struggling to reach a sensible result despite confusion engendered by the irreparable injury rule. Plaintiff vigorously argued from precedents that had minimized the irreparable injury requirement on facts where there was no real reason to deny specific relief, and the court did not know how to distinguish those cases on facts where there *was* strong reason to deny specific relief. The mere fact that there was good reason to deny specific relief did not seem to be enough; irreparable injury appeared as a separate question that required three columns of judicial prose to resolve.

The undue hardship rules are not limited to comparisons of legal and equitable remedies, or of substitutionary and specific remedies. Courts also recognize that some forms of specific relief are more burdensome than others. Established doctrine reserves especially intrusive remedies, such as receiverships[20] and corporate dissolution,[21] for situations where no other remedy will work. These rules are sometimes stated in terms of irreparable injury, but the comparison is to other remedies of all sorts. The basis for these rules is hardship to defendant, and not any distinction between law and equity.

There are even undue hardship cases at law. Undue hardship is the best explanation of cases like *Peevyhouse v. Garland Coal & Mining Co.*,[22] in which plaintiff sought damages based on the cost of specific performance, and the court awarded damages based on the value that performance would have created. The Restatement rule for breached construction contracts is that plaintiff is entitled

to the cost of completion unless that cost is "clearly disproportionate" to the benefit.[23] The Restatement's standard for refusing
specific performance is "unreasonable hardship."[24] The drafter
does not appear to have intended a distinction between these two
standards, and the cases use these and similar phrases interchangeably.[25]

This equivalence makes sense. If the court would deny specific
performance because the cost is disproportionate to the benefit,
plaintiff should not be able to evade the rule by claiming the cost
of specific performance as the measure of damages. But the effect
of this equivalence is that courts must sometimes balance the equities in a damage action at law. That is anomalous only if you think
the separation of law and equity still matters.

B. Freedom of Speech

Two related rules inhibit injunctions against unlawful speech. One
is the constitutional rule against prior restraints,[26] and one is the
nonconstitutional rule that equity will not enjoin a libel.[27] For
convenience, I will refer to the two rules collectively as the rules
against prior restraints. If these rules were absolute, injunctions
would never issue against speech; the only remedies for unlawful
speech would be damage judgments and criminal prosecutions. In
fact, neither rule absolutely bans injunctions against speech, and
a surprising number have been upheld.

Courts usually invoke the rules against prior restraints explicitly,
without additional talk about irreparable injury or adequate remedies. But occasionally, a court feels compelled to say that the
subsequent remedy is adequate.[28] In *Willing v. Mazzocone*, the
court said that a damage judgment would be an adequate remedy
for defamation, even though defendant was indigent and the judgment would be worthless![29] The court correctly saw that it could
not enjoin indigent speakers if it would not enjoin wealthy speakers: "conditioning the right of free speech upon the monetary worth
of an individual" would be intolerable. But the claim that an uncollectible damage judgment would be an adequate substitute for
reputation added nothing to the analysis.

The policy base of the rules against prior restraint is our commitment to freedom of speech and the traditional belief that prior restraints are more dangerous to free speech than subsequent penalties. Whether prior restraints are really a greater threat to liberty has been the subject of much debate,[30] but the belief that they are a greater threat is embedded in precedent and supports both the rules against prior restraints. For present purposes, I accept the rules as I find them; I need not enter the debate over prior restraints.

The important point here is that the rules against prior restraints cannot possibly be derived from the irreparable injury rule, and in fact have very little to do with it. It is not the law that plaintiff can get a prior restraint only when no other remedy is as clear, practical, and efficient as a prior restraint. Indeed, that is almost exactly backwards. The justification for the rules against prior restraints depends precisely on the claim that other remedies are *not* as effective. The prior restraint rules limit plaintiffs to less effective remedies because we fear over enforcement of rules against tortious or criminal speech.

On the usual criteria of irreparable injury, both damages and criminal prosecution are grossly inadequate. Humans have long understood that corrections never catch up to defamations. A medieval parable taught that retrieving a lie was like bursting a feather pillow from the highest tower in Rome and then trying to retrieve all the feathers. Money damages cannot replace a reputation once lost,[31] or erase emotional distress once suffered.[32] Neither reputation nor distress is sold in market transactions, so neither can be accurately valued in dollars. Consequential damages from defamation are usually speculative and always uncertain in amount. I do not mean to suggest that actual damages in defamation cases are generally large, but only that they are unusually difficult to measure. Both because the thing lost is irreplaceable and because the loss is hard to measure, damages are a seriously inadequate remedy for defamation.

The same analysis could be applied to any other category of unprotected speech. If seditious speech harms the nation, that harm is unmeasurable. If secrets are once revealed, they cannot be recalled, and the harm of their revelation can rarely be valued in dollars.[33] Nor is criminal punishment an adequate remedy. Criminal punishment neither undoes the harm nor compensates for it. It may be good for revenge or deterrence, but it is not a remedy.

So the subsequent remedies for speech torts and speech crimes are grossly inadequate, in the sense in which adequacy is usually measured under the irreparable injury rule. Courts do not forbid prior restraints because other remedies are adequate, but because they are affirmatively hostile to prior restraints.

The rule against enjoining a libel is historically related to the rule against enjoining a crime and to protection of defendant's right to jury trial.[34] If we value jury trial in speech cases, that becomes part of the rationale for the rules against prior restraints. If not, the jury argument is a makeweight. I think it is largely but not entirely the latter.

Jury trial rarely protects speech in a republic. In typical contemporary defamation cases, juries award large sums against media corporations, and judges reduce or set aside the verdicts.[35] The jury is a majoritarian institution; it is not our principal reliance for protection of individual rights. Our legal ancestors once looked to juries to protect popular dissent from royal charges of seditious libel,[36] but juries are much less likely to protect dissidents from a popularly elected government.

Even so, juries sometimes provide an additional layer of protection for speech. Juries might have protected labor speakers in the heyday of the antistrike injunction,[37] or antiwar speakers in the late stages of the Vietnam War. An occasional defamation case pits a well-off plaintiff against a not-so-well-off defendant, and the jury may protect the little guy there,[38] but not because the case involves speech.[39] In any event, the interaction of the rules against prior restraint and the sometime desire for jury trial does not make the resulting rules any more like the irreparable injury rule. Once again, we have a set of particular reasons for avoiding injunctions in particular situations.

The point is further illustrated by the cases permitting prior restraints. The Supreme Court has allowed injunctions against speech after a final judicial determination that the speech is unprotected,[40] and against movies if a judicial determination of obscenity is provided within the "shortest fixed period compatible with sound judicial discretion."[41] It has also enjoined disclosure of information obtained in discovery and subject to protective order.[42]

Legal remedies are no less adequate in these cases than in other cases where plaintiff seeks to suppress speech. But the Court believed that a final judicial determination,[43] or the limitation to information obtained in discovery,[44] removed most of the dangers associated with prior restraints. It also mattered that the regulation in most of these cases was aimed at commercial advertisements and sexually explicit movies,[45] which are not among the more important forms of speech even when they are protected. Whatever the relative weight of these factors, the point here is clear: these cases allow prior restraints because of variations in the perceived harm from the restraint, not because of variations in the adequacy of other remedies.

The same is true of the cases and statutes authorizing injunctions against securities fraud,[46] false advertising,[47] and disparagement of commercial products.[48] At least de facto, the prior restraint rule does not apply to misleading commercial speech, and the Court has suggested that the rule does not apply to commercial speech at all.[49]

Repeated dicta say that prior restraints might be available when the threatened harm from unprotected speech is especially severe; the standard example is Zechariah Chafee's hypothetical case of disclosing wartime troop movements.[50] To say that some information is especially dangerous is to say that the subsequent remedy for that speech is especially inadequate. Where the speech is so harmful that the ineffectiveness of the damage and criminal remedies is intolerable, the Court says it will enjoin despite the dangers to speech. But it is hard to find such an injunction that stood up on appeal.[51]

The most plausible candidates are the decisions enforcing the Central Intelligence Agency's system of administrative prior restraints. All CIA employees agree not to publish information relating to the agency without the agency's prior approval. The Fourth Circuit, which gets these cases because the CIA is headquartered in Virginia, has held that the agency must review manuscripts promptly and allow publication of unclassified material. Subject to that limitation, it enforces the secrecy agreement with injunctions not to publish manuscripts until the agency approves.[52]

The Supreme Court has also enforced the agreement, but in the context of a subsequent remedy for a book that had already been published in breach of the agreement.[53]

These cases depend as much on the employee's contract, and on the fact that he would never have acquired the information if he had not promised to keep it secret, as on the dangers of disclosure. That is, the validity of the prior restraint depended as much on considerations of substantive law as on the allegedly extreme inadequacy of subsequent remedies.

Presumably, there is some speech so dangerous that appellate courts would suppress it on that ground alone. Whether such a case will ever arise is much more doubtful. Information so dangerous would also be of great interest, and in an age of computer networks, fax machines, and photocopiers, it seems unlikely that the judicial process could prevent its dissemination to the people most interested.[54] Prior restraints based on the special inadequacy of the legal remedy will remain rare to nonexistent. But prior restraints will continue to be permitted in situations where they are perceived to do relatively little harm to First Amendment values.

C. Personal Service Contracts

It is generally said that equity will not specifically enforce a contract for personal services.[55] This maxim is related to several policies: that enforcement would be difficult,[56] that enforcement against employees would be involuntary servitude,[57] that enforcement against employers would lack mutuality[58] and deprive the employer of the right to choose agents in which he had confidence.[59] The maxim has become misleading as a maxim, but it survives to the extent of its policies.

1. Specific Relief Against Employees

Courts will specifically enforce some provisions of personal service contracts even against employees; the most important example is reasonable covenants not to compete.[60] The real target of the traditional maxim is not personal service contracts, but personal service: courts will not make a human being work.[61]

The reason for this rule is a substantive law commitment to free labor. Despite the vast social distance between chattel slavery and specific performance of contracts with professional athletes and entertainers, similar policies apply to both. The contractual promise to work is voluntary, but litigation arises only when the employee has changed his mind. An order to work on pain of contempt produces servitude that is involuntary when the services are performed.

The difficulties of enforcing such orders are real but secondary. These difficulties are partly a function of the discretionary skills involved in most of the modern cases. But they also result from our lack of stomach for enforcement. Judges were not deterred by these remedial difficulties until they recognized a substantive policy of free labor. In colonial America, yearly or longer employment contracts were common, quitting during the term of service was forbidden, and runaway servants were forcibly returned to their masters.[62] The practice declined in response to economic changes in the early national period; it surely would not have survived the bitter debate over the fugitive slave law.[63]

By the late nineteenth century, there was a settled rule against specific performance of personal service contracts, and some northern courts insisted that the rule was constitutionally required.[64] Modern opinions emphasize involuntary servitude and difficulty of enforcement, but courts occasionally invoke the irreparable injury rule as well.[65]

The doctrine is that we will not order employees to work, but the reality seems to be that neither will we make them pay damages for refusing to work. Except for the very rich and the very poor— those who can pay and those who have no assets or credit rating to lose—most Americans quitting their jobs would find any significant damage award almost as bad as an order to work.

Culturally, Americans have come to think of the employment contract as binding only the employer. Many Americans think employees are free to leave at any time if they find a better or more lucrative job, but that it would be outrageous for employers to discharge employees just because they found better or cheaper workers. These expectations do not seem much affected by whether the contract is for life tenure, a fixed term, or employment at will. No legal doctrine makes employment contracts so one-sided, but courts and employers respond to the prevailing ethos. My impression is that employers rarely seek damages for breach of the promise to work, and that they get a hostile reception when they do.

A clear example is *Lemat Corp. v. Barry*,[66] refusing to award damages against basketball star Rick Barry. Barry had jumped from the Golden State Warriors to the rival Oakland Oaks. Enjoined from playing for the Oaks, he refused to play for anybody. The trial judge found that the Warriors' damages for lost attendance in the first year without Barry were $356,000, but he entered judgment that the Warriors take nothing.[67] The court of appeal affirmed.

The court's first reason was clearly specious: it said that damages in addition to the injunction would be a double recovery. It is true that the injunction avoided the additional damages the Warriors would have suffered if Barry had played for the competition. But the injunction did nothing to compensate for the loss of Barry's services to the Warriors. The trial court found the damages suffered *with* the injunction, and found that damages would have been greater without the injunction. The injunction enforced the promise not to play for anyone else, but not the promise to play for the Warriors. This distinction between the promise not to compete and the promise to work is well recognized; it is a key part of the doctrinal justification for enforcing employee covenants not to compete.[68]

The court's second reason was only a little better. It said the damages were too speculative to be recovered. In fact, the evidence for the first season was pretty good. The trial court measured damages on the basis of a sharp decline in attendance in a year in which attendance elsewhere in the league had increased. Such comparisons to similarly situated businesses in the same time period, and to the plaintiff's business before and after the wrong, are standard means of proving lost profits. But they were not sufficient in a suit against an employee.

It is even more revealing to contrast *Barry* with the Houston Rockets' claim against the Los Angeles Lakers for the loss of another basketball player, Rudy Tomjanovich.[69] Kermit Washington of the Lakers threw a punch that quite literally smashed Tomjanovich's face and ended his career. Tomjanovich and his wife sued the Lakers, got a $3.4 million judgment, and eventually settled the case pending appeal.

The Rockets sued the Lakers for the loss of Tomjanovich's services. Like the Warriors in *Barry*, they offered evidence of lost attendance, including statistical analysis of games with and without Tomjanovich. After the jury found liability, but before the jury found damages, the case settled.

The amounts of the two settlements were initially confidential, but they were revealed in subsequent litigation over insurance coverage. The Tomjanoviches got $2.13 million for personal injury and loss of consortium; the Rockets got $750,000 for loss of their star player.[70] Adjusting for inflation, the settlement put about the same value on Tomjanovich's services as the trial judge had put on Barry's services a decade before. Lost attendance resulting from loss of a basketball player was too speculative in a contract suit against the employee, but not in a tort suit against a corporation.

If I am right that employees rarely or never pay damages for refusing to work, the rule against specific performance is merely part of a larger cultural reluctance to enforce employment contracts against employees at all. The substantive policy is not just hostility to work on pain of contempt, but hostility to any liability on promises to work. This broader substantive policy has little to do with the choice between specific and substitutionary relief. It is true that the policy is stronger, and supported by clearer precedent, with respect to specific relief. But the irreparable injury rule is not the reason. Far from having an adequate remedy at law, the disappointed employer rarely gets any remedy at all.

The inadequacy of the employer's nonremedy matters in only one situation. One of the principal grounds for enforcing covenants not to compete is that the employee has unique and extraordinary skills.[71] Thus, the employers of entertainers and athletic stars are more likely than other employers to get an injunction enforcing covenants not to compete.[72]

These injunctions against employees with unique skills obviously draw on the uniqueness thread of irreparable injury doctrine. But because of the countervailing policy of avoiding anything that hints at involuntary servitude, the rule reaches only the most extreme cases of unique services. Antebellum slave law was different. Contract and property rights in slaves were specifically enforced, on the sensible ground that each slave was unique.[73] Minor variations among the different slave states are explained in note 73.

We still believe that every human being is unique; that is not what has changed. What has changed is the belief that any human being can be made to work against his will.

2. Specific Relief Against Employers

The other side of the maxim has been largely superseded by modern regulation of employment. Specific relief against employers, including orders to hire, retain, reinstate, and promote, with the seniority that would have accrued but for the wrong, are the standard remedy in unfair labor practice,[74] employment discrimination,[75] and civil service[76] cases, and in discharge cases submitted to arbitration.[77] These remedies are the practical equivalent of specific performance of personal service contracts.

In litigation under the Age Discrimination in Employment Act, courts have actually reversed the traditional presumption, holding that reinstatement is the preferred remedy and that employees cannot recover compensation for lost future income unless the court finds that reinstatement would be unworkable.[78] Why this issue should arise repeatedly under the Age Act, but rarely anywhere else, is a bit of a puzzle. The apparent reason is that Age Act plaintiffs are entitled to jury trial,[79] and that makes it more attractive to seek lost future income. For similar reasons, employers in some states are now urging statutory reinstatement remedies in lieu of common law damages for wrongful discharge.[80]

Half a century ago, Indiana reached a similar conclusion with respect to tenured school teachers.[81] The tenure statute created contractual rights but said nothing about remedy. The state supreme court said that specific performance would be the only remedy, because it was "inconceivable" that "public funds exacted through taxation should be used to pay for services that were never rendered, or that a teacher should receive remuneration for services that were never performed." Such refusals to award damages remain exceptional, but the willingness to order reinstatement is routine.

Courts no longer presume that friction between employer and employee will make reinstatement unworkable. Courts do accept evidence of such friction, especially in cases where plaintiff must work closely with the employer or a particular supervisor, and deny reinstatement if it appears to be an unworkable remedy.[82] But courts sometimes go to extraordinary lengths to coerce working relationships in the face of bitter resentment.[83]

Some commentators have questioned the wisdom of these efforts, citing studies showing that reinstatement is often unsuccessful.[84] Workers offered reinstatement often decline, and those who accept often quit or get fired within a short time. Reinstatement is more successful when ordered by an arbitrator under a collective bargaining agreement, presumably because the reinstated worker then has the support of a recognized union in a functioning bargaining relationship.[85]

The risk of friction and the difficulties of reinstatement have nothing to do with the adequacy of back pay or damages. No two jobs are identical, and an employee who wants his job back can never be exactly compensated for taking some less desirable job instead.[86] Damages compensate for lost pay and little else. But the difficulty of coercing close personal relationships is a powerful reason for sometimes denying specific relief, even when damage remedies are inadequate. And not surprisingly, when courts refuse reinstatement for these reasons, they often invoke the irreparable injury rule as well.[87]

The old rule against specific performance survives in common law actions for breach of contract or wrongful discharge,[88] and in that context it is codified in some states.[89] The common law rule survives partly from the inertia of precedent, and partly because discharged employees seem rarely to seek reinstatement in common law actions. I found only a handful of recent common law cases granting or denying reinstatement,[90] and they seem not to be in the main line of contemporary wrongful discharge litigation. Two recent commentaries carefully consider the arguments for and against common law reinstatement without citing a single recent case either way.[91]

There are several possible explanations for the relative scarcity of common law actions for reinstatement. In those states where wrongful discharge is a tort, permitting recovery of emotional distress and punitive damages, damage awards are often in six figures. This makes damages far more lucrative than reinstatement.[92] Elsewhere, plaintiffs' lawyers may hope to create such liability, or they may assume that reinstatement is unavailable. Perhaps most likely, in common law actions with no provision for attorneys' fees, only a damage judgment produces a fund to pay the lawyer. It seems unlikely that most employees with statutory claims naturally prefer reinstatement, but that most employees with common law claims naturally prefer damages.

An absolute rule against reinstatement in common law actions, side by side with routine reinstatement in statutory and arbitral actions, is an unstable combination. Already a few courts have explicitly rejected the common law rule, ordering reinstatement without the authority of either a statute or an arbitration award.[93] Courts regularly order reinstatement of public employees discharged in violation of their First Amendment rights, without statutory authority and without noting that they are doing something that is supposed to be unusual.[94] Other Supreme Court cases obviously assume that reinstatement will be the remedy for a successful plaintiff, but do not squarely address the issue.[95]

I do not venture to predict the future course of the law in this area. But I expect future developments to depend on arguments about the workability and effectiveness of reinstatement, about the reasonableness and deterrent effect of damage awards, and about the proper balance between the employee's need for job security and the employer's need for discipline and productivity. I do not expect that developments will be significantly influenced either by the irreparable injury rule or by the maxim that personal service contracts cannot be specifically enforced.

Notes on Over Enforcement

1. [hardship disproportionate to benefit] See generally Dan B. Dobbs, *Handbook on the Law of Remedies* § 2.4 at 52–54, §§ 5.6–5.7 at 355–64 (West 1973); Zygmunt J.B. Plater, *Statutory Violations and Equitable Discretion*, 70 Cal. L. Rev. 524, 533–45 (1982).

2. [attacks on doctrine] See Daniel A. Farber, *Reassessing Boomer: Justice, Efficiency, and Nuisance Law*, in *Property Law and Legal Education: Essays in Honor of John E. Cribbet* (Peter Hay & Michael Harlan Hoeflich, eds.) (Univ. Ill. Press 1988); David S. Schoenbrod, *The Measure of an Injunction: A Principle* *to Replace Balancing the Equities and Tailoring the Remedy*, 72 Minn. L. Rev. 627, 636–70 (1988).

3. [tort applications] Myers v. Caple, 258 N.W.2d 301 (Iowa 1977) (refusing to enjoin construction of levee that would protect defendant's land in all years, and increase flooding of plaintiff's land only in extraordinary years); Boomer v. Atlantic Cement Co., 26 N.Y.2d 219, 223–28, 257 N.E.2d 870, 872–75, 309 N.Y.S.2d 312, 314–16 (1970) (refusing to order closing of $45-million dollar cement plant to prevent pollution that damaged plaintiffs in amount of $185,000); Restatement (Second) of Torts § 941 (1979) ("relative hardship" to parties is factor to be considered in determining whether to enjoin a tort).

4. [contract applications] Tex. v. N.M., 482 U.S. 124, 131–32 (1987) (court must consider relative hardships to contracting states before ordering retroactive specific performance of compact allocating water of Pecos River); N. Ind. Public Serv. Co. v. Carbon County Coal Co., 799 F.2d 265, 279–80 (7th Cir. 1986) (refusing to specifically enforce long-term contract for sale of coal, where performance would require reopening closed mine that was uneconomical to operate); 3615 Corp. v. N.Y. Life Ins. Co., 717 F.2d 1236, 1238 (8th Cir. 1983) (refusing to specifically enforce seller's promise to repair any damage that happened to building before closing of sale, where repairs would cost $1,125,000 and sale price was $35,000) (alternate holding); Sanitary Dist. v. Martin, 227 Ill. 260, 267–69, 81 N.E. 417, 419–20 (1907) (refusing to specifically enforce contract to build levee to protect plaintiff's land from flooding, where cost of levee would be disproportionate to value of land); Concert Radio Inc. v. GAF Corp, 73 N.Y.2d 766, 768–69, 532 N.E.2d 1280, 1282, 536 N.Y.S.2d 52, 54 (1988) (refusing to enforce option to buy radio station if it were offered for sale within five years, where station was offered for sale just before expiration of five-year period, purpose of option had been largely achieved and plaintiff collected substantial damages, and specific performance would impose hardship on defendant); Sternberg v. Bd. of Trustees of Kent State Univ., 37 Ohio St. 2d 115, 308 N.E.2d 457 (1974) (refusing specific performance of contract that would require defendant to reopen a closed high school); Restatement (Second) of Contracts § 364(1)(b) (1981) ("specific performance or injunction will be refused if such relief would be unfair because . . . the relief would cause unreasonable hardship or loss to the party in breach or to third persons"). But see W. Edmond Hunton Lime Unit v. Stanolind Oil & Gas Co., 193 F.2d 818 (10th Cir. 1951) (holding that doctrine does not apply to contract claims).

5. [property applications] Golden Press, Inc. v. Rylands, 124 Colo. 122, 125–29, 235 P.2d 592, 594–96 (1951) (reversing order to remove footings of wall that encroached three inches into plaintiff's property at point seven feet below surface); Brewer v. Hibbard, 424 So.2d 988 (Fla. App. 1983) (directing trial court to balance "relative conveniences" before ordering removal of encroaching buildings); Chesarone v. Pinewood Builders, Inc., 345 Mass. 236, 241, 186 N.E.2d 712, 715 (1962) (diversion of water should be enjoined unless "cost of an alternative is outrageously disproportionate to the benefit to be derived"); Cox v. City of N.Y., 265 N.Y. 411, 413–14, 193 N.E. 251, 252 (1934) (refusing to order reconstruction of destroyed bridges carrying highway over railroad track, where cost of reconstruction would greatly exceed value of plaintiff's easement entitling him to use bridges). For a survey of older cases, see M.T. Van Hecke, *Injunctions to Remove or Remodel Structures Erected in Violation of Building Restrictions*, 32 Tex. L. Rev. 521 (1954).

6. [names of doctrine] See Ariola v. Nigro, 16 Ill. 2d 46, 51–52, 156 N.E.2d 536, 540 (1959) (balancing the equities); Dobbs, *Remedies* § 2.4 at 52–54 (cited in note 1) (balancing the equities and hardships); Douglas Laycock, *Modern American Remedies* 908–29 (Little, Brown 1985) (undue hardship defense); W. Page Keeton & Clarence Morris, *Notes on "Balancing the Equities,"* 18 Tex. L. Rev. 412 (1940); Schoenbrod, 72 Minn. L. Rev. 627 (cited in note 2) (balancing the equities).

7. [defendant's culpability] Welton v. 40 E. Oak Street Bldg. Corp., 70 F.2d 377, 381–83 (7th Cir. 1934) (ordering demolition of twenty-story building deliberately constructed in violation of setback ordinance); Agmar v. Solomon, 87 Cal. App. 127, 142, 261 P. 1029, 1034–35 (1927) (refusing to balance equities "where the encroachment is not due to accident or innocent mistake"); Ariola v. Nigro, 16 Ill. 2d 46, 51–52, 156 N.E.2d 536, 540 (1959) ("where the encroachment is intentional . . . courts have refused to balance the equities"); Tyler v. City of Haverhill, 272 Mass. 313, 172 N.E. 342 (1930) (ordering removal of encroaching wall that was built over plaintiff's objections); Soergel v. Preston, 141 Mich. App. 585, 590, 367 N.W.2d 366, 369 (1985) (ordering removal of sewer line across plaintiff's property, where defendant erroneously believed it had an easement and continued building despite plaintiff's objections).

8. [public interest] City of Harrisonville v. W.S. Dickey Clay Mfg. Co., 289 U.S. 334, 338 (1933) (refusing to enjoin pollution from municipal sewer plant; "where an important public interest would be prejudiced, the reasons for denying the injunction may be compelling"); Boomer v. Atlantic Cement Co., 26 N.Y.2d 219, 225 n.*, 257 N.E.2d 870, 873 n.*, 309 N.Y.S.2d 312, 316 n.* (1970) (refusing to enjoin operation of cement plant that employed three hundred people); Storey v. Cent. Hide & Rendering Co., 148 Tex. 509, 514–15, 226 S.W.2d 615, 618–19 (1950) (refusing to enjoin operation of rendering plant; "some one must suffer these inconveniences rather than that the public interest should suffer"); Kuntz v. Werner Flying Serv., Inc., 257 Wis. 405, 409–11, 43 N.W.2d 476, 478–79 (1950) (refusing to enjoin operation of airport; "the interest of the public in injunctional cases of this nature has been recognized").

9. [plaintiff's culpability] Welton v. 40 E. Oak Street Bldg. Corp., 70 F.2d 377, 379 (7th Cir. 1934) (plaintiffs protested building permit and sued to prevent construction; their failure to seek preliminary injunction excused because they could not post bond for value of twenty-story building); Ariola v. Nigro, 16 Ill. 2d 46, 56, 156 N.E.2d 536, 541–42 (1959) ("plaintiffs at no time lulled defendants into proceeding with the construction").

10. [matters only if damages are inadequate] This relationship is also noted in Schoenbrod, 72 Minn. L. Rev. at 669–70 n.195 (cited in note 2).

11. [irreparable injury opinions] City of Harrisonville v. W.S. Dickey Clay Mfg. Co., 289 U.S. 334, 338–39 (1933) (damages for pollution of land give "substantial redress" and injunction against nuisance would impose "grossly disproportionate hardship"); N. Ind. Public Serv. Co. v. Carbon County Coal Co., 799 F.2d 265, 279–80 (7th Cir. 1986) (refusing to specifically enforce long-term contract for sale of coal, where performance would require reopening closed mine that was uneconomical to operate); Sims Varner & Assoc., Inc. v. Blanchard, 794 F.2d 1123, 1125, 1128 (6th Cir. 1986) (refusing to enjoin performance of government contract in response to delayed challenge by competing bidder); Kealey Pharmacy & Home Care Serv., Inc. v. Walgreen Co., 539 F. Supp. 1357, 1370–71 (W.D. Wis. 1982) (refusing to enjoin termination of plaintiff's franchise, where defendant was closing all franchise operations), damage award aff'd, 761 F.2d 345 (7th Cir. 1985); Matthews v. U.S., 526 F. Supp. 993, 1005–06 (M.D. Ga. 1981) (refusing to enjoin construction of dock that interfered with view of lake), rev'd, 713 F.2d 677, 681–82 (11th Cir. 1983) (ordering removal of dock); Para-Medical Ambulance, Inc. v. City of Torrington, 37 Conn. Supp. 124, 126, 444 A.2d 236, 238 (1981) (refusing to enjoin city from operating ambulance service); Cantrell v. Henry County, 250 Ga. 822, 824–26, 301 S.E.2d 870, 872–74 (1983) (reversing injunction ordering that subdivision be disconnected from public water supply); Paloukos v. Intermountain Chevrolet Co., 99 Idaho 740, 745–46, 588 P.2d 939, 944–45 (1978) (refusing specific performance of contract to sell 1974 three-quarter-ton Chevrolet pickup truck, where plaintiff did not claim that truck was uniquely different from other trucks, and shortage of that model made it impossible for defendant dealer to perform); Green v. Advance Homes, Inc., 293 N.W.2d 204, 208–09 (Iowa 1980) (vacating and remanding injunction ordering defendant to restore lateral support for land, where $48,000 retaining wall would add $6,000 in value); Myers v. Caple, 258 N.W.2d 301, 304, 306 (Iowa 1977) (refusing to enjoin levee that would protect defendant's land and increase flooding of plaintiff's land only occasionally); Keich v. Barkley Place, Inc., 424 So.2d 1194, 1199–200 (La. App. 1982) (reversing injunction against development of 146-acre tract, issued to reduce risk of flooding of plaintiffs' homes); Padilla v. Lawrence, 101 N.M. 556, 562, 685 P.2d 964, 970 (App. 1984) (refusing to enjoin operation of $2-million fertilizer plant); Burke v. Bowen, 40 N.Y.2d 264, 267, 353 N.E.2d 567, 569, 386 N.Y.S.2d 654, 656 (1976) (refusing to order city, "in the throes of a grave financial crisis," to specifically perform contract to employ fixed number of firefighters); Sternberg v. Bd. of Trustees of Kent State Univ., 37 Ohio St. 2d 115, 308 N.E.2d 457 (1974) (refusing specific performance of contract that would require defendant to re-open a closed high school); Morgan v. Morgan, 657 S.W.2d 484, 493–94 (Tex. App. 1983) (reversing injunction that precluded ex-husband from using any of his business assets as collateral for loans); Warner v. Haught, Inc., 329 S.E.2d 88, 95–96 (W. Va. 1985) (refusing to order forfeiture of mineral lease for late payment of rent); Kuntz v. Werner Flying Serv., Inc., 257 Wis. 405, 410–11, 43 N.W.2d 476, 479 (1950) (refusing to enjoin operation of airport); Gitlitz v. Plankinton Bldg. Properties, Inc., 228 Wis. 334, 339–40, 280 N.W. 415, 418 (1938) (refusing to enjoin redevelopment of building in which plaintiff had a short-term lease of one shop).

12. [irreparable injury for harm to others] Liza Danielle, Inc. v. Jamko, Inc., 408 So.2d 735, 738–40 (Fla. App. 1982) (lengthy discussion of how difficulty of proving lost profits does not make legal remedy inadequate, followed by recognition of hardship as "most compelling reason" to deny injunction); Watkins v. Paul, 95 Idaho 499, 501, 511 P.2d 781, 783 (1973) (damages adequate and specific performance denied where buyer wanted land only for resale; court noted but did not rely on fact that rights of innocent third party had intervened); Conger v. N.Y., W.S. & B.R. Co., 120 N.Y. 29, 23 N.E. 983 (1890) (refusing to specifically enforce contract to build railroad station on side of steep mountain in sparsely settled district, where station would delay travel and inconvenience the public); Vt. Nat'l Bank v. Chittenden Trust Co., 143 Vt. 257, 266–67, 465 A.2d 284, 290 (1983) (refusing to extend lease as specific remedy for earlier violations of restrictive covenant, because such relief would run against a person not party to the suit, and because plaintiff had not shown that damages would be an inadequate remedy; court enjoined further violations of the covenant without discussing irreparable injury).

13. [building trumps billboard] *Van Wagner*, 67 N.Y.2d 186, 492 N.E.2d 756, 501 N.Y.S.2d 628 (1986).

14. [disproportionate harm] Id. at 195, 492 N.E.2d at 761, 501 N.Y.S.2d at 633.

15. [leases not specifically enforced] Id. at 192 & n.3, 492 N.E.2d at 759 & n.3, 501 N.Y.S.2d at 631 & n.3. For New York cases specifically enforcing covenants in leases, see Yorkville Restaurant, Inc. v. Perlbinder, 34 A.D.2d 14, 308 N.Y.S.2d 922 (1970) (option to lease restaurant and bar in any new building constructed on site of building where plaintiff originally leased space), judgment vacated and reentered mem., 34 A.D.2d 637, 311 N.Y.S.2d 250 (1970), aff'd mem., 28 N.Y.2d 647, 269 N.E.2d 192, 320 N.Y.S.2d 521 (1971); Daitch Crystal Dairies, Inc. v. Neisloss, 8 A.D.2d 965, 190 N.Y.S.2d 737 (1959) (covenant not to lease space to tenant's competitors), aff'd mem., 8 N.Y.2d 723, 167 N.E.2d 643, 201 N.Y.S.2d 101 (1960). See also Braschi v. Stahl Assoc. Co., 74 N.Y.2d 201, 543 N.E.2d 49, 544 N.Y.S.2d 784 (1989) (reversing Appellate Division's reversal of preliminary injunction against eviction of gay life partner of deceased tenant in rent-controlled apartment; because case was submitted on certified question, issue of irreparable injury was not presented to Court of Appeals). For similar cases from other jurisdictions, see ch. 2 note 15.

16. [uniqueness as hard to measure damages] *Van Wagner*, 67 N.Y.2d at 192–94, 492 N.E.2d at 759–60, 501 N.Y.S.2d at 631–32, citing Anthony T. Kronman, *Specific Performance*, 45 U. Chi. L. Rev. 351, 359 (1978).

17. [preliminary injunction] ABC Trans Nat'l Transp., Inc. v. Aeronautics Forwarders, Inc., 62 Ill. App. 3d 671, 686–87, 379 N.E.2d 1228, 1239 (1978).

18. [permanent injunction] ABC Trans Nat'l Transp., Inc. v. Aeronautics Forwards, Inc., 90 Ill. App. 3d 817, 833, 413 N.E.2d 1299, 1312 (1980).

19. [lesser showing required for preliminary] Explaining why the right to a permanent injunction does not follow from right to preliminary injunction plus success on merits, the court said: "That this is so may be readily understood when the distinction between temporary and permanent injunctions is borne in mind. On a petition for preliminary injunction, the court is concerned with maintaining the status quo between the parties until a full hearing on the merits can be held." Id. at 833, 413 N.E.2d at 1311.

20. [receiverships] Remco Ins. Co. v. State Ins. Dep't, 519 A.2d 633, 636 (Del. 1986) ("receivership is an extreme remedy which should not be used unless other less drastic remedies are shown to be inadequate"); Poulakidas v. Charalidis, 68 Ill. App. 3d 610, 614, 386 N.E.2d 405, 408 (1979) (standards for appointment of receiver are "exceptionally stringent"); Ziffrin Truck Lines, Inc. v. Ziffrin, 242 Ind. 544, 547, 180 N.E.2d 370, 372 (1962) ("axiomatic that a receiver should not be appointed if the plaintiff has an adequate remedy at law or by way of temporary injunction"); In re Marriage of Gore, 527 N.E.2d 191 (Ind. App. 1988) (vacating appointment of receiver over defendant's corporation, but affirming receiver for defendant's personal assets, reciting many maxims about the high standard for appointment of receivers).

21. [corporate dissolutions] In the Matter of the Judicial Dissolution of Kemp & Beatley, Inc., 64 N.Y.2d 63, 69–74, 473 N.E.2d 1173, 1177–80, 484 N.Y.S.2d 799, 803–06 (1984).

22. [undue hardship at law] Peevyhouse v. Garland Coal & Mining Co., 382 P.2d 109 (Okla. 1962) (restoring strip-mined land, at cost of $29,000, would increase value of land by $300).

23. [disproportionate damages] Restatement (Second) of Contracts § 348(2)(b) (1981).

24. [disproportionate hardship] Id. § 364(1)(b) ("unreasonable hardship or loss").

25. [interchangeable standards] See 3615 Corp. v. N.Y. Life Ins. Co., 717 F.2d 1236, 1238 (8th Cir. 1983) ("unreasonable and disproportionate hardship"); Van Wagner Advertising Corp. v. S & M Enterprises, 67 N.Y.2d 186, 195, 492 N.E.2d 756, 761, 501 N.Y.S.2d 628, 633 (1986) ("disproportionate in its harm": "not an undue hardship").

26. [no prior restraints] Vance v. Universal Amusement Co., 445 U.S. 308, 315–17 (1980) (invalidating public nuisance statutes that authorized courts to order that movie theater be closed for one year); Neb. Press Ass'n v. Stuart, 427 U.S. 539, 556–70 (1976) (reversing injunction ordering press not to report testimony at preliminary hearing in criminal case); Southeastern Promotions, Ltd. v. Conrad, 420 U.S. 546, 552–62 (1975) (invalidating city's refusal to let plaintiff produce the musical *Hair* in municipal auditorium); N.Y. Times Co. v. U.S., 403 U.S. 713, 714 (1971) (reversing injunctions ordering press not to reprint Pentagon Papers); Org. for a Better Austin v. Keefe, 402 U.S. 415 (1971) (reversing injunction ordering defendants not to distribute leaflets); Near v. Minn., 283 U.S. 697, 711–23 (1931) (invalidating public nuisance statute that authorized courts to enjoin publication of newspaper); Cliffs Notes, Inc. v. Bantam Doubleday Dell Pub. Group, Inc., 886 F.2d 490, 497 (2d Cir. 1989) (reversing preliminary injunction against publication of parody); People v. Sequoia Books, Inc., 127 Ill. 2d 271, 537 N.E.2d 302 (1989) (reversing injunction that ordered adult bookstore closed for one year), cert. denied, 110 S. Ct. 835 (1990); Basarich v. Rodeghero, 24 Ill. App. 3d 889, 894–95, 321 N.E.2d 739, 743 (1974) (refusing to enjoin publication of newsletter that defamed teachers' union and its leaders); Am. Broadcasting Co. v. Smith Cabinet Mfg. Co., 160 Ind. App. 367, 372–79, 312 N.E.2d 85, 88–92 (1974) (refusing to enjoin broadcast of television show portraying fire hazard of baby crib manufactured by plaintiff); Unified School Dist. No. 503 v. McKinney, 236 Kan. 224, 233–36, 689 P.2d 860, 869–71 (1984) (reversing injunction ordering defendants not to hold press conference); Krebiozen Research Found. v. Beacon Press, Inc., 334 Mass. 86, 94–99, 134 N.E.2d 1, 6–9 (1956) (refusing to enjoin publication of book criticizing alleged cancer cure); J.Q. Office Equip., Inc. v. Sullivan, 230 Neb. 397, 432 N.W.2d 211 (1988) (reversing injunction against use of automatic dialing machine and trade-show demonstrations to complain about plaintiff's allegedly defective product). See also Carroll v. President of Princess Anne, 393 U.S. 175, 179–85 (1968) (reversing ex parte injunction against racist political rally).

27. [equity will not enjoin libel] Kuhn v. Warner Bros. Pictures, Inc., 29 F. Supp. 800, 801 (S.D.N.Y. 1939) (refusing to enjoin distribution of movie that portrayed German American Bund as a disloyal organization engaged in espionage for the Nazis); Gariepy v. Springer, 318 Ill. App. 523, 525–30, 48 N.E.2d 572, 573–75 (1943) (refusing to enjoin defendant from falsely claiming that plaintiff was associated with another lawyer, imprisoned for failing to account for trust funds); Greenberg v. De Salvo, 254 La. 1019, 1026–27, 229 So.2d 83, 86 (1969) (refusing to enjoin defendant from calling plaintiff a "crook" and a "slimy kike"); Willing v. Mazzocone, 482 Pa. 377, 382–83, 393 A.2d 1155, 1158 (1978) (reversing injunction ordering defendant not to picket courthouse with sign saying her lawyer stole her money and sold her out to the insurance company); Kwass v. Kersey, 139 W. Va. 497, 508–09, 81 S.E.2d 237, 243 (1954) (refusing to enjoin defendant from circulating letter charging lawyer with fraud); Rodney A. Smolla, *Law of Defamation* § 9.13[1][a] at p. 9–35 (Clark Boardman 1989) ("one of the unwavering precepts of the American law of remedies has long been the axiom that equity will not enjoin a libel"); Annotation, *Injunction as Remedy Against Defamation of Person*, 47 A.L.R.2d 715 (1956). But see Lothschuetz v. Carpenter, 898 F.2d 1200, 1206, 1208–09 (6th Cir. 1990) (enjoining repetition of specific defamatory statements; Spahn v. Julian Messner, Inc., 21 N.Y.2d 124, 233 N.E.2d 840, 286 N.Y.S.2d 832 (1967) (enjoining publication of false and "fictionalized" biography).

   28. [damages adequate for defamation] Kuhn v. Warner Bros. Pictures, Inc., 29 F. Supp. 800, 801 (S.D.N.Y. 1939); Basarich v. Rodeghero, 24 Ill. App. 3d 889, 894, 321 N.E.2d 739, 743 (1974); Unified School Dist. No. 503 v. McKinney, 236 Kan. 224, 227–28, 689 P.2d 860, 865 (1984); Greenberg v. De Salvo, 254 La. 1019, 1026–34, 229 So.2d 83, 86–88 (1969); Prucha v. Weiss, 233 Md. 479, 484–85, 197 A.2d 253, 256 (1964); Ryan v. City of Warrensburg, 342 Mo. 761, 771–72, 117 S.W.2d 303, 308 (1938); Kwass v. Kersey, 139 W. Va. 497, 508–09, 81 S.E.2d 237, 243 (1954).

   29. [even if defendant insolvent] Willing v. Mazzocone, 482 Pa. 377, 382–83, 393 A.2d 1155, 1158 (1978). Older cases to the same effect are collected in Annotation, 47 A.L.R.2d at 725–26.

   30. [debate over prior restraints] Compare Lucas A. Powe, *The Fourth Estate and the Constitution*, ch. 5 (Univ. Cal. Press 1991) (forthcoming), and Vincent A. Blasi, *Toward a Theory of Prior Restraint: The Central Linkage*, 66 Minn. L. Rev. 11 (1981) (both defending the traditional rule), with John Calvin Jeffries, Jr., *Rethinking Prior Restraint*, 92 Yale L.J. 409 (1983) (attacking the traditional rule).

   31. [reputation irreplaceable] Gibson v. Berryhill, 411 U.S. 564, 577 n.16 (1973) (publicity from revocation of optometrists' licenses); Adams v. Att'y Registration & Disciplinary Comm'n, 801 F.2d 968, 974 (7th Cir. 1986) (disciplinary proceedings against lawyer); Penthouse Int'l, Ltd. v. Barnes, 792 F.2d 943, 949–50 (9th Cir. 1986) (specific performance of contract not to publish nude photographs except under pseudonym; irreparable injury not discussed); Regents of the Univ. of Cal. v. Am. Broadcasting Co., 747 F.2d 511, 520 (9th Cir. 1984) (damage to reputation of college football program); Dino de Laurentiis Cinematografica, S.p.A. v. D-150, Inc., 366 F.2d 373, 376 (2d Cir. 1966) (breach of contract to launch new product); Black & Yates, Inc. v. Mahogany Ass'n, Inc., 129 F.2d 227, 234–36 (3d Cir. 1942) (product disparagement); Miller Brewing Co. v. Carling O'Keefe Breweries, Ltd., 452 F. Supp. 429, 437–38 (W.D.N.Y. 1978) (trademark infringement inflicts irreparable injury, because plaintiff's reputation is damaged if infringing product is inferior); Oppenheimer Mendez v. Acevedo, 388 F. Supp. 326, 337 (D.P.R. 1974) (government attorney discharged for conflict of interest), aff'd, 512 F.2d 1373 (1st Cir. 1975); Martin v. Reynolds Metal Co., 224 F. Supp. 978, 984–85 (D. Or. 1963) (billboard accusing company of pollution that killed cattle and endangered human life); Carter v. Knapp Motor Co., 243 Ala. 600, 603–04, 11 So.2d 383, 385 (1943) (Hudson automobile with white elephants painted on the sides, parked near Hudson dealership); City of Waterbury v. Comm'n on Human Rights and Opportunities, 160 Conn. 226, 231, 278 A.2d 771, 774 (1971) (irreparable harm to city's reputation from unauthorized investigation of alleged civil rights violations); Menard v. Houle, 298 Mass. 546, 548–49, 11 N.E.2d 436, 437 (1937) (false statements that automobile dealer had sold lemon and refused to repair it); Webb Pub. Co. v. Fosshage, 426 N.W.2d 445, 449 (Minn. App. 1988) (damage to business reputation); Univ. of Notre Dame du Lac v. Twentieth Century-Fox Film Corp., 44 Misc. 2d 808, 814, 820, 255 N.Y.S.2d 210, 217, 223 (1964) (enjoining distribution of movie depicting university in unfavorable light), rev'd on other grounds, 22 A.D.2d 452, 256 N.Y.S.2d 301 (no viewer would think movie was true, and injunction would infringe on speech), aff'd mem., 15 N.Y.2d 940, 207 N.E.2d 508, 259 N.Y.S.2d 832 (1965); Restatement (Second) of Torts § 944 comment b (1979) (money obviously inadequate for loss of personal reputation); Roscoe Pound, *Equitable Relief Against Defamation and Injuries to Personality*, 29 Harv. L. Rev. 640, 640–41 (1916) ("no pecuniary measure can possibly be applied to the interest and no pecuniary standard to the wrong"); Smolla, *Defamation* § 9.13[1][b] at p. 9–36 (cited in note 27) ("defamation is precisely the form of nonquantifiable injury for which damages are ill-suited").

32. [emotional distress irreparable] See cases cited in ch. 2 note 85.

33. [secrets irretrievable] Snepp v. U.S., 444 U.S. 507, 508–09, 514 (1980) (unauthorized publication by former intelligence agent inflicted "irreparable harm and loss"); Maness v. Meyers, 419 U.S. 449, 460 (1975) (compelled testimony "could cause irreparable injury because appellate courts cannot always 'unring the bell' once the information has been released"); U.S. v. Progressive, Inc., 467 F. Supp. 990, 996, 999 (W.D. Wis. 1979) (publication of information essential to the construction of hydrogen bombs would cause "grave, direct, immediate and irreparable harm to the United States"); Loveall v. Am. Honda Motor Co., 694 S.W.2d 937, 939–40 (Tenn. 1985) (release of trade secrets obtained in discovery would cause severe irreparable injury). See also Cent. Intelligence Agency v. Sims, 471 U.S. 159, 175 (1985) (identification of intelligence sources could have "devastating impact on the Agency's ability to carry out its mission"); Seattle Times Co. v. Rhinehart, 467 U.S. 20, 35–36 (1984) (public release of information produced in discovery could be "damaging to reputation and privacy"); Abbotts v. Nuclear Regulatory Comm'n, 766 F.2d 604, 608 (D.C. Cir. 1985) (accepting government's claim that release of any part of plans for protecting nuclear plants from terrorists could damage national security).

34. [protection of jury trial] Willing v. Mazzocone, 482 Pa. 377, 384, 393 A.2d 1155, 1159 (1978) (Roberts concurring).

35. [juries give excessive verdicts] For empirical data, see Randall P. Bezanson, Gilbert Cranberg, & John Soloski, *Libel Law and the Press* 129 (Macmillan, Free Press 1987); Marc A. Franklin, *Suing Media for Libel*, 1981 Am. Bar Found.

Research J. 797, 804–06; Marc A. Franklin, *Winners and Losers and Why: A Study of Defamation Litigation*, 1980 Am. Bar Found. Research J. 455, 472–76. The jury as a threat to freedom of the press is a recurring theme of Powe, *The Fourth Estate* (cited in note 30).

36. [jurors protected dissent under king] The famous American case is that of John Peter Zenger. For a modern account of the Zenger trial, see the Introduction to Powe (cited in note 30). For an accessible older account, see James Alexander, *A Brief Narrative of the Case and Trial of John Peter Zenger* (Stanley Katz, ed.) (Belknap Press of Harvard Univ. 1963). For an account of the English experience that goes beyond the most famous cases, see Thomas A. Green, *The Jury, Seditious Libel, and the Criminal Law*, in R.H. Helmholz & Thomas A. Green, *Juries, Libel, and Justice: The Role of English Juries in Seventeenth- and Eighteenth-Century Trials for Libel and Slander* 37 (William Andrews Clark Memorial Library, Univ. Cal. Los Angeles, 1984).

37. [antistrike injunctions] For the classic history of and attack on the use of injunctions to break strikes, see Felix Frankfurter & Nathan Greene, *The Labor Injunction* (Macmillan 1930). For a vigorous defense of those injunctions, see Sylvester Petro, *Injunctions and Labor Disputes 1880–1932, Part I: What the Courts Actually Did—and Why*, 14 Wake Forest L. Rev. 341 (1978). For contemporary uses of labor injunctions, see Henry H. Perritt, Jr., *Labor Injunctions* (Wiley 1986).

38. [defamation of better-off victims] Consider the three cases cited in note 27 in which lawyers sued former clients for defamation—*Gariepy*, *Willing*, and *Kwass*.

39. [propensities of juries] On the role of juries, see ch. 9 part A.

40. [prior restraint after final judgment] Pittsburgh Press Co. v. Pittsburgh Comm'n on Human Relations, 413 U.S. 376, 389–90 (1973).

41. [movies] Freedman v. Md., 380 U.S. 51, 59 (1965).

42. [information obtained in discovery] Seattle Times Co. v. Rhinehart, 467 U.S. 20, 33–34 (1984).

43. [final judicial determination] *Pittsburgh Press*, 413 U.S. at 390 ("the special vice of a prior restraint is that communication will be suppressed . . . before an adequate determination that it is unprotected by the First Amendment").

44. [source of information] *Seattle Times*, 467 U.S. at 34 ("the party may disseminate the identical information covered by the protective order as long as the information is gained through means independent of the court's processes").

45. [less important speech] For obscenity, see N.Y. Times v. U.S., 403 U.S. 713, 726 n.* (1971) (Brennan concurring) (cases upholding prior restraints against obscenity rest on the proposition that obscenity is not protected speech); Near v. Minn., 283 U.S. 697, 716 (1931) (obscenity is an exceptional case not protected against prior restraint). For commercial speech, see notes 46–49.

46. [securities fraud] Aaron v. Securities & Exchange Comm'n, 446 U.S. 680 (1980) (authorizing injunctions against misrepresentations in connection with sale of securities); Securities & Exchange Comm'n v. Great Am. Indus., Inc., 407 F.2d 453, 456–58 (2d Cir. 1968) (en banc) (enjoining misrepresentations in connection with sale of securities). See also Securities & Exchange Comm'n v. Capital Gains Research Bureau, Inc., 375 U.S. 180, 181–84 (1963) (ordering investment adviser to make disclosures).

47. [false advertising] Fed. Trade Comm'n v. Colgate-Palmolive Co., 380 U.S. 374, 377, 392–95 (1965) (enforcing order not to use simulations in television commercials without disclosing that commercial depicted a simulation; neither irreparable injury nor prior restraint discussed); Fed. Trade Comm'n v. Raladam, 316 U.S. 149 (1942) (enforcing order to stop making false claims on behalf of weight-loss product; neither irreparable injury nor prior restraint discussed); McNeilab, Inc. v. Am. Home Prod. Corp., 848 F.2d 34, 38 (2d Cir. 1988) (enjoining misleading claim that Advil was no more likely than Tylenol to cause upset stomach); Fed. Trade Comm'n v. Brown & Williamson Tobacco Corp., 778 F.2d 35, 43–45 (D.C. Cir. 1985) (enjoining deceptive claims for low tar cigarette, but holding that prior restraint can be no broader than necessary to prevent the deception); Sears Roebuck & Co. v. Fed. Trade Comm'n, 676 F.2d 385, 399 (9th Cir. 1982) ("the doctrinal question whether prior restraint analysis is properly applicable to any commercial speech remains open"); Jay Norris, Inc. v. Fed. Trade Comm'n, 598 F.2d 1244, 1251–52 (2d Cir. 1979) (order forbidding any claim about safety or performance of product without prior written substantiation does not violate rule against prior restraints); Elec. Corp. v. Honeywell, Inc., 428 F.2d 191, 196 (1st Cir. 1970) (enjoining defendant's false claims for its replacement part designed to fit in plaintiff's product; neither irreparable injury nor prior restraint discussed); *Developments in the Law—Deceptive Advertising*, 80 Harv. L. Rev. 1005, 1079–80, 1111 (1967) (cease and desist order is Federal Trade Commission's principal remedy against false advertising); id. at 1111 (for some false advertising violations of the Food, Drug, and Cosmetic Act, injunction is the only civil remedy).

48. [commercial disparagement] McNeilab, Inc. v. Am. Home Prod. Corp., 848 F.2d 34 (2d Cir. 1988) (enjoining misleading comparative advertising without discussing free speech); U-Haul Int'l, Inc. v. Jartran, Inc., 681 F.2d 1159, 1162 (9th Cir. 1982) (same); Black & Yates, Inc. v. Mahogany Ass'n, Inc., 129 F.2d 227, 234–36 (3d Cir. 1942) (distinguishing disparagement of property from defamation); Am. Home Prod. Corp. v. Johnson & Johnson, 654 F. Supp. 568, 590–91 (S.D.N.Y. 1987) (interest in eliminating false advertising "prevails over advertiser's right of commercial speech"); Systems Operations, Inc. v. Scientific Games Dev. Corp., 414 F. Supp. 750, 764 (D.N.J. 1976) (enjoining "false and disparaging statements, whether direct or indirect, regarding plaintiffs' instant lottery tickets"), rev'd on other grounds, 555 F.2d 1131 (3d Cir. 1977); Carter v. Knapp Motor Co., 243 Ala. 600, 11 So.2d 383 (1943) (authorizing injunction against painting white elephants on Hudson automobile and parking it near Hudson dealership); Lawrence Trust Co. v. Sun-American Pub. Co., 245 Mass. 262, 139 N.E. 655 (1923) (authorizing injunction against newspaper editorials falsely stating that plaintiff bank was mismanaged and failing); 15 U.S.C. §§ 1114(2), 1125 (1988) (authorizing injunction against publication of "commercial advertising or promotion" that "misrepresents the nature, characteristics, qualities, or geographic origin of his or another person's goods, services, or commercial activities"). But see J.Q. Office Equip. v. Sullivan, 230 Neb. 397, 399–401, 432 N.W.2d 211, 213–14 (1988) (reversing injunction against use of automatic dialing machine and trade-show demonstrations to complain about plaintiff's allegedly defective product). For analysis, see Dobbs, *Remedies* § 6.7 at 505–08 (cited in note 1); Marie V. Driscoll, *The "New" § 43(a)*, 79 Trademark Rptr. 238, 239–41, 244 (1989).

49. [commercial speech] Friedman v. Rogers, 440 U.S. 1, 10 (1979) (special characteristics of commercial speech "may also make inapplicable the prohibition against prior restraints," quoting Va. State Bd. of Pharmacy v. Va. Citizens Consumer Council, Inc., 425 U.S. 748, 772 n.24 (1976)) (dictum in both cases). See also Lorain Journal Co. v. U.S., 342 U.S. 143, 155–56 (1951) (finding that newspaper violated antitrust laws by refusing to sell advertising space to customers who also advertised with competing radio station, and ordering paper to publish these customers' ads).

50. [disclosing troop movements] Haig v. Agee, 453 U.S. 280, 308 (1981); Neb. Press Ass'n v. Stuart, 427 U.S. 539, 591 (1976) (Brennan concurring); Young v. Am. Mini Theatres, Inc., 427 U.S. 50, 66 (1976) (plurality opinion); Pittsburgh Press Co. v. Pittsburgh Comm'n on Human Relations, 413 U.S. 376, 400 n.1 (1973) (Stewart dissenting); N.Y. Times Co. v. U.S., 403 U.S. 713, 726 (1971) (Brennan concurring); Times Film Corp. v. City of Chicago, 365 U.S. 43, 47 (1961); Near v. Minn., 283 U.S. 697, 716 (1931); U.S. v. Progressive, Inc., 467 F. Supp. 990, 992 (W.D. Wis. 1979). For the first use of this example, see Zechariah Chafee, *Freedom of Speech* 10 (Harcourt, Brace & Howe 1920).

51. [restraints on dangerous speech vacated] See N.Y. Times v. U.S., 403 U.S. 713 (1971) (reversing injunction against publication of secret Pentagon study of the war in Vietnam); U.S. v. Progressive, Inc., 467 F. Supp. 990, 992 (W.D. Wis.), appeal dis'd mem. 610 F.2d 819 (7th Cir. 1979) (preliminary injunction granted, but case dismissed pending appeal when similar information was published elsewhere).

52. [enjoining violations of CIA censorship] U.S. v. Snepp, 897 F.2d 138 (4th Cir. 1990), cert. filed, 58 U.S.L.W. 3787 (May 29, 1990); U.S. v. Snepp, 595 F.2d 926, 934–35 (4th Cir. 1979), aff'd in revelant part, 444 U.S. 507, 509 n.3 (1980); Alfred A. Knopf, Inc. v. Colby, 509 F.2d 1362, 1370 (4th Cir. 1975); U.S. v. Marchetti, 466 F.2d 1309, 1317 (4th Cir. 1972).

53. [upholding CIA censorship] Snepp v. U.S., 444 U.S. 507, 509 n.3 (1980).

54. [prior restraints ineffective] See Powe, *Fourth Estate*, ch. 5 (cited in note 30).

55. [personal service contracts] Sampson v. Murray, 415 U.S. 61, 83 (1974) ("traditional unwillingness of courts of equity to enforce contracts for personal service either at the behest of the employer or of the employee"); Arthur Linton Corbin, 5A *Corbin on Contracts* § 1204 at 398–402 (West, 2d ed. 1964); Samuel Williston & Walter H.E. Jaeger, 11 *A Treatise on the Law of Contracts* § 1423 at 782–88 (Baker Voorhis, 3d ed. 1968); Martha S. West, *The Case Against Reinstatement in Wrongful Discharge*, 1988 U. Ill. L. Rev. 1, 10–12.

56. [hard to enforce] Bethlehem Engineering Export Co. v. Christie, 105 F.2d 933, 934–35 (2d Cir. 1939) (refusing to specifically enforce plaintiff's right to be exclusive selling agent); Wm. Rogers Mfg. Co. v. Rogers, 58 Conn. 356, 20 A. 467 (1890) (refusing to enforce contract to serve as general agent of company for twenty-five years); N. Am. Fin'l Group, Ltd. v. S.M.R. Enterprises, Inc., 583 F. Supp. 691, 699 (N.D. Ill. 1984) (refusing to specifically enforce franchise agreement at request of franchisor); Clark v. Truitt, 183 Ill. 239, 244–46, 55 N.E. 683, 685 (1899) (refusing to specifically enforce plaintiff's right to become part owner and editor of newspaper); Zannis v. Lake Shore Radiologists, Ltd., 73 Ill. App. 3d 901, 904–05, 392 N.E.2d 126, 128–29 (1979) (refusing to reinstate discharged physician); Am. Broadcasting Co. v. Wolf, 52 N.Y.2d 394, 401–02, 420 N.E.2d 363, 366, 438 N.Y.S.2d 482, 485 (1981) (refusing to enjoin sports announcer from moving to another network); State ex rel. Schoblom v. Anacortes Veneer, Inc., 42 Wash. 2d 338, 341–42, 255 P.2d 379, 381 (1953) (refusing to specifically enforce stockholder's right to be employed by corporation).

57. [involuntary servitude] In re Taylor, 103 Bankr. 511, 517 (D.N.J. 1989) (bankrupt musician with long-term contract with recording studio could reject contract in bankruptcy, i.e., could not be forced to perform contract for benefit of his creditors); In re Noonan, 17 Bankr. 793 (S.D.N.Y. Bankr. 1982) (same); Bloch v. Hillel Torah N. Suburban Day School, 100 Ill. App. 3d 204, 205, 426 N.E.2d 976, 977 (1981) (refusing to specifically enforce private school's contract to teach student); Case of Clark, 1 Blackf. 122 (Ind. 1821) (refusing to specifically enforce black woman's promise to serve employer for twenty years); H.W. Gossard Co. v. Crosby, 132 Iowa 155, 170, 109 N.W. 483, 488 (1906) (refusing to specifically enforce promise to sell plaintiff's product for three years); Am. Broadcasting Co. v. Wolf, 52 N.Y.2d 394, 402, 420 N.E.2d 363, 366, 438 N.Y.S.2d 482, 485 (1981) (refusing to enjoin sports announcer from moving to another network); Robert S. Stevens, *Involuntary Servitude by Injunction*, 6 Cornell L. Q. 235, 244–50 (1921).

58. [mutuality] Shubert v. Woodward, 167 F. 47, 59 (8th Cir. 1909) (theater manager); Ex parte Jim Dandy Co., 286 Ala. 295, 299–300, 239 So.2d 545, 548–49 (1970) (corporate executive; court relies on mutuality, long supervision, and adequate remedy at law); Poultry Producers, Inc. v. Barlow, 189 Cal. 278, 288–89, 208 P. 93, 97 (1922) (cooperative marketing agreement); Fiedler v. Coast Fin. Co., 129 N.J. Eq. 161, 165–68, 18 A.2d 268, 270–71 (1941) (exclusive sales agency); Gage v. Wimberley, 476 S.W.2d 724, 731–32 (Tex. Civ. App. 1972) (contract to care for parents in exchange for conveyance of dairy farm); Corbin, 5A *Contracts* § 12.04 at 401 (cited in note 55).

59. [choice of agents] Greene v. Howard Univ., 271 F. Supp. 609, 615 (D.D.C. 1967) ("intolerable for the courts to . . . require an educational institution to hire or to maintain on its staff a professor or instructor whom it deemed undesirable"), aff'd, 412 F.2d 1128, 1135–36 (D.C. Cir. 1969) (plaintiffs entitled to damages but not specific performance); Zannis v. Lake Shore Radiologists, Ltd., 73 Ill. App. 3d 901, 905, 392 N.E.2d 126, 129 (1979) ("courts will avoid the friction that would be caused by compelling an employee to work, or an employer to hire or retain someone against their wishes"); Dobbs, *Remedies* § 12.25 at 929–30 (cited in note 1). See also U.S. Postal Serv. v. Nat'l Ass'n of Letter Carriers, 481 U.S. 1301 (1987) (reinstatement of carrier convicted of criminal delay of mail would irreparably harm Postal Service) (Rehnquist in chambers).

60. [covenants not to compete] See notes 71–72; see ch. 2 note 114.

61. [will not make human being work] Linseman v. World Hockey Ass'n, 439 F. Supp. 1315, 1323 (D. Conn. 1977) (refusing to enjoin hockey player from changing teams); St. Joseph School v. Lamm, 288 Ala. 68, 70, 257 So.2d 318, 319 (1972) (refusing to enforce contract to admit student to private school, on ground that contract required school to perform personal services); Am. Broadcasting Co. v. Wolf, 52 N.Y.2d 394, 401–02, 420 N.E.2d 363, 366, 438 N.Y.S.2d 482, 485 (1981) (refusing to enjoin sports announcer from changing networks); Pierce v. Douglas School Dist. No. 4, 297 Or. 363, 371, 686 P.2d 332, 337 (1984) (refusing to enforce schoolteacher's contract to teach); Pingley v. Brunson, 272 S.C. 421, 423, 252

S.E.2d 560, 561 (1979) (refusing to specifically enforce organist's contract to play at restaurant); Restatement (Second) of Contracts § 367 (1981); Edward Yorio, *Contract Enforcement: Specific Performance and Injunctions* §§ 14.1–14.2 at 355–59 (Little, Brown 1989).

62. [colonial law different] For a summary of the law in this period, with citations to more extensive literature, see West, 1988 U. Ill. L. Rev. at 5–10 (cited in note 55).

63. [fugitive slave law] On Northern opposition to the fugitive slave law and the recapture of runaway slaves, see Stanley W. Campbell, *The Slave Catchers: Enforcement of the Fugitive Slave Law 1850–1860* (Univ. N.C. Press 1970); James M. McPherson, *Battle Cry of Freedom* 78–91 (Oxford Univ. Press 1988); Thomas D. Morris, *Free Men All: The Personal Liberty Laws of the North 1780–1861* (Johns Hopkins Univ. Press 1974).

64. [free labor opinions] Arthur v. Oakes, 63 F. 310, 317–18 (7th Cir. 1894) (Harlan, Circuit Justice) ("It would be an invasion of one's natural liberty to compel him to work for or to remain in the personal service of another. One who is placed under such constraint is in a condition of involuntary servitude,—a condition which the supreme law of the land declares shall not exist within the United States"); Case of Clark, 1 Blackf. 122, 123 (Ind. 1821) ("the [state] constitution, having determined that there shall be no involuntary servitude in this state, seems at first view to settle this case" in favor of black woman seeking release from contract for personal service); H.W. Gossard Co. v. Crosby, 132 Iowa 155, 170, 109 N.W. 483, 488 (1906) (if employee is ordered to specifically perform, "his position becomes one of involuntary servitude, a condition utterly incompatible with our institutions, and the fundamental law of the land").

65. [irreparable injury opinions] Infusaid Corp. v. Intermedics Infusaid, Inc., 739 F.2d 661, 668–70 (1st Cir. 1984) (refusing to specifically enforce partnership agreement between two corporations, unless legal remedies were inadequate and performance did not require personal services of principals in either corporation); Bloch v. Hillel Torah N. Suburban Day School, 100 Ill. App. 3d 204, 205–06, 426 N.E.2d 976, 977 (1981) (refusing to reinstate student expelled from private school, on grounds that contract required personal services from the school and legal remedy was adequate).

66. [no damages against basketball player] Lemat Corp. v. Barry, 275 Cal. App. 2d 671, 678–80, 80 Cal. Rptr. 240, 245–46 (1969).

67. [but court found damages] Id. at 675–76, 80 Cal. Rptr. at 243.

68. [promises to work and not to compete] Williston & Jaeger, 5 *Contracts* § 1450 at 1044 (cited in note 55) ("if the defendant's performance of his negative obligation has no value to the plaintiff in itself, an injunction will not generally be granted"); David Tannenbaum, *Enforcement of Personal Service Contracts in the Entertainment Industry*, 42 Cal. L. Rev. 18, 20 (1954) ("the injunction should only be granted where the performance of defendant's negative obligation has some value in itself to plaintiff over and above the possibility that defendant may thus be induced to perform his affirmative obligation"); M.T. Van Hecke, *Changing Emphases in Specific Performance*, 40 N.C. L. Rev. 1, 17 (1961) (injunction against working for competitor is "justified in cases where because of the employer's competitive situation the enforcement of the employee's negative promise has a significance separate from that of the enforcement of the employee's affirmative promise to work for the plaintiff, [but] this use of the injunction has been severely criticised when that element was lacking and the injunction was granted merely as an indirect compulsion of personal service for the plaintiff").

69. **[damages for loss of basketball player]** Tomjanovich v. Cal. Sports Inc., Civ. No. H–78–243 (S.D. Tex. 1979). The litigation is described in Cent. Nat'l Ins. Co. v. Prudential Reins. Co., 241 Cal. Rptr. 773, 775–76 (Cal. App. 1987) (not officially published, by order of state supreme court). Jeff Dykes, the attorney for the Rockets, and Nick Nichols, the attorney for the Tomjanoviches, also described the case to me and gave me copies of the jury submission.

70. **[settlements revealed]** Cent. Nat'l Ins. Co., 241 Cal. Rptr. at 776.

71. **[unique and extraordinary skills]** See Tannenbaum, 42 Cal. L. Rev. at 21–23 (cited in note 68); Yorio, *Contract Enforcement* § 14.3 at 360–66 (cited in note 61). For analysis of this and other reasons, see Dobbs, *Remedies* § 12.26 at 934 (cited in note 1).

72. **[athletes and entertainers]** See Schubert Theatrical Co. v. Rath, 271 F. 827, 829–33 (2d Cir. 1921) (acrobat); Nassau Sports v. Peters, 352 F. Supp. 870, 875–76 (E.D.N.Y. 1972) (hockey player); Washington Capitols Basketball Club, Inc. v. Barry, 304 F. Supp. 1193, 1197 (N.D. Cal.) (basketball player), aff'd, 419 F.2d 472, 474, 479 (9th Cir. 1969); Am. Broadcasting Co. v. Wolf, 52 N.Y.2d 394, 402–03, 420 N.E.2d 363, 367, 438 N.Y.S.2d 482, 486 (1981) (sports announcer; injunction denied because covenant had expired); Philadelphia Ball Club v. Lajoie, 202 Pa. 210, 215–19, 51 A. 973, 973–74 (1902) (baseball player); Lumley v. Wagner, 42 Eng. Rep. 687, 1 DeG., M. & G. 604 (Ch. 1852) (singer); Cal. Civ. Code § 3423 Fifth (services of "special, unique, unusual, extraordinary or intellectual character").

73. **[specific relief for rights in slaves]** Sanders v. Sanders, 20 Ark. 610, 613–14 (1859) (plaintiff need not prove "peculiar circumstances," because "from the very nature of the property itself, Chancery is authorized to interfere"); Williams v. Howard, 7 N.C. (3 Murphey) 74, 81 (1819) ("all the principles which induce a court of Equity to compel a specific execution of a contract for a sale of lands, or some favorite personal chattel, apply with equal, if not stronger force, to the case of slaves"); Young v. Burton, 1 S.C. Eq. 255, 262–63, 1 McMullan 257, 264–66 (1841) ("there are no two human beings, black, white, or mixed, which are exactly alike in all their moral, physical, or acquired qualities"); Henderson v. Vaulx, 18 Tenn. (10 Yerger) 29, 38 (1836) ("a court of chancery will protect the possession and enjoyment of this peculiar property—a property in intellectual and moral and social qualities, in skill, in fidelity, and in gratitude, as well as in their capacity for labor"); Summers v. Bean, 54 Va. (13 Grattan) 404, 412–13, 418 (1856) ("Slaves are not only property but rational beings; and are generally acquired with reference to their moral and intellectual qualities. . . . I am therefore of opinion . . . that a court of equity has jurisdiction to enforce the specific execution of a contract for the sale or delivery of slaves, though it be neither alleged in the bill nor proved that they have any peculiar value."); Mark V. Tushnet, *The American Law of Slavery 1810–1860* at 158–69 (Princeton Univ. Press 1981); A. Leon Higginbotham

& Barbara K. Kopytoff, *Property First, Humanity Second: The Recognition of the Slave's Human Nature in Virginia Civil Law*, 50 Ohio St. L.J. 511, 514–17 (1989). See also Sevier v. John M. Ross & Co., 1 Freeman's Chancery 519, 531 (Miss. Ch. 1842) ("the importance which has been attached to slave property" requires specific relief "even without any allegation of peculiar and special value").

Tushnet treats Georgia and Alabama as exceptions, but as is so often the case, decisions denying equitable relief in these states turned on reasons other than the adequacy of damages. Georgia required plaintiffs to prove the slave's special skills or their special affection for the slave, let defendants prove their special affection for the slave, and let an advisory jury decide where the slave should stay. This approach arose in a suit by the owner of a reversion interest in a fifteen-year-old house slave who had been with defendant since the age of four; the court thought it would be "an act of flagrant cruelty" to return this slave to her rightful owner. Mallery v. Dudley, 4 Ga. 52, 65–66 (1848).

In Alabama, reported requests for injunctions appear to have arisen only in contexts in which the choice between damages and specific relief was not clearly presented. Moreover, in the two cases in which the court denied equitable relief, the court rejected or plainly doubted plaintiff's claim on the merits. Compare Savery v. Spence, 13 Ala. 561, 563–64 (1848) (refusing specific performance of alleged oral contract that plaintiff would acquire a half-interest in six slaves in exchange for finding them in the hands of a judgment debtor; plaintiff sought only to have the slaves sold by the court and his share paid to him in cash); and Hardeman v. Sims, 3 Ala. 747 (1840) (refusing to order delivery of "family slave" to plaintiff, where slave had been with defendant from age six to age fifteen, plaintiff's claim was barred by statute of limitations, and if plaintiff succeeded on the merits, he could get specific relief at law in detinue); with Baker v. Rowan, 2 Stewart & Porter 361, 371–72 (Ala. 1832) (for "family slaves, to which owners are attached," or in other circumstances where "a peculiar value or interest attaches to slaves," equity should grant specific relief and not rely on the less certain specific remedy in detinue, but "peculiar value or attachment" must be stated with precision; equitable relief granted because of defendant's fraud).

74. [unfair labor practices] 29 U.S.C. § 160(c) (1988) (National Labor Relations Board shall order "such affirmative action including reinstatement of employees with or without back pay, as will effectuate the policies of this subchapter"); Nat'l Labor Relations Bd. v. Fleetwood Trailer Co., 389 U.S. 375, 381 (1967) ("if and when a job for which the striker is qualified becomes available, he is entitled to an offer of reinstatement"); Phelps Dodge Corp. v. Nat'l Labor Relations Bd., 313 U.S. 177, 189–97 (1941) (Board can order reinstatement even of employees who have found equivalent work elsewhere, if it states its reasons for doing so); Nat'l Labor Relations Bd v. Jones & Laughlin Steel Corp., 301 U.S. 1, 47–48 (1937) (statute authorizes Board to order reinstatement); David R. Webb Co. v. Nat'l Labor Relations Bd., 888 F.2d 501 (7th Cir. 1989) (former strikers who have been permanently replaced are entitled to reinstatement to first opening in former or substantially equivalent position, and this right is not terminated by unsatisfactory performance in position that is not substantially equivalent); S. Tours, Inc. v. Nat'l Labor Relations Bd., 401 F.2d 629, 633 (5th Cir. 1968) (Board "normally" orders reinstatement); Douglas S. McDowell & Kenneth C. Huhn, *NLRB Remedies for Unfair Labor Practices* 103–46 (Wharton School 1976); Clyde W. Summers,

Individual Protection Against Unjust Dismissal: Time for a Statute, 62 Va. L. Rev. 481, 491–92 (1976).

75. [employment discrimination] 42 U.S.C. § 2000e-5(g) (1982) (to remedy employment discrimination, court may "order such affirmative action as may be appropriate, which may include, but is not limited to, reinstatement or hiring of employees, with or without back pay"); Franks v. Bowman Transp. Co., 424 U.S. 747, 763–66 (1976) (adequate relief will "ordinarily" require reinstatement with seniority, "slotting the victim in that position in the seniority system that would have been his had he been hired at the time of his application"); Ford v. Nicks, 866 F.2d 865, 875–77 (6th Cir. 1989) (reinstating college professor without tenure; stating that reinstatement with tenure is available only if court is convinced that plaintiff could not receive fair consideration); Darnell v. City of Jasper, 730 F.2d 653, 655 (11th Cir. 1984) ("except in extraordinary cases," reinstatement is "required"); Maceira v. Pagan, 649 F.2d 8, 12–14 (1st Cir. 1981) (reinstating union officer discharged for protected speech); Aguilar v. Baine Serv. Systems, Inc., 538 F. Supp. 581, 585 (S.D.N.Y. 1982) (prohibiting discharge of employee who complained about discrimination); Ostrowski v. Local 1–2, Util. Workers Union, 530 F. Supp. 208, 215–16 (S.D.N.Y. 1980) (reinstating union officer discharged for protected speech). Most states have similar statutes. Summers, 62 Va. L. Rev. at 492–95. For an example, see Mass. Gen. Laws Ann. ch. 151B, § 5 (Supp. 1990) ("hiring, reinstatement, or upgrading" of employees).

76. [civil service] See 5 U.S.C. §§ 7512–7513 (1988) (right to hearing and appeal before removal from federal employment); Duchesne v. Williams, 821 F.2d 1234, 1242–46 (6th Cir. 1987) (plaintiff reinstated pending hearing on discharge for cause), vacated on other grounds, 849 F.2d 1004 (6th Cir. 1988) (en banc), cert. denied, 109 S.Ct. 1535 (1989); Bishop v. Tice, 622 F.2d 349, 356 (8th Cir. 1980) (improperly dismissed federal employee "is entitled to reinstatement and back pay"); Int'l Ass'n of Firefighters, Local 2069 v. City of Sylacauga, 436 F. Supp. 482, 492 (N.D. Ala. 1977) (rescinding unlawful promotions so that plaintiffs could compete for the positions); Oppenheimer Mendez v. Acevedo, 388 F. Supp. 326, 337–38 (D.P.R. 1974) (reinstating government attorney), aff'd, 512 F.2d 1373, 1375 (1st Cir. 1975); Madison County Bd. of Educ. v. Wigley, 288 Ala. 202, 207, 259 So.2d 233, 236 (1972) (reinstating public schoolteacher); Farmer v. McClure, 172 Ill. App. 3d 246, 256, 526 N.E.2d 486, 493 (1988) (reinstating "apprehension specialist," discharged during his period of probationary employment); State ex rel. Bardo v. City of Lyndhurst, 37 Ohio St. 3d 106, 524 N.E.2d 447 (1988) (mandamus ordering that police officer be promoted to vacant lieutenant's position); Summers, 62 Va. L. Rev. at 497–99. For an illustrative state statute, see Ohio Rev. Code Ann. § 124.34 (1990).

77. [arbitration] Staklinski v. Pyramid Elec. Co., 6 N.Y.2d 159, 188 N.Y.S.2d 541, 160 N.E.2d 78 (1959) (enforcing arbitration award reinstating corporate executive with 11-year contract); Frank Elkouri & Edna Asper Elkouri, *How Arbitration Works* 688–91 (BNA, 4th ed. 1985) (reviewing many variations of reinstatement in arbitration under collective bargaining agreements; damages remedy not mentioned as an option). For a survey of the arbitrator-made law of reinstatement, see Summers, 62 Va. L. Rev. at 499–508.

78. [reinstatement preferred] Equal Employment Opportunity Comm'n v. Prudential Fed. Sav. & Loan Ass'n, 763 F.2d 1166, 1172 (10th Cir. 1985) ("reinstatement is the preferred remedy"); Goldstein v. Manhattan Indus., Inc., 758 F.2d 1435, 1448–49 (11th Cir. 1985) (denying plaintiff's request for lost pay, and ordering reinstatement or nothing); McKelvy v. Metal Container Corp., 674 F. Supp. 827, 832 (M.D. Fla. 1987) ("employee does not have the power to select front pay as a remedy instead of reinstatement"), vacated in part, on other grounds, 854 F.2d 448 (11th Cir. 1988). See also Ford Motor Co. v. Equal Employment Opportunity Comm'n, 458 U.S. 219, 230–34 (1982) (victims of sex discrimination cannot recover lost pay accrued after employer offers reinstatement); City of Ingleside v. Kneuper, 768 S.W.2d 451, 458 (Tex. App. 1989) (where jury awarded damages for lost fringe benefits, and judge awarded reinstatement, plaintiff received double recovery and one remedy must be eliminated; by seeking reinstatement on motion for temporary injunction, plaintiff irrevocably elected reinstatement and could not now elect damages).

79. [jury trial for age discrimination] Lorillard, A Div. of Loew's Theatres, Inc. v. Pons, 434 U.S. 575, 580–85 (1978).

80. [reinstatement cheaper than damages] West, 1988 Ill. L. Rev. at 3–4 & n.7 (cited in note 55).

81. [damages pay for work not done] Lost Creek School Township v. York, 215 Ind. 636, 643, 21 N.E.2d 58, 61 (1939).

82. [hostility prevents reinstatement] Cooper v. Asplundh Tree Expert Co., 836 F.2d 1544, 1553 (10th Cir. 1988) ("tension and animosity between the parties in a working environment in which there were relatively few employees and close contact with supervisors"); McIntosh v. Jones Truck Lines, Inc., 767 F.2d 433, 435 & n.1 (8th Cir. 1985) ("animosity between the parties and the likelihood that they could not work together in peace"); Equal Employment Opportunity Comm'n v. Red Baron Steak Houses, 47 Fair Empl. Prac. Cases 49, 52 (N.D. Cal. 1988) ("given the small size of the defendant, it would be impossible to reinstate Mrs. Amick to her former position without substantial distress to her and to the defendant"); Toth v. Am. Greetings Corp., 40 Fair Empl. Prac. Cases 1768 (N.D. Ohio 1985) (mutual "antagonism" and "aggressive personalities"), aff'd mem., 811 F.2d 608 (6th Cir. 1986); Zahler v. Niagara County Ch. of the N.Y. State Ass'n for Retarded Children, Inc., 112 A.D.2d 707, 708, 491 N.Y.S.2d 880, 881 (1985) ("hostility between the parties" in employee's suit for specific performance).

83. [reinstatement despite hostility] Anderson v. Group Hospitalization, Inc., 820 F.2d 465, 473 (D.C. Cir. 1987) ("ill will" toward plaintiff "on part of management generally" is common in employment discrimination cases, and not sufficient reason to deny reinstatement; hostility "such that no meaningful relationship could be re-established" with plaintiff's supervisors is irrelevant where plaintiff can be assigned to "equivalent position" elsewhere in company); Holt v. Cont'l Group, Inc., 708 F.2d 87, 91 (2d Cir. 1983) ("considerable hostility" between plaintiff attorney and other attorneys in corporate legal department does not bar reinstatement in retaliation case, but trial court can give it some weight at preliminary injunction stage); Taylor v. Teletype Corp., 648 F.2d 1129, 1138–39 (8th Cir. 1981) (reinstating a public relations officer found to have lied at trial; "to deny reinstatement to a victim of discrimination merely because of the hostility engendered by the prosecution of a discrimination suit would frustrate the make-whole purpose of Title VII"); Nat'l Labor Relations Bd. v. Yazoo Valley Elec. Power Ass'n, 405 F.2d 479, 480 (5th Cir. 1968) (reinstating employee who had, in profane language, challenged supervisor to fight). See also Jordan v. Wilson, 851 F.2d 1290, 1291 (11th Cir. 1988) (reversing finding of civil contempt against mayor who said that "only person who thinks [plaintiff] is qualified to be a [police] captain is Judge Thompson, and he has no responsibility for her actions;" reinstatement order apparently not appealed).

84. [reinstatement often unsuccessful] Studies are collected in West, 1988 U. Ill. L. Rev. at 28–40 (cited in note 55).

85. [unionized reinstatements work better] See Julius G. Getman & Bertrand B. Pogrebin, *Labor Relations: The Basic Processes, Law, and Practice* 214–15 (Foundation Press 1988).

86. [damages inadequate for loss of job] Carson v. Am. Brands, Inc., 450 U.S. 79, 88–89 (1981) ("training and competitive advantages"); Black Ass'n of New Orleans Firefighters v. City of New Orleans, 853 F.2d 347, 353 (5th Cir. 1988) ("non-monetary distinction and perquisites"); Hewitt v. Magic City Furniture & Mfg. Co., 214 Ala. 265, 107 So. 745 (1926) (conceding that damages are never adequate remedy for loss of employment contract, but denying specific performance on grounds of mutuality); Farmer v. McClure, 172 Ill. App. 3d 246, 256, 526 N.E.2d 486, 493 (1988) ("remedy at law is inadequate to furnish the benefits of reinstatement to his job"); Endress v. Brookdale Community College, 144 N.J. Super. 109, 131, 364 A.2d 1080, 1091 (A.D. 1976) ("uncertainty in admeasuring damages because of the indefinite duration of the contract and the importance of the status of plaintiffs in the milieu of the college teaching profession"); Baker v. Minot Public School Dist. No. 1, 253 N.W.2d 444, 451 (N.D. 1977) (damages hard to measure because of "lost stature and reputation" and "indefinite duration" of employment contract); Yorio, *Contract Enforcement* § 14.4.1.2 at 380 (cited in note 61).

87. [damages adequate for loss of job] Millcarek v. Miami Herald Pub. Co., 388 F. Supp. 1002, 1005 (S.D. Fla. 1975) (damages are adequate and personal service contracts are not specifically enforced); Cahill v. Bd. of Educ., 187 Conn. 94, 97–98, 444 A.2d 907, 910 (1982) (jury had awarded $24,000); Waters v. School Bd., 401 So.2d 837, 838 (Fla. App. 1981) ("mere loss of employment does not constitute irreparable injury"); Bd. of Trustees v. Benetti, 492 N.E.2d 1098, 1104 (Ind. App. 1986) (plaintiff made "no showing of uniqueness"); Zahler v. Niagara County Ch. of the N.Y. State Ass'n for Retarded Children, Inc., 112 A.D.2d 707, 708, 491 N.Y.S.2d 880, 881 (1985) (adequate remedy at law and "hostility between the parties"); Clark v. Pa. State Police, 496 Pa. 310, 312–14, 436 A.2d 1383, 1384–85 (1981) (alleged contract to promote plaintiff from corporal to captain upon completion of law school; court held that damages were readily calculable by difference in pay).

88. [no common law reinstatement] Millcarek v. Miami Herald Pub. Co., 388 F. Supp. 1002, 1005 (S.D. Fla. 1975) (refusing preliminary injunction reinstating plaintiff as independent contractor to deliver newspapers); Ex parte Jim Dandy Co., 286 Ala. 295, 299–300, 239 So.2d 545, 548–49 (1970) (refusing to reinstate business executive); Cahill v. Bd. of Educ., 187 Conn. 94, 97–98, 444 A.2d 907, 910 (1982) (refusing to reinstate schoolteacher); Waters v. School Bd., 401 So.2d 837 (Fla. App. 1981) (same); Zannis v. Lake Shore Radiologists, Ltd., 73 Ill. App. 3d 901, 904–05, 392 N.E.2d 126, 129 (1979) (refusing to reinstate physician); Bd. of Trustees v. Benetti, 492 N.E.2d 1098, 1104 (Ind. App. 1986) (refusing to reinstate school teacher); Bussard v. College of St. Thomas, Inc., 294 Minn. 215, 227–28, 200 N.W.2d 155, 163 (1972) (discharged publisher of religious magazine is entitled to damages if he prevails, but not to specific performance); Zahler v. Niagara County Ch. of the N.Y. State Ass'n for Retarded Children, Inc., 112 A.D.2d 707, 491 N.Y.S.2d 880, 881 (1985) (refusing to reinstate executive director of not-for-profit corporation, discharged before expiration of contract term); Clark v. Pa. State Police, 496 Pa. 310, 312–14, 436 A.2d 1383, 1384–85 (1981) (refusing to enforce contract to promote plaintiff from corporal to captain upon completion of law school).

89. [statutory prohibitions] For example, Ala. Code § 8–1–41(2) (1984); Cal. Civ. Code § 3390.2 (1970).

90. [common law reinstatement cases] See notes 88 and 93.

91. [cases not in main line of authority] West, 1988 U. Ill. L. Rev. at 10–12 (cited in note 55); Note, *Remedies for Employer's Wrongful Discharge of an Employee Subject to Employment of Indefinite Duration*, 21 Ind. L. Rev. 547, 571–86 (1988). See also Paul H. Tobias, *Current Trends in Employment Dismissal Law: The Plaintiff's Perspective*, 67 Neb. L. Rev. 178 (1988) (surveying field without considering reinstatement).

92. [damages in six figures] See West at 3 n.4; Tobias at 187.

93. [common law reinstatement granted] Giron v. Housing Auth., 393 So.2d 1267, 1272 (La. 1981) (executive director discharged in breach of contract is "entitled either to damages or specific enforcement of the contract or to a dissolution of the contract"; choice of remedy appears to be largely plaintiff's); Duhon v. Slickline, Inc., 449 So.2d 1147, 1153 (La. App. 1984) (reinstating corporate officer in closely held family corporation); Am. Ass'n of Univ. Professors, Bloomfield College Ch. v. Bloomfield College, 136 N.J. Super 442, 448, 346 A.2d 615, 618 (A.D. 1975) (specific performance of professors' tenure contracts); Baker v. Minot Public School Dist. No. 1, 253 N.W.2d 444, 451–52 (N.D. 1977) (reinstating discharged school teacher).

94. [First Amendment reinstatements] Elrod v. Burns, 427 U.S. 347, 373–74 (1976) (affirming preliminary injunction against discharge of patronage workers for affiliation with Republican Party); Vitarelli v. Seaton, 359 U.S. 535, 545–46 (1959) (reinstating defense worker who lacked civil service protection); Savarese v. Agriss, 883 F.2d 1194, 1198–99, 1209 (3d Cir. 1989) (reinstating transportation workers discharged for political reasons); Mariani Giron v. Acevedo Ruiz, 834 F.2d 238, 239–40 (1st Cir. 1987) (preliminary injunction reinstating discharged patronage worker); Endress v. Brookdale Community College, 144 N.J. Super. 109, 130–31, 364 A.2d 1080, 1091 (A.D. 1976) (reinstating college professor discharged for failing to censor the student newspaper, explicitly rejecting rule that contracts for personal service can never be specifically enforced).

95. [reinstatement assumed] Perry v. Sindermann, 408 U.S. 593, 598, 603 (1972) (college professor discharged, allegedly in retaliation for speech and in violation of de facto tenure rights); Pickering v. Bd. of Educ., 391 U.S. 563, 564–65, 574–75 (1968) (schoolteacher discharged for writing letter to the editor).

8

Other Substantive Reasons

This chapter reviews a variety of cases in which the real basis of decision is the substantive merits of plaintiff's case. Plaintiff simply loses; he will get no remedy. But the court explains this result in terms of the irreparable injury rule, or it adds lack of irreparable injury as an additional ground of decision. There are vast numbers of these cases; they are surely the most common source of irreparable injury opinions at the permanent injunction stage.

A. Deference to More Particular Law

Litigants sometimes invoke the court's general equity powers to evade more particular rules of law. The court may cooperate if it considers the more particular law unjust, inapplicable, or not exclusive.[1] Thus, the real question in these cases is whether the more particular law controls, and the answer to that question is the proper ground of decision. But courts often add that the more particular law provides an adequate remedy that precludes equity jurisdiction.

Two recent examples illustrate the pattern. In *Sheets v. Yamaha Motors Corp.*,[2] plaintiff sued for theft of an alleged trade secret. The suit failed because he had not kept his device sufficiently secret. A second count alleged that defendant was unjustly enriched by use of plaintiff's device. The court dismissed this claim for several reasons, one of which was that an equitable claim for unjust enrichment would lie only if there were no adequate remedy at law. But the court also recognized the real reason for decision:

193

"An action for unjust enrichment will not be allowed to defeat the purpose of a rule of law directed to the matter at issue." The court might also have said that defendant's enrichment was not unjust if it were acquired consistently with the policies of patent and trade secret law.

The second example is *Emry v. American Honda Motor Co.*[3] Plaintiff moved to reinstate a personal injury claim that had been dismissed for want of prosecution. The court held that the statutory grounds for modifying the earlier judgment were not met. The statute was not exclusive; the court acknowledged uncodified equitable power to reinstate plaintiff's claim. But that power would not be used: "to proceed in equity the litigant must show that he was without a remedy at law; more specifically, that [the statute] could not serve him."[4] Of course, the court had just held that the statute could not serve him, but that was no longer the point. The uncodified equity power was reserved for fraud, and perhaps for similar situations where faultless plaintiffs were deprived of their statutory remedy. It would not be used where plaintiff's claim was barred by his own neglect.

There are many similar cases.[5] In each of them, plaintiff has lost on the merits. The court has not denied one remedy in favor of another; it has rejected two substantive theories and denied any remedy at all. Viewed as of the time of decision, the reason for denying relief on the more general theory is to avoid undermining the substantive restrictions in the more particular theory. Equitable relief is denied, not because some other remedy is adequate, but precisely because no other remedy is available.

Quite similar analysis applies to the many cases in which plaintiff asserts her general equity claim before it is clear that she has no claim under the more particular law. Courts will dismiss the equity claim if the dispute is one that should be governed by more particular substantive law or decided under more particular procedural law,[6] or if plaintiff has irretrievably elected another remedy by pursuing an earlier action.[7] In all these cases, courts sometimes reinforce their result with talk about adequate remedies at law.

Viewed *ex ante*, from the beginning of the controversy, a connection appears between these cases and the irreparable injury rule. The proper course for plaintiff in *Emry* was to not let his claim languish to the point of dismissal; the proper course for plaintiff in *Sheets* was to keep his device secret. If we conceive of these options as remedies, they would have been adequate if they had not been neglected. Plaintiffs are required to use these "remedies," and that requirement would be illusory if plaintiffs could neglect these "remedies" and seek an equitable remedy later. The denial of later equitable relief coerces plaintiffs into the preferred "remedy," just as the irreparable injury rule coerced plaintiffs into law courts before the merger. The analogy is even clearer when plaintiff is still free to try the more particular remedy.

The analogy is clear enough to explain why courts invoke it, but it diverts attention from the real basis for decision. It does not matter whether the choice is between two remedies or two substantive theories. It does not matter whether the less particular theory is legal or equitable. It may not even matter whether the more particular remedy would have been adequate if it had been used. In *Sheets*, the more difficult it would have been to qualify the device as a trade secret, the less adequate any remedy based on trade-secret law would have been, and the more important it would be not to let plaintiff get equivalent protection by another route. The *Emry* court was willing to relieve from fraud that precluded use of the statutory remedy; this may be thought of as rendering the statutory remedy inadequate, or more directly, as excusing the failure to use it.

The real issue in these cases is not law and equity, irreparable injury, or adequate and inadequate remedies. The issue is the policy of the more particular law. If plaintiff's general equity theory undermines a policy that the court or legislature is committed to preserving, relief should be denied. If the alternate theory fills a gap or corrects an injustice that the court is empowered to correct, and if the corrective is a good thing on balance, then the court should probably correct it. This is indeed a traditional function of substantive equity; it is Aristotle's conception of equity.[8] But the courts will perform it best if they focus directly on the competing substantive policies. Talk of irreparable injury and adequate remedy at law is usually a label for conclusions reached on other grounds. If the label guides decision, it is likely to mislead. The more particular remedy is important not because it might be adequate, but because it might be barred, and equity should not permit an end run around the more particular law.

The policy of preventing evasion of other substantive law plainly applies to damage remedies as well as to specific relief. If a legislature creates a cause of action specifying certain elements of recovery, plaintiffs generally cannot evade those limits by tacking common law measures of recovery onto the statutory cause of action.[9] If a legislature creates a set of remedies that are intended to be exclusive, plaintiffs cannot invoke other remedies, whether legal or equitable.[10] When the legislature fails to create any private remedy at all, conservative judges are reluctant to imply one, and again this reluctance extends to law[11] as well as equity.[12] (Notes 11 and 12 contain further explanation.) For constitutional violations, judicial conservatives concede the legitimacy of implied injunctive remedies but denounce implied damage remedies as a usurpation.[13] When protection of other substantive law requires courts to deny an equitable remedy, they may talk about the irreparable injury rule. But that is not the basis of their decision.

B. Hostility to the Merits of Plaintiff's Case

Courts frequently invoke the irreparable injury rule when they are hostile to plaintiff's case on the merits. Sometimes the hostility is justified, because the case is very weak; sometimes, the hostility is more akin to prejudice. Either way, once a court is inclined against plaintiff on the merits, it will often also conclude that plaintiff faces no irreparable injury.

I have already reviewed some special cases of this phenomenon. Cases denying equitable relief to prevent evasion of more particular substantive policies are really decisions on the merits. Decisions on preliminary injunctions openly and legitimately adjust the required degree of irreparable injury in light of plaintiff's chance of success on the merits.[14] Deference to other authorities is often accompanied by hostility to plaintiff's effort to bypass the other authority.[15] But the tendency of the merits to infect the court's views on irreparable injury extends beyond these special cases.

Sometimes the merits intrude as a well-considered deference to private arrangements or activities that the court is loath to disrupt. For example, courts are reluctant to enjoin payment on a letter of credit, because much international trade depends on nearly absolute certainty of payment.[16] So courts solemnly say that plaintiff has an adequate remedy by suing to get its money back in some foreign court, often in the Third World.[17] A significant split of authority arose only with respect to the adequacy of suit in the courts of revolutionary Iran on contracts with the former imperial government.[18]

American courts do not really mean that the foreign remedy is as complete, practical, and efficient as the domestic remedy. Rather, they mean that plaintiff agreed to the risk of foreign litigation when it put up the letter of credit, and now it must be held to its bargain.[19] Litigation in the United States is likely to be equally inconvenient and disconcerting for the foreign trading partner, and the letter of credit is a way of allocating that risk. It is the substantive law that forbids these injunctions, not the irreparable injury rule.

The point is equally well illustrated by the cases that do enjoin payment. Courts will enjoin payment if plaintiff sufficiently proves violation of the terms of the letter of credit,[20] or if she proves certain narrowly defined and serious frauds.* A later suit to recover the money would be no less adequate in these cases; rather, courts believe that plaintiff did not agree to bear these risks and that the flow of trade does not require her to do so. Where the substantive law permits courts to enjoin payment, the irreparable injury rule does not prevent the injunction even in wholly domestic cases.[22] Equally revealing, courts apply the same standards to suits to collect on the letter of credit,[23] although these are ordinary money claims and the irreparable injury rule does not apply to them.

Changes in the Michigan law of labor injunctions provide another clear example. Modern Michigan courts rarely find sufficient irreparable injury to justify an injunction against labor picketing.[24] A generation ago, they issued such injunctions routinely, finding it "self evident" that even temporary picketing

---

* A court may enjoin payment where the demand for payment is based on "forged or fraudulent" documents or where "there is fraud in the transaction." UCC § 5–114(2). "Fraud in the transaction" means fraud in the letter-of-credit transaction with the issuing bank; fraud in the underlying transaction between the buyer and seller is irrelevant, except for "egregious" fraud that "vitiates the entire transaction."[21]

would irreparably injure business, and that preliminary injunctions against picketing would inflict no "material ultimate damage" on workers.[25] There has been no general change in the Michigan law of irreparable injury. Instead, this change in irreparable injury doctrine reflects a fundamental change in Michigan labor policy.

Often a court decides the merits in favor of defendant, and then adds lack of irreparable injury as an additional ground.[26] This is harmless enough to the parties, as long as the court gives full consideration to the merits, but it creates odd precedents on the irreparable injury issue. Occasionally, a court will treat a defect in plaintiff's case on the merits as precluding the possibility of irreparable injury.[27] The reasoning here, logical but indirect, is that injury cannot be irreparable if it is not legally cognizable. A variation is to find that plaintiff has shown no injury at all, and thus that he has shown no irreparable injury.[28] This inference is valid enough, but misleading. The result in such cases is that plaintiff gets no remedy at all, not that he gets a legal remedy instead of an equitable remedy.

Another way to conflate the merits and remedies issues is to hold that a less effective remedy is good enough for such a weak claim.[29] This can be principled when the court recognizes what it is doing, but it carries the danger that the court will not squarely decide either issue. That danger is greater when the court is not clear about what it is doing. Courts will almost but not quite reject plaintiff's position on the merits, or ambiguously seem to reject it, and then fall back to irreparable injury, or to a mix of irreparable injury and the merits.[30]

Most troubling are cases where the court appears to be motivated by hostility to plaintiff's position on the merits, but decides the case only on the ground of no irreparable injury. In these cases, the court's reaction to the merits is not tested by the discipline of writing an opinion, and the court's avoidance of the merits may signal that an opinion for defendant would be hard to write. The holding of no irreparable injury is usually dubious or worse.

Covert grounds for decision are easy to suspect but hard to prove. I have included cases in this category only when the court's hostility to plaintiff's position is apparent in its statement of the case,[31] or when the court dismisses solely on the ground of no irreparable injury but the legal remedy is grossly inadequate,[32] or when I know that individual justices are being inconsistent. A simple example is Justice Brennan's suggestion that bankruptcy would be an acceptable result for Texaco but not for the NAACP.[33]

A more extended example is the shifting position of the justices on irreparable injury in free speech cases. In *Snepp v. United States*,[34] a former intelligence agent published a book about his experiences, without getting the required clearance from the agency. The Court imposed a constructive trust, giving the government all profits from the book. Justices Stevens, Brennan, and Marshall dissented on numerous grounds, including the ground that the equitable remedy of constructive trust should not be granted until the legal remedy of punitive damages had been tried and found wanting.[35]

The dissenters' proposal would have been an extraordinary application of the irreparable injury rule. The adequacy of the legal remedy is normally assessed at the time plaintiff requests the equitable remedy. Courts rarely follow the dissent's proposal of trying a doubtful legal remedy to see if it works. Punitive damages are inadequate in other ways as well. They are discretionary, and they depend on defendant's culpability. They are punitive rather than remedial. That is, they do not attempt to restore any version of the status quo prior to the violation. They are a dubious supplement to the specific, compensatory, or restitutionary remedy to which plaintiff is entitled, but they have never been considered a substitute for that remedy.

Contrast *Snepp* with the cases in which federal plaintiffs sought to enjoin prosecutions in state court. In those cases, the conservative wing of the Court invoked the irreparable injury rule to minimize the federal remedy.[36] Justices Stevens, Brennan, and Marshall frequently dissented,[37] or filed concurrences seeking to minimize the impact of the holdings.[38] Many of these cases involved speakers seeking protection from state authorities.[39] In short, justices in the *Snepp* majority invoke the irreparable injury rule against speakers; the dissenters invoke it against censors. How adequate a remedy you are entitled to may depend on who you are and which side of the dispute you are on.

C. Miscellaneous Reasons

A few unusual reasons for denying specific relief do not fit neatly in any of the foregoing categories. But these cases are consistent with my thesis: courts that invoke the irreparable injury rule have some additional reason for denying the relief plaintiff seeks.

One case invoked the irreparable injury rule in tandem with the unclean hands doctrine to deny a preliminary injunction against a tender offer. Unclean hands, the usual risks of preliminary relief, and deference to another court's injunction against plaintiff's competing tender offer all contributed to the decision.[40] Another vacated an injunction to make future payments as they came due, on the ground that the trial court had not found that the present value of the payments was too uncertain to be assessed in a money judgment.[41] The court did not mention the general reluctance to personally command the payment of money, but that reluctance justifies the result.[42]

In *Kowalski v. Chicago Tribune Co.*,[43] Judge Posner converted a limitation of remedy clause into an apparently conclusive presumption of adequate legal remedy. The Tribune's contract with its distributors provided that if the Tribune changed its method of distribution, the distributors would be compensated in an amount to be determined by negotiation or arbitration, but that there could be no judicial remedy, and no arbitrator could reinstate a terminated distributor. When the Tribune changed from independent distributors to agents selling on consignment, the distributors went to court and sought reinstatement. The trial court denied a preliminary injunction, and the court of appeals affirmed, holding that the contractual remedy provisions proved that the legal remedy was adequate.

Undoubtedly this is the right result, but it is not the right explanation. Courts regularly hold that damages are not an adequate remedy for the destruction of a small business, because going concern value is notoriously hard to measure and because small proprietors have a right to their business.[44] The parties can bargain for an exclusive damage remedy if they want, but that does not make damages adequate. It does not even suggest that the parties assumed that damages would be adequate. Rather, it suggests that the Tribune insisted on the right to change its distribution system and limited its distributors to remedies that would not prevent a change.

The Tribune's no-reinstatement provision should be analyzed as a limitation of remedies clause.[45] The very purpose of such clauses is to limit plaintiffs to remedies that are less effective than the remedy they would choose—to remedies that are inadequate under the usual definition. Such clauses are generally enforced unless they render the contract illusory or unconscionable,[46] a standard very different from the adequacy standard of equally complete, practical, and efficient.

Finally, a North Carolina case presented an apparently meaningless choice between substantive theories.[47] A buyer of land, who got less than he was promised, plead for damages or restitution in the alternative. After holding that the damage theory stated a claim, the court dismissed the restitution theory on the ground that the damage remedy was adequate. So far as one can tell from the facts, the measure of plaintiff's damages and of defendant's unjust enrichment would be identical. Either remedy would be substitutionary; plaintiff had already resold the land and no form of specific relief was possible.

Thus, once the court upheld the damage theory, the restitution theory became irrelevant. Here the irreparable injury rule is invoked as an explanation for eliminating redundant legal theories and thus simplifying the litigation. But there is a caveat: the court does not appear to have determined the measure of recovery under either theory. It may not have known whether the damage remedy was just as good as the restitution remedy. If not, this may arguably be counted as a real application of the irreparable injury rule. But the rule was not invoked to choose substitutionary relief over specific relief. Rather, it was invoked to choose the legal measure of substitutionary relief over the equitable measure of substitutionary relief.

D. Conclusion

In all the cases in this chapter, the irreparable injury rule was a handy but misleading label for a judgment on the merits. Resort to the irreparable injury explanation means that the court need not explain the substantive basis for the decision, and therefore, that the court need not think it through. The judgment on the merits may be based on little more than judicial intuition. What is clear in these cases is that the irreparable injury rule distracts the court's attention from the substantive questions that are really at issue.

Notes on Substantive Reasons

1. [use of equity to evade other law] Hoyne Sav. & Loan Ass'n v. Hare, 60 Ill. 2d 84, 88–90, 322 N.E.2d 833, 834 (1974) (equitable relief from fraudulent tax assessment where inadequate and untimely notice caused plaintiff to miss deadline for legal remedy); Hatcher v. Graddick, 509 N.E.2d 258, 260 (Ind. App. 1987) (preliminary injunction against reducing court's budget, where statutory remedy entailed substantial delay); Long v. Kistler, 72 Pa. Commw. 547, 553, 457 A.2d 591, 593 (1983) (allowing suit to enjoin discriminatory assessments, where state tax assessment law made no provision for such challenges); Cook v. Smith, 673 S.W.2d 232, 236 (Tex. App. 1984) (estoppel to assert limitations); Blum v. Mott, 664 S.W.2d 741, 743–44 (Tex. App. 1983) (allowing bill of review to consider claims that child custody agreement was obtained by fraud, where statutory proceeding to change custody was limited to change of circumstances).

2. [unjust enrichment from trade secret] Sheets v. Yamaha Motors Corp., 849 F.2d 179, 184 (5th Cir. 1988).

3. [motion to reinstate claim] Emry v. Am. Honda Motor Co., 214 Neb. 435, 334 N.W.2d 786 (1983).

4. [equity available only if statute is not] Id. at 447, 334 N.W.2d at 794.

5. [no irreparable injury; merits barred] Austin v. N. Am. Forest Prod., 656 F.2d 1076, 1088–89 (5th Cir. 1981) (no general claim for unjust enrichment where specific statutory claim for rescission was barred by limitations); Prudential Ins. Co. v. Crouch, 606 F. Supp. 464, 472 (S.D. Ind. 1985) (refusing to enjoin former agent from soliciting old customers to cancel policies, where agent did not promise not to compete, but allowing damage remedy for unearned premiums on cancelled policies, with respect to which agent had fiduciary duty); Rodgers v. Easterling, 270 Ark. 255, 603 S.W.2d 884 (1980) (Chancery Court can not enjoin tax assessment where taxpayer could have sought judicial review of assessment in County Court); Cook v. Oberly, 459 A.2d 535, 540–41 (Del. Ch. 1983) (refusing to enjoin suspension of plaintiff's driver's license where plaintiff failed to seek administrative hearing on suspension); Marshall v. Dist. of Columbia, 458 A.2d 28, 29–30 (D.C. App. 1982) (no injunction ordering trial judges to pay attorney full amount requested under Criminal Justice Act, where attorney failed to raise issue by motion before trial judges); Barnes v. White County Bank, 170 Ga. App. 681, 318 S.E.2d 74 (1984) (no counterclaim to enjoin continuation of plaintiff's lawsuit, where effect would be to evade state law on attorneys' fees and malicious prosecution); Bank of Danielsville v. Seagraves, 167 Ga. App. 135, 142–43, 305 S.E.2d 790, 796 (1983) (insurer cannot assert equitable subrogation after its failure to take assignment of insured's claim prejudicially misled insured and wrongdoer); Robinson v. Jones, 186 Ill. App. 3d 82, —, 542 N.E.2d 127, 131 (1989) (refusing to enjoin run-off election, because election contest of earlier election would be adequate remedy at law, and dismissing plaintiff's complaint for election contest because not filed within five-day statute of limitations); Scott & Fetzer Co. v. Montgomery Ward & Co., 129 Ill. App. 3d 1011, 1021–22, 473 N.E.2d 421, 429–30 (1984) (no rescission of contract where effect would be to give plaintiff refund much greater than sums recoverable under liquidated damages clause), aff'd as to other issues, 112 Ill. 2d 378, 493 N.E.2d 1022 (1986); Lowry v. Decks & Tapes, Inc., 415 So.2d 632, 634 (La. App. 1982) (no equity power to discharge consumer sales contract for late delivery, where more particular law of sales controlled); Northwoods Environmental Inst. v. Minn. Pollution Control Agency, 370 N.W.2d 449, 451 (Minn. App. 1985) (no mandamus against agency where adequate statutory remedies were not invoked); Chartiers Valley School Dist. v. Va. Mansions Apts., Inc., 489 A.2d 1381, 1386–92 (Pa. Super. 1985) (refusing to enjoin allegedly fraudulent conveyance of taxpayer's property, where taxing authority had failed to invoke statutory procedures to preserve its tax lien); Sprecher v. Weston's Bar, Inc., 78 Wis. 2d 26, 50, 253 N.W.2d 493, 504 (1977) (no injunction against transfer of liquor license, where plaintiff failed to mitigate loss by purchasing identical liquor license when chance to do so was offered).

  6. [no irreparable injury; use other law] Scruggs v. Moellering, 870 F.2d 376, 378 (7th Cir.) (refusing to order court reporter to prepare accurate transcript, where postconviction review would provide adequate remedy for alleged falsification of record), cert. denied, 110 S. Ct. 371 (1989); Stewart v. Gen'l Motors Corp., 756 F.2d 1285, 1291–92 (7th Cir. 1985) (regularized promotion system created by collective bargaining agreement is legal remedy for informal and discriminatory promotions, eliminating need for injunction against informal system); System Fed'n No. 30, Ry. Employees' Dep't, AFL-CIO v. Braidwood, 284 F. Supp. 607, 609–10 (N.D. Ill. 1968) (statutory review of decision of National Railroad Adjustment Board is adequate remedy, precluding injunction or mandamus against individual members of board); Dep't of Business Regulation v. Provende, Inc., 399 So.2d 1038 (Fla. App. 1981) (no trial court injunction against emergency suspension of liquor license, where judicial review of agency action in court of appeal would be adequate remedy); Punohu v. Sunn, 66 Hawaii 485, 666 P.2d 1133 (1983) (no injunction against reduction in welfare benefits where administrative review would be adequate remedy); Paul L. Pratt, P.C. v. Blunt, 140 Ill. App. 3d 512, 523, 488 N.E.2d 1062, 1070 (1986) (no injunction ordering production of documents in absence of showing that ordinary discovery procedures would be inadequate); Sanner v. Champaign County, 88 Ill. App. 3d 491, 497–98, 410 N.E.2d 656, 660–61 (1980) (refusing to order refund of improperly collected criminal fines, where motion in court supervising probation would be adequate remedy); Mayor of Morgan City v. Jesse J. Fontenot, Inc., 460 So.2d 685, 688–89 (La. App. 1984) (no equity action for causing fire, where tort law controlled): Nunez v. Erbelding, 442 So.2d 1335, 1337–38 (La. App. 1983) (no injunction against sale of assets by executor when all disputed issues should be raised and resolved in probate proceeding); LeBlanc v. Lyons, 401 So.2d 626, 628 (La. App. 1981) (refusing to enjoin ex-husband from alienating ex-wife's share of former community property, where proper remedy was suit to partition property); Schantz v. Ruehs, 348 Mich. 680,

83 N.W.2d 587 (1957) (no injunction against involuntary commitment and guardianship, where mental health law provided more specific remedies); Las Vegas Valley Water Dist. v. Curtis Park Manor Water Users Ass'n, 98 Nev. 275, 646 P.2d 549 (1982) (no general equity review of water permit revocation, where review at law would be limited to abuse of discretion); D.C. Trautman Co. v. Fargo Excavating Co., 380 N.W.2d 644, 645–46 (N.D. 1986) (no action for unjust enrichment where suit on express contract would be adequate remedy); State ex rel. Tudor v. Indus. Comm'n, 45 Ohio St. 3d 251, 543 N.E.2d 800 (1989) (no mandamus to agency where appeal would be adequate remedy); State ex rel. Pressley v. Indus. Comm'n, 11 Ohio St. 2d 141, 228 N.E.2d 631 (1967) (no mandamus in appellate court where injunction in trial court would be adequate remedy); City of Chickasha v. Ark. La. Gas Co., 625 P.2d 638, 641–42 (Okla. App. 1981) (no injunction against local ordinance allegedly pre-empted by state regulation, where application to state regulatory agency would be adequate remedy); Aquarian Church of Universal Serv. v. County of York, 90 Pa. Commw. 290, 293, 494 A.2d 891, 892–93 (1985) (refusing to enjoin tax foreclosure sale of allegedly exempt property, where owner never applied for exemption); Lashe v. N. York County School Dist., 52 Pa. Commw. 541, 551–52, 417 A.2d 260, 265 (1980) (refusing to enjoin allegedly unconstitutional tax ordinance, where plaintiffs failed to invoke specific statutory remedy); Barrett v. Miller, 283 S.C. 262, 263–64, 321 S.E.2d 198, 199 (App. 1984) (no general equity claim for unjust enrichment if case fell within Betterment Statutes); Sisco v. Hereford, 694 S.W.2d 3, 7 (Tex. App. 1984) (no implied access easement where restoration of road on existing easement would be adequate remedy); Truby v. Broadwater, 332 S.E.2d 284 (W. Va. 1985) (no injunction against enforcement of scholastic eligibility rules, where administrative remedy for challenging grades would be adequate).

  7. **[no irreparable injury; remedy elected]** Myshko v. Galanti, 453 Pa. 412, 416, 309 A.2d 729, 730–32 (1973) (by suing for damages, plaintiffs "not only manifested their belief that there was an adequate remedy at law but also precluded themselves from bringing a simultaneous action in equity" to recover specific property and an accounting of defendant's profits); Redmond Finishing Co. v. Ginsburg, 446 A.2d 1330, 1331–32 (Pa. Super. 1982) (no equitable action for constructive trust over land acquired by fraud, where plaintiff earlier elected adequate legal remedy of suit for damages).

  8. **[Aristotle on equity]** Aristotle, *Nicomachean Ethics* 1137b ("this is the nature of the equitable, a correction of law where it is defective owing to its universality") (W.D. Ross, trans.), in 2 *The Complete Works of Aristotle* 1796 (Jonathan Barnes, ed.) (Princeton Univ. Press 1984); Aristotle, *Rhetoric* 1374a ("for equity is regarded as just; it is, in fact, the sort of justice which goes beyond the written law") (W. Rhys Roberts trans.), in 2 *Works* at 2188.

  9. **[statutory damages exclusive]** DeGrace v. Rumsfeld, 614 F.2d 796, 808 (1st Cir. 1980) (no compensatory or punitive damages under employment discrimination statute that authorizes only back pay, reinstatement, and other equitable relief); Mack A. Player, *Employment Discrimination Law* § 5.67b (West 1988) (same).

  10. **[statutory remedies exclusive]** Smith v. Robinson, 468 U.S. 992, 1009–13, 1016–21 (1984) (remedy under Education of the Handicapped Act as it then stood precluded suit under Rehabilitation Act or Civil Rights Act of 1871); Middlesex County Sewerage Auth. v. Nat'l Sea Clammers Ass'n, 453 U.S. 1, 19–21 (1981)

(administrative remedies under federal environmental laws preclude suit under Civil Rights Act of 1871); City of Milwaukee v. Ill., 451 U.S. 304 (1981) (remedy under Federal Water Pollution Control Act precludes suit for common law nuisance); Great Am. Fed. Sav. & Loan Ass'n v. Novotny, 442 U.S. 366, 370–78 (1979) (rights created by Civil Rights Act of 1964 may not be enforced through remedial provisions of 42 U.S.C. § 1985(3), derived from Civil Rights Act of 1871); Brown v. Gen'l Serv. Admin., 425 U.S. 820 (1976) (remedy under Civil Rights Act of 1964, for racial discrimination against federal employee, precludes suit under Constitution); Preiser v. Rodriguez, 411 U.S. 475, 482–500 (1973) (habeas corpus remedy, for prisoner challenging length of his confinement, precludes suit under Civil Rights Act of 1871); U.S. v. Demko, 385 U.S. 149 (1966) (remedy under 18 U.S.C. § 4126, providing compensation for federal prisoner injured in prison work assignment, precludes suit under Federal Tort Claims Act); Patterson v. U.S., 359 U.S. 495 (1959) (remedy under Federal Employees' Compensation Act, for civilian sailor killed in course of federal employment, precludes suit under Suits in Admiralty Act); Johansen v. U.S., 343 U.S. 427 (1952) (remedy under Federal Employees' Compensation Act as it then stood, for civilian sailor killed or injured while employed on military vessel, precluded suit under Public Vessels Act); Makovi v. Sherwin-Williams Co., 316 Md. 603, 561 A.2d 179 (1989) (remedy under civil rights laws, for employee alleging sex-motivated discharge, precludes tort suit for abusive discharge); Lamphere Schools v. Lamphere Fed'n of Teachers, 400 Mich. 104, 252 N.W.2d 818 (1977) (remedy under Public Employment Relations Act precludes common law damage remedy for illegal strike); Karst v. F.C. Hayer Co., 447 N.W.2d 180 (Minn. 1989) (remedy under Workers Compensation Act, for worker injured on job and then denied re-employment, precludes remedy under handicap discrimination statute); Note, *Comprehensive Remedies and Statutory Section 1983 Actions: Context as a Guide to Procedural Fairness*, 67 Tex. L. Rev. 627 (1989). Compare Byrd v. Richardson-Greenshields Securities, Inc., 552 So.2d 1099 (Fla. 1989) (Workers Compensation Law does not provide remedy for sexual harassment, and thus does not preclude tort suit for assault and battery, emotional distress, and negligent hiring; question whether civil rights laws provide exclusive remedy not presented).

11. [implied damage remedies] Since 1975, the Court has implied only one private damage remedy. Merrill Lynch, Pierce, Fenner & Smith v. Curran, 456 U.S. 353 (1982) (Commodity Exchange Act). For decisions refusing to imply such remedies, see Mass. Mut. Life Ins. Co. v. Russell, 473 U.S. 134 (1985) (Employment Retirement Income Security Act); Daily Income Fund v. Fox, 464 U.S. 523 (1984) (§ 36(b) of Investment Company Act); Northwest Airlines, Inc. v. Transp. Workers Union, 451 U.S. 77 (1981) (contribution among civil rights defendants); Tex. Indus., Inc. v. Radcliff Materials, Inc., 451 U.S. 630 (1981) (contribution among antitrust defendants); Univ. Research Ass'n, Inc. v. Coutu, 450 U.S. 754 (1981) (Davis–Bacon Act); Transamerica Mortgage Advisors, Inc. v. Lewis, 444 U.S. 11, 18–24 (1979) (§ 206 of Investment Company Act); Touche Ross & Co. v. Redington, 442 U.S. 560 (1979) (§ 17(a) of Securities Act of 1933); Cort v. Ash, 422 U.S. 66 (1975) (18 U.S.C. § 610, since repealed, which prohibited campaign contributions by federally chartered corporations).

12. [implied equitable remedies] The Court has generally not distinguished damages from injunctions in its implied private remedy opinions. Claims for implied specific relief have fared slightly better than claims for implied damage remedies, but this may be just random variation. For opinions applying its standard implied remedy analysis to requests for injunctions, see Cal. v. Sierra Club, 451 U.S. 287 (1981) (refusing to enjoin violation of Rivers and Harbors Act); Cannon v. Univ. of Chicago, 441 U.S. 677, 705 (1979) (finding implied right to enjoin sex discrimination in university admission); Chrysler Corp. v. Brown, 441 U.S. 281, 316–17 (1979) (refusing to enjoin violation of criminal statute prohibiting disclosure of confidential private information furnished to government regulators). However, *Chrysler Corp.* found a right to substantially equivalent relief under the Administrative Procedure Act. Id. at 317–19. Another case in this line, which should have been decided on other grounds, is Thompson v. Thompson, 484 U.S. 174 (1988). *Thompson* refused to imply a private right to a federal judgment declaring the validity of conflicting state judgments in child custody cases. The issue here was not private enforcement, but whether the private remedy should be a new lawsuit or an appeal if the second state court rejected a plea of res judicata. For a case distinguishing legal from equitable relief, and preferring equitable, see Transamerica Mortgage Advisors, Inc. v. Lewis, 444 U.S. 11, 18–19 (1979) (implying private right to rescission, injunction, and restitution from statutory provision making contract "void," but refusing to imply private right to damages or other monetary relief).

13. [implied constitutional remedies] See Carlson v. Green, 446 U.S. 14, 42–43 (1980) (Rehnquist dissenting) (conceding that "federal courts have historically had broad authority to fashion equitable remedies," but insisting that judicially created damage remedy was a usurpation).

14. [merits and preliminary relief] See ch. 5. For especially clear examples, see Calvin Klein Cosmetics Corp. v. Lenox Labs., Inc., 815 F.2d 500, 505 (8th Cir. 1987) (irreparable injury insufficient to support preliminary injunction where trial court erred in finding probable success on merits); Friends of the Earth, Inc. v. Coleman, 518 F.2d 323, 330 (9th Cir. 1975) (irreparable injury not controlling where there is little likelihood of success on merits); Palm Beach County Classroom Teacher's Ass'n v. School Bd., 411 So.2d 1375, 1376–77 (Fla. App. 1982) (giving several reasons for rejecting plaintiff's position on merits, but denying preliminary injunction solely on less plausible ground of no irreparable injury).

15. [hostility to attacks on deference] See ch. 6.

16. [letters of credit] See John F. Dolan, *The Law of Letters of Credit* ¶ 11.04 (Warren, Gorham & Lamont, 1984 and Cum. Supp. 1990).

17. [foreign remedy adequate] Enterprise Int'l, Inc. v. Corporacion Estatal Petrolera Ecuatoriana, 762 F.2d 464, 474 (5th Cir. 1985) (Ecuador; "showing of a substantial threat of irreparable injury" is "to be strictly exacted" in letter-of-credit cases); Foxboro Co. v. Arabian Am. Oil Co., 805 F.2d 34, 36–37 (1st Cir. 1986) (Saudi Arabia).

18. [Iranian cases] Compare KMW Int'l v. Chase Manhattan Bank, N.A., 606 F.2d 10, 14–17 (2d Cir. 1979) (refusing injunction); with Itek Corp. v. First Nat'l Bank, 730 F.2d 19, 22 (1st Cir. 1984) (granting injunction); Rockwell Int'l Systems, Inc. v. Citibank, N.A., 719 F.2d 583, 586–88 (2d Cir. 1983) (granting injunction); Harris Corp. v. Nat'l Iranian Radio & Television, 691 F.2d 1344, 1356–57 (11th Cir. 1982) (granting injunction). See Note, *"Fraud in the Transaction": Enjoining Letters of Credit During the Iranian Revolution*, 93 Harv. L. Rev. 992 (1980).

19. [plaintiff accepted risk] Trans Meridian Trading, Inc. v. Empresa Nacional de Comercializacion de Insumos, 829 F.2d 949, 956 (9th Cir. 1987) (remitting plaintiff to suit in Peru, on ground that plaintiff knowingly undertook that risk; not relying on irreparable injury rule). The cases cited in note 17 invoke similar grounds in addition to the irreparable injury rule.

20. [enjoining payment in breach of terms] Atlas Mini Storage, Inc. v. First Interstate Bank, 426 N.W.2d 686, 688 (Iowa App. 1988).

21. [fraud in the transaction] See Cromwell v. Commerce & Energy Bank, 464 So.2d 721, 730–36 (La. 1985) (reviewing cases from several jurisdictions); Brown v. U.S. Nat'l Bank, 220 Neb. 684, 692–96, 371 N.W.2d 692, 698–700 (1985) (plaintiff must show fraud "vitiating the entire transaction"); Sztejn v. J. Henry Schroder Banking Corp., 177 Misc. 719, 31 N.Y.S.2d 631 (Sup. 1941) (payment of draft on letter of credit may be enjoined where seller shipped crates of worthless cowhair and rubbish, provided that draft has not been negotiated to a holder in due course); Intraworld Indus., Inc. v. Girard Trust Bank, 461 Pa. 343, 357–63, 336 A.2d 316, 323–27 (1975) (plaintiff must show that documents presented with demand for payment have "no basis in fact"); Philipp Bros., Inc. v. Oil Country Specialists, Ltd., 787 S.W.2d 38, 40 (Tex. 1990) ("fraud in which the wrong doing of the beneficiary has so vitiated the entire transaction that the legitimate purposes of the independence of the issuer's obligation would no longer be served"); Paris Sav. & Loan Ass'n v. Walden, 730 S.W.2d 355, 365–66 (Tex. App. 1987) (fraud and irreparable injury do not justify enjoining payment of letter of credit, unless fraud is "egregious, intentional and unscrupulous" and "vitiate[s] the entire transaction"). For a more complete account, see James J. White & Robert S. Summers, *Uniform Commercial Code* § 19–7 (West 3d ed. 1988). For an argument that customers who agree to pay through letters of credit deserve somewhat greater protection from fraudulent draws on letters of credit, see E.P. Ellinger, *Fraud in Documentary Credit Transactions*, 1981 J. Bus. L. 258.

22. [enjoining payment in domestic cases] Atlas Mini Storage, Inc. v. First Interstate Bank, 426 N.W.2d 686, 689 (Iowa App. 1988) (finding irreparable injury without explaining why); Shaffer v. Brooklyn Park Garden Apts., 311 Minn. 452, 462–68, 250 N.W.2d 172, 181–82 (Minn. 1977) (finding irreparable injury on erroneous ground that plaintiff could not recover money if it were once erroneously paid, confusing issues of irreparable injury and holder in due course); O'Grady v. First Union Nat'l Bank, 296 N.C. 212, 234–36, 250 S.E.2d 587, 602 (1978) (plaintiff "would be entitled to a permanent injunction and cancellation of the letter of credit" if on remand they sufficiently prove fraud; irreparable injury not discussed).

23. [collecting on letter of credit] Philadelphia Gear Corp. v. Cent. Bank, 717 F.2d 230, 236–40 (5th Cir. 1983) (failure to comply with terms of letter of credit); United Bank Ltd. v. Cambridge Sporting Goods Corp., 41 N.Y.2d 254, 258–61, 360 N.E.2d 943, 947–49, 392 N.Y.S.2d 265, 269–71 (1976) (fraud in the transaction).

24. [Michigan labor cases] Holland School Dist. v. Holland Educ. Ass'n, 380 Mich. 314, 326, 157 N.W.2d 206, 210 (1968) ("it is basically contrary to public policy in this State to issue injunctions in labor disputes absent a showing of violence, irreparable injury, or breach of the peace"; showing that schools would not open is insufficient); Cross Co. v. United Auto. Workers Local No. 155, 371 Mich. 184, 197, 123 N.W.2d 215, 221–22 (1963) (in labor cases, injunction may issue without adversary hearing only on "a clearly persuasive showing of imminent and irreparable injury beyond the power of the regularly constituted police authorities of the community to control"); Acorn Bldg. Components v. Local Union No. 2194, 164 Mich. App. 358, 365, 416 N.W.2d 442, 446 (1987) ("labor injunction regulating picketing cannot be issued unless there is a clearly persuasive showing that the plaintiff will suffer imminent and irreparable injury which is beyond the power of the regularly constituted police authorities to control").

25. [old Michigan labor cases] Cohen v. Detroit Joint Bd. Amalgamated Clothing Workers, 327 Mich. 606, 611, 42 N.W.2d 830, 833 (1950) (preliminary injunction against picketing dry cleaning business; "quite self-evident that . . . plaintiff's business will be completely ruined or at least suffer irreparable damage pending final decision"; "equally apparent that granting the temporary injunctive relief sought will not subject defendant [union] to any material ultimate damage or deprivation of rights"); Niedzialek v. Journeymen Barbers Int'l Union, Local No. 552, 331 Mich. 296, 300–01, 49 N.W.2d 273, 275 (1951) (same, quoting *Cohen*).

26. [irreparable injury opinions; no merit] Sheets v. Yamaha Motors Corp., U.S.A., 849 F.2d 179, 184 (5th Cir. 1988) (refusing to award equitable restitution for use of trade secret, on grounds that plaintiff had not made reasonable efforts to preserve secrecy, and that his legal remedy was adequate); Thorbus v. Bowen, 848 F.2d 901, 904 (8th Cir. 1988) (refusing to enjoin plaintiff's exclusion from eligibility for Medicare reimbursement, on grounds that he had received adequate hearing and that he failed to show irreparable injury); Holly Sugar Corp. v. Goshen County Co-op. Beet Growers Ass'n, 725 F.2d 564, 569–70 (10th Cir. 1984) (refusing to enjoin efforts to enforce cooperative marketing agreement, on grounds that agreement was lawful and that its enforcement would not inflict irreparable injury; stating that damages from loss of crop and closing of factory would be measurable, and that harm to community was irrelevant); Cont'l Bank & Trust Co. v. Am. Bonding Co., 462 F. Supp. 123, 130 (E.D. Mo. 1978) (refusing to order specific performance of contract to build recreational facilities, on grounds that there was no contract, and if there were, legal remedies would be adequate), rev'd in part, as to other parties, 605 F.2d 1049 (8th Cir. 1979); Robinson v. Kitchin, 78 F.R.D. 691, 692 (E.D. Mo. 1978) (vague allegations of mistreatment of black prisoners do not state claim on which relief can be granted and do not show irreparable injury); 7978 Corp. v. Pitchess, 41 Cal. App. 3d 42, 46, 115 Cal. Rptr. 746, 748 (1974) (refusing to enjoin dance-hall curfew, on grounds that curfew is not unconstitutional and does not inflict irreparable injury); Para-Medical Ambulance, Inc. v. City of Torrington, 37 Conn. Supp. 124, 126–29, 444 A.2d 236, 238–39 (1981) ("the issue before the court is whether the plaintiff has demonstrated irreparable harm," followed by decision that defendant's challenged conduct—operation of ambulance service—is entirely lawful); Meerbrey v. Marshall Field & Co., 169 Ill. App. 3d 1014, 1017–18, 524 N.E.2d 228, 230 (1988) (refusing to order defendant to let plaintiff enter its store, on grounds that plaintiff had no right to be there and that inability to shop there would not be irreparable injury); Commonwealth Revenue Cabinet v. Graham, 710 S.W.2d 227, 228–29 (Ky. 1986) (refusing writ of prohibition to prevent in camera inspection of allegedly privileged executive-branch documents, on ground that the inspection was necessary to determine claim of privilege and therefore could not inflict "great injustice and irreparable injury");

Ingraham v. Univ. of Maine, 441 A.2d 691, 692–93 (Me. 1982) (refusing to order prosecutor to expunge a criminal conviction, on grounds of failure to state a claim, prosecutorial immunity, and no irreparable injury); Barkau v. Ruggirello, 100 Mich. App. 617, 300 N.W.2d 342, 345–46 (1980) (refusing to enforce administrative rule entitling owners of mobile homes to sell them on rented lots, on grounds that rule was "invalid and unenforceable," and that plaintiffs had adequate remedy at law); Reno v. Clark, 33 Ohio App. 3d 41, 43, 514 N.E.2d 456, 458 (1986) (trial court awarded proceeds of insurance policy to plaintiff "in equity and in conscience"; appellate court reversed on ground that plaintiff had adequate remedy at law and defendant was entitled to one-half the proceeds); Quirk v. Schuylkill County Mun. Auth., 54 Pa. Commw. 619, 622, 422 A.2d 904, 905 (1980) (considering "the questions of lack of standing and an adequate remedy at law," court concludes that "equity has no jurisdiction" over private suit to enforce statute that only the state can enforce); Southwestern Sav. & Loan Ass'n v. Mullaney Constr. Co., 771 S.W.2d 205, 207 (Tex. App. 1989) (legal remedies are adequate, and "there is no probative evidence" of plaintiff's claim); Vt. Div. of State Bldgs. v. Town of Castleton Bd. of Adjustment, 138 Vt. 250, 256–57, 415 A.2d 188, 193 (1980) (refusing to enjoin enforcement of valid zoning laws, reciting that injunctions will be issued only to prevent irreparable injury); George E. Warren Co. v. A.L. Black Coal Co., 85 W. Va. 684, 102 S.E. 672, 673–74 (1920) (refusing to order specific performance of contract, on grounds that defendant was not party to contract and damages would be adequate); Rapids Assoc. v. Shopko Stores, Inc., 96 Wis. 2d 516, 520–21, 292 N.W.2d 668, 671 (App. 1980) (refusing to enjoin sublease of retail premises, on ground that lease permitted sublease, and commenting that there was no evidence of irreparable injury); Kuntz v. Werner Flying Serv., Inc., 257 Wis. 405, 410–11, 43 N.W.2d 476, 479 (1950) (refusing to enjoin operation of airport, on grounds that airport is not a nuisance, injunction would impose undue hardship, and damage remedy would be adequate). See also Tri-State Generation & Transmission Ass'n, Inc. v. Shoshone River Power, Inc., 874 F.2d 1346, 1361–63 (10th Cir. 1989) (trial court rejected plaintiff's interpretation of contract and also held that damages would be adequate remedy; court of appeals reversed on merits, but could "not say that the district court was clearly erroneous in finding that [plaintiff] would not be irreparably harmed").

27. [irreparable injury requires right] Anne Arundel County v. Whitehall Venture, 39 Md. App. 197, 200–01, 384 A.2d 780, 783 (1978) ("existence of some *right*, which will be irreparably injured, is a prerequisite to the *extraordinary* relief of an injunction" (emphasis in original)); Hollenkamp v. Peters, 358 N.W.2d 108, 111–12 (Minn. App. 1984) ("trial court's finding appellants would not suffer irreparable harm was not clearly erroneous because appellants did not even demonstrate an interest in the [disputed] name or trademark").

28. [no injury means no irreparable injury] New Castle Orthopedic Assoc. v. Burns, 481 Pa. 460, 467–69, 392 A.2d 1383, 1387 (1978) (violation of covenant not to compete did no harm where plaintiff had more customers than it could serve); In re Marriage of Strauss, 183 Ill. App. 3d 424, —, 539 N.E.2d 808, 812 (1989) (declining academic performance of children is not irreparable harm, because not causally connected to misconduct of ex-spouse); R.I. Turnpike & Bridge Auth. v.

Cohen, 433 A.2d 179, 182–84 (R.I. 1981) (operator of toll bridge failed to show that resale of fare tokens reduced its revenues); Parkem Indus. Serv., Inc. v. Garton, 619 S.W.2d 428, 430–31 (Tex. Civ. App. 1981) (violation of covenant not to compete did no harm where defendants solicited only one customer, and that customer gave plaintiff as much business as before).

29. [weak remedy good enough for weak merits] Hill v. State, 382 Mich. 398, 404–06, 170 N.W.2d 18, 22 (1969) ("We do not base our decision herein so much upon the adequacy of plaintiffs' remedy in the Court of Claims as we do upon the tenuousness of the claims themselves. In a case in which there was a clear fact situation of an unconstitutional taking of private property, the argument of an adequate remedy in the Court of Claims might not prevail.").

30. [mix of merits and irreparable injury] Lewis v. S.S. Baune, 534 F.2d 1115, 1121–24 (5th Cir. 1976) (refusing to enjoin parties from settling personal injury case without consent of plaintiff's counsel, stating that such settlements were lawful and that if defendant overreached, plaintiff would have adequate remedy at law); Josten's, Inc. v. Cuquet, 383 F. Supp. 295, 297–99 (E.D. Mo. 1974) (refusing to enjoin violation of covenant not to compete, on grounds of no irreparable injury, stating that covenant was unreasonable, one-sided, and a restraint of trade, but that "this is not to be taken as a decision on the merits as to the validity of the contract"); State ex rel. Gen'l Dynamics Corp. v. Luten, 566 S.W.2d 452, 460 (Mo. 1978) (refusing to enjoin litigation in sister state, stating that plaintiff had adequate remedy in courts of other state, that plaintiff had unclean hands, and that equities were with courts of other state); Herron v. Sisk, 625 S.W.2d 909, 911–12 (Mo. App. 1981) (refusing to enjoin harassment of prison inmate, stating that the claim was trivial, outside the scope of the statute, unripe, and that it failed to allege irreparable injury); Stanklus v. County of Montgomery, 86 A.D.2d 908, 909, 448 N.Y.S.2d 536, 537–38 (1982) (refusing to enjoin drainage of surface water across plaintiff's land, stating that defendant had not caused flow to exceed capacity of stream, that case should be dismissed, that plaintiff had adequate remedy at law, and that an action for damages might lie); Lloyd Corp. v. Whiffen, 307 Or. 674, 773 P.2d 1294 (1989) (refusing to enjoin circulation of political petitions in shopping mall, disclaiming constitutional holding, but relying on public interest in petition process, balance of hardship, and lack of "great and irreparable injury," and opining that judgment permitting limited circulation of petitions would not violate speech, due process, or takings clause).

31. [hostility in statement of case] Skates v. Hartsfield, 216 Ala. 618, 114 So. 10 (1927) (refusing to order sheriff to return plaintiff's slot machines, on ground that damages would be adequate remedy for loss of personal property); Perkins v. Village of Quaker City, 165 Ohio St. 120, 133 N.E.2d 595 (1956) (refusing to enjoin enforcement of village weight limit against trucks that were destroying streets); Griscom v. Childress, 183 Va. 42, 31 S.E.2d 309 (1944) (refusing to order specific performance of sale to high bidder at sale foreclosing lien on personal property, on ground that damages would be adequate remedy, and that even if damages were inadequate, plaintiff could not get specific performance because he concealed his insolvency and failed to pay the amount of his bid in timely fashion).

32. [grossly inadequate remedy held adequate] Stewart v. Walton, 254 Ga. 81, 82, 326 S.E.2d 738, 739 (1985) (refusing to enjoin alleged fraudulent transfer of all defendant's assets, on ground that damages would be adequate remedy; court appeared not to believe the allegations of the complaint); New Club Carlin, Inc., v. City of Billings, 237 Mont. 194, 196–97, 772 P.2d 303, 305 (1989) (refusing to enjoin enforcement of ban on nude dancing, stating that money damages would be adequate remedy).

33. [bankruptcy irreparable for some] Pennzoil Co. v. Texaco, Inc., 481 U.S. 1, 22 (1987) (Brennan & Marshall concurring).

34. [conservatives ignore rule for CIA] Snepp v. U.S., 444 U.S. 507 (1980).

35. [liberal dissenters invoke rule] Id. at 526.

36. [conservatives invoke rule for states] Trainor v. Hernandez, 431 U.S. 434 (1977) (federal court cannot enjoin state proceeding to recoup welfare benefits from claimant alleged to have fraudulently concealed assets); Juidice v. Vail, 430 U.S. 327, 333–39 (1977) (federal court cannot enjoin state civil contempt proceeding); Hicks v. Miranda, 422 U.S. 332, 348–52 (1975) (federal court cannot enjoin subsequent state prosecution begun before substantial proceedings on the merits in federal court); Huffman v. Pursue, Ltd., 420 U.S. 592, 599–613 (1975) (federal court cannot enjoin enforcement of state civil nuisance judgment); Perez v. Ledesma, 401 U.S. 82, 83–85 (1971) (federal court may not order return of books seized as evidence for pending obscenity prosecution); Younger v. Harris, 401 U.S. 37, 43–54 (1971) (federal court cannot enjoin pending state prosecution).

37. [liberal dissenters minimize rule] Trainor v. Hernandez, 431 U.S. 434, 450–60 (1977) (Brennan & Marshall dissenting); id. at 460–70 (Stevens dissenting); Juidice v. Vail, 430 U.S. 327, 341–47 (1977) (Brennan & Marshall dissenting); Hicks v. Miranda, 422 U.S. 332, 353–57 (1975) (Stewart, Douglas, Brennan, & Marshall dissenting); Huffman v. Pursue, Ltd., 420 U.S. 592, 613–18 (1975) (Brennan, Douglas, & Marshall dissenting).

38. [liberal concurrences minimize rule] Juidice v. Vail, 430 U.S. 327, 339–41 (1977) (Stevens, concurring on ground that the challenged law was constitutional, but rejecting the Court's irreparable injury holding); Younger v. Harris, 401 U.S. 37, 56–57 (1971) (Brennan, White, & Marshall concurring); Perez v. Ledesma, 401 U.S. 82, 93–136 (1971) (Brennan, White, & Marshall, dissenting in part, in opinion attempting to limit the consequences of Younger v. Harris, decided the same day).

39. [free speech cases] Of the cases cited in note 36, *Hicks*, *Huffman*, *Perez*, and *Younger* presented free speech claims.

40. [refusing to enjoin tender offer] Samjens Partners I v. Burlington Indus., Inc., 663 F. Supp. 614, 621 (S.D.N.Y. 1987) (treating plaintiff as mere shareholder and not as competing tender offeror, on ground that its competing tender offer had been enjoined by the other court).

41. [refusing to order payment of money] Nat'l Souvenir Center, Inc. v. Historic Figures, Inc., 728 F.2d 503, 517 (D.C. Cir. 1984).

42. [no injunctions to pay money] See ch. 1 part B.2, at 17–18.

43. [limitation of remedy clause] Kowalski v. Chicago Tribune Co., 854 F.2d 168, 170–73 (7th Cir. 1988).

44. [right to business] See ch. 2 parts C and D.

45. [limitation of remedy] Compare Brademas v. Real Estate Dev. Co., 175 Ind. App. 239, 370 N.E.2d 997 (1977) (clause excluding specific performance of real estate contract treated as limitation of remedy of clause).

46. [clauses generally enforced] See UCC §§ 2–718 and 2–719 (limitation of remedies clauses and clauses liquidating damages in a small sum are enforceable unless unconscionable, or unless exclusive remedy "fails of its essential purpose"); Restatement (Second) of Contracts § 356 comment d (a term fixing unreasonably small damages is not subject to the limits on liquidated damages, but it may be unconscionable).

47. [duplicate substantive theory] Hawks v. Brindle, 51 N.C. App. 19, 25, 275 S.E.2d 277, 282 (1981).

9

Other Procedural Reasons

Concerns for full and fair procedure explain the most important source of irreparable injury opinions, the preliminary relief cases examined in Chapter 5. Other procedural reasons for irreparable injury opinions are jury trial, ripeness, mootness, and practicality.

A. Jury Trial

Perhaps the most plausible defense of the irreparable injury rule is that it protects the right to jury trial.[1] The federal[2] and most state[3] constitutions guarantee the right to jury trial in criminal cases and in suits at common law. But only a handful of states use jury trials in equity.*

1. Civil Jury Trial

Whether a civil suit is at law or in equity often depends on the remedy sought. If plaintiffs had a free choice between legal and equitable relief, they could sometimes use that choice to deprive defendant of jury trial. The irreparable injury rule could prevent this abuse by restricting plaintiffs' choice of remedy. Thus, a plaintiff can avoid jury trial if, and only if, his legal remedy is inade-

---

* The standard article on jury trial in equity, written in 1953, lists Georgia, North Carolina, Tennessee, and Texas.[4] A 1988 survey of state jury trial practice lists North Carolina, Texas, and Virginia, a few remaining cases in Tennessee, and the former practice in Arizona.[5] The two lists appear to disagree over Arizona, Georgia, and Virginia.

213

quate. The Supreme Court reinvigorated and extended this argument in two famous opinions by Justice Black, *Beacon Theatres v. Westover*[6] and *Dairy Queen v. Wood*.[7]

This argument is inapplicable to the great bulk of civil cases. In most civil litigation, it is plaintiffs and not defendants who demand juries. Some plaintiffs prefer juries because they hope to benefit from the jury's sympathy or sense of equity. Of more general importance, jury trial exposes defendant to the risk of a much higher assessment of damages, and thus increases the settlement value of any case.[8] Some plaintiffs may manipulate the choice of remedy to deprive defendants of their right to jury trial, but this risk does not extend widely across the range of civil litigation. This risk of manipulation in a small number of cases cannot justify a preference for legal remedies in all cases. Indeed, it is more common for defendants to manipulate the law-equity distinction to eliminate the jury, and this tactic sometimes succeeds.[9]

Defendant's right to jury trial does not get much weight in deciding the adequacy of legal remedies. If plaintiff were generally limited to legal remedies in any case that could be tried to a jury, the law would have to be that legal remedies are generally adequate. In fact, as we have seen, courts hold that legal remedies are generally inadequate in cases that present a viable choice.

Indifference to preservation of jury trial goes beyond plaintiff's choice of remedy. Under the equitable cleanup doctrine, once a case is in equity, whether because of the substantive claim or the requested remedy, the judge can decide any legal issues presented as well.[10] This subordinates the civil jury to judicial efficiency as well as to plaintiff's choice of remedy. Federal courts abandoned the equitable cleanup doctrine in *Beacon*[11] and *Dairy Queen*,[12] holding that it violated the right to jury trial. A recent survey by Gregory Gelfand reports that state courts have rejected the federal rule by a ratio of three to one.* And in several contexts since

* Gelfand lists eleven states as following the federal rule: Alabama, Alaska, Florida, Georgia, Hawaii, Kentucky, Montana, Rhode Island, Utah, Vermont, and West Virginia. He lists Arkansas, California, Colorado, Connecticut, Idaho, Illinois, Indiana, Iowa, Kansas, Maryland, Massachusetts, Michigan, Minnesota, Missouri, Nebraska, Nevada, New Hampshire, New Mexico, New York, North Dakota, Ohio, Oklahoma, Oregon, Rhode Island, South Carolina, South Dakota,

Beacon and *Dairy Queen*, federal courts have invoked substantive equity to deny defendants' jury demands, usually where the court feared that jury trial would hamper enforcement of federal rights.[14]

But there are still some contexts where courts care about defendant's right to jury trial. Sometimes the usual preferences are reversed, as when a large corporation sues a consumer or small business, or when a potential defendant sues for a declaration of nonliability, thus reversing the normal party alignment. Courts sometimes invoke the irreparable injury rule to protect jury trial in these contexts, but they do not force plaintiff to accept a less effective remedy.

I have shown elsewhere that this was true even at the peak of the Supreme Court's solicitude for jury trial.[15] Both *Beacon* and *Dairy Queen* presented the unusual alignment where defendant wanted jury trial and plaintiff did not.[16] The Court refused to let either plaintiff manipulate the pleadings for the sole purpose of depriving defendant of jury trial, but it did not require either plaintiff to accept less relief than it sought.

The Dairy Queen chain sued one of its franchisees for some $60 thousand in back franchise payments, and for injunctions against further use of the Dairy Queen trademark. The trial court issued a preliminary injunction, and everyone agreed that the chain was entitled to the injunction if it proved its case.[17]

The jury–trial dispute affected only the claim for money. The chain requested an accounting for trademark infringement instead of damages for breach of contract.[18] Its theory was that the franchisee infringed by continuing to use the trademark after it materially breached the franchise agreement by falling behind in its payments. This is a classic example of a large plaintiff manipulating its pleadings to avoid jury trial against a small defendant. A successful damage suit for breach of contract would produce a money judgment for an identical sum. The Court held the contract remedy adequate, so that defendant was entitled to jury trial. But the actual

Washington, Wisconsin, and Wyoming as retaining some version of equitable cleanup doctrine; and Delaware, Mississippi, New Jersey, and Pennsylvania as having largely unmerged equity courts that exercise cleanup jurisdiction. I cannot make his listing of individual states match his summary statistic of thirty-one states rejecting the federal rule.[13]

relief was not affected—only the legal theory and the mode of trial.[19]

Beacon Theatres v. Westover illustrates the juxtaposition-of-parties cases. Beacon threatened to bring an antitrust suit against the Fox Theatre. Fox responded by suing for a declaratory judgment that its practices were lawful and for an injunction to prevent Beacon from making threats or filing suits.[20] Beacon then filed its antitrust suit as a counterclaim. So the party who would in normal course be the antitrust defendant was cast as the plaintiff, and vice versa. The Court held that Fox was entitled to preliminary and permanent injunctions as needed to avoid any harm from Beacon's threats, but that the underlying issue of whether Fox was violating the antitrust laws must be tried to a jury on the counterclaim, not to the judge on Fox's suit for an injunction. Trial of Beacon's antitrust claim on Fox's suit for an injunction would grant Fox "no additional protection unless the avoidance of jury trial be considered as such."[21] Fox was entitled to all the remedies it sought, but it was not entitled to avoid jury trial.

Defendants in juxtaposition-of-parties cases do not always respond with a counterclaim. Sometimes they prefer to harass and threaten out of court, but to avoid any forum in which their charges might actually be decided. Some older decisions denied potential defendants relief in this situation. The cases sometimes acknowledged that waiting to be sued was a terribly unsatisfactory remedy, but held that the resulting difficulties are the cost of preserving the potential plaintiff's right to jury trial.[22] This problem has largely disappeared with the advent of declaratory judgment acts.[23] In any event, I doubt that many modern courts would leave a potential defendant remediless out of concern for the jury trial rights of a potential plaintiff who resisted all attempts to have his claims decided.[24]

One other revealing example comes from the law of Pennsylvania. Pennsylvania offers three remedies to a disappointed seller of real estate: a suit for damages, measured by the contract price less the market value; a suit in assumpsit for the full contract price; and specific performance. When land is sold for cash, assumpsit for the contract price gives the seller everything she would get from specific performance. In that situation, Pennsylvania refuses specific performance on the ground that assumpsit is an adequate legal remedy.[25] As in *Beacon* and *Dairy Queen*, the result is to protect the defaulting buyer's right to jury trial without reducing the relief available to sellers. There is an analogous practice in the trespass cases that preliminarily enjoin the trespass pending jury trial of conflicting claims to title.[26]

2. Criminal Jury Trial and Associated Rights of Criminal Procedure

In the criminal context, courts occasionally invoke the irreparable injury rule, and sometimes its more specific corollary, the fading rule that equity will not enjoin a crime.[27] The difference matters little, because a more complete statement of the corollary is that equity will not enjoin a crime where criminal prosecution would be an adequate remedy.[28] Some courts say that equity will not enjoin a crime merely because it is a crime, but will enjoin a crime if there are other grounds for equitable relief.[29] This formulation explicitly subjects threatened crimes to the general rules of equity.

A good example of reluctance to enjoin crime is *City of Chicago v. Festival Theatre Corp.*[30] The court refused to enjoin a live sex show, on the ground that the city had not shown the inadequacy of criminal prosecution. Criminal prosecution would be inadequate if "a risk to public health" required immediate action, or if criminal conviction and punishment failed to deter repeated violations. But it was not enough that repeated arrests and criminal prosecutions not carried to judgment failed to deter repeated violations.

The court recited the definition that legal remedies are inadequate unless they are as clear, complete, practical, efficient, and prompt as the equitable remedy. But that was not the standard it actually applied. Under the court's remedy, live sex shows would continue several times a day, at least until a criminal prosecution could be brought to judgment. Whatever harm the shows inflicted would be irremediably suffered. No one would be compensated for that harm; compensation could not undo the harm in any event. Punishment would not undo the harm either, and realistically, only a few of the shows would be punished.

Given defendant's willingness to run the risk of criminal prosecution, and its ability to find performers who would run those risks, criminal prosecution would not end the shows as quickly as an injunction and vigorous use of the contempt power. The criminal remedy put the city to the expense of indictment, criminal jury trial, and appeal, to impose a single punishment. If defendant persisted, the city would have to repeat the whole process to get a second punishment. But once even a preliminary injunction issued, every violation would be a new act of contempt, providing the basis for immediate coercive sanctions on motion. From the city's perspective, the criminal remedy was simply not as good as the equitable remedy. That is why both sides found it worth their money to litigate the choice of remedy to the state supreme court.[31]

But the city had to make do with the criminal remedy, because there were countervailing considerations. Defendant was entitled to jury trial, and the city was not entitled to avoid "the supposed shortcomings of jurors," a reference to possible jury nullification.[32] Defendant was entitled to the "definite penalties fixed by the Legislature" instead of the open-ended sanctions of contempt. And courts should not be perceived to engage in "government by injunction." The court might have added that the injunction suit avoided all the other protections of criminal procedure, including proof beyond a reasonable doubt. It was precisely these protections for defendants that made the criminal remedy undesirable from the city's perspective.

So despite the court's recitation that the legal remedy must be just as good as the injunction, the city was left with a remedy that was not as good. As in the prior restraint cases in chapter 7, the court preferred the legal remedy because it was inadequate. The analytic tool of adequate legal remedy could not produce that result without distortion, but the court got to the result it wanted because it understood what else was at stake. The city would be required to tolerate, perhaps for an extended period, minor criminal violations that did not harm an identifiable victim, in order to protect defendant's rights in the criminal process.

Equally plainly, the court was balancing. If the violation did more tangible harm, the city would not have to tolerate any violations. And if convictions failed to deter, the city could get an injunction; it would not have to tolerate even minor violations forever.

Festival Theatre may plausibly be viewed as a speech case. But the court did not write it that way. It concluded that the shows were legally obscene and hence unprotected by the First Amendment, and that the injunction issued was not a prior restraint.[33] The holding rested unambiguously on the lack of necessity to enjoin a crime.

I began this research thinking that *Festival Theatre* represented a significant line of cases. I now think it is exceptional. Despite widespread recitations of the "rule," I found only a handful of modern cases that actually refused to enjoin crimes.[34] Some of those appear to have been decided largely on the merits,[35] or on some other ground unrelated to defendant's rights to criminal procedure.[36]

If the crime is serious, the court is likely to enjoin on the ground that no violations can be tolerated.[37] If the crime is not serious, the criminal penalties may be too small to deter repeated violations, so that the criminal remedy is inadequate.[38] Courts say the injunction can issue if the crime would do enjoinable harm to the plaintiff,[39] or if it would endanger an important public interest,[40] or if the crime is also a nuisance.[41] Some opinions offer two or three of these reasons; together, they cover any case one can imagine.

If the statute is perceived as administrative or regulatory, courts will enjoin violations even if the statute also imposes "incidental" criminal penalties.[42] Criminal prosecution is not the principal means of enforcement in this context, and the potential criminal-jury-trial rights of regulated industries are not allowed to interfere with the smooth functioning of the administrative state. At least since the New Deal, agencies have relied principally on injunctions or cease-and-desist orders for all but the most egregious cases.[43]

Scores of cases enjoin violations of statutes.[44] Many of those statutes carry criminal penalties, but few cases note the fact. Two scholars have attacked equitable rules that occasionally prevent injunctions against violating statutes, but these scholars found it unnecessary to consider the supposed rule that equity will not enjoin a crime. One gives the rule a passing mention as a "lowered barrier";[45] the other mentions the criminal law only to note that it is reserved for the most egregious cases and is usually irrelevant.[46] These scholars were attacking the judicial propensity to balance equities; reluctance to enjoin crimes was not an obstacle to their goals.

The few cases that still raise the issue tend to involve state-licensing statutes and municipal ordinances. Dan Dobbs's thoughtful review of these cases concludes that the reasons courts give do not explain differences in result.[47] I agree, but I do not find much remaining variation to explain. Half a century ago the tendency to enjoin threatened crimes seemed "constantly to be broadening and extending itself."[48] That trend has continued. At least in the contexts where the issue arises, the reluctance to enjoin crimes is as dead as all the other variations of the irreparable injury rule.

B. Ripeness and Mootness

Plaintiffs may seek specific relief either too early or too late. A plaintiff may fear wrongful conduct and seek an injunction against it before he can convince a court that his fear is reasonable; in this case, his suit is not ripe.[49] Or he may continue to seek an injunction after the danger has passed or after it is too late either to prevent the harm or repair it in kind. In this case, his suit is moot.[50]

Ripeness and mootness are jurisdictional doctrines and also equitable doctrines.[51] They are the subject of considerable debate and manipulation,[52] but they are reasonably well understood on their own terms. They have in common that an injunction will be denied if there is not a sufficient threat of future harm. Sometimes the underlying policy is to restrict the role of the judiciary;[53] sometimes the policy is to allow defendants to experiment with activity that may turn out to be socially useful despite plaintiff's fears of its risks.[54]

Ripeness opinions frequently contain irreparable injury talk. It is easy to see why in light of the doctrinal structure. There are two doctrinal requirements: that the threat be ripe, and that the injury that is threatened be irreparable.[55] These are analytically distinct, but they can be verbally combined into a single sentence: that there be a ripe threat of irreparable injury. It is tautologically true that if there is no ripe threat of injury, then there is no ripe threat of irreparable injury. Thus, a court may summarize its conclusion either way. But "irreparable" is surplusage in a ripeness holding. When a court finds no threat of injury, and goes on to say no threat of irreparable injury, "irreparable" adds nothing to its analysis.

This distinction is not just verbal hairsplitting. A finding of injury that is not irreparable remits plaintiff to damages; a finding of no ripe threat of injury leaves plaintiff with no remedy at all unless something further happens. If the threat ripens and there is still time before it comes to fruition, plaintiff may return to court and get an injunction. In most ripeness cases, the feared injury will be irreparable if it happens at all. A court that finds no ripe threat of injury, and says no ripe threat of irreparable injury, does not really mean that if the threat comes to fruition the damage remedy will be adequate.

A dramatic illustration is *City of Los Angeles v. Lyons*, a suit to enjoin the Los Angeles police from using chokeholds that had killed fifteen persons.[56] The Supreme Court said that plaintiff had not shown a threat of irreparable injury. Plainly it did not mean that being choked to death is not irreparable injury. Rather, the Court unambiguously meant that plaintiff had not shown a sufficient likelihood that he would ever again be choked. It said that the irreparable injury requirement "cannot be met where there is no showing of any real or immediate threat that the plaintiff will be wronged again."[57] Despite the language of irreparable injury, this is a ripeness holding.

The distinctions between ripeness and irreparable injury inhere in the two doctrines. But only occasionally does a court explicitly distinguish between them. One example is an opinion refusing to preliminarily enjoin defendant from destroying evidence.[58] The court recited the rule that injunctions issue only to prevent irreparable injury. It agreed that the destruction of evidence would be irreparable if it occurred. But, it said, "potential irreparable injury" is only one requirement. Plaintiff must also demonstrate "real danger that the acts to be enjoined will occur."

More typical is the Supreme Court's opinion in *Lyons*, running the two doctrines together. Many invocations of the irreparable injury rule are ripeness holdings in which the court says that there is no threat of irreparable injury.[59]

Mootness cases present similar issues. Indeed, whether a case is categorized in terms of mootness or ripeness is a matter of emphasis. Consider *Lyons*, in which the police had already choked plaintiff once. A suit to enjoin that choking was moot; a suit to enjoin future chokings was not ripe. Mootness focuses on the past, ripeness on the future, but cases look both ways when plaintiff's fears for the future are based on an incident in the past.

Courts are more likely to talk of irreparable injury when they focus on the future and conceive these cases as ripeness cases. But sometimes they say the case is moot and the legal remedy is adequate.

A clear example is *Rondeau v. Mosinee Paper Corp.*[60] The Court said it granted certiorari "to determine whether a showing of irreparable harm is necessary" in a private suit under § 13(d) of the Securities Exchange Act.[61] But the case had nothing to do with threatened harm that would not be irreparable. Defendant had committed one technical violation of § 13(d), had promptly complied when the violation was pointed out, and had promised to comply in the future. The Court concluded that there was "no cognizable danger" of recurrent violation, that "none of the evils" to which the statute is directed "has occurred or is threatened," and that anyone who claimed to have been hurt by the original violation had an adequate damage remedy.[62]

The Court did not say that damages would be adequate if there were still a choice between damages and prevention. Damages were the only remedy still possible, and the Court commented that they would be adequate. Despite the talk of irreparable injury and adequate remedy at law, the holding is that any claim for injunction against the original violation was moot, and that no claim directed to future violations was ripe. Other cases are similar.[63]

C. Practicality

It is commonly said that equity will not specifically enforce a contract that is too difficult to supervise,[64] or issue an injunction that is impractical to enforce.[65] Like undue hardship, these rules matter doctrinally only when plaintiff's legal remedy is inadequate.[66]

In this context, both practicality and adequacy are matters of degree. Forced to choose between one remedy that is inadequate and another that is impractical, any mature legal system must ask how inadequate and how impractical. It is one thing to deny specific performance of a commercial contract where the legal remedy will be a substantial damage award with uncertainty in the measurement;[67] it is quite different to deny an injunction where plaintiff will lose fundamental political rights and the defendant is immune from damages anyway.[68]

Plainly our courts distinguish such cases. Sometimes they specifically enforce construction contracts,[69] and sometimes not,[70] depending on the difficulty of supervising the job, the plaintiff's need for specific performance, and the court's ambition. But specific relief is routine in cases that are much more complex, such as restructuring prison systems,[71] school districts,[72] or public-housing authorities,[73] reapportioning state legislatures,[74] breaking monopolies into competing companies,[75] and reorganizing insolvent businesses.[76] The less adequate the damage remedy, the more willing courts are to undertake complex specific relief. Surprisingly few cases make the point explicitly, but some do.[77]

A New York case illustrates the point nicely, but not quite explicitly. The court refused to enjoin violations of the warranty of habitability. It held that the injunction would be impractical, because it would require the court to run a large apartment building. It added that damages were adequate anyway.[78] It retained jurisdiction to consider damages, and then noted that there might be "drastic continuous" breaches for which damages would not be an adequate remedy, such as cutting off heat, water, or elevator service.[79] So where the harm was great enough, and the required injunction discrete enough, the court was prepared to enjoin.

There is also a long line of cases holding that equity will be more ambitious where the public interest is affected.[80] This doctrine has been invoked where railroads or utilities seek specific performance of contracts,[81] where the government seeks relief,[82] and in the enforcement of the labor laws.[83] It makes sense only on the ground, not clearly articulated, that inadequate remedies are less acceptable in these contexts than where purely private interests are at stake.

Once a court has decided that the impracticality of the equitable remedy outweighs the inadequacy of the legal remedy, it is almost inevitable that the opinion will maximize the impracticality of the one and minimize the inadequacy of the other. Sometimes impracticality opinions specifically invoke the irreparable injury rule as an additional ground of decision. That is plausible where damages are readily measurable and the money can be used to replace the very thing plaintiff seeks from defendant.[84] But often, the court simply assumes the adequacy of the legal remedy,[85] or ignores serious inadequacies.[86]

An example is *Northern Delaware Industrial Development Corp. v. E.W. Bliss Co.*,[87] involving a contract to modernize a steel plant. Plaintiff sought specific performance of a promise to put on a second shift for a part of the work that required the plant to be shut down. The court denied specific performance for fear that it would wind up supervising the whole project. It briefly commented that plaintiffs could "resort to law for a fixing of their claimed damages." It did not consider whether the law court could accurately measure lost profits, or determine whether the delay might cause a permanent loss of customers. The damage remedy plainly was not as complete, practical, and efficient as specific performance. But the defects of the damage remedy might have been outweighed by the difficulties of the specific remedy.

Notes on Procedural Reasons

1. [rule protects jury trial] Buzard v. Houston, 119 U.S. 347, 351 (1886) (if legal remedy is adequate, defendant has constitutional right to jury); Cappetta v. Atlantic Rfg. Co., 74 F.2d 53, 55 (2d Cir. 1934) (same); Dan B. Dobbs, *Handbook on the Law of Remedies* § 2.5 at 61 (West 1973) ("the main reason today for observing the adequacy test as a limit on equitable relief is that the plaintiff who gets his case into equity has foreclosed the possibility of a jury trial for the defendant"); Doug Rendleman, *The Inadequate Remedy at Law Prerequisite for an Injunction*, 33 U. Fla. L. Rev. 346, 354–55 (1981) ("inadequacy decision determines whether to preclude a binding jury verdict").

2. [federal right to jury] U.S. Const. Amend. VII ("In Suits at common law, where the value in controversy shall exceed twenty dollars, the right of trial by jury shall be preserved"); U.S. Const. Amend. VI ("In all criminal prosecutions, the accused shall enjoy the right to a speedy and public trial, by an impartial jury"). The federal right to criminal jury trial binds the states. Duncan v. La., 391 U.S. 145 (1968). The federal right to civil jury trial does not. Walker v. Sauvinet, 92 U.S. (2 Otto) 90 (1876); Letendre v. Fugate, 701 F.2d 1093, 1094 (4th Cir. 1983).

3. [state right to jury] Fleming James, Jr., & Geoffrey C. Hazard, Jr., *Civil Procedure* § 8.1 at 409 (Little, Brown, 3d ed. 1985).

4. [jury in equity] M.T. Van Hecke, *Trial by Jury in Equity Cases*, 31 N.C. L. Rev. 157 (1953).

5. [jury in equity] Gregory Gelfand, *Smith v. University of Detroit: Is There a Viable Alternative to Beacon Theatres?* 45 Wash. & Lee L. Rev. 159, 178 n.78 (1988).

6. [extending protection of jury trial] Beacon Theatres, Inc. v. Westover, 359 U.S. 500 (1959).

7. [extending protection of jury trial] Dairy Queen, Inc. v. Wood, 369 U.S. 469 (1962).

8. [juries award higher damages] For empirical verification of this view in one narrow set of cases, see David W. Leebron, *Final Moments: Damages for Pain and Suffering Prior to Death*, 64 N.Y.U. L. Rev. 256, 307 (1989) (in suits for conscious pain and suffering prior to death, juries award five times as much as judges on average, two-and-one-half to three times as much if the largest awards are disregarded).

9. [defendants trying to avoid jury] Bernstein v. Universal Pictures, Inc., 79 F.R.D. 59 (S.D.N.Y. 1978) (holding legal remedy inadequate where case is too complex for jury to understand, but changing only the mode of trial and not the remedy); Hill v. State, 382 Mich. 398, 170 N.W.2d 18 (1969) (refusing to order state to file condemnation proceeding triable to jury, because plaintiff had adequate remedy by inverse condemnation suit in Court of Claims, triable to court). For cases where such arguments failed, see Ross v. Bernhard, 396 U.S. 531 (1970) (plaintiff entitled to jury trial in shareholder's derivative suit for damages); Dixon v. Northwestern Nat'l Bank, 297 F. Supp. 485 (D. Minn. 1969) (plaintiff entitled to jury trial in suit for breach of trust where any recovery would be paid directly to plaintiff and not into trust); Arbor Acres Farm, Inc. v. Benedict, 278 Ark. 14, 15–17, 642 S.W.2d 893, 894–95 (1982) (dismissing defendant's counterclaim for reformation and transferring case from chancery court to circuit court, where plaintiffs sought only damages and claimed no interest in land, so that reformation would be "useless act"); Raedeke v. Gibraltar Sav. & Loan Ass'n, 10 Cal. 3d 665, 673–75, 517 P.2d 1157, 1161–63, 111 Cal. Rptr. 693, 697–99 (1974) (plaintiff entitled to jury trial on promissory estoppel claim where he also alleged ordinary breach of contract); Holter v. Moore & Co., 681 P.2d 962, 966–67 (Colo. App. 1983) (plaintiff entitled to jury trial in suit against real estate agent for breach of fiduciary duty); Sanguinetti v. Strecker, 94 Nev. 200, 207–09, 577 P.2d 404, 409–10 (1978) ("permissible" to try damage claims to jury, and reserve to court equitable claim for cancellation of deeds and counterclaim for specific performance); S.P.C.S., Inc. v. Lockheed Shipbuilding & Constr. Co., 29 Wash. App. 930, 631 P.2d 999 (1981) (issues not so complex that jury trial is inadequate remedy).

10. [equitable cleanup] Porter v. Warner Holding Co., 328 U.S. 395, 398, 399, 403 (1946) (ordering landlord to comply with rent control laws and to refund past overcharges; "where, as here, the equitable jurisdiction of the court has properly been invoked for injunctive purposes, the court has the power to decide all relevant matters in dispute and to award complete relief even though the decree includes that which might be conferred by a court of law"); Rice & Adams Corp. v. Lathrop, 278 U.S. 509, 515 (1929) (suit to enjoin infringement of patent, filed forty-one days before patent expired; equity retained jurisdiction to award damages for past infringement); Salton Sea Cases, 172 F. 792, 802–03 (9th Cir. 1909) (enjoining future flooding and awarding damages for past flooding); Frank v. Coyle, 310 Mich. 14, 17, 16 N.W.2d 649, 650 (1944) (ordering specific performance of agreement to remove tourist cabins from plaintiff's land, and awarding damages for delay in removal); Jamaica Sav. Bank v. M.S. Inv. Co., 274 N.Y. 215, 219, 8 N.E.2d 493, 494 (1937) (equity court can give judgment for deficiency in suit to foreclose mortgage); John Norton Pomeroy, 1 *A Treatise on Equity Jurisprudence as Administered in the United States of America* §§ 231–32 at 239–40 (Bancroft-Whitney Co. 1881). For a brief description of the historical development of this rule, see Fleming James, Jr., *Right to Jury Trial in Civil Actions*, 72 Yale L.J. 655, 658–59 (1963).

    11. [federal courts reject cleanup] *Beacon*, 359 U.S. 500, 509 (1959).

    12. [federal courts reject cleanup] *Dairy Queen*, 369 U.S. 469, 472–73 (1962).

    13. [survey of state jury-trial rules] Gelfand, 45 Wash. & Lee L. Rev. at 168–72 (cited in note 5).

    14. [federal courts avoid jury trial] Katchen v. Landy, 382 U.S. 323 (1966) (striking defendant's jury demand, in suit by bankruptcy trustee to recover preference); Securities & Exchange Comm'n v. Commonwealth Chem. Securities, 574 F.2d 90 (2d Cir. 1978) (striking defendant's jury demand, on ground that suit seeking restitution of profits is equitable); Harkless v. Sweeny Indep. School Dist., 427 F.2d 319, 323–24 (5th Cir. 1970) (striking defendant's jury demand, on ground that civil rights suit for lost wages seeks equitable restitution).

    15. [remedy never restricted] Douglas Laycock, *Injunctions and the Irreparable Injury Rule* (Book Review), 57 Tex. L. Rev. 1065, 1078–83 (1979).

    16. [some defendants prefer jury] For other cases where defendant wanted jury trial, see Granfinanciera, S.A. v. Nordberg, 109 S.Ct. 2782 (1989) (trustee in bankruptcy seeking to recover alleged fraudulent conveyance); Mitchell v. Robert De Mario Jewelry, Inc., 361 U.S. 288 (1960) (defendant demanded jury as a way of severing individual back pay suits from government enforcement action); Sun Oil Co. v. Fleming, 469 F.2d 211, 213–14 (10th Cir. 1972) (oil company seeking to cancel franchise agreement with service station operator); Christian v. Porter, 340 Mich. 300, 65 N.W.2d 779 (1954) (executor seeking to recover treasury bonds allegedly given to person who had cared for deceased in last illness).

    17. [injunction granted] Dairy Queen, Inc. v. Wood, 369 U.S. 469, 479 n.20 (1962).

    18. [identical legal and equitable claims] Id. at 475.

    19. [identical legal and equitable claims] For a similar but simpler case, see Christian v. Porter, 340 Mich. 300, 65 N.W.2d 779 (1954) (suit for damages is triable to jury, and allegations of fraud do not automatically move the case to equity).

    20. [injunction granted] Beacon Theatres, Inc. v. Westover, 359 U.S. 500, 502–03, 505 (1959).

    21. [plaintiff sought only to avoid jury] Id. at 508.

    22. [waiting to be sued not a remedy] Johnson v. Swanke, 128 Wis. 68, 70, 107 N.W. 481, 482 (1906).

    23. [declaratory judgment acts solved problem] See ch. 3 part A.4 at 79.

    24. [modern courts will not deny remedy] See Restatement (Second) of Torts § 933(2) (1979) (injunction not rendered inappropriate by need for jury trial).

    25. [assumpsit as adequate remedy] Trachtenburg v. Sibarco Stations, Inc., 477 Pa. 517, 523–24, 384 A.2d 1209, 1212–13 (1978).

26. **[injunction pending jury trial of title]** See ch. 2 at notes 24–28.

27. **[equity will not enjoin a crime]** W. Allis Memorial Hosp., Inc. v. Bowen, 852 F.2d 251, 254, 256 (7th Cir. 1988) (assuming plaintiff would suffer "great irreparable harm" from competitor's allegedly unlawful discount program, court would not enjoin crime in absence of national emergency, widespread public nuisance, or specific statutory authority); Commonwealth v. Stratton Fin. Co., 310 Mass. 469, 474, 38 N.E.2d 640, 643 (1941) (denouncing "criminal equity" and "government by injunction"); State ex rel. Fairchild v. Wisconsin Auto. Trades Ass'n, 254 Wis. 398, 402, 37 N.W.2d 98, 100 (1949) ("any attempt of equity to restrain purely criminal acts would be a denial to the defendant of his right to a trial by jury").

28. **[where criminal prosecution is adequate]** State ex rel. McLeod v. Holcomb, 245 S.C. 63, 67, 138 S.E.2d 707, 709 (1964) (equity may enjoin crime where criminal prosecution is not adequate to protect public interest); State ex. rel. Kirk v. Gail, 373 P.2d 955, 958 (Wyo. 1962) ("ordinarily, when a criminal prosecution will constitute an effectual protection against the acts complained of, no grounds exist for relief by injunction"); Restatement (Second) of Torts § 949 (1979) (where plaintiff seeks injunction against tort that is also a crime, court should consider adequacy of prosecution or police protection).

29. **[criminal nature of acts irrelevant]** In re Debs, 158 U.S. 564, 593–96 (1895) (enforcing injunction against blocking trains, stating that jurisdiction to enjoin acts interfering with property rights "is not destroyed by the fact that they are accompanied by or are themselves violations of the criminal law"); Meyer v. Seifert, 216 Ark. 293, 297, 225 S.W.2d 4, 6 (1949) (enjoining construction of nonfireproof building; "if grounds for equity jurisdiction exist in a given case, the fact that the act to be enjoined is incidentally violative of a criminal enactment will not preclude equity's action to enjoin it"); Eagle Books, Inc. v. Jones, 130 Ill. App. 3d 407, 415, 474 N.E.2d 444, 450 (1985) ("as a general rule, courts will not enjoin criminal activity unless the conduct that constitutes the crime also serves as a basis for equitable intervention"); State v. Red Owl Stores, Inc., 253 Minn. 236, 249, 92 N.W.2d 103, 112 (1958) (enjoining unlicensed sale of nonprescription drugs; "the mere fact that the act, or series of them, constitutes a crime, does not bar injunctive relief if otherwise there are grounds for it"); Lanvin Parfums, Inc. v. Le Dans, Ltd., 9 N.Y.2d 516, 523, 174 N.E.2d 920, 922, 215 N.Y.S.2d 257, 260–61, (1961) (authorizing injunction against sale of misbranded goods, because "the alleged criminal acts also threaten plaintiff's property rights"); Everett v. Harron, 380 Pa. 123, 128, 110 A.2d 383, 386 (1955) (enjoining exclusion of blacks from public accommodations; "the mere fact that the act complained of is a crime neither confers equitable jurisdiction nor ousts it"); Utah County v. Baxter, 635 P.2d 61, 64–65 (Utah 1981) ("injunction should not be issued to prevent the commission of a crime, if the only reason for preventing it is that it is a crime"); State ex rel. Fairchild v. Wis. Auto. Trades Ass'n, 254 Wis. 398, 402, 37 N.W.2d 98, 100 (1949) ("the mere fact that the act complained of is a crime neither confers equitable jurisdiction nor ousts it").

30. **[refusing to enjoin sex show]** City of Chicago v. Festival Theatre Corp., 91 Ill. 2d 295, 313–15, 438 N.E.2d 159, 167–68 (1982).

31. **[defects of criminal remedy]** For judicial comparisons of the enforcement procedures, see Ark. State Bd. of Pharmacy v. Troilett, 249 Ark. 1098, 1102–03,

463 S.W.2d 383, 386 (1971) (Harris dissenting); State ex rel. McLeod v. Holcomb, 245 S.C. 63, 69, 138 S.E.2d 707, 709 (1964). For a more detailed analysis, see Note, *The Statutory Injunction as an Enforcement Weapon of Federal Agencies*, 57 Yale L.J. 1023 (1948).

32. [jury nullification not an inadequacy] *Festival Theatre*, 91 Ill. 2d at 313, 438 N.E.2d at 167, quoting Commonwealth v. Stratton Fin. Co., 310 Mass. 469, 474, 38 N.E.2d 640, 643 (1941).

33. [not a prior restraint case] *Festival Theatre*, 91 Ill. 2d at 311, 438 N.E.2d at 166.

34. [actual refusals to enjoin crimes] U.S. v. Jalas, 409 F.2d 358, 360 (7th Cir. 1969) (refusing to enjoin felon from holding office in labor union); Commonwealth v. Stratton Fin. Co., 310 Mass. 469, 474–75, 38 N.E.2d 640, 642–44 (1941) (refusing to enjoin usury); Mo. Veterinary Medical Ass'n v. Glisan, 230 S.W.2d 169, 171–72 (Mo. App. 1950) (refusing to enjoin unlicensed practice of veterinary medicine); State ex rel. Fairchild v. Wis. Auto. Trades Ass'n, 254 Wis. 398, 402, 37 N.W.2d 98, 100 (1949) (refusing to enjoin operation of unlicensed collection agency); State ex. rel. Kirk v. Gail, 373 P.2d 955, 957–58 (Wyo. 1962) (refusing to enjoin unlicensed sale of milk, because criminal prosecution would be adequate remedy).

35. [motivated by merits] W. Allis Memorial Hosp., Inc. v. Bowen, 852 F.2d 251, 254–56 (7th Cir. 1988) (court found no private right of action, doubted that defendant's conduct was unlawful, and said that equity would not enjoin crime); Eagle Books, Inc. v. Jones, 130 Ill. App. 3d 407, 415, 474 N.E.2d 444, 450 (1985) (refusing to enjoin picketers from harassing customers of adult bookstore, invoking rule against enjoining crime only after concluding that picketers were protected by First Amendment).

36. [other collateral motivations] Ark. State Bd. of Pharmacy v. Troilett, 249 Ark. 1098, 1101, 463 S.W.2d 383, 385 (1971) (law against unlicensed sale of condoms was widely ignored, so that enforcement would require many prosecutions; this caseload would be better handled by state's many criminal judges than by its twenty-three chancellors).

37. [enjoining dangerous crimes] U.S. v. Zenon, 711 F.2d 476 (1st Cir. 1983) (trespass on military base); State v. Red Owl Stores, Inc., 253 Minn. 236, 251, 92 N.W.2d 103, 113–14 (1958) (court found threat to public health from unlicensed sale of nonprescription drugs); State ex rel. Kirk v. Gail, 373 P.2d 955, 957 (Wyo. 1962) (refusing to enjoin unlicensed sale of milk, but noting that there would be more reason to enjoin if defendant were charged with selling unsafe milk).

38. [enjoining crimes with small penalties] Harvey v. Prall, 250 Iowa 1111, 1118, 97 N.W.2d 306, 310 (1959) (enjoining unlicensed garbage collection); Commonwealth ex rel. Grauman v. Cont'l Co., 275 Ky. 238, 250, 121 S.W.2d 49, 54 (1938) (enjoining unlicensed operation of small loan business); State v. Red Owl Stores, Inc., 253 Minn. 236, 251, 92 N.W.2d 103, 113 (1958) (enjoining unlicensed sale of nonprescription drugs); Wychavon Dist. Council v. Midland Enterprises (Special Event) Ltd., [1988] 1 Common Market Law Reports 397 (Eng. Ch. 1987) (enjoining flea market in violation of Sunday closing law).

39. [enjoining crimes that harm plaintiff] In re Debs, 158 U.S. 564, 593–96 (1895) (enforcing injunction against blocking trains); Meyer v. Seifert, 216 Ark. 293, 299, 225 S.W.2d 4, 6 (1949) (enjoining construction of nonfireproof building); Lanvin Parfums, Inc. v. Le Dans, Ltd., 9 N.Y.2d 516, 523, 174 N.E.2d 920, 922, 215

N.Y.S.2d 257, 260–61 (1961) (authorizing injunction against sale of misbranded goods); Everett v. Harron, 380 Pa. 123, 128, 110 A.2d 383, 386 (1955) (enjoining exclusion of blacks from public accommodations).

40. [enjoining crimes that harm public] State v. Red Owl Stores, Inc., 253 Minn. 236, 251, 92 N.W.2d 103, 113 (1958) (enjoining unlicensed sale of nonprescription drugs); State ex rel. McLeod v. Holcomb, 245 S.C. 63, 69, 138 S.E.2d 707, 709 (1964) (enjoining unlicensed practice of dentistry).

41. [enjoining crimes that are nuisances] Harvey v. Prall, 250 Iowa 1111, 1118, 97 N.W.2d 306, 310 (1959) (enjoining unlicensed garbage collection); State ex rel. Fairchild v. Wis. Auto. Trades Ass'n, 254 Wis. 398, 402, 37 N.W.2d 98, 100 (1949) ("equity exercises jurisdiction over the act as a nuisance as distinguished from a crime").

42. [where criminal penalties are incidental] Harvey v. Prall, 250 Iowa 1111, 1118, 97 N.W.2d 306, 310 (1959) (ordinance forbidding unlicensed garbage collection "is regulatory in nature," and "the penal provision thereof is merely incidental"); Commonwealth ex rel. Grauman v. Cont'l Co., 275 Ky. 238, 250, 121 S.W.2d 49, 54 (1938) ("while the Small Loan Statute provides for a penalty for its violation, yet it is not, strictly speaking, a criminal or penal statute"); State v. Red Owl Stores, Inc., 253 Minn. 236, 250, 92 N.W.2d 103, 112–13 (1958) (statute forbidding sale of nonprescription drugs without license "was not passed for the purpose of punishing crime").

43. [injunctions as principal remedy] Note, 57 Yale L.J. at 1023–25 (cited in note 31).

44. [enjoining violation of statutes] See ch. 3 part B. For an opinion that does note the issue, see Ariz. State Bd. of Dental Examiners v. Hyder, 114 Ariz. 544, 547, 562 P.2d 717, 720 (1977) (where statute authorizes both injunction and criminal prosecution, "remedies will be construed as cumulative").

45. [dismissing reluctance to enjoin crimes] Zygmunt J.B. Plater, *Statutory Violations and Equitable Discretion*, 70 Cal. L. Rev. 524, 545 n.70 (1982).

46. [criminal law usually irrelevant] Daniel A. Farber, *Equitable Discretion, Legal Duties, and Environmental Injunctions*, 45 U. Pitt. L. Rev. 513, 514, 522 n.64, 536 (1984).

47. [reasons given do not explain results] Dobbs, *Remedies* § 2.11 at 115–18 (cited in note 1).

48. [willingness to enjoin increasing] Robert A. Leflar, *Equitable Prevention of Public Wrongs*, 14 Tex. L. Rev. 427, 428 (1936). See also Note, 57 Yale L.J. at 1024 (cited in note 31) (rule against enjoining crime "has been so whittled away that the government can obtain such an injunction to protect 'the general welfare'").

49. [ripeness] For a general survey, see Charles Alan Wright, Arthur R. Miller, & Edward H. Cooper, 13A *Federal Practice & Procedure* §§ 3532–3532.6 (2d ed. 1984).

50. [mootness] For a general survey, see id. §§ 3533–3533.11.

51. [both equitable and jurisdictional] On the equitable and jurisdictional dimensions of ripeness, see Douglas Laycock, *Modern American Remedies* 223–25 (Little, Brown 1985). On the equitable and jurisdictional dimensions of mootness, see U.S. v. W.T. Grant Co., 345 U.S. 629, 632–33 (1953).

52. [doctrines debated] See Lea Brilmayer, *The Jurisprudence of Article III:*

Perspectives on the "Case or Controversy" Requirement, 93 Harv. L. Rev. 297 (1979); Mark V. Tushnet, *The Sociology of Article III: A Response to Professor Brilmayer*, 93 Harv. L. Rev. 1698 (1980); Lea Brilmayer, *A Reply*, 93 Harv. L. Rev. 1727 (1980); Henry Monaghan, *Constitutional Adjudication: The Who and When*, 82 Yale L.J. 1363, 1383–86 (1973); Note, *The Mootness Doctrine in the Supreme Court*, 88 Harv. L. Rev. 373 (1974).

53. [doctrines restrict judiciary] Brilmayer, 93 Harv. L. Rev. at 303–15.

54. [doctrines protect risk taking] Laycock, *Remedies* at 223 (cited in note 51).

55. [two requirements] See Flowers Indus. v. Fed. Trade Comm'n, 849 F.2d 551, 552 (11th Cir. 1988) (plaintiff "would suffer irreparable injury if its assets were divested," but "no immediate danger of divestiture exists"); Humble Oil & Rfg. Co. v. Harang, 262 F. Supp. 39, 42–43 (E.D. La. 1966) (plaintiff must show "potential irreparable injury" plus "real danger" that it will occur); System Concepts, Inc. v. Dixon, 669 P.2d 421, 428 (Utah 1983) (plaintiff must show "the likely or threatened occurrence of such harm and the irreparability thereof").

56. [refusing to enjoin chokeholds] City of Los Angeles v. Lyons, 461 U.S. 95, 100 (1983).

57. [no irreparable injury] Id. at 111.

58. [distinguishing the two requirements] Humble Oil & Rfg. Co. v. Harang, 262 F. Supp. 39, 43 (E.D. La. 1966).

59. [irreparable injury opinions; ripeness] O'Shea v. Littleton, 414 U.S. 488, 502 (1974) (refusing to enjoin "conjectural" threat of racial discrimination by state criminal judges); Flowers Indus. v. Fed. Trade Comm'n, 849 F.2d 551, 552–53 (11th Cir. 1988) ("because no immediate danger of divestiture exists, [plaintiff] cannot suffer irreparable harm"); Caribbean Marine Serv. Co. v. Baldrige, 844 F.2d 668, 674–76 (9th Cir. 1988) (refusing preliminary injunction against female inspectors on commercial tuna boats, where court found that fears of harmful consequences were only speculative); Quechan Tribe of Indians v. Rowe, 531 F.2d 408, 410 (9th Cir. 1976) (refusing to order state officials not to arrest tribal officials, where they had not threatened to do so); Sellers v. Regents of the Univ. of Cal., 432 F.2d 493, 497 (9th Cir. 1970) (refusing to enjoin university from enforcing its rule against unlawful activities on campus, where court found that university had not invoked the rule against plaintiffs' continuing draft-resistance activities); Kamakazi Music Corp. v. Robbins Music Corp., 534 F. Supp. 57, 69 (S.D.N.Y. 1981) (alleged copyright infringement; "the possible irreparable injury has not been shown to be actual and imminent and is at best speculative"); Smith Oil Corp. v. Viking Chem. Co., 127 Ill. App. 3d 423, 468 N.E.2d 797, 803 (1984) (refusing to enjoin defendants from using trade secrets, where court found that defendants had not taken trade secrets and did not have access to them); Tubular Threading, Inc. v. Scandaliato, 443 So.2d 712, 715–16 (La. App. 1983) (refusing to enjoin misappropriation of trade secret where court found no evidence of intent to misappropriate); Campbell v. City of Annapolis, 44 Md. App. 525, 536, 409 A.2d 1111, 1117 (1980) (refusing to order landlord to permit city inspections of rental property, where inspections had neither been sought nor refused), rev'd in part, on other grounds, 289 Md. 300, 424 A.2d 738 (1981); Grein v. Bd. of Educ., 216 Neb. 158, 169, 343 N.W.2d 718, 725 (1984) (refusing to enjoin violations of Public Meetings Law, where court did not believe that one past violation showed propensity to further violations); Franzese v. Franzese, 108 Misc. 2d 154, 158, 436 N.Y.S.2d 979,

980–81 (1981) (refusing to enjoin transfer of marital property pending divorce, where court found no evidence defendant intended to make improper transfers); Duke Power Co. v. City of High Point, 69 N.C. App. 335, 337–38, 317 S.E.2d 699, 700–01 (1984) (refusing to enjoin municipally owned electric utility from serving customers outside city limits, where city had no plans to serve such customers); Philadelphia Ass'n of School Admin'rs v. School Dist., 80 Pa. Commw. 242, 246–47, 471 A.2d 581, 583–84 (1984) (school administrators sought injunction against being ordered to teach during teacher's strike, alleging fear of physical injury when crossing picket line; injunction denied for failure to prove danger); Ark. La. Gas Co. v. Fender, 593 S.W.2d 122, 123–24 (Tex. Civ. App. 1979) (refusing to enjoin gas company from cutting trees outside its right-of-way, where court found no evidence that it would do so).

60. [mootness as no irreparable injury] Rondeau v. Mosinee Paper Corp., 422 U.S. 49 (1975).

61. [Court said issue was irreparable injury] Id. at 51.

62. [issue was mootness] Id. at 59–60.

63. [irreparable injury opinions; mootness] Ramirez de Arellano v. Weinberger, 788 F.2d 762, 764 (D.C. Cir. 1986) (refusing to enjoin use of private land for military base, after military had withdrawn); Ghandi v. Police Dep't, 747 F.2d 338, 343–44 (6th Cir. 1984) (refusing to enjoin police surveillance that had ended seven years before, commenting that injunctions are extraordinary remedy that should be granted only sparingly and for compelling reasons); Black United Fund, Inc. v. Kean, 763 F.2d 156, 160–61 (3d Cir. 1985) (refusing preliminary injunction against enforcement of repealed statute); Posada v. Lamb County, 716 F.2d 1066, 1070 (5th Cir. 1983) (refusing to enjoin discriminatory apportionment of county commissioner districts, after county adopted nondiscriminatory reapportionment); Sires v. Luke, 544 F. Supp. 1155, 1166 (S.D. Ga. 1982) (refusing injunction on ground that "the issue has been mooted and there exists an adequate remedy at law"); Nissan Motor Corp. v. Md. Shipbuilding & Drydock Co., 544 F. Supp. 1104, 1121–22 (D. Md. 1982) (refusing to enjoin spray painting that had damaged plaintiff's cars on two occasions in four years, where defendant had taken effective corrective measures), aff'd mem., 742 F.2d 1449 (4th Cir. 1984); Teleprompter, Inc. v. Bayou Cable TV, 428 So.2d 17 (Ala. 1983) (refusing to enjoin one cable company from cutting another's cables, where cables had been cut only during installation of competing cable in same right-of-way, and installation was complete); Daiquiri Factory, Ltd. v. City of Lafayette, 429 So.2d 523, 525–26 (La. App. 1983) (refusing to enjoin police from issuing traffic tickets to lines of motorists approaching plaintiff's business, where tickets had been issued only in traffic jam resulting from plaintiff's grand opening); S. Kane & Son, Inc. v. City of Philadelphia, 74 Pa. Commw. 172, 176–77, 459 A.2d 866, 868–69 (1983) (city awarded contract to second-lowest bidder, and lowest bidder sued; court refused to order award of contract to plaintiff because city had cancelled the award and rebid the contract); Gross v. Conn. Mut. Life Ins. Co., 361 N.W.2d 259, 264–67 (S.D. 1985) (refusing to enjoin diversion of polluted water onto plaintiffs' land, where defendants had repaired their dam and thus ended the flow of water); Orwick v. City of Seattle, 103 Wash. 2d 249, 253, 692 P.2d 793, 796 (1984) (refusing to enjoin mishandling of traffic prosecutions that had already been dismissed). See also State ex rel. Stephan v. Pepsi-Cola Gen'l Bottlers, Inc., 232 Kan. 843, 844–45, 659 P.2d 213,

215 (1983) (discussing mootness in conjunction with adequate remedy at law, but holding case not moot and deciding merits).

64. [contracts hard to supervise] Tex. & Pacific Ry. v. Marshall, 136 U.S. 393, 405–07 (1890) (contract to perpetually operate railroad maintenance facilities in city); Marble Co. v. Ripley, 77 U.S. (10 Wall.) 339, 358–59 (1870) (perpetual contract to supply marble); Black Diamond Coal Co. v. Jones Coal Co., 200 Ala. 276, 277, 76 So. 42, 43 (1917) (coal mining); Long Beach Drug Co. v. United Drug Co., 13 Cal. 2d 158, 170–72, 88 P.2d 698, 704–05 (1939) (drugstore franchise); N. Del. Indus. Dev. Corp. v. E.W. Bliss Co., 245 A.2d 431, 432–34 (Del. Ch. 1968) (expansion and modernization of steel fabrication plant); Yonan v. Oak Park Fed. Sav. & Loan Ass'n, 27 Ill. App. 3d 967, 972–73, 326 N.E.2d 773, 778–79 (1975) (construction of building); Security Builders, Inc. v. Southwest Drug Co., 244 Miss. 877, 883–86, 147 So.2d 635, 638–39 (1962) (ten-year lease of space in shopping center, where specific performance would require supervision of the business); Standard Fashion Co. v. Siegel-Cooper Co., 157 N.Y. 60, 66–68, 51 N.E. 408, 409–10 (1898) (refusing specific performance of contract to sell plaintiff's goods, but granting specific performance of contract not to sell competitor's goods); Canteen Corp. v. Republic of Tex. Properties, Inc., 773 S.W.2d 398, 400 (Tex. App. 1989) (building and operating restaurant); Edward Yorio, *Contract Enforcement: Specific Performance and Injunctions* § 3.1 at 46 (Little, Brown 1989).

65. [injunctions hard to enforce] U.S. v. Paramount Pictures, Inc., 334 U.S. 131, 161–66 (1948) (vacating injunction ordering motion picture industry to distribute films by competitive bids); Restatement (Second) of Torts § 943 (1979) ("practicability of drafting and enforcing" injunction is factor to be considered in deciding whether to issue it); Gene R. Shreve, *Federal Injunctions and the Public Interest*, 51 Geo. Wash. L. Rev. 382, 394 (1983) (court should not issue injunctions that would not be "manageable").

66. [undue hardship and adequacy] See ch. 7 part A.

67. [contract with uncertain damages] N. Del. Indus. Dev. Corp. v. E.W. Bliss Co., 245 A.2d 431, 432–34 (Del. Ch. 1968) (delay in reopening of steel fabrication plant).

68. [political rights with immune defendants] Reynolds v. Sims, 377 U.S. 533, 585 (1964) (reapportionment of state legislature).

69. [specific performance of construction] Ammerman v. City Stores Co., 394 F.2d 950 (D.C. Cir. 1968) (construction of department store in shopping mall); Lee Builders, Inc. v. Wells, 33 Del. Ch. 315, 321–22, 92 A.2d 710, 714 (1952) (contract to move buildings and erect them on new foundations, with new basements, and connect utilities); Pa. R.R. v. City of Louisville, 277 Ky. 402, 408–10, 126 S.W.2d 840, 843–44 (1939) (contract to build elevated railroad crossings); Daniel v. Kensington Homes, Inc., 232 Md. 1, 11–12, 192 A.2d 114, 120 (1963) (holding contract to construct curbs and gutters specifically enforceable, but denying relief on grounds unrelated to the remedy issues); Jones v. Parker, 163 Mass. 564, 566–67, 40 N.E. 1044, 1045 (1895) (contract to install heating and lighting equipment in building); Zygmunt v. Ave. Realty Co., 108 N.J. Eq. 462, 463–65, 155 A. 544, 545 (1931) (construction of street and sidewalks); Grayson-Robinson Stores v. Iris Constr. Corp., 8 N.Y.2d 133, 137–38, 168 N.E.2d 377, 379, 202 N.Y.S.2d 303, 306–07 (1960) (enforcing arbitration award ordering defendant to construct building, and suggesting that difficulty of supervision is exaggerated and trend is to specific performance); McDonough v. S. Or. Mining Co., 177 Or. 136, 149–56, 159 P.2d 829, 834–37 (1945) (restoration of fields after mining); Goldman v. McShain, 432 Pa. 61, 74, 247 A.2d 455, 461 (1968) (complaint for specific performance of contract to build and operate movie theater states claim on which relief may be granted; whether contract is too complex to specifically enforce depends on evidence at trial); Joseph Story, 2 *Commentaries on Equity Jurisprudence as Administered in England and America* §§ 725–28 (Little, Brown 1836) (noting that cases were divided, but arguing that damages were rarely adequate); M.T. Van Hecke, *Changing Emphases in Specific Performance*, 40 N.C. L. Rev. 1, 13–16 (1961); Annotation, *Specific Performance of Lease of, or Binding Option to Lease, Building or Part of Building to Be Constructed*, 38 A.L.R.3d 1052 (1971).

70. [no specific performance of construction] Hannah v. Butz, 445 F. Supp. 503, 506 (N.D. Miss. 1977) (construction of house); Big State Barging Co. v. Calmes, 138 F. Supp. 891, 892 (E.D. La. 1956) (construction of tugboat); Nelson v. Darling Shop, Inc., 275 Ala. 598, 608, 157 So.2d 23, 33 (1963) (remodeling of retail space); Ryan v. Ocean Twelve, Inc., 316 A.2d 573, 575 (Del. Ch. 1973) (repair of defective condominiums); Levene v. Enchanted Lake Homes, Inc., 115 So.2d 89 (Fla. App. 1959) (construction of house); Besinger v. Nat'l Tea Co., 75 Ill. App. 2d 395, 221 N.E.2d 156 (1966) (construction of supermarket).

71. [reforming prisons] Hutto v. Finney, 437 U.S. 678, 683–85 (1978) (reviewing judicially supervised reform of Arkansas prison system); Eng v. Smith, 849 F.2d 80 (2d Cir. 1988) (ordering state to provide mental health services in state prison).

72. [reforming schools] Milliken v. Bradley, 433 U.S. 267 (1977) (affirming injunction ordering special programs in reading, teacher training, testing, and career counseling in school undergoing desegregation); Swann v. Charlotte-Mecklenburg Bd. of Educ., 402 U.S. 1 (1971) (affirming widespread busing of students and revision of attendance zones); Brown v. Bd. of Educ., 349 U.S. 294, 301 (1955) (ordering district courts to "effectuate a transition to a racially nondiscriminatory school system"); U.S. v. Bd. of School Comm'rs, 637 F.2d 1101, 1112–17 (7th Cir. 1980) (metropolitan desegregation of Indianapolis schools).

73. [reforming public housing] Hills v. Gautreaux, 425 U.S. 284, 286–92 (1976) (reviewing judicial efforts to desegregate Chicago Housing Authority); Perez v. Boston Housing Auth., 379 Mass. 703, 400 N.E.2d 1231 (1980) (appointing receiver for housing authority, and reviewing history of injunctions against it).

74. [reapportioning legislatures] Reynolds v. Sims, 377 U.S. 533, 585–87 (1964) (directing courts to insure, except in unusual cases, that no further elections are conducted under apportionment plans found to be invalid).

75. [dissolving monopolies] Cal. v. Am. Stores Co., 110 S. Ct. 1853, 1859 (1990) ("divestiture is the preferred remedy"); Schine Chain Theatres, Inc. v. U.S., 334 U.S. 110, 126–30 (1948) (ordering dissolution of theater chain); Standard Oil Co. v. U.S., 221 U.S. 1, 77–82 (1911) (dissolving Standard Oil combination, without discussing irreparable injury or difficulty of supervision); U.S. v. Am. Tobacco Co., 221 U.S. 106, 184–88 (1911) (directing trial court to design plan for dissolving American Tobacco combination); U.S. v. Am. Tel. & Tel. Co., 552 F. Supp. 131, 160–226 (D.D.C. 1982) (dissolution of AT&T), aff'd mem. as Md. v. U.S., 460 U.S. 1001 (1983).

76. [reorganizing businesses] Regional Rail Reorganization Act Cases, 419 U.S. 102 (1974) (rejecting constitutional challenges to scheme for reorganizing bankrupt northeastern railroads); Theodore Eisenberg & Stephen C. Yeazell, *The Ordinary and the Extraordinary in Institutional Litigation*, 93 Harv. L. Rev. 465, 485–86 (1980).

77. [balancing practicality and adequacy] Laclede Gas Co. v. Amoco Oil Co., 522 F.2d 33, 39 (8th Cir. 1975) ("the public interest in providing propane to the retail customers is manifest, while any supervision required will be far from onerous"); Kearns-Gorsuch Bottle Co. v. Hartford-Fairmont Co., 1 F.2d 318, 319 (S.D.N.Y. 1921) (specifically enforcing patent license; "everything depends on how insistently the justice of the case demands the court's assumptions of difficult, unfamiliar, and contentious business problems"); Zygmunt v. Ave. Realty Co., 108 N.J. Eq. 462, 465, 155 A. 544, 545 (1931) (with respect to construction contracts, "if the difficulties attendant upon enforcement are not impressive, and the actual performance of the contract seems of much moment to complainants, courts are apt to grant equitable relief"); McDonough v. S. Or. Mining Co., 177 Or. 136, 152, 159 P.2d 829, 835 (1945) (with respect to construction contracts, "where the inadequacy of damages is great, and the difficulties not extreme, specific performance will be granted," quoting Williston); Gerety v. Poitras, 126 Vt. 153, 154–55, 224 A.2d 919, 921 (1966) (same). For the current edition of the passage quoted from Williston, see Samuel Williston & Walter H.E. Jaeger, 11 *A Treatise on the Law of Contracts* § 1422A at 762 (Baker Voorhis, 3d ed. 1968). For a similar synthesis of specific performance cases, see Yorio, *Contract Enforcement* § 3.1 at 46–49, § 3.3.3 at 60–65 (cited in note 64).

78. [refusing to repair apartments] Bartley v. Walentas, 78 A.D.2d 310, 312–15, 434 N.Y.S.2d 379, 382–83 (1980).

79. [except for drastic defects] Id. at 314, 434 N.Y.S.2d at 383.

80. [will do more for public interest] Cal. v. Am. Stores Co., 110 S. Ct. 1859, 1867 (1990) (antitrust); U.S. v. Morgan, 307 U.S. 183, 194 (1939) (Packers and Stockyards Act); Water Resources Comm'n v. Conn. Sand & Stone Corp., 170 Conn. 27, 33, 364 A.2d 208, 212 (1975) (water pollution laws); Reppun v. Bd. of Water Supply, 65 Hawaii 531, 557 n.18, 656 P.2d 57, 74 n.18 (1982) (water rights); Thornton, Ltd. v. Rosewell, 72 Ill. 2d 399, 407, 381 N.E.2d 249, 253 (1978) (protection of bidders at tax foreclosure sales).

81. [railroad and utility contracts] Joy v. City of St. Louis, 138 U.S. 1, 47 (1891) (railroad); Laclede Gas Co. v. Amoco Oil Co., 522 F.2d 33, 39 (8th Cir. 1975) (gas utility); Orange & Rockland Util., Inc. v. Amerada Hess Corp., 67 Misc. 2d 560, 563, 324 N.Y.S.2d 494, 498 (1971) (electric utility); Edison Illum. Co. v. E. Pa. Power Co., 253 Pa. 457, 464, 98 A. 652, 654 (1916) (electric utility).

82. [government as plaintiff] Porter v. Warner Holding Co., 328 U.S. 395, 398 (1946) (enforcement of Emergency Price Control Act of 1942); Walling v. James V. Reuter, Inc., 321 U.S. 671, 674–75 (1944) (enforcement of Fair Labor Standards Act).

83. [labor laws] Golden State Bottling Co. v. Nat'l Labor Relations Bd., 414 U.S. 168, 179–80 (1973) (claim under National Labor Relations Act); Virginian Ry. v. System Fed'n, 300 U.S. 515, 552 (1937) (claim under Railway Labor Act).

84. [services replaceable in market] Ryan v. Ocean Twelve, Inc., 316 A.2d 573, 575 (Del. Ch. 1973) (plaintiffs could hire another contractor to repair their condominium units, and recover cost from defendant); McCormick v. Proprietors, Cemetery of Mt. Auburn, 285 Mass. 548, 550–51, 189 N.E. 585, 586 (1934) (plaintiff could hire another contractor to raise grade of cemetery monument, and recover cost from defendant); Gerety v. Poitras, 126 Vt. 153, 155, 224 A.2d 919, 921 (1966) (defendant refused to honor warranty on house sold to plaintiff; plaintiff had already retained contractor who had itemized the necessary work). See also Cont'l & Vogue Health Studios, Inc. v. Abra Corp., 369 Mich. 561, 564–67, 120 N.W.2d 835, 837–38 (1963) (damages from refusal to reconstruct destroyed building was difference between rent plaintiff paid and rent plaintiff charged sublessees; potential claims of sublessees not discussed).

   85. [adequacy assumed] Dworman v. Mayor of Morristown, 370 F. Supp. 1056, 1078 (D.N.J. 1974) (specific performance of construction contracts is generally impractical and damages are generally adequate); Levene v. Enchanted Lake Homes, Inc., 115 So.2d 89 (Fla. App. 1959) (refusing specific performance of contract to build house); Suchan v. Rutherford, 90 Idaho 288, 410 P.2d 434 (1966) (refusing specific performance of promise to buy land, where damages based on market value would be adequate remedy, and it would be difficult to supervise buyer's payments over term of years); King Features Syndicate v. Courrier, 241 Iowa 870, 873–74, 43 N.W.2d 718, 721 (1950) (stating general rule that contracts for delivery of services are not specifically enforced because of impossibility of supervision "and of course the adequacy of the legal remedy"); 13 Am. Jur. 2d, *Building and Construction Contracts* § 112 (1964) ("as a general rule, contracts for building construction will not be specifically enforced, partly because damages are an adequate remedy at law, and partly because of the incapacity of the court to superintend the performance").

   86. [inadequacies ignored] Thayer Plymouth Center, Inc. v. Chrysler Motors Corp., 255 Cal. App. 2d 300, 306–07, 63 Cal. Rptr. 148, 152 (1967) (damages from termination of automobile dealership can be measured, albeit with difficulty); Bissett v. Gooch, 87 Ill. App. 3d 1132, 1139–41, 409 N.E.2d 515, 520–21 (1980) (damages are adequate remedy for breach of contract to construct house on defendants' lot and to convey house and lot to plaintiffs); London Bucket Co. v. Stewart, 314 Ky. 832, 834–35, 237 S.W.2d 509, 510 (1951) (construction contracts are hard to supervise and remedy at law is adequate, even where damages are hard to measure); Lester's Home Furnishers v. Modern Furniture Co., 1 N.J. Super. 365, 370, 61 A.2d 743, 746 (Ch. 1948) (tenant can hire contractor to construct improvements promised by landlord, and recover cost from landlord; court noted defendant's claim of insolvency, and noted that "frequent disputes" would arise over scope of needed repairs, but did not view either of these as affecting the adequacy of the damage remedy); Petry v. Tanglwood Lakes, Inc., 514 Pa. 51, 54–60, 522 A.2d 1053, 1054–57 (1987) (damages are adequate remedy for failure to build lake in front of plaintiff's cottage); George E. Warren Co. v. A.L. Black Coal Co., 85 W. Va. 684, 687–89, 102 S.E. 672, 673–74 (1920) (refusing specific performance of contract to mine and sell coal, principally on ground of no irreparable injury, but also on ground that court could not supervise coal mining; legal remedy was in fact inadequate because defendant was insolvent, and specific performance would not have been a preference because plaintiff had not paid in advance). See also Arnold v. Engelbrecht, 164 Ill. App. 3d 704, 709–10, 518 N.E.2d 237, 240–41 (1987) (refusing to review allegedly retaliatory performance rating of public employee, on grounds of deference to agency, no irreparable injury, no substantive right, ripeness, and impracticality).

87. [assuming measurable damages] N. Del. Indus. Dev. Corp. v. E.W. Bliss Co., 245 A.2d 431, 433 (Del. Ch. 1968).

10

The Disparate Uses of a Code Phrase

The cases reveal judicial behavior very different from what the irreparable injury rule would predict. Courts do not deny plaintiff's preferred remedy without a functional reason. They do not deny specific relief just because that is the rule, because of some lingering hostility to equity, or because it was so laid down in the time of Edward III.

The irreparable injury rule is not a significant barrier to equitable relief, because the legal remedy is almost never adequate. Principled doctrine and ample precedent support any articulable need for equitable relief. A plaintiff with any plausible need for an equitable remedy has a prima facie malpractice claim against a lawyer who fails to fit his need into a doctrinal niche.

The real reasons for denying specific relief are themselves rather specific. A fairly short list accounts for nearly all the cases, but it is hard to generalize about the items on the list. They are a quite miscellaneous group, and irreparable injury talk is put to a variety of different uses. But there are some patterns, or at least some groups of similar cases.

In some cases, courts more or less consciously balance the costs to defendant or the judiciary of granting specific relief against the costs to plaintiff of denying it. The cases on preliminary relief, undue hardship, and impracticality fit this pattern, as do some of the cases on deference to other tribunals or branches of government. These are the cases in which the traditional understanding of the irreparable injury rule most nearly applies. Plaintiff is required to accept a less desirable or less effective remedy, because it is good enough under the circumstances. In these cases, the relative adequacy of the legal remedy actually affects the analysis.

But even these cases do not fit the traditional understanding. The standard for denying specific relief is not that the damage remedy meets some threshold of adequacy, but that the costs or risks of granting specific relief outweigh the costs or risks of denying it. The relative adequacy of some other remedy is not enough to trigger this inquiry; courts compare remedial choices only if there is some identifiable cost to the remedy plaintiff prefers. The ensuing balance of costs and benefits turns on the facts of individual cases, not on generalizations about large groups of cases.

Moreover, there are distinct approaches to balancing, each highly sensitive to context. In the preliminary relief cases, the merits are unresolved, so the balance is struck in light of the probability of success. In the undue hardship cases, defendant is an adjudicated wrongdoer and plaintiff is an adjudicated victim, so the balance is tilted sharply against defendant. But if the hardship falls on an innocent third party, the balance will be more even, or even tilt against plaintiff. Balancing is less explicit in the impracticality cases, but courts are willing to incur more burdens if plaintiff's claim is thought to serve the public interest or if damages are especially inadequate.

In most of the other cases denying specific relief, courts apply a rule that does not require balancing and in which the relative adequacy of other remedies is largely irrelevant. Cases that fit this pattern are those decided on grounds of prior restraint, personal service contracts, ripeness and mootness, evasion of other law, hostility to the merits, and many of the cases deferring to the jurisdiction of other tribunals. The rules applied in these cases may be simple or complex; they may serve substantive, jurisdictional, or remedial policies. But their application does not vary with the adequacy of other remedies, and the adequacy of other remedies is not a significant policy base for the rule.

Thus, exceptions to the rules against prior restraints turn on free speech policies, not on variations in the adequacy of legal remedies. Courts will not make an employee work, or reinstate an employee where the resulting personal friction would be too disruptive. The working of these rules does not depend on the court's assessment of the adequacy of damage remedies. Remedial choices based on preventing evasion of substantive law or on the court's reaction to the merits are obviously driven by substantive law policies.

Policies of ripeness and mootness are connected to irreparable injury talk only by their common connection to the risk of injury. Surely the seriousness and irreparable nature of the injury sometimes matters to courts, but the probability of injury matters more.

Courts will generally not interfere with the jurisdiction of an administrative agency until administrative remedies have been exhausted, and a showing of unusual hardship in a particular case is usually insufficient to create an exception. When courts will interfere, the relevant policies are usually found in the relationship between the court and the agency, or in the substantive law committed to the agency. Serious inadequacy of the administrative remedy is sometimes relevant but never sufficient.

In some of these cases, the legal remedy is preferred precisely because it is inadequate; specific relief is denied because it is too effective. This is most obviously true in the rules against prior restraints and involuntary servitudes, and in the old rule against enjoining crimes. In these cases, plaintiff's claim conflicts with countervailing constitutional rights, and we fear over enforcement. The undue hardship cases are a little different, but they also respond to fears of unduly burdensome enforcement.

Sometimes the reasons for denying specific relief also apply to damages. Courts will not give preliminary damage relief; they create immunities that often insulate governments and government employees from damage liability; and they will not allow plaintiffs to evade specific provisions of applicable law either with generalized equity or generalized damage remedies. Courts seem reluctant to award damages against breaching employees. The governing policies in these cases are full deliberation before decision, deference to other branches of government, adherence to particularly applicable law, and free labor. These policies may sometimes have different implications for specific relief than for damages, but a general bias against specific relief is not part of the relevant policies.

The same pair of phrases—"irreparable injury" and "adequate remedy at law"—is used to perform these varied functions and to describe all these different sets of cases. Obviously, these phrases cannot have a single meaning. Their meaning must vary with the circumstances, and courts must assess the circumstances first to determine the meaning. When there is no reason to deny specific relief, legal remedies are inadequate unless they are as complete, practical, and efficient as equitable remedies. When there is a reason to deny specific relief, legal remedies are much more likely to be judged adequate.

The catch phrases can label the conclusion, but they are not much help in reaching it. If a judge thinks in terms of "irreparable injury" without first deciding on other grounds what the phrase means or how the case should come out, she has only a very small chance of reaching the right result. As Judge Friendly once said, the phrase "generally produces more dust than light."[1]

The research technique of finding new cases through citations in known cases oddly confirmed how little meaning the catch phrases have. Judicial citations to irreparable injury opinions sometimes collect factually similar cases, so that the cases cited are actually in point. But often, the citations are simply to the catch phrase, and the cases themselves are wholly irrelevant.

A good example is the Supreme Court's string cite in *Weinberger v. Romero-Barcelo*.[2] The Court says that "the basis for injunctive relief in the federal courts has always been irreparable injury and the inadequacy of legal remedies." It then cites *Rondeau v. Mosinee Paper Corp.*,[3] a mootness case; *Sampson v. Murray*,[4] a case about preliminary relief and deference to administrative agencies; *Beacon Theatres v. Westover*,[5] a jury trial case; and *Hecht Co. v. Bowles*,[6] a case about the risk of future violations and whether an injunction would do any good. *Weinberger* itself is about undue hardship and deference to the military.[7]

These cases have nothing in common except the phrase, "irreparable injury." *Hecht Co. v. Bowles* does not even have that. *Hecht* denied an injunction on the ground that it would be futile, and avoided the temptation to describe that result in terms of irreparable injury. Neither "inadequate," nor "remedy," nor "irreparable," nor "injury," appears in the opinion. "Adequate" appears only in a statement about the lack of "adequate records."[8] *Hecht* is simply miscited in *Weinberger*. Perhaps the law clerk assumed that any case that denied an injunction and mentioned discretion must have been an irreparable injury case.

The only context in which one of these catch phrases may do more good than harm is the stage of preliminary relief. In that context, "irreparable injury" nicely captures the fundamental point. If the phrase could be confined to that context, it could come as close to coherence as most phrases. At the stage of preliminary relief, courts will balance the risk of injury against the risk of error, and injury does not count for much if it can be repaired or replaced in kind, even approximately, by a permanent injunction or with a damage award, or if it can be valued in dollars even approximately, or if it is temporary and the temporary loss is not especially compelling. The equally complete, practical, and efficient standard does not apply; plaintiff cannot demand a complete remedy before he proves his case.

It would eliminate much confusion if we eliminated all other uses of the irreparable injury rule, all other uses of the phrases "irreparable injury" and "adequate remedy," and all other definitions of either phrase. Phrases with so many different meanings cannot convey any of them.

Some defenders of the irreparable injury rule imply that the phrases are proxies for the many disparate considerations that actually govern the choice of remedies.[9] But this proxy is too crude to help. In many contexts, it is affirmatively misleading. Most notably, it suggests that some policies are limited to equity when in fact they are equally applicable at law. And in all contexts, one has to ignore the proxy and get down to the underlying policies in order to think clearly about a case. Ultimately, the desire to retain the irreparable injury rule as a proxy for the real rules wholly abandons any link to ordinary English usage. "No irreparable injury to plaintiff" has a range of plausible English meanings, but that range simply does not cover "undue hardship to defendant," or "no involuntary servitude," or "preserve the role of agencies in the administrative state."

If "irreparable injury" has come to mean such things, it is only as a code phrase. It would be just as plausible to agree that "orange banana" will be the code phrase. The rule could be that equity will not act unless plaintiff has an orange banana. To a reader who understood the real reasons for choosing remedies, "orange banana" would communicate as well as "irreparable injury." To a reader who does not understand the real reasons, it would com-

municate about as badly—a little worse at first perhaps, but no
worse after we got used to the new code.

Edward Yorio's new book avoids avoids speaking in code. He
would explicitly balance competing interests, and he would treat
the irreparable injury rule as identifying only plaintiff's side of the
balance. This is an advance over more traditional formulations,
and he is right that courts must assess the strength of plaintiff's
interest in specific relief. But Yorio's formulation does not avoid
the substantive and procedural difficulties of a general irreparable
injury rule.

Yorio offers a single model: plaintiff must show some degree of
irreparable injury to initiate a cost-benefit analysis in which plaintiff's need for specific relief is balanced against the costs of specific
relief.[10] That model may fit a large proportion of the specific performance cases, although it does not fit all of them. Certainly when
analysis is expanded to the full range of litigation over specific
relief, Yorio's model no longer fits all the cases. Irreparable injury
cases include several different balancing tests, and often, as in the
employment contract cases, the operative rules are fixed and do
not require balancing at all.

I think that Yorio's model also errs in assigning to plaintiff the
initial burden of showing that legal remedies are inadequate. Plaintiff always has a corrective justice claim to specific relief if he wants
it, so defendant should bear the intitial burden of showing that
there is some reason to deny specific relief. This disagreement
between us would rarely affect the result. But it would affect the
efficiency of litigation. In vast numbers of cases, plaintiff wants
specific relief and there is no reason to deny it. Yorio's approach
would require plaintiffs in these cases to address the irreparable
injury issue in pleadings, evidence, and briefs; they would get no
equitable remedy without some showing of irreparable injury. The
inadequacy of legal remedies might be obvious, and the effort to
prove the point a ritual, but if plaintiff bears the burden, he must
go through the ritual. My approach would dispense with all this
unless defendant raised the issue and showed some reason to deny
equitable relief.

I suspect that when Yorio proposes that plaintiff bear the initial
burden of showing irreparable injury, he is thinking of the fungible
goods cases. Why make defendant show some difficulty in specific

performance when damages seem perfectly adequate? Why decide the second issue—whether there is some reason to deny specific performance—when the first issue seems so easy? But there are only a tiny number of cases in which plaintiff seeks specific performance of a contract to sell fungible goods in an orderly market. Indeed, there are only a tiny number of cases, if any, in which a competently represented plaintiff seeks specific relief and cannot show irreparable injury.

When I propose that defendant bear the burden of showing some reason to deny specific relief, I am thinking of the thousands of cases in which plaintiff seeks specific relief because there is indeed something inadequate about the legal remedy. The defect may be obvious or subtle, but a well-advised plaintiff with any plausible need for specific relief can always show irreparable injury. In only some of these cases will there be any reason to deny specific relief. Why make plaintiff prove his need for specific relief in all the cases when it is really at issue only in some fraction of the cases?

At this point, I am speaking normatively, but also to some extent positively. I do not claim that courts consciously think in terms of requiring defendant to raise the issue that there is some reason to deny specific relief. But I do observe that courts frequently grant specific relief without discussing irreparable injury. In this large number of cases, the de facto operative rule is that equitable relief is not extraordinary, and that there is no need to discuss irreparable injury unless the defendant raises the issue. And when defendant raises the issue, the real issue is some alleged reason to withhold specific relief on the facts of the particular case. As a description of defendant's real reason, "no irreparable injury" remains a code phrase.

Notes on a Code Phrase

1. **[rule yields more dust than light]** Studebaker Corp. v. Gittlin, 360 F.2d 692, 698 (2d Cir. 1966).

2. **[string cite for rule]** Weinberger v. Romero-Barcelo, 456 U.S. 305, 312 (1982).

3. **[mootness case]** Rondeau v. Mosinee Paper Corp., 422 U.S. 49, 61 (1975).

4. **[preliminary relief and deference case]** Sampson v. Murray, 415 U.S. 61, 88 (1974).

244 THE DEATH OF THE IRREPARABLE INJURY RULE

5. **[jury trial case]** Beacon Theatres, Inc. v. Westover, 359 U.S. 500, 506–07 (1959).

6. **[futility case]** Hecht Co. v. Bowles, 321 U.S. 321, 329 (1944).

7. **[hardship and deference case]** See *Weinberger*, 456 U.S. at 309–10.

8. **[not an irreparable injury case at all]** *Hecht*, 321 U.S. at 325.

9. **[rule as proxy for real considerations]** Doug Rendleman, *The Inadequate Remedy at Law Prerequisite for an Injunction*, 33 U. Fla. L. Rev. 346, 358 (1981) ("the legal conclusion that the legal remedy is inadequate masks the intellectual process of identifying and evaluating interests"); Gene R. Shreve, *Federal Injunctions and the Public Interest*, 51 Geo. Wash. L. Rev. 382, 394–95 (1983) (irreparable injury rule should be part of "a framework of considerations that is sensitive to the way factors in the injunction dispute will register and combine differently in each case").

10. **[plaintiff bears burden]** See Edward Yorio, *Contract Enforcement: Specific Performance and Injunctions* § 2.5 at 41 (Little, Brown 1989) For further explanation of Yorio's position, see ch. 1 part A.2 at 10–11.

11

Holmes, Posner,
and Efficient Breach

The mistaken belief that specific remedies are exceptional and damages the norm is central to one of the most famous and provocative claims in legal scholarship. This is the claim that in a wide range of circumstances, people are entitled to violate the rights of others so long as they pay the resulting damages.[1] But if courts generally stand ready to grant specific relief where feasible, then there is no such entitlement.

The argument over this asserted right to violate the law ranges over most substantive areas of law. But I wish to explore the question with particular reference to breach of contract, where the issues are most sharply posed and where belief in a right to breach is most entrenched. The original formulation of the right to breach is Justice Holmes's famous aphorism about contract, "The duty to keep a contract at common law means a prediction that you must pay damages if you do not keep it,—and nothing else."[2]

More recently, the claim has become part of the economic theory of efficient breach. Efficient breach theory argues that contracting parties will breach and pay damages only when it is profitable for them to do so, and that the law should encourage such breaches because they will lead to a more efficient allocation of scarce resources. The best known formulation of this claim is Judge Posner's, who argues that the law does and should encourage parties to profit by breaching their contracts.[3]

A. The Positive Law and Efficient Breach

The essential point of positive law is the replaceability rules described in chapter 2. The emphasis on replaceability turns the traditional remedial hierarchy on its head. Money is an adequate remedy if, and only if, it can be used to replace the specific thing that was lost. That is to say, *money is never an adequate remedy in itself.* It is either a means to an end or an inadequate substitute that happens to be the best courts can do at reasonable cost. But the legal system's preference is to give plaintiff specific relief if she wants it—to replace her loss with as identical a substitute as possible.

The preference for specific relief squarely rejects Holmes's aphorism. It is technically true that damages are the only universal consequence of breach at common law, excluding equity. But when our legal system is viewed whole, the duty to keep a contract means a duty to deliver to plaintiff the specific thing she was promised or the means of acquiring it, if either is feasible. This duty is commuted into a duty to pay substitutionary damages only if plaintiff agrees or if there is some other substantial reason to deny specific relief.

Holmes dismissed specific performance as so exceptional that it did not affect the general theory. Specific performance may be numerically exceptional, for reasons already discussed.[4] But Holmes's broader point is untrue: our legal system does not generally give obligors an option to perform or pay damages.

The emphasis on replaceability separates the positive law from efficient breach theory as well. Opportunities for efficient breach typically arise in two sets of cases. The first is when there arises a more profitable use of some resource allocated by the contract, *and* that resource is in short supply. The relevance of shortage is this: if there is enough of the scarce resource to satisfy both plaintiff and defendant, or plaintiff and defendant's new customer, then neither performance nor breach will change the allocation of resources. Plaintiff will be supplied at the contract price, and all other parties will be supplied at the market price.

If there is a shortage, so that one side must do without, it becomes meaningful to speak of allocating the resource to the more efficient use. But in time of shortage, damages are an inadequate remedy and the positive law allocates the resource to the party who was promised it under a valid contract.[5] The principle of allocation is entitlement, and the entitlement is created by contract. Whatever its normative or heuristic merits, efficient breach theory does not describe the law in shortage cases.

Nor can efficient breach theorists take comfort in the minority of cases that deny specific performance in the face of less-than-absolute shortage. Those cases are written on the premise that plaintiff can replace the lost goods despite the difficulties.[6] They do not hold that plaintiff should do without so that defendant can auction the goods to the buyer with the most valuable use. I found no case that denied specific performance and acknowledged that plaintiff would be unable to replace the goods. That is, I found no positive law support for efficient breach theory in the context of shortage.

There is a conceivable exception, a hypothetical shortage case to which efficient breach theory might offer a solution consistent with the replaceability rules. Suppose that defendant's product is in short supply, that it has close substitutes that are entirely adequate for plaintiff's purposes, but that a third party has a unique use for which only defendant's product will work.

This hypothetical has been discussed in the literature,[7] although I found no example of it in the cases. If such a case were ever litigated, we might not identify it from the opinion, because the third party and his use are doctrinally irrelevant to the irreparable injury rule. (The possibility of undue hardship to the third party will be considered soon.)

Whether plaintiff's injury would be irreparable would depend on whether the court focused on the goods themselves, in which case they would be irreplaceable, or on plaintiff's use of the goods, in which case they would be replaceable with functional equivalents. The cases tend not to pose the issue in those terms. Probably functional equivalence would suffice in most courts, but only if the substitutes were truly equivalent in every characteristic of any importance to plaintiff.[8]

If this rare combination of facts is the entire potential domain of efficient breach analysis in shortage cases, a general preference for damages would be an extraordinarily overbroad solution to a tiny problem. Indeed, if substitute goods really are adequate for plaintiff, his claim to specific performance can surely be terminated more efficiently by negotiation than by litigation. Instead of litigating the adequacy of substitute goods, the third party can pay plaintiff to release his entitlement. Any problems in plaintiff's use of substitutes will be reflected in the price. If plaintiff refuses to sell at any price, that simply means that the goods are more valuable to him than money. There is no basis in economics to override plaintiff's judgment on that question.

It is possible that plaintiff will drive a hard bargain even though substitute goods are adequate for his use. Plaintiff might extract a premium from the third party's need; because plaintiff is not in the business of selling such goods, he may be less concerned about good will and more aggressive about the premium than the original seller would have been. Owners of scarce resources do such things, and efficient breach theorists should be the last to complain, even though such premiums would reduce the incentive to identify and complete potentially efficient transactions with third parties. To limit plaintiff to a damage remedy to keep him from profiteering is a form of price control administered exclusively through litigation. It would be hard to imagine a less efficient form of regulation. Courts should not make every plaintiff prove the inadequacy of substitute goods in order to reduce profiteering by the rare plaintiff who bought scarce goods that he does not really need.

The second set of opportunities for efficient breach consists of cases where performance becomes burdensomely expensive.[9] The irreparable injury rule cannot solve these cases, because it is fortuitous whether plaintiff's loss is readily replaceable when defendant's performance is burdensome. Defendant must rely on the defense that explicitly addresses the burden of performance, variously labeled undue hardship, balancing the equities,[10] or the straightforward proposition that seriously uneconomic contracts should not be performed.[11]

It is clear that the law recognizes such a defense. It is equally clear that the law does not recognize the efficient breach version of the defense, in which defendant may breach and pay damages at his own election, no matter how small the resulting gain. The law's standard is not precisely defined, but only substantial or unreasonable hardship will lead courts to refuse specific performance.[12] Defendant can breach and pay damages if the cost of performance is seriously disproportionate to the benefits, but not just because it is economically efficient to breach. Something like efficient breach theory is part of our positive law to this limited extent, but we do not need the irreparable injury rule to implement it.

Courts can also consider undue hardship to third parties.[13] This doctrine might conceivably be used in a shortage case to take account of a third party's desperate need for the goods. I know of no cases, but hypotheticals are easy to imagine. If children in the desert are dying for lack of water, one might expect that courts would refuse specific performance of a contract to deliver water to a car wash in Palm Springs. The court could say that the children's disproportionate hardship outweighed the car wash's contractual entitlement to the water.

This hypothetical case could be described as shifting the promised resources to a more valuable use. But its source in the undue hardship cases reveals a normative theory very different from efficient breach. Efficient breach is an economic theory. To an economist, the third party's use for the goods is more valuable if, and only if, the third party is willing to pay a higher price. The reason he is willing to pay a higher price is irrelevant. The relevant economic concept is "demand" or "willingness to pay."

The undue hardship defense turns on the distinctly noneconomic concepts of "hardship" and "disproportionate." Hardship often arises from "need," another noneconomic concept that contrasts sharply with demand. To an economist, need without willingness to pay is nothing. Willingness to pay is everything, whether based on need or whim or something in between. Willingness to pay is both necessary and sufficient; need is neither.[14]

These conceptual differences have important practical implications. Whether to deny specific performance because of undue hardship is necessarily a question committed to courts. If efficient breach theory were the law, whether to perform or breach would be a question committed to promisors. A central feature of efficient breach theory is that the promisor should breach and pay damages when he can profit by doing so. Efficient breach theorists can leave the decision to the promisor, because they believe that his individual interest is an adequate proxy for social interests. This equivalence of individual and social interests depends on the assumption that social value is fully reflected in the prices offered by potential buyers and in the damages awarded to victims of breach. These assumptions depend on willingness to pay as the measure of value.

If value is measured in any other way—by hardship, or need, or utility—then the promisor's opportunities for profit are not an adequate proxy, and the choice must be committed to a neutral decision maker. This would be true even if courts excused specific performance for slight gains in social utility. Such a rule would require courts to compare the utility of performance and breach, assessing social utility without regard to willingness to pay. Such a regime would be fundamentally different from efficient breach. Current positive law, in which specific performance is excused only for *disproportionate* hardship, is even more different from efficient breach.

The difference between hardship and willingness to pay produces differences in result, both in extreme cases and in close cases. Variations on the hypothetical water contract will serve to illustrate. Suppose the children were unable to pay for their water, but the seller was willing to breach his contract with the car wash and give it to them. It is inconceivable that the children's inability to pay would affect the court's decision on the car wash's claim for specific performance. By contrast, suppose the third party were a wealthy homeowner, willing to pay a higher price to get water for his private swimming pool. His willingness to pay would satisfy the criterion for efficient breach, but I suspect that few judges would be impressed by his claim of hardship.

To sum up, the positive law allocates scarce resources principally by enforcing entitlements. Entitlements to performance are occasionally reduced to entitlements to money in response to claims of disproportionate hardship. Willingness to pay is not relevant to either determination; neither entitlement nor hardship implements the theory of efficient breach.

The alleged connection between efficient breach theory and the irreparable injury rule depends entirely on the cases that refuse specific performance of contracts for the sale of fungible and near-fungible goods in orderly markets. But those cases do not support the theory, because they cannot affect the allocation of resources. When they are rightly decided—when the goods are really replaceable—these cases are trivial. They are trivial whether one's criterion is economic efficiency, distributive justice, corrective justice, or any combination of such theories.

The irreparable injury rule survives in these cases only because so little turns on it. If identical goods are available on the market, then damages are as good as specific performance, and if quite similar goods are available, then damages are almost as good. Because plaintiff can get the specific thing he was promised from either damages or specific relief, the choice of remedy matters only to secondary considerations affecting the costs of implementation. There is a large literature on the costs of implementing each remedy, much of it devoted to tiny and speculative differences.[15] But any slight difference in the cost of administering the two remedies would be dwarfed by the costs of litigation to remedy the greater number of breaches that would occur if efficient breach were the law. Any argument for the efficiency of legal rules must assume that people know the rules and respond to them. But on that assumption, if judges were seriously to proclaim the legitimacy and desirability of breaching contracts, they would increase the frequency of breaches.

The principal consequence of the irreparable injury rule as it actually exists is to permit wasteful litigation over the choice of remedy in marginal cases. The potential for such litigation creates bargaining leverage for defendants in cases where replacement is difficult but arguably not impossible. It creates a risk of erroneous decision; the court may underestimate the difficulty of replacement and deny specific performance to a plaintiff who needed it and was entitled to it under the replaceability rules. It creates friction with our civil law trading partners, who believe that plaintiffs should be entitled to specific performance on demand.[16] Its benefits are hard to identify.

The law's preference for specific relief if plaintiff wants it could be deduced from the first principle of remedies, which I have called the rightful position principle.[17] Remedies are designed to restore plaintiff as nearly as possible to the position he would have occupied but for the wrong.[18] If plaintiff has been deprived of a painting, or land, or red-cored carrots, but for the wrong he would have had the painting, the land, or the carrots. He would not have had an extra sum of money in his pocket. In some situations money damages will be almost as good, and in all situations money will be better than nothing. Money is the medium of exchange and therefore the most nearly universal substitute. If it can be conveniently exchanged for the lost painting, land, or carrots, and if only contract rights and not property rights have been violated, our courts will treat the money as equivalent to the painting, land, or carrots. But if the painting, the land, or the carrots are available only from defendant, then the only way to fully restore plaintiff to the position he would have occupied but for the wrong is to give him the painting, the land, or the carrots.

If the traditional understanding were correct—if our law seriously preferred substitutionary remedies—plaintiffs would have to accept less-exact substitutes. Money would be an adequate remedy if it could be exchanged for a similar painting, similar land, or a similar variety of carrots, or even if it could be exchanged for some work of art, some land, or some vegetable. Indeed, the law could say that all values are fungible and prescribe money damages as the universal remedy. But the cases do none of these things. If money cannot be exchanged for the specific painting, the specific land, or wholly fungible carrots, or even if the exchange will for some reason be seriously inconvenient, the money remedy is inadequate. The painting, the land, or the carrots is the rightful position, and thus the preferred remedy where possible.

This analysis of efficient breach and the replaceability rules has necessarily emphasized cases where the party in breach may be called the seller—a seller of goods, a provider of services, someone whose obligation under the contract is to expend or transfer real resources and not merely to pay money.

Where the buyer breaches, analysis is much simpler. In the great bulk of cases, the seller sought only money from the transaction. Money damages will give him exactly what he sought, and the replaceability issue does not arise. Damages for the difference between the contract price and the resale price, plus the incidental costs of resale, give him the very thing he expected from the contract. But if the seller is stuck with something hard to sell or burdensome to own, he is entitled to specific performance.[19]

Probably the most common reason for buyers to breach is that they no longer need or want the goods or services they agreed to buy. It would be wasteful to insist that the services be performed to no end, or even to insist that the goods be delivered.[20] Certainly the seller, who is in the business of selling goods of that kind, is in better position to resell them. And because money will make the seller completely whole even within the meaning of the replaceability rules—money is all he wanted—the cost of specific performance is always disproportionate to the benefit. Damages are rarely difficult to measure, because sellers do not suffer the consequences of doing without needed goods or services. So, cases where buyer no longer needs the goods are plainly cases where breach is efficient. But they are uncontroversial because they do not require any sacrifice of the promisee's rights. The law had solved these cases with mitigation of damage rules long before efficient breach theory came on the scene.

B. A Note on the Normative Argument

In this chapter as elsewhere, my principal point is positive: the law does not support efficient breach theory. But a credible account of the positive law must make normative sense. Why does the law prefer specific relief? What is the normative basis of the replaceability rules? A full exploration of those questions is beyond the scope of this project, but I can outline the main points. The law's preference for specific relief makes sense on both moral and economic grounds.

1. The Economic Argument

Efficient breach theory is plausible in shortage cases only if one focuses narrowly on the moment of breach and asks which use of the resources is most valuable at that moment. Perhaps it is not plausible even then. Richard Wright has suggested in conversation that the most efficient way to compare the value of competing uses is to have the two users—the original buyer and the new customer—negotiate directly with each other. It is hard to see why efficient breach theorists want the seller and the courts to resolve that issue.

Even assuming efficiency gains at the moment of breach, other costs overwhelm the immediate advantage when the time horizon is expanded in either direction. It is common ground that one economic function of contract is to allocate risk. One of the risks that is allocated by contracts is the risk of doing without in time of shortage. Those who plan ahead when shortage is merely a risk should reap the benefits when shortage comes to pass. Converters and breaching sellers should not be able to reallocate the risk after the fact by taking or keeping the specific thing and paying damages that cannot be used to replace it.

The allegedly efficient breach defeats the risk allocation functions of property and contract rights, deprives plaintiff of the benefits of having planned ahead to cover his needs, and thereby reduces the incentive for long-term planning. As others have effectively pointed out, the allegedly efficient breach disrupts commercial relationships and creates unnecessary litigation.[21]

An economist who read this chapter said he was puzzled by the preceding paragraph. If we fully compensate the plaintiff who planned ahead to avoid the risk of doing without in time of shortage, why should plaintiff care, and how have we defeated the risk allocation functions of his contract? Of course, the economist mused, the consequential damages will be hard to measure, and you have to consider not just the profits he loses immediately, but also the risk that he might lose some customers permanently. I would add that you have to consider the transaction costs of reallocating plaintiffs' other factors of production, and the cost of communicating his problems to his customers and trying to placate them, and his liability to customers with whom he had already contracted, and so on through his chains of supply and distribution. But assuming you could measure all that, the economist said, all the problems go away. Then he reluctantly volunteered, "But I suppose you have to take reality into account somewhat if you are going to do this seriously."

Indeed. The replaceability rules recognize that in the real world courts cannot accurately measure all the damages from doing without in time of shortage, and that any serious attempt to do so would impose inordinate litigation costs. These rules also recognize that only specific performance enables contracts to allocate the risk of doing without, as distinguished from the risk of not being compensated for doing without. At least some buyers care about the risk of doing without; they are the ones who sue for specific performance.

2. The Moral Argument

The law's preference for specific relief also rests on views of morality and justice that run deep in Western culture. A promise creates an entitlement that should be honored. Our children absorb that belief from an early age; they quickly learn to argue, "But Daddy, you promised." Circumstances sometimes excuse the duty to keep promises, or extenuate their breach, but that lesson is more complicated and tends to come later.

Our major religious traditions teach the duty to keep promises,[22] and our language and our literature reflect our sense of moral obligation: I gave my word; I have promises to keep.[23] One who keeps his promises is a man of his word; one who does not is a welsher or a deadbeat.

Ethicists and moral theologians offer a variety of explanations for the duty to keep promises, and they disagree over the frequency of exceptions to the duty, but an extraordinarily broad consensus agrees that there is such a duty. Kantians emphasize autonomy, trust, the categorical imperative, and the duty not to use another as a mere means.[24] (Kant's personal position is further explained in the note.) Utilitarians emphasize the role of promises in facilitating cooperation and exchange,[25] an argument traceable to Hume.[26] The mature John Rawls derived the duty from his fairness principle: if you accept benefits from the social practice of keeping promises, you incur an obligation to keep promises you make.[27] Intuitionists find the duty self-evident.[28] Some theologians emphasize God's example: a central theme of both Christian and Jewish theology is that God makes promises to His people and keeps them.[29] Hannah Arendt saw promising and promise keeping as an essential part of the human condition, arising "directly out of the will to live together with others in the mode of acting and speaking."[30]

Philosophers have sufficient confidence in the existence of a duty to keep promises that they use the duty to test their explanations more often than they use their explanations to test the duty. The consensus in favor of promise keeping is one of the principal arguments against act-utilitarianism, the claim that the moral worth of each act must be assessed by its utility in the particular instance. For act-utilitarians, like efficient breach theorists, whether to perform a promise depends not on any obligation arising from the promise, but on a new calculation of costs and benefits when performance is due. Critics argue that act-utilitarianism would make promises worthless, and that this is a powerful refutation of act-utilitarianism.[31] Act-utilitarians respond that even under their system, something like promises would be made and kept often enough to be relied on.[32]

Ethicists from different camps acknowledge that the culture's intuitive sense of the matter is older and more confident than their explanations.[33] Holmes and Posner were startling and provocative precisely because they so openly and self-consciously challenged a moral consensus.

Of course the culture's beliefs about the duty to keep promises are complex. Nearly everyone recognizes exceptions, and there is less consensus about the exceptions than about the basic duty. Uncontroversial applications of efficient breach theory are uncontroversial because they fit widely recognized exceptions to the duty of promise keeping. But efficient breach theory as a whole does not fit any widely recognized exception. Break your promises whenever you find it profitable, or break your promises whenever a better deal comes along, is not the common man's conception of promise keeping.

Some promises are binding in law, some only in morals. Most of us morally distinguish promises by their seriousness: the more solemnly we make a promise, the more we urge the promisee to rely on the promise, the more important the promise is to the promisee, the stronger the sense of obligation to keep the promise.[34] The promise itself counts in any weighing of costs and benefits; we think that breach is justified only when it does enough good to outweigh the breach of promise.[35]

We tend to discount "unfair" promises extracted by too much bargaining power, but we disagree sharply over how much bargaining power is too much. Many of us think that promises and conditions buried in the fine print of form contracts are not promises at all. My former colleague Elizabeth Warren likes to say that the real contract is not the writing, but only "dickered terms plus trade usage."

Some agreements that appear to be promises are often treated by trade usage as mere options, involving no promise at all. The

most obvious and important example is a customer's offer to buy
out of a seller's inventory. Most consumer customers, and many
commercial customers, can cancel orders without fear of liability.
Patrick Atiyah treats this practice as evidence of a declining belief
in the importance of keeping promises, and of his broader claim
that reliance is the real basis of liability in contract.[36] But he also
recognizes the more plausible explanation that neither side considers that the buyer has promised.[37] This trade usage results from
competition for the good will of customers. On Atiyah's primary
account, the customer would become bound when the seller relied.
But in fact, trade usage often allows buyers to return goods for a
full refund even after full performance on both sides. The measure
of the right to cancel orders or return goods is trade usage, subject
to the seller's right to announce his own policy if he has the market
strength to do so.

Often, without denying that a promise has created an entitlement, we think the decent, virtuous, and even customary thing for
the promisee to do is to release his entitlement—that it is selfish
and inconsiderate for him not to do so. We do not like promise
breakers, but neither do we like Giles Corey, who knew his rights
and would have them, and was thirty-three times a plaintiff against
his neighbors in Salem.[38] Corey was indicted for witchcraft, and
pressed to death for refusing to plead.[39]

However clear it is that it would be better for a promise not to
be performed, most of us think it morally better for the promisee
to excuse the promise than for the promisor to break it. When the
promisee excuses performance, no entitlement is violated. And
the promisee's decision that the promise should be excused is not
clouded by self-interest.

None of these exceptions has much bearing on the case of specific
performance of a contract for something irreplaceable. These are
nearly always cases where the promise is of great importance to
the plaintiff—where she bargained for the promise, agreed to pay
a price, now finds the thing promised irreplaceable in the market,
and cares enough to sue for specific performance. In commercial
cases, plaintiff typically relied on the promised supply in the operation of her business; in shortage cases (but usually not in monopoly or one-of-a-kind-item cases), plaintiff also relied by not
arranging for a supply elsewhere. In all irreplaceability cases, the

breach goes to the central point of the promise, and not to some collateral provision in the fine print. The moral duty to keep these promises is very strong, and that duty is reflected in the law.

I am not subscribing to Charles Fried's claim that the duty to keep promises explains all of contract law.[40] But I do believe that the moral argument for specific performance is based on the entitlement created by promises, and that it is principally this sense of moral entitlement that motivates the judges in the irreplaceability cases. Supporters of specific performance in the United Nations Commission on International Trade Law explicitly invoked this claim of entitlement. They relied on the right to have a promise honored even where the goods were replaceable.[41] American law does not go so far, but the replaceability rules protect plaintiff's entitlement whenever it matters. One who breaches his contract without legal excuse is a wrongdoer, and the wrongdoer should not profit while his victim does without the thing he was promised.

If the *buyer* can make a larger profit by reselling the goods to a third party—suppose the contract is for scarce carrots—he is entitled to choose between the carrots and the larger profit. But the original seller is no longer entitled to either; she promised the carrots, and all the benefits of owning the carrots, to the buyer. What is at stake in the normative debate over efficient breach is not whether resources can move to more valuable uses. What is at stake is the allocation of entitlements: whether the promise breaker or her victim gets to profit from a new and more valuable use, and whether the victim or the court gets to value the victim's use and decide whether the new use is really more valuable.[42]

Richard Craswell has recently argued that the moral obligation to keep promises is irrelevant to the choice of remedy, because the law's rules about remedy are part of the content of the promise. In his view, one can keep a promise by satisfying the legally prescribed remedy, and the remedy might be expectancy damages, reliance damages, rescission, or "any number under the sun."[43] It is tautologically true that in a court, a promise of carrots can mean anything under the sun if we have a legal rule that says it means anything under the sun. But outside a court, a promise of carrots usually means carrots. A legal rule commuting a promise of carrots into anything under the sun would be inconsistent with the widespread moral sense that promises should be kept.

I have argued that the moral claim to specific performance depends on the entitlement created by the promise. The moral entitlement depends on the terms of the promise, not on the law of remedies. Providing a remedy for breaking the promise is not a form of keeping the promise.

Sellers should be able to promise carrots or money, if that is really the intended transaction, but they should also be able to promise carrots. "I promise carrots" is readily distinguished in ordinary language from, "I promise carrots or an equivalent sum of money, at my election." If the law were to treat these two statements as equivalent, then one who wanted to really promise carrots would have to say something like, "I promise carrots, and I mean that this promise can be fulfilled only by delivering carrots, and that no substitute will satisfy this promise."

Ordinary people will never learn that they must go through these extra steps if they mean to do something that seems as simple as promising carrots. Craswell concedes that "most promisors probably do not explicitly have in mind anything like" the range of remedies that he would treat as equivalent to keeping the promise, and that "it seems inherently correct or natural" to treat the choice of remedy as a question of what to do about a broken promise and not as a question of interpreting the promise.[44] I agree. The claim that a promise of carrots can be commuted to a promise of carrots or money depends on an unstated background rule, and interpreting promises in light of such a background rule is inherently deceptive to promisees who do not know the unstated rule. The dominant cultural understanding appears to match the ordinary meaning of the language—that a promise of carrots creates a moral entitlement to carrots.[45] The law enforces this entitlement by specific performance when carrots cannot be replaced on the market. And because the law has traditionally granted specific performance when damages cannot be used to replace the promised thing in kind, it cannot even be said that legally sophisticated promisees know a background rule that routinely commutes promises into money remedies for breach.

C. Conclusion

It is important to distinguish the normative arguments for and against efficient breach theory from positive arguments about the current state of the law. The two arguments are independent of each other. Readers who believe that efficient breach would be a good thing must still face up to the implications of the replaceability rules. Efficient breach theory does not describe the law; Holmes and Posner got things backwards.

Courts do not limit remedies so that promised resources can be reallocated to their most valued use, and courts do not recognize a general right to breach and pay damages. Whenever anything important depends on the choice of remedy, courts protect plaintiff's entitlement to the specific thing he was promised. Efficient breach theory is an academic theory of what the law might be, or of what some people think the law should be. But it is not the law.

Notes on Efficient Breach

1. [right to violate law and pay damages] See Richard A. Posner, *Economic Analysis of Law* § 3.8 at 58–62, § 4.11 at 117–19 (Little, Brown, 3d ed. 1986); Gary S. Becker, *Crime and Punishment: An Economic Approach*, 76 J. Pol. Econ. 169, 199 (1968); Guido Calabresi & A. Douglas Melamed, *Property Rules, Liability Rules, and Inalienability: One View of the Cathedral*, 85 Harv. L. Rev. 1089, 1105–10 (1972).

2. [contract means only a duty to pay damages] Oliver Wendell Holmes, Jr., *The Path of the Law*, 10 Harv. L. Rev. 457, 462 (1897).

3. [efficient breach theory] See Posner, *Economic Analysis* § 4.8 at 107 (cited in note 1).

4. [specific performance often not an option] See ch. 1 part B.2 at 16–17.

5. [damages inadequate in shortage] See ch. 2 parts A.2. and B.

6. [no court says money adequate in itself] See ch. 2 at notes 53–55, 86, and ch. 4 at note 10.

7. [unique use vs. unique goods] See William Bishop, *The Choice of Remedy for Breach of Contract*, 14 J. Legal Stud. 299, 314 (1985); Peter Linzer, *On the Amorality of Contract Remedies—Efficiency, Equity, and the Second Restatement*, 81 Colum. L. Rev. 111, 114–15 (1981); Alan Schwartz, *The Case for Specific Performance*, 89 Yale L.J. 271, 289–90 (1979).

8. [functional equivalence may be adequate] See Campbell Soup Co. v. Wentz, 172 F.2d 80, 82–83 (3d Cir. 1948) (assuming in principle that one variety of carrot could substitute for another, but holding that other varieties were not adequate where plaintiff cared about uniform color); Graves v. Key City Gas Co., 83 Iowa 714, 718, 50 N.W. 283, 284 (1891) ("he could use candles, oils, or electricity, but he contracted for gaslight, and is entitled to it"). Compare Kirsch v. Zubalsky, 139 N.J. Eq. 22, 24–26, 49 A.2d 773, 775 (1946) (one model car is adequate substitute for another model); Welch v. Chippewa Sales Co., 252 Wis. 166, 168–69, 31 N.W.2d 170, 171 (1948) (same).

9. [**burdensome performance inefficient**] See Posner, *Economic Analysis* § 4.11 at 118 (cited in note 1); N. Ind. Public Serv. Co. v. Carbon County Coal Co., 799 F.2d 265, 279 (7th Cir. 1986) (refusing to order specific performance of contract to deliver coal, where performance would require reopening of abandoned mine).

10. [**undue hardship defense**] See ch. 7 part A.

11. [**uneconomic contracts should be breached**] N. Ind. Public Serv. Co. v. Carbon County Coal Co., 799 F.2d 265, 279 (7th Cir. 1986) (specific performance would "force the continuation of production that has become uneconomical").

12. [**substantial or disproportionate hardship**] See 3615 Corp. v. N.Y. Life Ins. Co., 717 F.2d 1236, 1238 (8th Cir. 1983) ("oppressive, unfair, inequitable or would work an unreasonable and disproportionate hardship"); Van Wagner Advertising Corp. v. S & M Enterprises, 67 N.Y.2d 186, 195, 492 N.E.2d 756, 761, 501 N.Y.S.2d 628, 633 (1986) ("disproportionate in its harm"; "undue hardship"); Restatement (Second) of Contracts § 364(1)(b) (1981) ("unreasonable hardship or loss"); Daniel Friedmann, *The Efficient Breach Fallacy*, 18 J. Legal Stud. 1, 15–18 (1989).

13. [**hardship to third parties**] See ch. 7 note 12.

14. [**hardship vs. willingness to pay**] See Posner, *Economic Analysis* § 1.2 at 11–15 (cited in note 1) ("the economic value of something is how much someone is willing to pay for it or, if he has it already, how much money he demands to part with it"). For further comparison of economic and other concepts of value, and a spirited defense of the morality of the willingness to pay definition, see Richard A. Posner, *Utilitarianism, Economics, and Legal Theory*, 8 J. Legal Stud. 103 (1979).

15. [**cost of implementing remedies**] See sources cited in ch. 1 notes 13–14.

16. [**friction with trading partners**] See Amy H. Kastely, *The Right to Require Performance in International Sales: Towards an International Interpretation of the Vienna Convention*, 63 Wash. L. Rev. 607, 614–16, 625–28 (1988) (describing sharp disagreement over specific performance in negotiation of United Nations Convention on Contracts for the International Sale of Goods).

17. [**rightful position principle**] Douglas Laycock, *Modern American Remedies* 15 (Little, Brown 1985).

18. [**plaintiff's position but for wrong**] Milliken v. Bradley, 433 U.S. 267, 280 (1977); Milliken v. Bradley, 418 U.S. 717, 746 (1974); U.S. v. Hatahley, 257 F.2d 920, 923 (10th Cir. 1958).

19. [**specific performance for seller**] See ch. 2 at note 103.

20. [**unneeded performance is wasteful**] See Posner, *Economic Analysis* § 4.8 at 106 (cited in note 1).

21. [**efficient breach causes litigation**] Daniel Friedmann, 18 J. Legal Stud. at 6–7 (cited in note 12); Ian R. Macneil, *Efficient Breach of Contract: Circles in the Sky*, 68 Va. L. Rev. 947 (1982).

22. [**religious traditions and promise keeping**] See *Deuteronomy* 23:24 ("That which is gone out of thy lips thou shall keep and perform; even a freewill offering"); P.K. Meagher, *Moral Obligation of a Promise*, in 11 *New Catholic Encyclopedia* 837 (Catholic Univ. of Am. 1967) (contractual promise "binds in virtue of commutative justice," and breach is "gravely sinful"; noncontractual promise "binds only in fidelity"; keeping such promises is "a matter of truthfulness" and "a most commendable quality of soul," but "violation under ordinary circumstances is not considered mortally sinful"); Thomas Aquinas, *Summa Theologica*, Part II (Second

Part), Question 89, art. 7, at p. 147 (Fathers of the English Dominican Province, trans.) (Burns, Oates & Washburne 1922) ("in the oath that is made about something to be done by us, the obligation falls on the thing guaranteed by oath. For a man is bound to make true what he has sworn, else his oath lacks truth.").

23. [I have promises to keep] Robert Frost, *Stopping by Woods on a Snowy Evening*, in *The Poetry of Robert Frost* 224, 225 (Edward Connery Latham, ed.) (Holt, Rinehart & Winston 1969).

24. [Kantian explanation of duty] Charles Fried, *Contract as Promise: A Theory of Contractual Obligation* 7–17 (Harvard Univ. Press 1981) ("obligation to keep a promise is grounded not in arguments of utility but in respect for individual autonomy and in trust"). Kant himself appears to have considered only the case of a person who makes a promise knowing he cannot keep it. Immanuel Kant, *Foundations of the Metaphysics of Morals* *402–03, *422 (false promises violate the categorical imperative, because universal false promises "would make the promise itself and the end to be accomplished by it impossible"); id. at *429–30 ("he who intends a deceitful promise to others sees immediately that he intends to use another man merely as a means"). These passages appear in the Lewis White Beck translation at 21–23, 45–46, 54 (Bobbs-Merrill 1969).

25. [utilitarian explanation of duty] Russell Hardin, *Morality Within the Limits of Reason* 59–65 (Univ. of Chicago Press 1988) ("promises have the function of strategically binding us to bring about better results than might otherwise occur with uncoordinated action" (p. 64)); John Rawls, *Two Concepts of Rules*, 64 Phil. Rev. 3, 13–18, 30–31 (1955); Donald Regan, *On Preferences and Promises: A Response to Harsanyi*, 96 Ethics 56, 58–64 (1985); Peter Singer, *Is Act-Utilitarianism Self-Defeating?* 81 Phil. Rev. 94, 100–01 (1972).

26. [Hume's explanation of duty] David Hume, *A Treatise of Human Nature* 516–25 (Oxford Univ. Press 1978) (original publication 1740) (without promises and promise keeping, commerce would be impossible "and every one reduc'd to his own skill and industry for his well-being and subsistence" (p. 520)).

27. [Rawlsian explanation of duty] John Rawls, *A Theory of Justice* 344–50 (Harvard Univ. Press 1971) ("Having, then, availed ourselves of the practice for this reason, we are under an obligation to do as we promised by the principle of fairness" (p. 347)).

28. [intuitionist explanation of duty] W.D. Ross, *The Right and the Good* 20–21 & n.1, 40 (Oxford Univ. Press 1930) ("it seems, on reflection, self-evident that a promise, simply as such, is something that *prima facie* ought to be kept, and it does *not*, on reflection, seem self-evident that production of maximum good is the only thing that makes an act obligatory" (emphasis in original)).

29. [theological explanation of duty] James F. Childress, *Promise*, in *The Westminster Dictionary of Christian Ethics* 505–06 (James F. Childress & John MacQuarrie, eds.) (Westminster Press, rev. ed. 1986) ("Jewish and Christian morality is largely founded on the biblical conception of God as one who makes promises and lives up to those promises, as reflected in his covenants and his fidelity to those covenants").

30. [promises arise out of living together] Hannah Arendt, *The Human Condition* 243–47 (Univ. Chicago Press 1958).

31. [act-utilitarians would ignore promises] D.H. Hodgson, *Consequences of Utilitarianism* 38–62 (Oxford Univ. Press 1967) ("in our act-utilitarian society, promising would be pointless" (p. 42)); David Lyons, *Ethics and the Rule of Law* 122–24 (Cambridge Univ. Press 1984) ("the obligation created by promising, for example, is not overridden merely by the fact that one can promote welfare to a greater degree by breaking it than by keeping it"); Ross, *Right and Good* at 17–18, 34–47 (cited in note 28) (promises are the case in which "it is easiest to see" the fallacy of utilitarianism (p. 34)); John C. Harsanyi, *Does Reason Tell Us What Moral Code to Follow and, Indeed, to Follow Any Moral Code at All?* 96 Ethics 42, 44–45 (1985) (utilitarian breach "would greatly reduce the social utility of promise making"). For a careful and evenhanded review of the arguments, see P.S. Atiyah, *Promises, Morals, and Law* (Oxford Univ. Press 1981) (concluding that "neither rule utilitarianism nor act utilitarianism seems able to offer an acceptable explanation of why (or whether) a promise remains binding when it would be best on the whole to break it").

32. [defenses of act-utilitarianism] See Hardin, *Morality* at 59–65; Regan, 96 Ethics at 58–64; Singer, 81 Phil. Rev. at 100–01 (all cited in note 25).

33. [cultural consensus] Atiyah, *Promises* at 4 (cited in note 31) (describing "the modern viewpoint, that promises per se are morally binding, and that insofar as the doctrine of consideration fails to give effect to this moral ideal, it is an anomaly"); Hodgson, *Consequences* at 40 (cited in note 31) ("in most cases, [promise-keeping] is required by a conventional moral rule, a rule which many persons also accept as a personal rule"); Ross, *Right and Good* at 17 (cited in note 28) ("when a plain man fulfills a promise because he thinks he ought to do so, it seems clear that he does so with no thought of its total consequences"); Harsanyi, 96 Ethics at 44 (cited in note 31) ("commonsense morality would say that [promise breaking] would be permissible only in some rare and rather exceptional cases where keeping his promise would cause him or some other people extreme hardship, or where the promisee would suffer only a very minor loss if the promise made to him were not fulfilled"); Regan, 96 Ethics at 60, 64 (cited in note 31) ("commonsense promising is a subtle and flexible practice," and justified breach is not rare, but "most people keep most of their promises most of the time"). See also Morris R. Cohen, *The Basis of Contract*, 46 Harv. L. Rev. 553, 572 (1933) ("there can be no doubt that common sense does generally find something revolting about the breaking of a promise").

34. [promises distinguished by seriousness] For a similar claim, see Regan, 96 Ethics at 60 (cited in note 25).

35. [good from breach must outweigh promise] For a general claim that violation of rights is a consequence that must be weighed with other consequences, see Douglas Laycock, *The Ultimate Unity of Rights and Utilities*, 64 Tex. L. Rev. 407 (1985). For a similar treatment of promises, see Ross, *Right and Good* at 34–35 (cited in note 28).

36. [right to cancel as breach] P.S. Atiyah, *The Rise and Fall of Freedom of Contract* 756–61 (Oxford Univ. Press 1979).

37. [right to cancel as trade usage] Id. at 760 ("in many situations contracting parties, particularly, but not exclusively, consumers, do not regard a contract as involving mutual promises").

38. [Giles Corey insisting on his rights] See Arthur Miller, *The Crucible* 95 (Viking Press 1952):

> GILES: I am thirty-three times in court in my life. And always plaintiff, too.
> DANFORTH: Oh, then you're much put-upon.
> GILES: I am never put-upon; I know my rights, sir, and I will have them.

39. [Corey pressed to death] Id. at 135. For the historical Giles Corey, see Marion L. Starkey, *The Devil in Massachusetts: A Modern Enquiry into the Salem Witch Trials* 64, 74–75, 106, 204–07, 267–68 (Doubleday, Dolphin Books 1961).

40. [promises explain all of contract law] Fried, *Contract as Promise* (cited in note 24).

41. [international trade and specific relief] See Kastely, 63 Wash. L. Rev. at 614 n.41 (cited in note 16), quoting Mr. Hjerner, the delegate from Sweden: "even if the buyer was able to purchase substitute commodities elsewhere on the market, he should still have the right to hold to the contract and to expect that the seller's promise would be honoured."

42. [argument is over entitlements] See Friedmann, 18 J. Legal Stud. at 5 (cited in note 12) ("the real issue . . . is who should benefit from C's willingness to pay a

43. [promise can mean anything under the sun] Richard B. Craswell, *Contract Law, Default Rules, and the Philosophy of Promising*, 88 Mich. L. Rev. 489, 512–13 (1989).

44. [but people do not understand promises this way] Id. at 513.

45. [cultural understanding of promise] See Randy E. Barnett, *Contract Remedies and Inalienable Rights*, 4 Soc. Phil. & Policy 179, 183 (1986) ("Persons with common sense—that is, those who have not taken a first-year contracts class (or been counseled by a lawyer who has)—would naturally assume, for example, that when a good is purchased the purchaser obtains a right to the good. They would not assume that the seller has an *option* to deliver or pay damages" (emphasis in original)). See also Joseph Story, 2 *Commentaries on Equity Jurisprudence as Administered in England and America* § 717 at 25 (Little, Brown 1836) ("it is against conscience, that a party should have a right of election, whether he should perform his covenant, or only pay damages for the breach of it").

12

Conforming Doctrine to Reality

In this chapter, I explore how judicial doctrine might be conformed to the reality of the decided cases. I offer a tentative restatement of the courts' operative rules, and a proposed statute abolishing the irreparable injury rule at final judgment. Finally, I briefly consider the need for courts and legislatures to adopt such reforms.

A. A Tentative Restatement

Chapter 1 promised a set of functional rules for choosing among remedies. Those rules should be apparent to the reader who has come this far, but it is helpful to state them succinctly and explicitly in a single place. As is so often the case, the attempt to formulate precise statements revealed ambiguities and extended my analysis.

I propose to restate existing law in general terms, in ways that focus attention on the real interests at stake, and without misleading references to irreparable injury. I do not offer a detailed analysis that would resolve close cases. I will focus on the most basic remedial choices—between specific and substitutionary relief, between preliminary and permanent relief, and between personal commands and impersonal judgments. These choices arise in all areas of substantive law. I am not trying to state particular remedies for particular wrongs, or to state measures of damage or define the scope of injunctions.[1] I am assuming the existing rules for these issues. That is, I am assuming that more detailed law tells us what the order should say if specific relief is awarded, and what the measure of recovery should be if substitutionary relief is awarded. I am addressing the choice among forms of relief.

The format of blackletter rule and explanatory comment, familiar from real Restatements, is well suited to its purpose. It highlights the careful formulation of general principles, while allowing for explanation, qualification, and detail that could be forced into the general principle only by writing sentences that sound like the Internal Revenue Code. I adopt that format for these functional reasons, and not to create illusions of official status.

Some of these rules would obviously benefit from further specification, and there may be other constraints on plaintiff's choice of remedy that I have not yet identified. But I am confident that I have stated most of the operative rules in general form, and that even this level of generality explains the cases far better than any version of the irreparable injury rule.

For readers who are unconvinced, I have offered a clear target. I will confess error, in whole or in part, if anyone shows me a substantial body of cases with results that cannot be explained by my rules and that can be explained by the irreparable injury rule.

§ 1 General Rule

A plaintiff who has prevailed on the merits is presumptively entitled to choose either a substitutionary or specific remedy. A court should refuse plaintiff's choice of remedy only when countervailing interests outweigh plaintiff's interest in the remedy he prefers.

This rule is stated at the same level of generality as the irreparable injury rule. Its rationale is that a victim of wrongdoing is presumptively entitled to be made completely whole, and that plaintiff is the best judge of what will make him whole.

In practice, countervailing interests often require plaintiff to accept a remedy different from what he would have preferred. Such interests include burdens on the defendant, the court, or the public, and countervailing policies of substantive law. But plaintiff's remedy should not be limited because of the mere possibility of such interests. Rather, plaintiff's remedy should be limited only when such interests are actually at stake and outweigh plaintiff's interests.

Countervailing interests are identified in the sections that follow. These sections are not exclusive; exceptional cases may arise in which considerations not anticipated here provide good cause to refuse the remedy elected by plaintiff. But the general rule stated in this section, together with the exceptions stated in the following sections, should cover all but the most unusual cases.

Only one of the rules that follow use "equitable remedy" as a relevant category. That is the rule about civil jury trial, where the category is determined by the Constitution. Most of these rules restrict "specific relief" or "permanent specific relief." But several apply to "any remedy," one applies to "preliminary substitutionary relief," and one applies to "the payment of money." One applies to specific performance but not to specific relief generally. These distinctions are carefully chosen. One reason the irreparable injury rule is a poor proxy for the operative rules is that the irreparable injury rule purports to restrict the role of equity. But law and equity are rarely relevant categories in the operative rules that actually govern the choice of remedy.

I have not stated a general rule about the public interest, but I believe that the rules I have stated will cover most of the legitimate considerations of public interest that require limitation on plaintiff's choice of remedy. Cases that fall outside these rules are likely to be so unusual that it is not possible to state a sensible general principle for deciding them. Few judges will ignore bona fide considerations of public interest, and I do not want them to do so. But I would be reluctant to limit plaintiff's remedy because of some vague notion of public interest or public policy that cannot be articulated as an identifiable harm to persons, property, or institutions.

I have stated no rule corresponding to the cases in which courts invoke the irreparable injury rule to disguise a decision on the merits. In my judgment, those cases are illegitimate under any understanding of present law.

§ 2 Undue Hardship

A court should deny permanent specific relief if:
(a) the relief would impose hardship on defendant, and
(b) that hardship is substantially disproportionate to the disadvantage to plaintiff of receiving only substitutionary relief.

In balancing the interests, a court should consider the relative fault of each litigant.

This section states the traditional rule of undue hardship or balancing the equities. A remedy will not be withheld merely because its expense exceeds the benefit to plaintiff. The standard is hardship that is substantially disproportionate to plaintiff's interest. This standard is supported by the cases, and it is justified by the interest in making plaintiff whole and by defendant's adjudicated wrongdoing.

§ 3 Burden on Innocent Third Parties

A court should deny permanent specific relief if:
(a) the relief would harm innocent third parties, and
(b) that harm is not outweighed by the disadvantage to plaintiff of receiving only substitutionary relief.

In balancing the interests, a court should consider the innocence of the third parties and the relative entitlements of the plaintiff and the third parties.

This section separates the problem of harm to third parties from hardship to defendants. It is difficult to justify imposing the cost of a remedy on innocent third parties. But incidental burdens on third parties are sometimes unavoidable. And in some areas of the law, such as the law of employment discrimination, quite substantial effects on third parties have been thought necessary to enforcement.

Some harm to innocent third parties is the incidental consequence of legal entitlements and is not to be considered under this section. Consider the case of a third party who wishes to buy goods already under contract to plaintiff. The third party may be innocent, and his inability to buy the goods may be a hardship. But plaintiff has an entitlement to the goods, and the third party does not. Furthermore, if the third party knowingly induced the seller to breach his contract with the plaintiff, the third party would no longer be innocent. His claim of hardship should be considered under the test of substantially disproportionate hardship stated in § 2.

§ 4 Impracticality

A court should deny permanent specific relief if:

(a) the relief would be impractical to implement or burdensome for the court to supervise, and

(b) these problems outweigh the disadvantage to plaintiff of receiving only substitutionary relief.

This section makes explicit that the burdens of enforcement are to be balanced against the need for the remedy. Courts will undertake more burdensome supervision in cases of civil or political rights, in cases where the public interest is affected, and in other cases where substitutionary remedies are especially ineffective.

§ 5 Personal Service Contracts

(a) A court in a civil case may not require a human being to perform personal services.

(b) A court should not require an employer to hire, retain, or promote an employee in circumstances of serious mistrust or personal friction, except where such an order is necessary to vindicate strong substantive policy.

The rule stated in § 5(a) implements strong policies against involuntary servitude and admits of no exceptions. However, this rule does not prevent a court from ordering a business entity to provide services through willing employees, or from ordering any defendant to provide services if performance can be delegated to a willing contractor.

§ 5(b) states what is left of the traditional reluctance to order employers to hire particular employees. This reluctance is supported by much weaker policies, and has been seriously eroded by statutes and collective bargaining agreements. The inevitable friction attendant on any employment dispute is not sufficient reason to refuse specific relief. But specific relief should generally be withheld where it would be impossible to restore a functioning working relationship with supervisors or co-workers and reassignment to another unit of the same employer is not an option.

When employees are discharged in violation of the labor laws or the civil rights laws, courts sometimes order reinstatement even in the face of serious personal friction. Such orders have been thought necessary to vindicate the statutory policy. The last clause provides for this line of cases.

§ 6 Prior Restraints on Speech

A court should refuse specific relief that would impose an unconstitutional prior restraint on speech.

Where specific relief is denied on grounds of prior restraint, the speech is often protected from subsequent damages or punishment as well. But prior restraints are thought to pose special dangers, and courts insist that sometimes the prior restraint will be refused even though subsequent remedies will be granted. This section states that traditional principle.

§ 7 Civil Jury Trial

A court should refuse an equitable remedy if:
(a) the demand for that remedy would deprive defendant of civil jury trial, and
(b) the remedy would give plaintiff no advantages over an equivalent legal remedy.

This section prevents plaintiff from manipulating the pleadings to deprive defendant of jury trial. It does not require that plaintiff accept an incomplete remedy in order that the case may be tried to a jury; it does not require that defendant's interest in jury trial be balanced against plaintiff's interest in a more complete remedy. The constitutional right to jury trial does not apply to equitable remedies, and plaintiff is entitled to an equitable remedy if it provides any practical benefit not provided by the legal remedy.

The court may try the equity case with an advisory jury. If further protection of jury trial is thought necessary, courts should be authorized to try equity cases to juries.

§ 8 Equality Among Creditors

A court should refuse specific relief if the relief would prefer plaintiff over other creditors of an insolvent defendant.

This section states the traditional rule by which courts of general jurisdiction have cooperated with bankruptcy courts. The court may enter a damage judgment against an insolvent defendant, and plaintiff may collect it from any assets available. If a bankruptcy proceeding ensues within the period provided by the Bankruptcy Code, the bankrupt estate may recover the funds thus collected. The rule of this section ensures that the bankruptcy court will not be presented with the problem of trying to recover the value of specific relief.

§ 9 Interference with Other Authorities

A court should deny any remedy that would require the court to inappropriately interfere with the jurisdiction of another tribunal or the discretion of another branch of government.

This section states a broad principle that subsumes many more specific rules. These more specific rules include exhaustion of administrative remedies; primary jurisdiction of agencies; sovereign, official, legislative, and judicial immunities; deference to the discretionary decisions of the executive branch; various abstention doctrines; and other considerations of comity and federalism. The content of these specific rules depends on the relationship between the court and the other authority, on the intrusiveness of the remedy requested, and on the needs of plaintiff. These rules do not depend on any distinction between law and equity. Rather, these rules distinguish cases of appropriate and inappropriate interference with other authorities.

§ 10 Interference with Other Law

A court should deny any remedy that would inappropriately evade or override the more particular provisions of other applicable law.

The principle stated in this section prevents plaintiffs from using general remedial principles to evade controlling provisions of more specific law. Thus, if a statute provides an exclusive remedy, plaintiff is not entitled to some other remedy that would have been available but for the statute. If a statute or legal doctrine includes a substantive restriction on plaintiff's right to a particular remedy, or to any remedy at all, plaintiff should not be able to evade that restriction by pleading some more general theory such as unjust enrichment, general equitable discretion, or full compensation for breach of legal duty.

This principle is not limited to remedies; it is an application of the principle that a more specific provision of law controls a more general provision. As in § 9, the ultimate question is whether it is appropriate or inappropriate to evade or override the more particular law.

§ 11 Ripeness

A court should deny any remedy if:
    (a) plaintiff has not yet been injured, and
    (b) there is no sufficient threat that unlawful acts by defendant will harm plaintiff in the future.

Plaintiff may not recover damages for harm he has not suffered. And he may not get an injunction against harm that is not sufficiently likely to justify judicial intervention.

The sufficiency of the threat may be judged in light of two policies. First, there must be a case or controversy for judicial resolution.

Second, it often happens that defendant plans a course of conduct that may or may not unlawfully harm plaintiff. For example, defendant may plan socially useful conduct that may or may not turn out to also be a nuisance. The requirement of a ripe threat of unlawful harm to plaintiff should be interpreted in light of the risk that the court will unnecessarily forbid useful conduct.

§ 12 Mootness

A court should deny permanent specific relief if:
    (a) such relief would not cure, in whole or in part, harm inflicted on plaintiff by past unlawful acts; and

(b) there is no sufficient threat that defendant will commit future unlawful acts that will harm plaintiff.

It is always possible to award substitutionary relief for past harm, or for unavoidable future harm, such as pain and suffering from a past accident.

When it is too late for specific relief to remedy harm already inflicted, the court may still enjoin future repetitions of defendant's unlawful conduct. But if there is no threat of future harm, the claim for specific relief is moot, and relief should be denied.

§ 13 *Preliminary Specific Relief*

A court should grant specific relief before final judgment only to prevent injury that cannot be remedied by later remedies of any kind. Specific relief before final judgment should be designed to minimize the risk of erroneously permitting such injury to the litigants or the public. In its attempt to minimize the risk of such harm, a court should consider:

(a) the severity and the likelihood of such harm to each litigant and to the public if the requested relief is granted and if it is denied;

(b) the interest of each litigant and the public in obtaining or avoiding the requested relief, as compared to the relief that would be available to that litigant or the public after final judgment; and

(c) the probability that the requested relief will be consistent with the final judgment.

The principle of this section could be stated in terms of irreparable injury or inadequacy of later remedies, if we could agree that the only meaning of these phrases would be the meaning they now carry in the case law on preliminary relief. The principle could also be stated in terms of irremediable harm. In ordinary English, "irremediable" means the same thing as "irreparable," but it does not carry the weight of precedent applying it interchangeably to preliminary and permanent relief.

The cases are in substantial agreement on what factors are to be balanced, but they disagree on how to describe the balancing test of which the factors are a part. Most courts now hold that a strong showing of irremediable harm will excuse a weaker showing of probable success, and vice versa. The implicit logic of such a trade off is to minimize the risk of erroneously inflicting irremediable harm. This section adopts that standard as an analytic approach, but without the pretense that any of the relevant factors can be quantified or manipulated algebraically.

The three factors listed in the subsections are more precise formulations of the traditional factors in the cases. Subsections (a) and (b) specify the balance of harms to the parties. Subsection (a) refers to the severity of harm and the likelihood that it will occur, factors that are explicit in the cases.

Subsection (b) refers to a factor that is implicit in the cases: the extent of the gap between the remedy before judgment and the remedy that would be available after judgment. This might be best described as the degree of inadequacy of the permanent remedy. But again, to describe it that way would require agreement on a new usage of the term.

Subsection (c) states more precisely the probability-of-success factor. What counts is not the probability of some judgment on the merits for plaintiff, but rather the probability of a judgment that will justify the particular grant of preliminary relief.

§ 14 Coercive Collection of Money

A court should not use the contempt power to coerce the payment of money, except
    (a) to collect child or spousal support, or
    (b) where expressly authorized by statute.

The main clause and exception (a) state the traditional rule. Exception (b) takes account of recent legislative innovations.

OPTIONAL SECTIONS, NOT RECOMMENDED

[§ 15 Sale of Fungible Goods

A court should refuse to order specific performance of a contract to sell goods, if
    (a) defendant is solvent, and
    (b) substantially identical substitutes are readily available in the market.]

This section states existing law. But it has no basis in policy. It produces wasteful litigation about which goods are substantially identical and whether they are readily available. These issues sometimes provide bargaining leverage to breaching sellers who have no defense on the merits. This rule should be abolished.

[§ *16 Preliminary Substitutionary Relief*

A court should not grant substitutionary relief before final judgment.]

This rule means that plaintiffs cannot collect partial damages in advance of judgment, however great their financial hardship and however much that hardship is attributable to defendant's wrongdoing. The rule is sometimes a source of injustice and hardship, and its justifications are weak. But it is well settled in the cases.

[§ *17 Criminal Procedure*

A court should refuse to enjoin criminal conduct where the injunction would deprive defendant of criminal jury trial or other rights of criminal procedure, if:

(a) the threatened crime would not impose significant harm on a person or property before it can be deterred by criminal prosecution and punishment;

(b) a criminal prohibition is the primary regulation of the conduct at issue; and

(c) repeated prosecution has not already proven ineffectual to deter repeated violations of the law.]

This section accurately states a rule that some will find worth saving, but which has been largely abandoned in the existing case law. The conditions required to make the rule plausible may make it so narrow that it is not worth preserving.

Subsection (a) effectively limits the section to victimless crimes, petty nuisances, minor violations of licensing regulations, and the like. The possibility of later criminal prosecution should not induce a court to stand by while a person seriously harms another.

Subsection (b) further limits the section by eliminating conduct that is principally regulated by civil penalties or administrative agencies. Such conduct sometimes carries criminal penalties as well, but the criminal penalties are generally reserved for the most egregious violations. The mere possibility of criminal penalties is not a reason to transfer cases from the primary enforcement agency to criminal courts that are already overcrowded with more serious offenses that are the primary concern of the criminal law.

The combined effect of subsections (a) and (b) is to permit injunctions against all crimes except for offenses that are both minor and normally prosecuted in criminal courts. Subsection (c) makes the injunctive remedy available even in these cases after criminal prosecution has proved ineffective.

B. A Proposal for Legislative Repeal

The rules just tentatively restated are supported by existing decisions. They are the operative rules by which courts really decide cases. Most courts could use these rules to clarify their thought and explain their decisions, forever abandon the irreparable injury rule, and do so without overruling a single modern case.

But the common law method of slowly spreading a reform through accumulating precedents has not begun, and may never begin. Because the irreparable injury rule no longer constrains results, judges feel no pressure to abandon it. What is needed is a single event that will crystallize the developments that have already occurred and focus judicial attention on a new line of development. A sweeping Supreme Court opinion would work, but a more promising solution is a statute.

Congress and each state should enact all or part of the following statute:

> **(a) The existence of another adequate remedy does not preclude a final judgment of injunction, specific performance, or other equitable relief, in cases where such relief is appropriate. The rule that equity will act only to prevent irreparable injury shall not be applied to the choice of remedy at final judgment.**
>
> **(b) A plaintiff who has prevailed on the merits is presumptively entitled to choose either a substitutionary or specific remedy. A court should refuse plaintiff's choice of remedy only when**

countervailing interests outweigh plaintiff's interest in the remedy he prefers.

Legislatures that find paragraph (b) too bold may enact paragraph (a) alone, or just the first sentence of paragraph (a). The first sentence is modeled directly on Federal Rule 57, which governs declaratory judgments.[2] The second sentence is for emphasis and clarity; it expressly repeals the irreparable injury rule at the final judgment stage. Together the two sentences eliminate both the adequacy and irreparable injury formulations of the rule. Paragraph (b) elaborates the meaning of "appropriate" in the first sentence of paragraph (a).

The first sentence of paragraph (a) should be sufficient in theory, but both paragraphs may be needed in practice. Emphasis, clarity, and elaboration are important in any effort to change even the empty shell of a rule that has been around as long as has the irreparable injury rule.

Consider the remarkable saga of Pennsylvania's efforts to free declaratory judgments from the irreparable injury rule. In 1923,[3] 1935,[4] 1943,[5] and 1976,[6] in increasingly emphatic and redundant terms, the legislature authorized declaratory judgments even if other remedies were available. The state supreme court ignored this aspect of the 1923 act,[7] construed away the 1935 amendment,[8] and changed its mind five times about the meaning of the 1943 amendment.[9] Its last opinion, in 1973, found the statute was "*clear and explicit*" and disavowed the court's earlier "indifference to the plain meaning."[10] The 1976 amendment was apparently designed to prevent a further change of mind, and so far it has worked.[11] Some of the cases defying the statute fit the pattern described in this book: the court had some other reason to deny declaratory relief, but it also treated other adequate remedies as a bar to relief.[12]

This fiasco is one more example of the costs of talking about irreparable injury and adequate remedies instead of the real reason for decision. But I tell this tale to make a different point. Legislatures seeking to repeal the irreparable injury rule should say it boldly and emphatically the first time, and they should say it redundantly at least to the extent of repealing both the irreparable injury and adequate remedy formulations of the rule. They should not risk waiting half a century for the statute to become effective.

Any version of my proposed statute would abolish the irreparable injury rule while encouraging continued judicial development of the real reasons for remedial choices under the rubric of appropriateness or countervailing interests. Precedent under the declaratory judgment acts would ensure that this statute is not misunderstood to give plaintiffs a free choice of remedy. The statute would give defendants strong incentives to argue functional objections to equitable remedies instead of arguing the irreparable injury rule. Such a statute is no panacea, but it would point courts in the right direction.

An attempt to go further, and to codify the competing interests, is premature and unnecessary. Codification is unnecessary because the competing considerations are well developed in the case law; the legislature need only force courts to disentangle the real reasons from irreparable injury talk and make the real reasons the primary tools of analysis. Codification is premature because the balancing of competing interests in individual cases is probably best left to case law development. It would be hard to get everything right with the precision required of workable statutes. The formulations in my tentative restatement are not ready for enactment, although they may be ready for insertion into legislative history.

Finally, some readers might wonder whether my proposed statute could be promulgated by supreme courts as a rule of civil procedure. Judicially promulgated rules of procedure are not supposed to change substantive law.[13] But if the irreparable injury rule is procedural for purposes of declaratory judgments, as Federal Rule 57 implies, why is it not procedural for other kinds of specific relief?

The answer is that the irreparable injury rule never applied to declaratory judgments. Federal Rule 57 states that point more clearly than the state and federal declaratory judgment acts, but the law would be the same with or without Rule 57. Because Rule 57 was merely a clarification, no one had occasion to question whether it was substantive or procedural.

A general repeal of the irreparable injury rule would change formal legal doctrine, and I have little doubt that the doctrine is substantive. The Supreme Court has generally treated remedies issues as substantive,[14] and there is sound reason for that categorization.[15] Even though the irreparable injury rule is an empty shell, it is a substantive empty shell, and it cannot be changed by a procedural rule. If reformers are to have any confidence of success, they must embody the change in a statute or in substantive adjudications of appellate courts.

C. The Need for Reform

I have proposed a set of rules and a statute that would sharply revise legal doctrine while changing the results of very few cases. Realists of a certain stripe might ask whether such a change is worth making. Doctrine does not control results; if the results are satisfactory, why worry about doctrine?

Doctrine does not control results because the rule has been swallowed by its exceptions. Students encounter this possibility in the first year of law school, and every competent lawyer understands it. Where the judicial sense of justice matches the exceptions, remarkably few cases are incorrectly decided under the nominal rule instead of the exceptions. And we can often expect that judicial intuitions will match the exceptions. It is the judges' sense of justice that caused them to proliferate the exceptions that swallowed the rule.

At some point, it makes sense to describe the exceptions as the rule, and the former rule as the exception. But this shift is a matter of relative advantage rather than necessity. Our language and modes of reasoning are flexible enough to describe the rule as a preference for legal remedies, and then describe a series of exceptions that cover 95% of the cases, or 99%, or even 100%. The legal system can function in this cumbersome way for decades without conforming the rhetoric of rule and exception to the reality of decided cases.

The system can function in this way, but the costs are substantial. Most obviously, it is hard for legal actors to understand what they are doing. A principal claim of this book is that we can understand the law of remedies more clearly when we state the rules directly— that we can see relationships and explanations that were hidden by the irreparable injury rule. I hope that readers found such insights in every chapter. If not, there is nothing more I could say here to support the claim.

The consequences of inverting rule and exception are practical as well as intellectual. The side that benefits from the nominal rule will sometimes invoke the rule and litigate the issue. The side that benefits from the exceptions must identify the appropriate exception and fit the case into it. The opinion must recite the nominal rule and then the exception. There is much wasted effort as lawyers and judges who know the rule puzzle through to the appropriate exception. Most of the cases cited in this book reflect the time of at least one judge and two lawyers—usually more lawyers and one or two panels of appellate judges—working on the irreparable injury rule. Clients and taxpayers pay for that effort.

The lawyers, the court, or both may get confused in this ritual; a few opinions will reach bad results, and many more will say strange things. As Grant Gilmore once noted, courts will reach sound decisions despite bad doctrine, but the cost will often be opinions that are "patently absurd."[16] Some irreparable injury opinions are patently absurd by any standard: consider the cases holding that an uncollectible damage judgment is an adequate remedy for defamation.[17]

There are probably more bad results than we can identify from reading the opinions. The opinions we read are all from cases where a judge went to the trouble of writing for publication, and mostly from cases where the parties went to the trouble of briefing an appeal. These are the cases in which the most legal effort was invested. The error rate is presumably higher in unappealed and unpublished trial court judgments. Overburdened trial judges must often rely on their memory of blackletter rules; bad doctrine can lead them into error.

Another hidden set of bad results is the winnable cases that never get filed. All living lawyers have been taught some version of the rule, and they must sometimes be deterred by it and advise clients to forget about specific performance or an injunction. I have no way to estimate the size of this effect. I assume that it occurs mostly in cases where either the client's claim is weak on the merits or his need for specific relief is marginal. If the lawyer has sufficient incentive to do even a little legal research, she is likely to find some similar case in which specific relief was granted. That is all she needs; she does not need to read fourteen hundred cases and conclude that the whole rule is dead.

Even if the lawyer files the case and the judge publishes an opinion, bad results can still be invisible. If the focus on irreparable injury distracts the court and the parties from more important reasons for choosing among remedies, the opinion may not reveal the facts that should have produced a different result. For example, I continue to puzzle over the cases seeking specific performance of contracts to sell fungible goods in an orderly market. Why would the parties litigate that issue through trial and appeal? Are they just mad and fighting over the principle of the thing? Are their lawyers focused on a theoretical victory or a higher fee, and oblivious to the lack of practical consequences? Or is there something else at stake that the court never tells us about? Reading only the published opinions, we have no way to know.

The reasons for choosing one remedy over another cannot be reliably applied by trial judges or openly argued by counsel unless they are openly stated in opinions. A meaningless code phrase cannot serve as an adequate proxy for sound doctrine. Many of the realists understood this perfectly well. It was the great realist Karl Llewellyn who said that "covert tools are never reliable tools."[18] The system will function better—lawyers will prepare cases better, try and argue them better, and settle them more efficiently, and judges will decide cases more efficiently and sometimes more justly—when doctrine reflects reality.

Covert tools have to do when nothing better is available. The problem is how to get the covert tools out of the way after we come to understand the problem well enough to devise better tools. The judges' intuitive sense of justice creates pressure to get the results right, but it creates no similar pressure to get the doctrine right.

The irreparable injury rule is an extreme example of the tenacity of obsolete rules. The rule was created to allocate jurisdiction between courts that have long been merged. Law and equity have been merged for more than half a century in the federal courts and for well over a century in England and many American states.[19] Even before the merger, Americans had largely eliminated the differences between law judges and equity judges. Law and equity were committed to the same federal judges from the beginning— the irreparable injury rule never served its original purpose even for a day in federal court.

It could hardly be clearer that this rule has outlived its purpose. Yet lawyers and academics made up new purposes, from jury trial to personal liberty to economic efficiency. But either the rule does not serve these purposes, or it serves them at too high a cost to our sense of remedial justice. These makeshift rationales have not been sufficient to sustain the rule in practice. But the rule persists in the conventional wisdom and judicial rhetoric.

The origins of this confusion lie in a familiar pattern of judicial behavior. When law and equity were administered by separate judges in separate and somewhat rival courts, it was in the equity court's interest to prominently repeat that it would not take jurisdiction if the legal remedy were adequate. Such pronouncements reassured the other actors in the system that equity knew its place and was not usurping authority, just as Supreme Court nominees assure the Senate that judges should never attempt to bring about social, economic, or political change.[20] It is not surprising that the equity court loudly proclaimed the irreparable injury rule while quietly finding that the legal remedy was usually inadequate. Nor is it surprising that many lawyers took the first-level statement of the rule at face value.

It is harder to explain why the traditional understanding lasted so long, but the most important reasons are clear enough. First, the traditional understanding seemed consistent with the experience that damage verdicts outnumber specific remedies. As noted, specific remedies are simply not an option in several important categories of routine litigation.[21]

Second, in a legal system based on precedent, lawyers and judges tend to repeat the sayings of the past until forced to repudiate them because there is no other way to reach a desired result. It has never been necessary to repudiate the irreparable injury rule, because it long ago ceased to function as a serious constraint on equitable remedies. But many judges find it comforting to declare the adequacy of the damage remedy in those cases where they have some other reason for denying specific relief. The irreparable injury rule has become an all-purpose rhetorical tool, almost irresistibly thrown into the opinion when judges have some good reason to deny equitable relief.

When a case is close, the rule is a way of hedging bets—of reducing the stakes that ride on difficult choices. It is as if the judge said, "I am denying the injunction, for a reason that is sound but debatable, but even if I am wrong, no harm is done, because your legal remedy is adequate." When the decision is easy, the rule is a way of piling on—of multiplying reasons without having to decide which, if any, is independently sufficient.

The rhetoric thrives, but the rule itself is dead. It does not decide cases of its own force, and it adds nothing to the other grounds of decision in cases where it is invoked. It is long past time to give it a decent burial. Legislatures and supreme courts should formally abolish the irreparable injury rule at final judgment. They should force judges to focus on their real reasons for choosing remedies. Only then will courts conform remedial doctrine to remedial reality.

Notes on Conforming Doctrine

1. [scope of injunction] See Douglas Laycock, *Modern American Remedies*, ch. 3 (Little, Brown 1985); David S. Schoenbrod, *The Measure of an Injunction: A Principle to Replace Balancing the Equities and Tailoring the Remedy*, 72 Minn. L. Rev. 627 (1988).

2. [declaratory judgment rule] See Fed. R. Civ. Proc. 57 ("The existence of another adequate remedy does not preclude a judgment for declaratory relief in cases where it is appropriate").

3. [1923 Declaratory Judgments Act]

Courts of record, within their respective jurisdictions, shall have power to declare rights, status, and other legal relations whether or not further relief is or could be claimed.

Act of June 18, 1923, 1923 Pa. Laws 840, Act No. 321, § 1, adopted verbatim from Uniform Declaratory Judgments Act, § 1, codified and still in effect at 32 Pa. Stat. § 7532 (Purdon 1982).

4. [1935 amendment]

[T]he mere fact that an actual or threatened controversy is susceptible of relief through a general common law remedy, or an equitable remedy, or an extraordinary legal remedy, whether such remedy is recognized or regulated by statute or not, shall not debar a party from the privilege of obtaining a declaratory judgment or decree in any case where the other essentials to such relief are present; (sic) but the case is not ripe for relief by way of such common law remedy, or extraordinary legal remedy, or where the party asserting the claim, relation, status, right or privilege and who might bring action thereon, refrains from pursuing any of the last mentioned remedies. Nothing herein provided is intended to or shall limit or restrict the general powers or jurisdiction conferred by the act hereby amended.

Act of April 25, 1935, 1935 Pa. Laws 72, Act. No. 33, § 1.

5. **[1943 amendment]** The 1943 amendment repealed all the language following the semicolon in the 1935 amendment. Act of May 26, 1943, 1943 Pa. Stat. 645, Act No. 285, § 1. This was thought to be necessary because the state supreme court had promptly found a negative implication in that language. Allegheny County v. Equitable Gas Co., 321 Pa. 127, 129, 183 A. 916, 917 (1936) ("if the case is 'ripe' for relief by the common law remedy, that remedy shall be preferred").

6. **[1976 amendment]**

§ 7537. Remedy discretionary

. . . as provided in section 7541(b) (relating to effect of alternative remedy), the existence of an alternative remedy shall not be a ground for the refusal to proceed under this subchapter.

. . .

§ 7541. Construction of subchapter

. . .

(b) Effect of alternative remedy.—The General Assembly finds and determines that the principle rendering declaratory relief unavailable in circumstances where an action at law or in equity or a special statutory remedy is available has unreasonably limited the availability of declaratory relief and such principle is hereby abolished. The availability of declaratory relief shall not be limited by the provisions of 1 Pa.C.S. § 1504 (relating to statutory remedy preferred over common law) and the remedy provided by this subchapter shall be additional and cumulative to all other available remedies except as provided in subsection (c). Where another remedy is available the election of the declaratory judgment remedy rather than another available remedy shall not affect the substantive rights of the parties, and the court may pursuant to general rules change venue, require additional pleadings, fix the order of discovery and proof, and take such other action as may be required in the interest of justice.

Act of July 9, 1976, 1976 Pa. Laws 305, Act No. 161, § 1, codified in 42 Pa. Stat. § 7541 (Purdon 1982). § 7541 (c) provides that declaratory judgments cannot be used to obtain divorce or annulment, to avoid the exclusive jurisdiction of an administrative agency, or to challenge an order that could be appealed.

7. **[cases under 1923 Act]** In re Sterret's Estate, 300 Pa. 116, 124, 150 A. 159, 162 (1930) ("this court has uniformly held that [declaratory] relief may not be granted . . . where another established remedy is available").

8. **[1935 amendment changed nothing]** Stofflet & Tillotson v. Chester Housing Auth., 346 Pa. 574, 577, 31 A.2d 274, 275 (1943) ("the fundamental principle so declared in numerous cases was not changed by the amendment of 1935").

9. **[five changes of mind]** See the following cases, each stating the opposite of the one before it: Friestad v. Travelers Indemnity Co., 452 Pa. 417, 423, 306 A.2d

295, 298 (1973) (1943 amendment "intended to remove any possible ambiguity in the Act's language in order to ensure that a declaratory judgment would lie even where an alternative remedy existed"); McWilliams v. McCabe, 406 Pa. 644, 653, 179 A.2d 222, 227 (1962) ("Act . . . was not intended for, and *should not be invoked in cases where the judgment sought can be had as expeditiously in the ordinary course of legal procedure as it can under the statute.* This fundamental principle so declared in numerous cases was not changed by the amendment of 1935." (emphasis in original)); In re Estate of Johnson, 403 Pa. 476, 488, 171 A.2d 518, 523 (1961) ("The existence of any other form of remedy will not per se bar declaratory judgment. Such is the mandate of the legislature."); Wirkman v. Wirkman, 392 Pa. 63, 66, 139 A.2d 658, 660 (1958) ("declaratory judgment should not be granted where a more appropriate remedy is available," citing pre-1943 cases); Philadelphia Mfrs. Mut. Fire Ins. Co. v. Rose, 364 Pa. 15, 23, 70 A.2d 316, 320 (1950) (granting declaratory judgment despite the availability of assumpsit and reformation; "the amendment of 1943 was obviously an effort to accomplish what had failed in 1935").

10. [statute clear and explicit] Friestad v. Travelers Indemnity Co., 452 Pa. 417, 421, 423, 306 A.2d 295, 297, 298 (1973) (emphasis in original).

11. [interpretation of 1976 amendment] Allegheny Ludlum Steel Corp. v. Pa. Public Util. Comm'n, 67 Pa. Commw. 400, 410–11, 447 A.2d 675, 680 (1981) (quoting, italicizing, and applying statutory language making declaratory judgment available despite existence of other remedies), aff'd on other grounds, 501 Pa. 71, 459 A.2d 1218 (1983); Wash. Township v. Slate Belt Vehicle Recycling Center, Inc., 58 Pa. Commw. 620, 624, 428 A.2d 753, 755 (1981) ("Act clearly provides that the availability of an alternative judicial, as opposed to administrative, remedy does not preclude declaratory relief"); Myers v. Commonwealth Dep't of Revenue, 55 Pa. Commw. 509, 513, 423 A.2d 1101, 1103 (1980) (1976 amendment "substantially broadened the availability of declaratory relief").

12. [real reasons to deny declaratory judgment] McWilliams v. McCabe, 406 Pa. 644, 656, 179 A.2d 222, 228 (1962) (hostility to plaintiff's claim; "how often do we have to reiterate that we intend to uphold the integrity of written contracts and that we will not permit them to be altered, modified, changed, circumvented, or effectually nullified by parol evidence"); Wirkman v. Wirkman, 392 Pa. 63, 139 A.2d 658 (1958) (plaintiff sought declaratory judgment on issues subject to arbitration); Stofflet & Tillotson v. Chester Housing Auth., 346 Pa. 574, 578, 31 A.2d 274, 275 (1943) (same).

13. [procedural rules not to change substance] See the federal Rules Enabling Act, 28 U.S.C. § 2072 (1988) ("general rules of practice and procedure" promulgated by the Supreme Court "shall not abridge, enlarge or modify any substantive right"). Provisions for rule-making authority in state courts vary widely.

14. [remedies law is substantive] See Monessen Southwestern Ry. v. Morgan, 486 U.S. 330, 335–36 (1988) (measure of recovery, including right to prejudgment interest and methods of discounting to present value, are substantive issues for purposes of deciding whether to apply state or federal law).

15. [nature of remedies law] See Laycock, *Remedies* at 1–2, 6–7 (cited in note 1) (arguing that remedies law is too important to be treated as procedural, but also that it must be distinguished from other substantive law).

16. [bad rules yield absurd opinions] See Grant Gilmore, 1 *Security Interests in Personal Property* 551–52 (1965) ("it is a fairly reliable rule of thumb that, when courts with some regularity begin to assign patently absurd reasons for their decisions, the decisions themselves are sound and the underlying rule of law has fallen out of touch with reality").

17. [examples of absurd opinions] See Willing v. Mazzocone, 482 Pa. 377, 382–83, 393 A.2d 1155, 1158 (1978), and Annotation cited in ch. 7 note 27.

18. [covert tools unreliable] Karl Llewellyn, Book Review, 52 Harv. L. Rev. 700, 703 (1939).

19. [merger of law and equity] For federal courts, see Fed. R. Civ. Proc. 2 (1988) (originally adopted in 1937). For England, see Judicature Act, 36 and 37 Vict. ch. 66, §§ 24, 25 (1873). For American states, see John Norton Pomeroy, 1 *A Treatise on Equity Jurisprudence as Administered in the United States of America* § 40 at 33 n.1 (Bancroft-Whitney Co. 1881) (New York merged law and equity in the Field Code in 1848, and sixteen states and six territories followed its lead by 1881).

20. [Supreme Court confirmation hearings] See 9 *The Supreme Court of the United States: Hearings and Reports on Successful and Unsuccessful Nominations of Supreme Court Justices by the Senate Judiciary Committee, 1916–1975*, at 105–06 (Roy Mersky & J. Myron Jacobstein, eds.) (W.S. Hein 1977) (quoting Justice Fortas at his confirmation hearing).

21. [specific relief often not an option] See ch. 1 part B.2.

Table of Cases

Cases from state courts, foreign courts, and the local courts of the District of Columbia are listed under their respective jurisdictions.

Cases from the Supreme Court of the United States are listed under that court. Cases from federal courts of appeals, district courts, and bankruptcy courts are listed under their respective circuits. Cases from federal district courts and bankruptcy courts in Alabama, Florida, and Georgia are listed under the Fifth Circuit if they were decided before 1982, and under the Eleventh Circuit if they were decided after 1981.

References are to chapter and footnote numbers. For example, Abbott Labs. v. Gardner is cited in Chapter 1 note 31, and in Chapter 6 notes 42 and 48. Italicized footnote numbers indicate that the case is discussed in text.

Supreme Court of the United States

287

Second Circuit

S.J. Groves & Sons Co. v. Warner Co., 1–44
Systems Operations, Inc. v. Scientific Games Dev. Corp., 7–48
Tully v. Mott Supermarkets, Inc., 3–13
U.S. Steel Plan for Employee Ins. Benefits v. Musisko, 6–26
United Steelworkers v. Fort Pitt Steel Casting, 2–84
Valentine v. Beyer, 3–78

Fourth Circuit

Alfred A. Knopf, Inc. v. Colby, 7–52
Blackwelder Furniture Co. v. Seilig Mfg. Co., 5–40
Capital Tool & Mfg. Co. v. Maschinenfabrik Herkules, 5–32
Carolinas Cotton Growers Ass'n, Inc. v. Arnette, 2–48
Environmental Defense Fund, Inc. v. Lamphier, 3–92, 94
In re Heritage Village Church & Missionary Fellowship, 6–7
In re Smith-Douglass, Inc., 3–26
James A. Merrit & Sons v. Marsh, 5–21
Klein v. PepsiCo, Inc., 2–86
Lankford v. Gelston, 2–74; 3–22
Letendre v. Fugate, 9–2
L.J. v. Massinga, 2–84; 5–40
Nissan Motor Corp. v. Md. Shipbuilding & Drydock Co., 9–63
Pantry Pride Enterprises, Inc. v. Stop & Shop Co., 2–15
Phillips v. Crown Cent. Petroleum Corp., 2–97, 113
S. Packaging & Storage Co. v. U.S., 3–41
Todd v. Sorrell, 2–84
U.S. v. Cent. Carolina Bank & Trust Co., 2–68
U.S. v. Marchetti, 7–52
U.S. v. Snepp (1979), 7–52
U.S. v. Snepp (1990), 7–52

Fifth Circuit

Allied Mktg. Group, Inc. v. CDL Mktg., Inc., 2–111
Atwood Turnkey Drilling, Inc. v. Petroleo Brasileiro, S.A., 1–56; 6–88
Austin v. N. Am. Forest Prod., 8–5
Bell v. Southwell, 2–65
Big State Barging Co. v. Calmes, 9–70
Black Ass'n of Firefighters v. City of New Orleans, 3–22; 7–86
Bolin Farms v. Am. Cotton Shippers Ass'n, 2–48
Canal Auth. v. Callaway, 2–78; 5–19, 21
Chisom v. Roemer, 5–21; 6–80

Eighth Circuit

Iowa

Kansas

314 THE DEATH OF THE IRREPARABLE INJURY RULE

State ex rel. Stephan v. Pepsi-Cola Gen'l Bottlers, Inc., 9–63
Unified School Dist. No. 503 v. McKinney, 7–26, 28

Kentucky

Commonwealth ex rel. Grauman v. Cont'l Co., 9–38, 42
Commonwealth Revenue Cabinet v. Graham, 8–26
London Bucket Co. v. Stewart, 9–86
Nat'l Gypsum Co. v. Corns, 6–67
Pa. R.R. v. City of Louisville, 9–69

Louisiana

Anzelmo v. La. Comm'n on Ethics for Public Employees, 6–62
Arbour v. Total CATV, Inc., 5–21
Caney Hunting Club, Inc. v. Tolbert, 2–79
Cashio v. Shoriak, 2–12
CDT, Inc. v. Greener & Sumner Architects, Inc., 1–52
Conway v. Stratton, 5–11, 12
Cromwell v. Commerce & Energy Bank, 8–21
Daigre Engineers, Inc. v. City of Winnfield, 3–74
Daiquiri Factory, Ltd. v. City of Lafayette, 9–63
Deer Slayers, Inc. v. La. Motel & Inv. Corp., 2–9
Duhon v. Slickline, Inc., 7–93
Forrest House Apts. v. La. Tax Comm'n, 6–1
Freeman v. Treen, 6–80
Giron v. Housing Auth., 7–93
Greenberg v. De Salvo, 1–6, 9; 7–27, 28
Keich v. Barkley Place, Inc., 7–11
Kliebert Educ. Trust v. Watson Marines Serv., Inc., 3–92
LeBlanc v. Lyons, 8–6
Lowry v. Decks & Tapes, Inc., 8–5
M & A Farms, Ltd. v. Town of Ville Platte, 4–14
Mayor of Morgan City v. Ascension Parish Police Jury, 2–77; 3–95
Mayor of Morgan City v. Jesse J. Fontenot, Inc., 8–6
National Co. v. Bridgewater, 2–17
Nunez v. Erbelding, 8–6
Perez v. Perez, 2–61; 6–85
Redfearn v. Creppel, 2–13
S. Cent. Bell Tel. Co. v. F. Miller & Sons, 2–84
Staple Cotton Co-op Ass'n v. Pickett, 2–48
Terrebonne Parish Police Jury v. Matherne, 2–8

Michigan

Minnesota

Mississippi

Missouri

Boeving v. Vandover, 2–52, 87
Estate of Cantonia v. Sindel, 1–76
Herron v. Sisk, 8–30
Landau v. St. Louis Public Serv. Co., 3–75
McCullough v. Newton, 2–2
McNulty v. Heitman, 1–51; 4–2
Public Serv. Co. v. Peabody Coal Co., 2–107
Mo. Veterinary Medical Ass'n v. Glisan, 9–34
Mut. Drug Co. v. Sewall, 1–32
Ryan v. City of Warrensburg, 7–28
St. Louis Smelting & Rfg. Co. v. Hoban, 2–10, 24
Sedmak v. Charlie's Chevrolet, Inc., 2–38, 47, 87, 94
Smith v. W. Elec. Co., 2–84; 3–1
State ex rel. Danforth v. Independence Dodge, Inc., 2–116; 4–27
State ex rel. Gen'l Dynamics Corp. v. Luten, 6–4; 8–30

Montana

Frame v. Frame, 2–24, 47
Ide v. Leiser, 2–1
New Club Carlin, Inc. v. City of Billings, 3–41; 8–32

Nebraska

Brown v. U.S. Nat'l Bank, 8–21
City of Lincoln v. Cather & Sons Constr., Inc., 6–6, 65
Credit Bureau, Inc. v. Moninger, 1–47
Czarnick v. Loup River Public Power Dist., 2–8, 20
Emry v. Am. Honda Motor Co., 8–3, 4, 7
Fred Gorder & Son v. Pankonin, 2–15
Ganser v. County of Lancaster, 1–81; 6–7
Graves v. Gerber, 2–16
Grein v. Bd. of Educ., 1–6; 9–59
J.Q. Office Equip., Inc. v. Sullivan, 7–26, 48
Koperski v. Husker Dodge, Inc., 1–77
OB-GYN, P.C. v. Blue Cross & Blue Shield, 1–33
Reed v. Williamson, 2–12, 22

North Carolina

North Dakota

Ohio

Bauer v. Bauer, 1–54
De Moss v. Conart Motor Sales, 2–52, 87
Fuchs v. United Motor Stage Co., 2–107
Garono v. State, 1–6; 6–8
Harris v. Harris, 1–51
Karches v. City of Cincinnati, 6–61
Perkins v. Village of Quaker City, 8–31
Reno v. Clark, 8–26
Schank v. Hegele, 2–72
Sloane v. Clauss, 2–17, 35; 6–5
State ex rel. Barton v. Butler County Bd. of Elections, 1–38
State ex rel. Bardo v. City of Lyndhurst, 7–76
State ex rel. P.O.B., Inc. v. Hair, 6–6
State ex rel. Pressley v. Indus. Comm'n, 8–6
State ex rel. Tudor v. Indus. Comm'n, 8–6
Stephan's Mach. & Tool, Inc. v. D & H Mach. Consultants, 2–37
Sternberg v. Bd. of Trustees of Kent State Univ., 7–4, 11
Valco Cincinnati, Inc. v. N & D Mach. Serv., Inc., 2–109

Oklahoma

Brook v. James A. Cullimore & Co., 2–57
Chadwell v. English, 2–44
City of Chickasha v. Ark. La. Gas Co., 8–6
Fortner v. Wilson, 2–53, 55, 94
Marquette v. Marquette, 2–81
McDaniel v. Moyer, 2–24, 108
Mid-Continent Pipe Line Co. v. Emerson, 2–16, 28
Peevyhouse v. Garland Coal & Mining Co., 7–22

Oregon

Harris v. Barcroft, 2–41
Jewett v. Deerhorn Enterprises, Inc., 2–7
Lauderback v. Multnomah County, 3–91
Lloyd Corp. v. Whiffen, 2–8; 8–30
McDonough v. S. Or. Mining Co., 9–69, 77
Paullus v. Yarbrough, 2–47, 87
Pierce v. Douglas School Dist. No. 4, 7–61
Wittick v. Miles, 2–1

Pennsylvania

Payne v. Clark, 2–1
Pechner v. Pa. Ins. Dept., 6–36, 63
Petry v. Tanglwood Lakes, Inc., 9–86
Philadelphia Ass'n of School Admin'rs v. School Dist., 9–59
Philadelphia Ball Club v. Lajoie, 7–72
Philadelphia Mfrs. Mut. Fire Ins. Co. v. Rose, 12–9
Quirk v. Schuylkill County Mun. Auth., 8–26
Redmond Finishing Co. v. Ginsburg, 8–7
S. Kane & Son, Inc. v. City of Philadelphia, 9–63
S. Coventry Township v. Philadelphia Elec. Co., 6–5
Schipper Bros. Coal Mining Co. v. Economy Domestic Coal, 2–107
Scholl v. Hartzell, 2–86
Schwartz v. Laundry & Linen Supply Drivers' Union Local, 2–113, 121
Stofflet & Tillotson v. Chester Housing Auth., 12–8, 12
Strank v. Mercy Hosp., 2–72, 97
Teacher v. Kijurina, 2–26
Trachtenburg v. Sibarco Stations, Inc., 1–79; 2–103; 9–25
Wash. Township v. Slate Belt Vehicle Recycling Center, Inc., 12–11
Willing v. Mazzocone, 3–22; 7–27, 29, 34, 38; 12–17
Wirkman v. Wirkman, 12–9, 12

Rhode Island

Belilove v. Reich, 1–79
Brown v. Amaral, 6–63
Landrigan v. McElroy, 1–55
Melrose Enterprises v. Pawtucket Form Constr. Co., 2–1
Newport Yacht Club, Inc. v. Deomatares, 2–8
O'Connors v. Helfgott, 1–6; 2–66
Raposa v. Guay, 2–6
R.I. Turnpike & Bridge Auth. v. Cohen, 1–9; 8–28
Tortolano v. Difilippo, 2–8

South Carolina

Barrett v. Miller, 8–6
Pingley v. Brunson, 7–61
State ex rel. McLeod v. Holcomb, 9–28, 31, 40
Young v. Burton, 7–73

Table of Secondary Sources*

Alexander, James. *A Brief Narrative of the Case and Trial of John Peter Zenger* (1963). 7–36

Am. Jur. 2d, *Actions* (1962). 3–15

Am. Jur. 2d, *Building and Construction Contracts* (1964). 9–85

Am. Jur. 2d, *Injunctions* (1969). 1–81

Anderson, Walter Houston. *Actions for Declaratory Judgments* (1940, 1951). 1–32, 33

Annotation, *"De minimis non curat lex,"* 44 A.L.R. 168 (1926). 3–15.

Annotation, *Injunction as Remedy Against Defamation of Person*, 47 A.L.R.2d 715 (1956). 7–27, 29; 12–17

Annotation, *Specific Performance of Agreement for Sale of Private Franchise*, 82 A.L.R.3d 1102 (1978). 2–42

Annotation, *Specific Performance of Lease of, or Binding Option to Lease, Building or Part of Building to Be Constructed*, 38 A.L.R.3d 1052 (1971). 9–69

Aquinas, Thomas. *Summa Theologica* (Fathers of the English Dominican Province, trans.) (1922). 11–22

Arendt, Hannah. *The Human Condition* (1958). 11–30

Aristotle. *Nicomachean Ethics* (W.D. Ross trans. in Jonathan Barnes, ed., *The Complete Works of Aristotle* (1984). 8–8

Aristotle. *Rhetoric* (W. Rhys Roberts, trans., in Jonathan Barnes, ed., *The Complete Works of Aristotle* (1984). 8–8

Atiyah, P.S. *Promises, Morals, and Law* (1981). 11–31, 33

Atiyah, P.S. *The Rise and Fall of Freedom of Contract* (1979). 11–36

Audain, Linz. *Of Posner, and Newton, and Twenty-First Century Law: An Economic and Statistical Analysis of the Posner Rule for Granting Preliminary Injunctions*, 23 Loyola L.A. L. Rev. 1215 (1990). 5–44

---

* References are to chapter and footnote numbers.

Bailyn, Bernard. See Stanley Katz.

Balkin, J.M. *Too Good to be True: The Positive Economic Theory of Law*, 87 Colum. L. Rev. 1447 (1987). 1–8

Balos, Beverly and Trotzky, Katie. *Enforcement of the Domestic Abuse Act in Minnesota: A Preliminary Study*, 6 L. & Inequality 83 (1988). 2–81

Barnes, Jonathan. See Aristotle.

Barnett, Randy E. *Contract Remedies and Inalienable Rights*, 4 Soc. Phil. & Policy 179 (1986). 1–22, 45

Beck, Lewis White. See Immanuel Kant.

Becker, Gary S. *Crime and Punishment: An Economic Approach*, 76 J. Pol. Econ. 169 (1968). 11–1

Berger, Raoul. *Exhaustion of Administrative Remedies*, 48 Yale L.J. 981 (1939). 6–40, 58

Bezanson, Randall, Cranberg, Gilbert, and Soloski, James. *Libel Law and the Press* (1987). 7–35

Bird, Robert and Fanning, William. *Specific Performance of Contracts to Convey Real Estate*, 23 Ky. L.J. 380 (1935). 2–1, 3

Bishop, William. *The Choice of Remedy for Breach of Contract*, 14 J. Legal Stud. 299 (1985). 1–14; 11–7

Black's Law Dictionary (1979). 2–36

Blasi, Vincent A. *Toward a Theory of Prior Restraint: The Central Linkage*, 66 Minn. L. Rev. 11 (1981). 7–30

Bowman, Cynthia Grant. *Bowen v. Massachusetts: The "Money Damages Exception" to the Administrative Procedure Act and Grant-in-Aid Litigation*, 21 Urban Law. 557 (1989). 3–61

Brilmayer, Lea. *A Reply*, 93 Harv. L. Rev. 1727 (1980). 9–52

Brilmayer, Lea. *The Jurisprudence of Article III: Perspectives on the "Case or Controversy" Requirement*, 93 Harv. L. Rev. 297 (1979). 9–52, 53

Brown, Gary Richard. *Battered Women and the Temporary Restraining Order*, 10 Women's Rights L. Rptr. 261 (1988). 2–81

Calabresi, Guido and Melamed, A. Douglas. *Two Views of the Cathedral: Property Rules, Liability Rules, and Inalienability*, 85 Harv. L. Rev. 1089 (1972). 2–60; 11–1

Campbell, Stanley W. *The Slave Catchers: Enforcement of the Fugitive Slave Law 1850–1860* (1970). 7–63

Casenote, *Sadat v. American Motors Corporation: Limiting Consumer Remedies Under Magnuson-Moss and the New Car Buyer Protection Act*, 19 John Marshall L. Rev. 163 (1985). 4–28

Chafee, Zechariah. *Freedom of Speech* (1920). 7–50

Chafee, Zechariah. *Some Problems of Equity* (1950). 3–83, 84

Chambers, David L. *Making Fathers Pay* (1979). 1–51

Driscoll, Marie V. *The "New"* § *43(a)*, 79 Trademark Rptr. 238 (1989). 7–48

Eisenberg, Theodore and Yeazell, Stephen C. *The Ordinary and the Extraordinary in Institutional Litigation*, 93 Harv. L. Rev. 465 (1980). 9–76

Elkouri, Edna Asper. See Frank Elkouri.

Elkouri, Frank and Elkouri, Edna Asper. *How Arbitration Works* (1985). 7–77

Ellinger, E.P. *Fraud in Documentary Credit Transactions*, 1981 J. Bus. L. 258. 8–21

Elliott, Byron K. and Elliott, William F. *Roads and Streets* (1890). 3–7, 8

Elliott, Ivan A. *Specific Performance*, 1960 U. Ill. L.F. 72. 2–3

Elliott, William F. See Byron K. Elliott.

Fanning, William. See Robert Bird.

Farber, Daniel A. *Reassessing Boomer: Justice, Efficiency, and Nuisance Law,* in Peter Hay and Michael Harlan Hoeflich, eds., *Property Law and Legal Education: Essays in Honor of John E. Cribbet* (1988). 7–2

Farber, Daniel A. *Equitable Discretion, Legal Duties, and Environmental Injunctions*, 45 U. Pitt. L. Rev. 513 (1984). 3–97; 9–46

Farnsworth, E. Allan. *Contracts* (1982). 3–27

Farnsworth, E. Allan. *Legal Remedies for Breach of Contract*, 70 Colum. L. Rev. 1145 (1970). 1–22, 36

Finn, Peter. *Statutory Authority in the Use and Enforcement of Civil Protection Orders Against Domestic Abuse*, 23 Family L.Q. 43 (1989). 2–82

Fiss, Owen M. and Rendleman, Doug. *Injunctions* (1984). 1–9, 22; 2–30

Fiss, Owen M. *The Civil Rights Injunction* (1978). 1–12, 15, 25, 26; 3–42

Fleming, Donald. See Stanley Katz.

Frankfurter, Felix and Greene, Nathan. *The Labor Injunction* (1930). 7–37

Franklin, Marc A. *Suing Media for Libel* (1981). Am. Bar Found. Research J. 797. 7–35

Franklin, Marc A. *Winners and Losers and Why: A Study of Defamation Litigation* (1980). Am. Bar Found. Research J. 455. 7–35

Fried, Charles. *Contract as Promise: A Theory of Contractual Obligation* (1981). 11–24, 40

Friedman, Lawrence M. *A History of American Law* (1973). 1–73, 75

Friedmann, Daniel. *The Efficient Breach Fallacy*, 18 J. Legal Stud. 1 (1989). 1–14; 11–12, 21, 42

Frost, Robert. *Stopping by Woods on a Snowy Evening*, in Edward Connery Latham, ed., *The Poetry of Robert Frost* (1969). 11–23

Galanter, Marc. *Why the "Haves" Come Out Ahead: Speculation on the Limits of Legal Change*, 9 L. & Soc'y Rev. 95 (1974). 4–26

Gelfand, Gregory. *Smith v. University of Detroit: Is There a Viable Alternative to Beacon Theatres?* 45 Wash. & Lee L. Rev. 159 (1988). 9–5, 13

Getman, Julius G. and Pogrebin, Bertrand B. *Labor Relations: The Basic Processes, Law, and Practice* (1988). 7–85

Gilmore, Grant. *Security Interests in Personal Property* (1965). 12–16

Green, Thomas A. *The Jury, Seditious Libel, and the Criminal Law*, in R.H. Helmholz and Thomas A. Green, *Juries, Libel, and Justice: The Role of English Juries in Seventeenth- and Eighteenth-Century Trials for Libel and Slander* (1984). 7–36

Greene, Nathan. See Felix Frankfurter.

Hardin, Russell. *Morality Within the Limits of Reason* (1988). 11–25, 32

Harsanyi, John C. *Does Reason Tell Us What Moral Code to Follow and, Indeed, to Follow Any Moral Code at All?* 96 Ethics 42 (1985). 11–31, 33

Hay, Peter. See Daniel A. Farber.

Hazard, Geoffrey C., Jr. See Fleming James, Jr.

Helmholz, R.H. See Thomas A. Green.

Higginbotham, A. Leon and Kopytoff, Barbara K. *Property First, Humanity Second: The Recognition of the Slave's Human Nature in Virginia Civil Law*, 50 Ohio St. L.J. 511 (1989). 7–73

Hodgson, D.H. *Consequences of Utilitarianism* (1967). 11–31, 33

Hoeflich, Michael Harlan. See Daniel A. Farber.

Holmes, Oliver Wendell, Jr. *The Path of the Law*, 10 Harv. L. Rev. 457 (1897). 11–2

Horack, H.C. *Insolvency and Specific Performance*, 31 Harv. L. Rev. 702 (1918). 3–27

Huhn, Kenneth C. See Douglas S. McDowell.

Hume, David. *A Treatise of Human Nature* (1740, 1978). 11–26

Jacobstein, J. Myron. See Roy Mersky.

Jaeger, Walter H.E. See Samuel Williston.

Jaffe, Louis. *Primary Jurisdiction*, 77 Harv. L. Rev. 1037 (1964). 6–37, 44

James, Fleming, Jr. *Right to Jury Trial in Civil Actions*, 72 Yale L.J. 655 (1963). 1–77; 9–10

James, Fleming, Jr. and Hazard, Geoffrey C., Jr. *Civil Procedure* (1985). 9–3

Jeffries, John Calvin. *Rethinking Prior Restraint*, 92 Yale L.J. 409 (1983). 7–30

Kane, Mary Kay. See Charles Alan Wright.

Kant, Immanuel. *Foundations of the Metaphysics of Morals* (Lewis White Beck, trans.) (1969). 11–24

Kastely, Amy H. *The Right to Require Performance in International Sales: Towards an International Interpretation of the Vienna Convention*, 63 Wash. L. Rev. 607 (1988). 1–22; 11–16, 41

Katz, Stanley. *The Politics of Law in Colonial America: Controversies over Chancery Courts and Equity Law in the Eighteenth Century*, in Donald Fleming and Bernard Bailyn, eds., *Law and American History* (1971). 1–73, 74

Katz, Stanley. See also James Alexander.

Keeton, W. Page and Morris, Clarence. *Notes on "Balancing the Equities,"* 18 Tex. L. Rev. 412 (1940). 2–3; 7–6

Kopytoff, Barbara K. See A. Leon Higginbotham.

Kronman, Anthony T. *Specific Performance*, 45 U. Chi. L. Rev. 351 (1978). 1–13; 2–98, 100; 7–16

Latham, Edward Connery. See Robert Frost.

Laycock, Douglas. *Federal Interference with State Prosecutions: The Cases Dombrowski Forgot*, 46 U. Chi. L. Rev. 636 (1979). 3–50, 51; 6–10, 12, 14, 19, 28

Laycock, Douglas. *Federal Interference with State Prosecutions: The Need for Prospective Relief*, 1977 S. Ct. Rev. 193. 3–48; 6–17, 20, 31, 32, 46

Laycock, Douglas. *Injunctions and the Irreparable Rule*, 57 Tex. L. Rev. 1065 (1979). 1–9, 16, 83; 3–42; 4–11; 9–15

Laycock, Douglas. *Modern American Remedies* (1985). 1–9, 12, 14, 34, 76; 2–25; 3–56; 5–3, 17, 35; 6–87, 95; 7–6; 9–51, 54; 11–17; 12–1, 15

Laycock, Douglas. *The Ultimate Unity of Rights and Utilities*, 64 Tex. L. Rev. 407 (1985). 11–35

Leebron, David W. *Final Moments: Damages for Pain and Suffering Prior to Death*, 64 N.Y.U. L. Rev. 256 (1989). 9–8

Leflar, Robert A. *Equitable Prevention of Public Wrongs*, 14 Tex. L. 427 (1936). 9–48

Leubsdorf, John. *The Standard for Preliminary Injunctions*, 91 Harv. L. Rev. 525 (1978). 5–37, 41, 50

Linzer, Peter. *On the Amorality of Contract Remedies—Efficiency, Equity, and the Second Restatement*, 81 Colum. L. Rev. 111 (1981). 1–13, 11–7

Llewellyn, Karl. Book Review, 52 Harv. L. Rev. 700 (1939). 12–18

Note, *Comprehensive Remedies and Statutory Section 1983 Actions: Context as a Guide to Procedural Fairness*, 67 Tex. L. Rev. 627 (1989). 8–10

Note, *"Fraud in the Transaction": Enjoining Letters of Credit During the Iranian Revolution*, 93 Harv. L. Rev. 992 (1980). 8–18

Note, *Remedies for Employer's Wrongful Discharge of an Employee Subject to Employment of Indefinite Duration*, 21 Ind. L. Rev. 547 (1988). 7–91

Note, *Specific Performance and Insolvency—A Reappraisal*, 41 St. John's L. Rev. 577 (1967). 3–28

Note, *The Mootness Doctrine in the Supreme Court*, 88 Harv. L. Rev. 373 (1974). 9–52

Note, *The Statutory Injunction as an Enforcement Weapon of Federal Agencies*, 57 Yale L.J. 1023 (1948). 9–31, 43, 48

Palmer, George E. *The Law of Restitution* (1978). 3–68

Perritt, Henry H. Jr. *Labor Injunctions* (1986). 7–37

Petro, Sylvester. *Injunctions and Labor Disputes 1880–1932, Part I: What the Courts Actually Did—and Why*, 14 Wake Forest L. Rev. 341 (1978). 7–37

Plater, Zygmunt J.B. *Statutory Violations and Equitable Discretion*, 70 Cal. L. Rev. 524 (1982). 3–97; 7–1; 9–45

Player, Mack A. *Employment Discrimination Law* (1988). 8–9

Plucknett, Theodore F.T. *A Concise History of the Common Law* (1956). 1–59, 60, 61, 62, 73; 2–59

Pogrebin, Bertrand B. See Julius G. Getman.

Pomeroy, John Norton. *A Treatise on Equity Jurisprudence as Administered in the United States of America* (1881–83, 1941). 1–2, 57, 64, 65, 68, 76, 77, 78, 80; 2–1, 20, 22, 31, 35, 67; 3–1, 9, 64, 65, 66, 67, 69, 80, 81, 82, 83, 85; 4–7; 9–10; 12–19

Pomeroy, John Norton, *A Treatise on the Specific Performance of Contracts as It Is Enforced by Courts of Equitable Jurisdiction in the United States of America* (1879). 2–46, 106

Posner, Richard A. *Economic Analysis of Law* (1973, 1986). 1–13; 2–91; 11–1, 3, 9, 14, 20

Posner, Richard A. *Utilitarianism, Economics, and Legal Theory*, 8 J. Legal Stud. 103 (1979). 11–14

Pound, Roscoe. *Equitable Relief Against Defamation and Injuries to Personality*, 29 Harv. L. Rev. 640 (1916). 7–31

Powe, Lucas A. *The Fourth Estate and the Constitution* (1991). 7–30, 35, 36, 54

Power, Robert C. *Help Is Sometimes Close at Hand: The Exhaustion*

Problem and the Ripeness Solution, 1987 U. Ill. L. Rev. 547. 6–36, 48, 59

Rawls, John. *A Theory of Justice* (1971). 11–27

Rawls, John. *Two Concepts of Rules*, 64 Phil. Rev. 3 (1955). 11–25

Regan, Donald. *On Preferences and Promises: A Response to Harsanyi*, 96 Ethics 56 (1985). 11–25, 32, 33, 34

Rendleman, Doug. *The Inadequate Remedy at Law Prerequisite for an Injunction*, 33 U. Fla. L. Rev. 346 (1981). 1–4, 7, 18, 20, 35, 43; 9–1; 10–9

Restatement (Second) of Contracts (1981). 1–44; 3–75; 7–4, 23, 24, 61; 8–46; 11–12

Restatement (Second) of Torts (1979). 1–17, 36, 44, 81; 2–8, 25, 36, 62, 97, 112, 116; 3–1; 7–3, 31; 9–24, 28, 65

Richards, Richard F. See Charles A. Sullivan

Roberts, W. Rhys. See Aristotle.

Ross, W.D. *The Right and the Good* (1930). 11–28, 31, 33, 35

Ross, W.D. See also Aristotle.

Sampson, John J. *Title 2. Parent and Child*, 17 Tex. Tech L. Rev. 1065 (1986). 1–51

Schoenbrod, David S. *The Measure of an Injunction: A Principle to Replace Balancing the Equities and Tailoring the Remedy*, 72 Minn. L. Rev. 627 (1988). 7–2, 6, 10; 12–1

Schuck, Peter H. *Suing Government* (1983). 6–95

Schwartz, Alan. *The Case for Specific Performance*, 89 Yale L.J. 271 (1979). 1–13, 46; 11–7

Shavell, Steven. *The Design of Contracts and Remedies for Breach*, 99 Q.J. Econ. 121 (1984). 1–14

Shreve, Gene R. *Federal Injunctions and the Public Interest*, 51 Geo. Wash. L. Rev. 382 (1983). 1–7, 10, 19, 21, 22, 82; 3–13; 9–65; 10–9

Silberman, Linda J. *Injunctions by the Numbers: Less Than the Sum of Its Parts*, 63 Chi.-Kent L. Rev. 279 (1987). 5–44, 48, 49

Singer, Peter. *Is Act-Utilitarianism Self-Defeating?* 81 Phil. Rev. 94 (1972). 11–25, 32

Smolla, Rodney A. *Law of Defamation* (1989). 7–27, 31

Soifer, Aviam and Macgill, H.C. *The Younger Doctrine: Reconstructing Reconstruction*, 55 Tex. L. Rev. 1141 (1977). 6–18

Soloski, James. See Randall Bezanson.

Spedding, James. *Letters and Life of Francis Bacon* (1869). 1–70

Starkey, Marion L. *The Devil in Massachusetts: A Modern Enquiry into the Salem Witch Trials* (1961). 11–39

Stevens, Robert S. *Involuntary Servitude by Injunction*, 6 Cornell L. Rev. 235 (1921). 7–57

Story, Joseph. *Commentaries on Equity Jurisprudence as Administered in England and America (1835–1836)*. 1–59, 60, 63, 64, 65, 66, 67, 68, 70, 77, 78, 79, 80; 2–1, 7, 8, 9, 10, 15, 34, 35, 97, 106, 110, 111; 3–66, 67, 80, 82, 83; 4–10; 9–69; 11–45

Subrin, Stephen N. *How Equity Conquered Common Law: The Federal Rules of Civil Procedure in Historical Perspective*, 135 U. Pa. L. Rev. 909 (1987). 3–86

Sullivan, Charles A., Zimmer, Michael J., and Richards, Richard F. *Federal Statutory Law of Employment Discrimination* (1980). 6–91

Summers, Clyde W. *Individual Protection Against Unjust Dismissal: Time for a Statute*, 62 Va. L. Rev. 481 (1976). 7–74, 75, 76, 77

Summers, Craig S. *Remedies for Patent Infringement in the Federal Circuit—A Survey of the First Six Years*, 29 Idea 333 (1989). 2–110

Summers, Robert S. See James J. White.

Tannenbaum, David. *Enforcement of Personal Service Contracts in the Entertainment Industry*, 42 Cal. L. Rev. 18 (1954). 7–68, 71

Tobias, Paul H. *Current Trends in Employment Dismissal Law: The Plaintiff's Perspective*, 67 Neb. L. Rev. 178 (1988). 7–91, 92

Trotzky, Katie. See Beverly Balos.

Tushnet, Mark V. *The American Law of Slavery 1810–1860* (1981). 7–73

Tushnet, Mark V. *The Sociology of Article III: A Response to Professor Brilmayer*, 93 Harv. L. Rev. 1698 (1980). 9–52

Ulen, Thomas S. *The Efficiency of Specific Performance: Toward a Unified Theory of Contract Remedies*, 83 Mich. L. Rev. 341 (1984). 1–14

Van Hecke, M.T. *Changing Emphases in Specific Performance*, 40 N.C. L. Rev. 1 (1961). 2–43, 44, 107; 7–68; 9–69

Van Hecke, M.T. *Equitable Replevin*, 33 N.C. L. Rev. 57 (1954). 1–36, 57; 2–36; 4–7

Van Hecke, M.T. *Injunctions to Remove or Remodel Structures Erected in Violation of Building Restrictions*, 32 Tex. L. Rev. 521 (1954). 7–5

Van Hecke, M.T. *Trial by Jury in Equity Cases*, 31 N.C. L. Rev. 157 (1953). 9–4

Vaughn, Lea. *A Need for Clarity: Toward a New Standard for Preliminary Injunctions*, 68 Or. L. Rev. 839 (1990). 5–37, 44, 51

Warren, Elizabeth and Westbrook, Jay Lawrence. *The Law of Debtors and Creditors* (1986). 1–47

Wasserman, Rhonda S. *Equity Transformed: Preliminary Injunctions to Require the Payment of Money*, 70 B.U. L. Rev. — (1990). 5–13

Weinberg, Louise. *The New Judicial Federalism*, 29 Stan. L. Rev. 1191 (1977). 6–15

West, Martha S. *The Case Against Reinstatement in Wrongful Discharge*, 1988 U. Ill. L. Rev. 1. 7–55, 62, 80, 84, 91, 92

Westbrook, Jay Lawrence. *A Functional Analysis of Executory Contracts*, 74 Minn. L. Rev. 227 (1989). 3–25, 30

Westbrook, Jay Lawrence. See also Elizabeth Warren.

White, James J. and Summers, Robert S. *Uniform Commercial Code* (1988). 8–21

Williston, Samuel and Jaeger, Walter H.E. *A Treatise on the Law of Contracts* (1968, 1972). 2–1, 107; 3–75; 7–55, 68; 9–77

Wright, Charles Alan and Miller, Arthur R. *Federal Practice & Procedure* (1973). 1–10; 2–75

Wright, Charles Alan, Miller, Arthur R., and Cooper, Edward H. *Federal Practice & Procedure* (1984, 1988). 6–47; 9–49, 50

Wright, Charles Alan, Miller, Arthur R., and Kane, Mary Kay. *Federal Practice & Procedure* (1986). 3–87

Yeazell, Stephen C. *From Medieval Group Litigation to the Modern Class Action* (1987). 3–84

Yeazell, Stephen C. See also Theodore Eisenberg.

Yorio, Edward. *Contract Enforcement: Specific Performance and Injunctions* (1989). 1–7, 13, 23, 24; 2–3; 3–22, 27; 7–61, 71, 86; 9–64, 77; 10–10

Yorio, Edward. *In Defense of Money Damages for Breach of Contract*, 82 Colum. L. Rev. 1365 (1982). 1–13

Zimmer, Michael J. See Charles A. Sullivan.

Index*

*References are to page numbers. References to text pages are in roman; refer-
ence to note pages are in italic.

preliminary relief, *124, 127,* 140–42
promotion, *63, 130, 189, 191–92,
203*
reinstatement
   common law, 173–74, *184–85,
   191–92,* 269–70
   hostility to employee, 173, *190,*
   238–39, 269–70
   preferred, 172, *189–90, 204*
   statutory, 141–42, 172–73, *188–91,*
   269–70
   seniority, 174, *189*
   specific performance, 105, *156,* 168–
   72
Encroachments. *See* Land
Entertainers, 169, 171, *184–87*
Environmental litigation
   air, 41, *50, 63, 67,* 73–74, *84–85,
   154, 175–76*
   endangered species, 41, *63*
   environmental impact statements,
   41, *63*
   generally, 45, *48, 60, 130, 143, 205*
   insolvent polluters, *87–88*
   preliminary relief, 116, *127*
   restoration of land, 163–64, *179, 233*
   toxic wastes, *87*
   water, 41, *50, 63–64, 127, 130, 176,
   205–6, 231, 234*
Equally complete, practical, and efficient standard
   definition of adequacy, 22, *35–36,*
   217, 224, 240
   not applied, 105, 162, 197, 201,
   217–18, 240–41
   satisfied, 100–1
Equipment, miscellaneous, *56, 60*
Equitable conversion, *34*
Equitable lien, *34, 88*
Equitable remedies. *See* Legal
remedies
Equity. *See* History of equity; Law-
equity distinction
"Equity, comity, and federalism,"
135, *148, 150*
Establishment of religion. *See* Reli-
gious liberty
Estoppel, *98, 202–3, 225*
Eviction, *52, 94, 124, 127, 178*
Evidence, destruction of, 221
Exclusionary rule, *62*
Execution

on body of defendant, *32*
on property, 15, 17, *31*
Executive branch, injunctions against,
133, 140–42, *145*
Exhaustion. *See* Administrative remedies; Labor law; State remedies
Expert witnesses, 103, *108*

Family law
   child custody, *202, 209*
   declaratory judgments, *284*
   marital property, *31–32, 94, 128,
   157, 177, 203, 231*
   support, 17, *31–32,* 73, *84–85, 107,*
   274
   violence, 41, *64*
Federal Rules of Civil Procedure
   Rule 2, *286*
   Rules 20–23.1, *95*
   Rules 26–37, *95*
   Rule 57, 278, *283*
   Rules 65–66, *123–24*
   Rule 69, *30*
Feedlots, *50, 84*
Fences, *50, 52–53*
Fertilizer plants, *87, 177*
Fiduciary duty, *129, 202, 225*
Filing fees, *85*
Fire codes, *227–28*
Fires, *203*
Fishing boats, *230*
Fish skins, *57–58*
Flooding, *50, 53, 108, 175, 177, 210,
225–26, 231*
Football teams, 114, *180*
Forcible entry and detainer. *See*
Eviction
Foreclosure. *See* Goods; Land;
Mortgages
Formalism, ix
Franchises, 40, *56, 67, 128–29, 177,
184,* 200–1, *226, 232. See also* Auto-
mobile dealerships
Fraud
   common law, *49, 71, 92–93, 204,
   226*
   concealment of assets, *211*
   consumer, *71, 109*
   defamatory charges of, *180*
   equitable defense, 20, *34, 188,* 194,
   202
   letters of credit, 197, *207*

from specific performance, 142,
158–59
Impersonal judgments. *See* Personal
commands
Implied rights of action, 196, *205–6,
209, 228*
Impracticality. *See* Practical difficulties
Imprisonment for debt. *See*
Collections
Inconvenience
to plaintiff, 44–45, *58, 66, 128,* 197,
252
to public, *176–77*
Indeterminacy, ix
Injunctions. *See also* various kinds of
injunctions, acts or harms to be prevented by injunction, and rights to
be protected by injunction
contrasted with mandamus, 15, *30*
contrasted with prohibition, 15, *30*
difficulty of supervision, 222, *232*
extraordinary remedy, 5, *24–25,
124, 209, 231*
immunity from, 142
specific remedy, 13, *29*
Insane delusions, *92*
Insolvent defendants. *See* Bankruptcy
Instruments
fraudulent, 80, *89*
lost, 20, *34,* 80, *93*
negotiable, *91, 207*
Insurance, 56, *64,* 81, *88–89, 92–93,
149, 156,* 171, *202–3, 209*
Intellectual property, *116, 121–22. See
also* Copyrights; Patents; Trademarks; Trade secrets
Interest, *30,* 141, *144–45, 285*
Interpleader, 82, *95*
Intuitionists, 255, *262*
Irreplaceability. *See also* Hard-to-mea-
sure damages; Uniqueness
defined, 37
goods
difficulty in replacement, 42–44,
65, 101, 247, 251
functional equivalence, 246, *260*
monopoly, 40, 257
shortage, 40, 42, 46, *57–59, 107,*
246–47, 253–54, 257
unique, 39
land, 37
preliminary relief, 113

reputation, 165, *180–81*
short-term losses, 114, 122, *128–29*
Irreparable injury
defined, 74
degrees of irreparability, 120–22,
273–74
Irreparable injury rule
applied, 100–4, *108–9*
contrasted with deference to
agency, 135
contrasted with exhaustion rules,
136–38, *149–50*
defended, 6, 9–11, *25, 28–29,* 241–
43, *244*
enforced by equity courts, 21, *34*
held inapplicable, 82, *95–96*
legislative repeal, 276–78
manipulation of rule, 5, 7, 239–42
minimum content of, *11*
nature of injury contrasted with seriousness, 74, *85*
origin of, 19–20
recited, 99, *106–7,* 110–11
tiebreaker, 100–1, *108*
traditional understanding of, vii, 3–
4, 9–10, *28–29,* 74
undermined by implementing rules,
4, 22–23, *28, 35–36*

Joinder rules, 74–75, 82, *95*
Judgments. *See also* Collections; Res
judicata; various means of
enforcement
injunctions against enforcement,
143, 147
means of enforcement generally, 15,
17–19, *30*
Jurisdiction. *See* Allocation of
jurisdiction
Jury trial
advisory, *188,* 270
bankruptcy, *226*
constitutional right
civil, viii, 12, 16, *34,* 213–17, *224–
26,* 240, *244,* 267
criminal, 217–20, *224*
declaratory judgments, *93, 226*
declining respect for civil, 19
equitable awards of money, *30,* 112
equitable remedies to avoid, *30,*
172, *190,* 214–15, *225–26*
in equity, 213, *225*

Limitations, statute of, *188, 202–3*
Lipstick, *107*
Liquidated damages, *203, 211–12*
Liquor licenses, *90, 142, 203*
Lis pendens, 100, *107*
Litigation costs as irreparable injury, 115, *129*, 138–40, *154–56*
Loan commitments, 45–46, 102
Lumber, *58*

Malicious prosecution, *202*
Mandamus, 13–15, *30, 57, 144–45, 189, 203–4*
Maps, *56*
Marble, *232*
Maritime shipping rates, *149*
Marketing agreements, *67*
Massage parlor, 74, *85*
Medical care, *64, 127*
Medicare and Medicaid, *142–43, 154, 208*
Mental health care, *64*
Mental health commitments, *204*
Merger of law and equity, 12, 19, 22, *34–36, 82, 95*, 195, 281, *286*
Mergers. *See* Antitrust
Merits as reason for denying remedy
   deference to more particular law, 193–96, *202–6*, 238–39
   generally, 105, 201–2
   hostility to plaintiff's claim
      analysis, 196–99, *206–11*, 238–39
      examples, *91, 188*, 219, *228, 285*
      illegitimate, 267
Milk, *228*
Minerals. *See* Land and specific minerals
Mistake, 20, *34*
Mitigation of damages. *See* Avoidable consequences
Mobile homes, *107, 209*
Modification of judgments, 194, *202*
Monetary remedies
   contrasted with equitable remedies, 197, *206*
   enforceable by contempt, 15, 17, 274
   granted in equity, 14, 18, *29–30, 32, 60, 84,* 112
   never adequate in themselves, 246
   preliminary, 112–13, *126–28*, 239, 275

Mootness, *91, 96–97, 144*, 220–22, *229–32*, 238–40, *243*, 272–73
Mortgages. *See also* Equitable lien
   enforcement, 20, *34, 53*, 226
   enjoining foreclosure, 38, *53, 60–61, 90, 94*
   foreclosure not irreparable, 141, *156*
Motion pictures, *56, 232–33*
Multi-District litigation, 75, *86*
Multiplicity of suits
   administrative remedies, *153, 155*
   covenants not to compete, *70, 86*
   land, 38, *54–55, 94–95*, 104
   litigation expense irreparable, 139, *155–56*
   repeated violations, 73–74, *84–86*, 217, 219, *228*, 275–76
   scattered litigation, 74–75, *84, 86*
Municipal ordinances. *See* State statutes and ordinances
Mutuality of remedy, 22, *35*, 168, *185, 191*

New Deal, 134, 219
Newspapers, *129, 183–84, 191*, 200–1
Noise, *50, 176*
Normative analysis, 7, *25, 243, 249*, 253–60
Nuclear plants, *158, 181*
Nudity, *90–91, 157, 180, 211*, 217–19, 227
Nuisance
   environmental, 38, *50, 67*, 73–74, *84–85, 175–77, 209*
   grounds for enjoining crime, 219, 229
   ripeness, 272
   sexual, *179, 211*

Obscenity. *See* Speech
Oil and gas
   leases, *49, 57, 84, 86*
   wells, *68, 128, 130*
Operative rules. *See* Rules for choosing remedies
Orders to reach and apply, *88*
Organ transplants, *64*
"Our Federalism," *146*
Output contracts, 46, *68*